An Illustrated Guide to the '03 Service Rifle

Bruce N. Canfield

ANDREW MOWBRAY PUBLISHERS · P.O. BOX 460 · LINCOLN, RI 02865

LIBRARY OF CONGRESS
CATALOG CARD NO: 2004114992
    Bruce N. Canfield
      An Illustrated Guide to the '03 Service Rifle
    Lincoln, R.I.: ANDREW MOWBRAY INCORPORATED — *PUBLISHERS*
    240 pp.

ISBN: 1-931464-15-4

©2004 by Bruce N. Canfield

All rights reserved. No part of this book may be reproduced in any form
or by any means without permission in writing from the author.

To order more copies of this book, call 1-800-999-4697
or visit our website at www.manatarmsbooks.com.

Printed in Canada.

This book was designed and set in type by Jo-Ann Langlois.
The typeface chosen was Souvenir.

Dedication

This book is dedicated to the men and women
of the United States Armed Forces who put their lives
on the line daily to protect us from the forces of evil
in this world. Our freedom must never be taken for
granted, and we should always be thankful for the
sacrifices our troops make to preserve our way of life.

Table of Contents

Historical Background and Prototypes 13

Experimental Magazine Rifle of 1900 14
1901 Prototype 16
The M1903 Rod Bayonet Rifle (1903–1904) 19
   German Patent Infringement Claims 26
     M1905 Bayonet 27
     M1905 Sights................................ 27
M1903 Rifle with the Modifications of 1905........ 27
     M1906 Cartridge 29
Springfield Armory and Rock Island Arsenal Rifles —
Circa late 1906–1908 31
   Finish.. 31
   Receivers 31
   Barrels 32
   Stocks 32
   Handguards 33
   Rear Sights................................... 34
   Rear Sight Fixed Base......................... 34
   Front Sight Covers 35
   Buttplates and Butt Trap Recess 35
   Triggers 35
   Stock Fore-end Tip Markings 35
Post-1907 Assembly of Rock Island Arsenal Rifles 35
Springfield Armory 1909–1917/Rock Island Arsenal
1909–1913 37
   Finish.. 37
   Receivers 37
   Barrels....................................... 37
   Upper Bands 38
   Stocks 38
   Handguards 38
   Rear Sights................................... 38
   Triggers 38
   Cessation of M1903 Rifle Production at Rock Island Arsenal
     Sniper Rifles 40
   Springfield Armory Sectionalized Rifles 42
   NRA-marked Rifles............................. 42
   Issuance of M1903 Rifles with Maxim Silencers 43
   Pre-WWI Combat Use of the M1903 Rifle......... 44

First World War: 1917-1918 46

   Resumption of Rock Island Arsenal Production 46
   M1917 U.S. Enfield............................. 54
   Mark I Rifle................................... 58
   Low-Numbered and *High-Numbered* Receivers 58
M1903 Sniper Rifles: 1908–1918.................... 61
   Warner & Swasey Musket Sights 62
   Model of 1908 Warner & Swasey Musket Sight....... 63
U.S Marine Corps Match Use of the M1908
Warner & Swasey Sight 66
   Model of 1913 Warner & Swasey Musket Sight........ 67
   Combat Use of the Warner & Swasey Sights...... 67
   M1903 Rifle with Winchester A5 Telescope 72

Pedersen Device and the M1903 Mark I Rifle 75
   M1903 Mark I Rifle............................. 81
Cameron-Yaggi Trench Periscope M1903 Rifle...... 82
M1903 Air Service Rifle............................ 90
   WWI Combat Use of the '03 Rifle 98

Post-WWI 99

     Avis Barrels 99
   Post-WWI Overhaul of M1903 Rifles 100
   Springfield Armory Assembly of Rifles with Rock Island
     Receivers, circa 1927 102
   The M1903 Experimental Cavalry Carbine 103
1920s Production M1903 Service Rifles 103
   Finish....................................... 103
   Receivers 103
   Barrels 104
   Bolts 104
   Stocks 105
   Handguards 106
   Buttplates................................... 106
   Rear Sights.................................. 106
   U.S.M.C. "No. 10" Sights 106
   Triggers 106
Other Springfield Armory Production 107
   M1903A1 Rifle 107
     The Hatcher Hole........................... 108
   Rifle Bolts Marked with Serial Numbers 108
   Use of the M1903 Rifle *Between the Wars* 108

World War II 112

Remington M1903 Rifles 112
M1903 Remington Rifle – circa October 1941 to
December 1941 112
   Receivers 113
   Barrels...................................... 113
   Stocks 114
   Handguards 114
   Rear Sights.................................. 115
   Finish....................................... 115
   Furniture 115
M1903 Modified Rifles – circa January 1942 to
March 1943 117
   Receivers 118
   Barrels...................................... 118
   Stocks 118
   Handguards 119
   Finish....................................... 119
   Rear Sights.................................. 120
   Furniture 120
   Scant Grip Stock............................. 120
Remington Factory Sectionalized M1903 Modified Rifles
.... 121
Remington Model 1903A3 Rifle 123
   Receivers 125
   Barrels...................................... 125

Stocks 125	
Handguards 126	
Rear Sights. 126	
Furniture 126	
Finish. 127	

M1903A4 Sniper's Rifle 128
Smith-Corona M1903A3 Rifle 128
    Receivers 128
    Barrels. 128
    Stocks 128
    Finish. 130
    Rear Sights. 130
    Bolts 130
    Furniture 131
    M1903A2 133
Other WWII M1903 Procurement 134
  WWII Assembled M1903A1 Rifles 134
  U.S. Marine Corps WWII M1903 Rifles 134
    Rifle Grenade Launchers. 137
  Bushmaster Carbine 137
World War II Sniper Rifles 139
Remington M1903A4 Sniper Rifle. 139
    Telescopes 141
    Mounts. 143
    Receivers 144
    Barrels. 144
    Stocks 144
    Barrel Guards. 145
    Rear Sights. 145
    Finish. 145
    Furniture 145
  Use of the M1903A4 Rifle by the U.S.M.C. 146
U.S. Marine Corps Sniper Rifles 150
  M1903 Rifles with Winchester A5 and
    Lyman 5A Telescopes. 150
  Consideration of Winchester Model 70 Rifle
    and Unertl Telescope 153
  M1903A1 Rifle and Unertl Telescope
    ("M1941 Sniper Rifle") 153
    Serial Number Range 156
    Barrels. 157
    Receivers 157
    Bolts 157
    Scope Mount Blocks 157
    Stocks 157
    Handguards 157
    Iron Sights 157
    Unertl Telescopes 157
    Carrying Can 158
  Post-WWII Use of the M1903A1/Unertl Sniper Rifle 161
  Postwar Disposition of M1903 Rifles 163

Accessories, Accouterments and Appendages 165

Slings 165
  M1887 Sling. 165
  M1903 Sling. 165
  1907 Sling 165
  M1917 Kerr Sling 168
  M1923 Sling 169
  M1 Sling. 170
Oiler and Thong Case 171
Spare Parts Container 171
Bayonets and Bayonet Scabbards 172
  M1905 Bayonet and Scabbard – 1905 to 1910. 172
  M1910 Bayonet Scabbard. 177
  Model of 1915 Bolo-Bayonet 178
  M1905 Bayonet and M1910 Scabbard – World War I . . . 179
  M1917 Bayonet Scabbard. 181
  M1905 Bayonet – Post-WWI. 181
  M1905 Bayonet – World War II. 181
  M1910 and M3 Bayonet Scabbards – WWII 183
  M1 Bayonet 185
  M7 Bayonet Scabbard 186
  Front Sight Covers 186
  Cavalry Saddle Scabbard 187
Cartridge Belts • Pre-World War I 189
  M1903 Cartridge Belt. 189
  M1909 Cavalry Cartridge Belt 190
  M1910 Cartridge Belt. 190
  M1912 Cavalry Equipment and M1912 Cartridge Belt . . . 191
  M1914 Mounted Cartridge Belt 192
  World War I Cartridge Belts. 192
  M1917/M1918 Cartridge Belts 193
World War II and Postwar Cartridge Belts 193
  M1923 Cartridge Belt. 193
Rifle Grenade Launchers 194
  V-B Grenade Launchers – WWI 194
  M1 Launcher – WWII 200
25-Round Extension Magazine. 206
Manuals, Handbooks and Ammunition 208

Tables

  Tables 1 and 2 211
  Table 3. 211–212
  Table 4. 213–217
  Table 5. 218–219
  Table 6. 220
  Table 7. 221
  Tables 8 and 9 222
  Tables 10 and 11 223–224
  Table 12 225–226
  Table 13. 226
  Table 14. 227

Bibliography 229

Index 233

Foreword

The U.S. Rifle Model of 1903, or simply the '03 Springfield, is America's greatest military bolt action. Back in 1903, at the time of its adoption, the airplane was just a novel contraption that managed to stay in the air for a few precious seconds and Henry Ford had just founded a motor company that bore his name. With slight modification and improvement, the basic rifle designed by the U.S. Ordnance Department to replace the U.S. Krag-Jorgensen rifle and carbine with a single rifle for both infantry and cavalry served American soldiers, sailors, Marines and airmen for more than half a century, from the Mexican Border to the frozen mountains of Korea.

The '03 has been many things to many people. Rock-solid and reliable in combat from the trenches of Flanders to the jungles of the South Pacific, accurate enough for target shooters and the 1,000-yard line at Camp Perry, and handy enough to be carried as a deer rifle in the woods back home, it became the benchmark for what a bolt-action rifle should be for generations of American soldiers, shooters and hunters. Its service to our nation, and its impact on the attitudes of shooter and soldier alike, is only surpassed — perhaps — by John Cantius Garand's *U.S. Rifle, Cal. .30 M1.*

In addition to its utility, the '03 represents craftsmanship of the like we will never see again. The machining, polishing and bluing work carried out by the craftsmen of Springfield and Rock Island can only be found on the highest priced custom rifles of today. The quality of the walnut, the fitting of the handguards and the hand-rubbed oil finish of the original '03's stock are, again, outside the realm of possibility for a factory-made rifle. These feats are even more impressive when you consider the fact that these were government employees, merely doing their jobs. It's a cliché, but when it comes to the '03 they just don't make them like they used to anymore.

Aesthetically, the '03 is simply a thing of beauty. While other rifles may have been a bit more robust, there is no military bolt rifle that has the grace and lines of the venerable '03. Even its likely progenitor, the Mauser Model 98, has angular Teutonic lines when compared to the svelte '03. A glance at some of its other contemporaries from just after the turn of the 20th century, such as the Short, Magazine Lee-Enfield or French Berthier, only make the case stronger.

Add together its combat record, myriad models and variations, and the grace of its design, and you have what is today a favorite rifle among collectors and shooters alike. The '03 offers the modern collector so many possibilities from rarities — such as the Rod Bayonet guns, Pedersen Device or Air Service rifles — to the common "plain Jane" M1903A3s likely to found at any decent gun show. Indeed, there is something for everyone regardless of the depth of your wallet. With the recent quantities of '03s and '03A3s offered by the Civilian Marksmanship Program, the rifle has made a return to the target range through matches such as the M1903 Match held at Camp Perry. It seems we are rediscovering what our grandfathers and great-grandfathers knew so well — the '03 can shoot, and shoot well.

For Bruce Canfield and me, it was the '03 that began our friendship. Bruce, who has one of the finest collection of U.S. martial arms in private hands, had managed to acquire a Cameron-Yaggi Trench Periscope rifle in about 1992 and was looking for a copy of the 1917 *Arms & The Man* article (*American Rifleman's* predecessor from 1903–1923) about the device. He wrote to the "Dope Bag" asking for a copy of the article. Bruce was doing what he does for all the arms about which he writes: his homework. As the owner of several already dog-eared copies of his books, I happily supplied him with it and asked if he would be interested in writing an article or two for *American Rifleman*. He readily agreed and soon thereafter became an *American Rifleman* contributing editor. Bruce is a gentleman in the truest sense of the word and has become one of the most important contributors to *American Rifleman*.

What Bruce does so well with his magazine articles for *American Rifleman* and *Man at Arms* and his arms books is to convey the historical background, development of evolution of American military arms in a conversation style, while at the same time giving the reader the detail to truly learn about almost every aspect of his gun or guns. He does an impressive job of weaving readable narrative together with original documents and reports, as well as supplying detail on aspects of the guns that the modern collecting fraternity has discerned. With his *Collector's Guide* series, he draws the arms enthusiast and collector into the subject, and he has managed to open up the world of collecting American military arms to a whole new generation. Whether an advanced collector or a beginner, the *Collector's Guides* are invaluable references that are readable and easy to use. As one who has reviewed hundreds of books on arms and equipment, I can assure you that those two traits are not commonly found when it comes to reference books on firearms.

When asked to recommend just one book on the '03 in the past, I have answered unequivocally: *A Collector's Guide to the '03 Springfield*. With the release of *An Illustrated Guide to the '03 Service Rifle*, I'll have to amend my response. If you need to know when your rifle was made, whether that is indeed the issue scope on your '03A4, who is represented by the "J.F.C." inspector's cartouche, or what should be on the ricasso of a typical World War II bayonet, it's just about all in here, and it's easy to find. Bruce's books are not the end-all and be-all in arms reference books, but there is no better place to start, and the revised edition of *Collector's Guide to the '03 Springfield* is no exception. After pouring through the manuscript, I believe it is Bruce's best yet. It is a fitting tribute to America's greatest military bolt-action rifle and the men who used it.

Mark A. Keefe, IV
Editor-In-Chief
American Rifleman
Fairfax, Virginia
December 2003

Author's Preface

The period of the last decade of the 20th century and the beginning of the 21st century has been a time of tremendous increase in collector interest regarding U.S. military arms of all types. Weapons that were only marginally popular with collectors and arms enthusiasts less than a decade ago are now avidly sought-after items with ever-escalating prices. The increased collector interest, along with upward spiraling prices, make it even more important that a collector acquire as much knowledge as possible about the weapons that he finds to be of interest.

Until the late 1970s and into the early 1980s, the '03 rifle was looked upon primarily as a candidate for sporterizing. Many books and magazine articles in the '40s, '50s and '60s detailed how to turn the old warhorse into an attractive (in the eyes of some) sporter for hunting or target use. This widespread practice of sporterizing the '03, and other surplus U.S. military rifles, partially accounts for the scarcity of examples remaining in their original military issue configuration today.

When my book *A Collector's Guide to the '03 Springfield* was published in 1989, collector interest in the genre was beginning to experience a noticeable increase. The encyclopedic book, *The Springfield '03*, by the late Col. William Brophy had been published a couple of years earlier and, despite some layout problems, had really raised the bar for other books on the subject. At the time, I was a fledgling author, and the late Andrew Mowbray, my publishing mentor and a first-class gentleman, encouraged me to do a basic collector's guide on the subject, to be, as he put it, "...a threshold to Brophy's book." I had some initial reservations, but Andy soon persuaded me that there was a place for both a book of this sort as well as Brophy's tome. As usual, he was right. My original '03 book has gone through several printings and has weathered the years pretty well. The time has come to thoroughly revise and expand my original '03 book in much the same manner as I did with my original M1 Garand/Carbine book a few years ago. Such a revision enables me to correct the errors and to expand on topics not covered, or only given cursory coverage, in my first Springfield guide.

This book will maintain the same basic format and scope as my first '03 book and will cover the variations of the M1903 rifle intended for service issue and/or combat use. In order to have a more focused work, such variations as the National Match rifles, .22 trainers and special target rifles will not be discussed. This is not any sort of disparagement of these rifles, as there are numerous, interesting, and quite valuable examples of these arms. However, the inclusion of these arms would result in a book about the size of the *Manhattan Yellow Pages*! Those interested in such noncombat variants of the M1903 rifle should consult Brophy's book which covers most of these weapons. This book is intended to be an intermediate collector's guide for anyone interested in the M1903 Springfield rifles. With books of this genre, an author is always faced with a striking an appropriate balance between presenting sufficient material in enough detail to provide a student of the subject with enough meat to make a book useful without delving into seemingly endless minutiae that will be of interest to only a small percentage of readers. A book that is too general in nature runs the risk of becoming an irrelevant coffee table tome, while a book that covers the most minor features in excruciating detail can easily make a casual reader's eyes glaze over in boredom and frustration. No book can be all things to all people. My goal with this book, as was the case with its predecessor, is to provide a general overview of M1903 service rifles and their variants, including some information on the historical background of the weapons. It is not intended to be an extremely detailed advanced collector's bible. This book was written to appeal to intermediate collectors, but is intended to be of sufficiently broad scope so as to be of interest to beginners as well. A person cannot have too many books or too many rifles. The study of different books by different writers will enable a reader to compare, contrast, and evaluate the information contained in each book to get a clearer and more accurate picture of the subject. No book is error-free and no author is immune from incorporating subtle, or sometimes not so subtle, bias into his work. Don't take everything you read in this or any other book as gospel and remember that any book is simply the best information that the writer has available to him at the time the book was written. New information is continually being discovered, which is one reason why I feel it is now time to update my first '03 book. Unlike some revised books, which consist of little more than a new cover, this book will be a totally different and greatly expanded work as compared to the original.

Collector interest in the '03 rifle has continued to increase over the years and was given a significant boost when the Civilian Marksmanship Program (CMP) received a large number of M1903 rifles, of various types, that were offered for sale to qualified purchasers beginning in 2002. Even though virtually all of the rifles were well used, and most were refinished/rebuilt one or more times, the CMP rifles have introduced many newcomers to the fascinating world of '03 collecting, and the interest shows no sign of abating in the near future. This growing collector interest in the '03 has resulted in some staggering price increases, along with some questionable specimens being offered for sale. This makes it even more important that a potential buyer be armed with reliable information before making a purchase decision. There are some Internet websites and forums devoted to the topic of '03 collecting and sometimes good information is exchanged there. Unfortunately, some of the information is also in the fantasy or *BS* category, or occasionally consists of unproven theories presented as fact. Whether a book or Internet site, do not always believe everything you read. As far as possible in this book, I will refrain from making idle speculation and will endeavor to clearly label theory or supposition as such. There is nothing wrong with a theory as long as it is not presented as proven fact and has some basis in logic. As readers of my previous books can attest, I like to interweave the historical aspects with details of the mechanical intricacies of the weapons. A book that consists of nothing but photographs and information about the hardware and leaving out the how, when and where the weapons were employed is a pretty sterile approach. I don't think it is possible to adequately discuss a weapon, even in a collector's guide type of book, without at least some discussion of the historical context in which the weapons were utilized.

The year 2003 marked the 100th anniversary of the M1903 rifle. Few American military weapons enjoy such widespread interest today among shooters, collectors and arms fanciers as does the venerable '03. It wouldn't be surprising if this interest is still alive and well when the 200th Anniversary of the rifle is celebrated in 2103!

Bruce N. Canfield
Shreveport, Louisiana
January 2004

Acknowledgements

I am most grateful to the individuals who helped make this book possible. Special thanks go to Cliff Feiler who provided invaluable assistance by helping to edit the initial manuscript and providing numerous suggestions. Cliff is a long-time collector and advanced student of the '03, and has owned or examined many rare and exotic variants. His extensive knowledge of the subject, eye for detail, and critical comments were important in making this book as accurate and informative as possible. His help is sincerely appreciated.

Thanks also to William Hansen, who has labored many hours in compiling information on the World War II production Remington and Smith-Corona rifles. His serial number/production date tables are the products of much scholarly research and dedication. His permission to allow the use of these tables in this book is gratefully acknowledged.

Thank you to Mark A. Keefe, IV, editor of *American Rifleman*, for writing the Foreword. Mark is not only the Editor-in-Chief of one of the most venerable arms-related publications in the world, he is also a devoted collector and has a wide-ranging interest in many types of military weaponry. I am grateful to have him as a friend.

I'm also greatly indebted to Frank Mallory of Springfield Research Service for information, photographs and encouragement. Frank, unfortunately, passed away prior to completion of this book. Researchers and collectors of U.S. martial arms owe a huge debt to Frank and his valuable contributions to the field of arms collecting. Others contributors who deserve my thanks are Hayes Otoupalik, Larry Reynolds, Frank Trzaska, John Gangel, Rick Slater, Billy Pyle, Scott Duff, Martin K.A. Morgan and Stuart Mowbray.

This is my ninth book to be published by Andrew Mowbray Publishing, Inc. I sincerely believe this is the finest organization of this type in existence today. Stuart Mowbray and his talented and helpful staff are the epitome of professionalism. I am fortunate to be associated with them and look forward to many more years of working with such a fine team.

Finally, thanks to my lovely wife Betty and my wonderful son Andrew for their patience, encouragement and inspiration and to God, our Heavenly Father, for all his blessings.

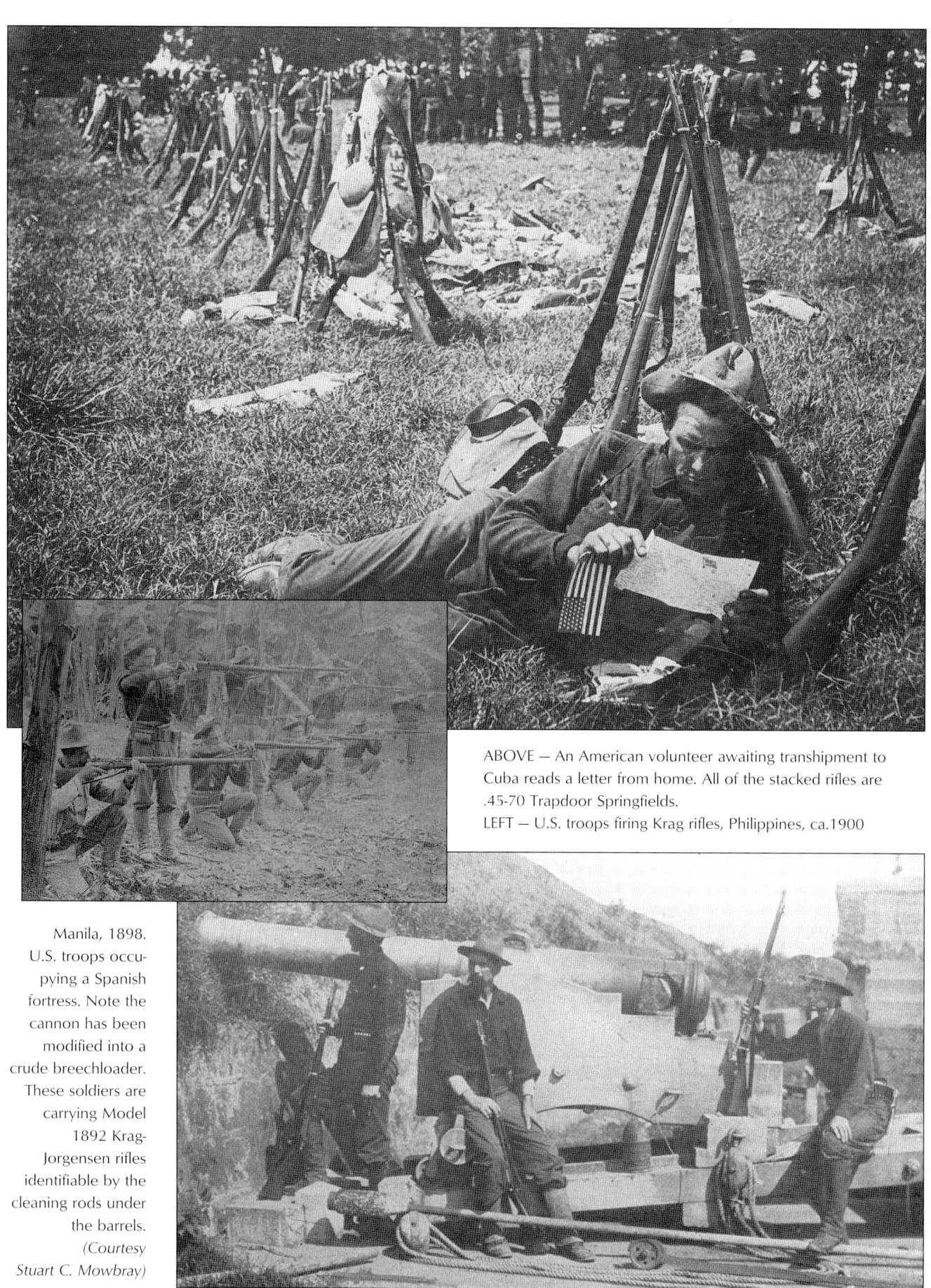

ABOVE — An American volunteer awaiting transhipment to Cuba reads a letter from home. All of the stacked rifles are .45-70 Trapdoor Springfields.
LEFT — U.S. troops firing Krag rifles, Philippines, ca.1900

Manila, 1898. U.S. troops occupying a Spanish fortress. Note the cannon has been modified into a crude breechloader. These soldiers are carrying Model 1892 Krag-Jorgensen rifles identifiable by the cleaning rods under the barrels.
(Courtesy Stuart C. Mowbray)

Historical Background and Prototypes

The development and adoption of the M1903 rifle can be directly traced back to the short-lived Spanish-American War of 1898. At the time of the conflict, the standard U.S. service rifle was the Norwegian-designed Krag-Jorgenson. The Krag had been adopted by the United States in 1892 after an exhaustive series of tests of many types of repeating rifles, both foreign and domestic. The Krag had an unusual side-mounted hinged magazine that was loaded by individual cartridges. The U.S. Krag was chambered for a .30 caliber round, the .30-40, and was the first smokeless powder United States service rifle cartridge. Due to protests from domestic arms inventors and delays in getting the production line set up, manufacture of the Krag did not get underway at Springfield Armory until 1894. The first pattern U.S. Krag service rifle was the Model of 1892. A couple of prototype cavalry Krag carbines were also fabricated, but a carbine version was not initially put into production. The Model of 1892 rifle was followed by the Model of 1896 rifle and carbine. The Model 1896 rifle differed from the Model 1892 primarily in deletion of the under-barrel full-length cleaning rod, the addition of a longer handguard and an improved rear sight, but functioning and performance of the two models were identical. The M1896 was followed by the Model of 1898, made in rifle and carbine configuration, and the Model of 1899 carbine. None of the Krag variants differed in any significant mechanical respects.

The outbreak of the Spanish-American War in 1898 found the United States Army woefully unprepared. The regular Army's primary arm was the M1892 Krag rifle, although a few of the later M1896 rifles and carbines were available. Due to the relative shortage of Krags, many of the old black-powder .45-70 Trapdoor Springfield rifles and carbines were issued to volunteer infantry and cavalry units. The Krag rifles of the regular U.S. Army units were soon pitted against the advanced German-designed Model 1893 Mausers in the hands of our Spanish adversaries. Once in combat, a number of problems inherent in the basic action and cartridge of the American Krag became glaringly apparent, especially when compared to the Mauser. The Mauser's much stronger double locking lug bolt enabled it to fire a flatter-shooting and more powerful cartridge than was possible with the Krag's single lug bolt. In addition, the Mauser was capable of being loaded by means of a five-round charger, often referred to as a stripper clip, which enabled the weapon to achieve a higher rate of fire than the Krag which could only be loaded with individual cartridges. Fortunately, the short duration of the Spanish-American War mitigated the Krag's shortcomings, so our troops did not have to pay an inordinate price for the deficiencies of our service rifle. However, the superiority of the Mauser and the relative inferiority of the Krag did not go unnoticed and, shortly after the war, a thorough evaluation of the Krag was begun by the U.S. Army Ordnance Department.

The deficiencies of the Krag were studied and methods to improve the weapon's performance were suggested and evaluated. One suggestion was to adapt the Krag's magazine to clip-loading capability. To this end, the Parkhurst Clip Loading Attachment was developed which enabled the Krag magazine to be loaded by means of a five-round charger. Circa 1901, Springfield Armory fitted one hundred M1898 Krag rifles and one hundred M1899 Krag carbines with the Parkhurst attachment to test the concept. Although marginally successful, the Parkhurst Attachment was not adopted and, in any event, did nothing to address the other deficiencies of the Krag, especially its ballistic performance.

Springfield Armory was ordered to begin development of a new service rifle cartridge with a minimum muzzle velocity of 2,300 feet per second (f.p.s.), compared to the Krag's 2,000 f.p.s. This increase in muzzle velocity resulted in chamber pressures in excess of 40,000 p.s.i., which was well above what the Krag action could safely handle. The proposed new cartridge was initially to be of the rimmed variety, as was the .30-40 Krag, although the option for a rimless cartridge was also considered.

Clearly, the Krag action had to be replaced by one capable of handling the increased chamber pressures of the newly proposed service rifle cartridge. Since a stronger two-lug bolt and clip-loading capability were desirable, and as the Mauser action incorporated both features, it was logical for our Ordnance Department engineers to base the new experimental prototype rifle on the Mauser. The Mauser's performance in the recently-concluded Spanish-American War gave further credence to the relative superiority of the basic design.

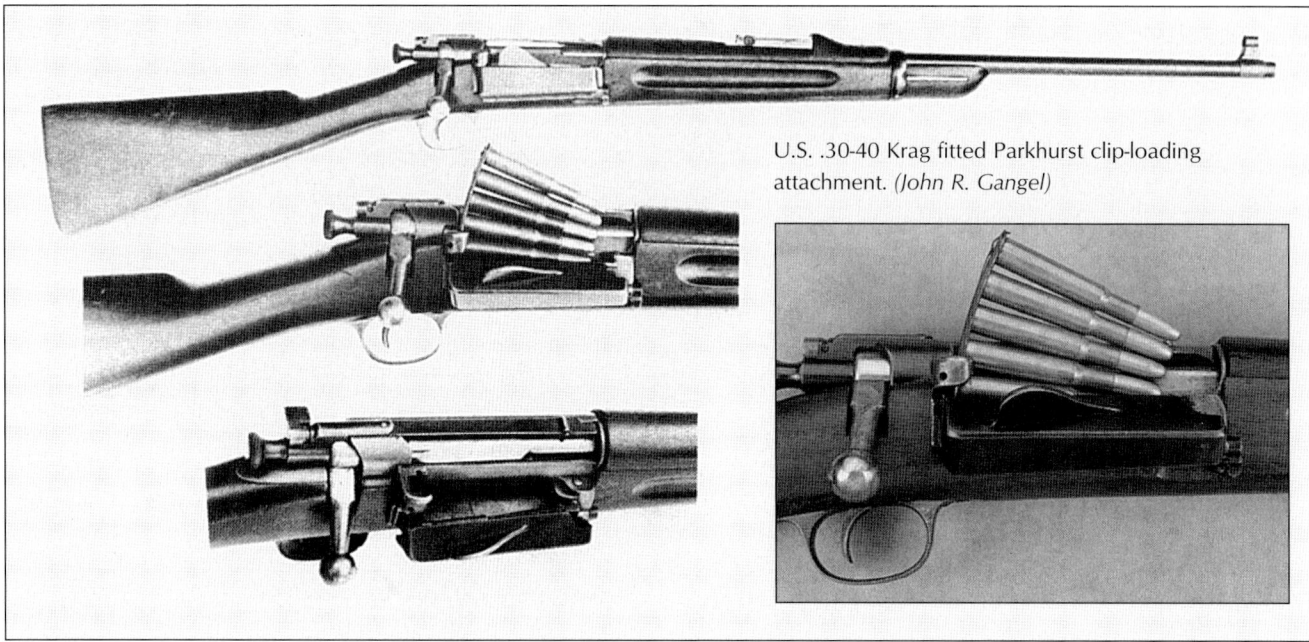

U.S. .30-40 Krag fitted Parkhurst clip-loading attachment. *(John R. Gangel)*

Experimental Magazine Rifle of 1900

Even while attempts to improve the Krag, such as the Parkhurst Attachment, were being conducted, an experimental rifle was fabricated by Springfield Armory in mid-1900. This rifle featured an action reflecting a number of features clearly based on the Mauser. These included clip-loading slots in the top of the receiver and a bolt with two locking lugs plus a separate safety lug. Otherwise, the rifle had features similar to the M1898 Krag including a 30-inch barrel, stock furniture (barrel bands, buttplate, etc.), provision for the Krag bayonet, a jointed cleaning rod housed in a hinged butt trap recess, and a magazine cut-off. The rear sight made for the 1900 rifle was later adopted as the M1901 rear sight for the Krag. One wag of the day described the new rifle as, "being sired by Mauser out of Krag." Perhaps the quip was funnier at the time!

On August 25, 1900, the rifle, designated as the Experimental Magazine Rifle of 1900, was delivered to the War Department for evaluation. The rifle was subsequently returned to Springfield Armory on October 2nd to be submitted to an Ordnance Department Board convened to evaluate the weapon. The Board tested the rifle for a few months, and on December 8, 1900, made its report and recommendations to the War Department. The suggestions included replacing the magazine that extended below the stock with an integral staggered-row magazine, improving the function of the magazine cut-off mechanism and adopting a cannelured (rimless) cartridge to improve the functioning of the magazine and make clip-loading easier.

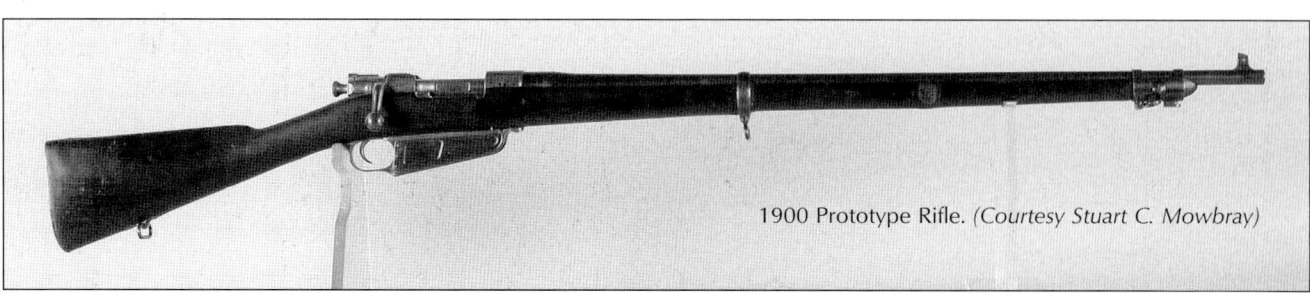

1900 Prototype Rifle. *(Courtesy Stuart C. Mowbray)*

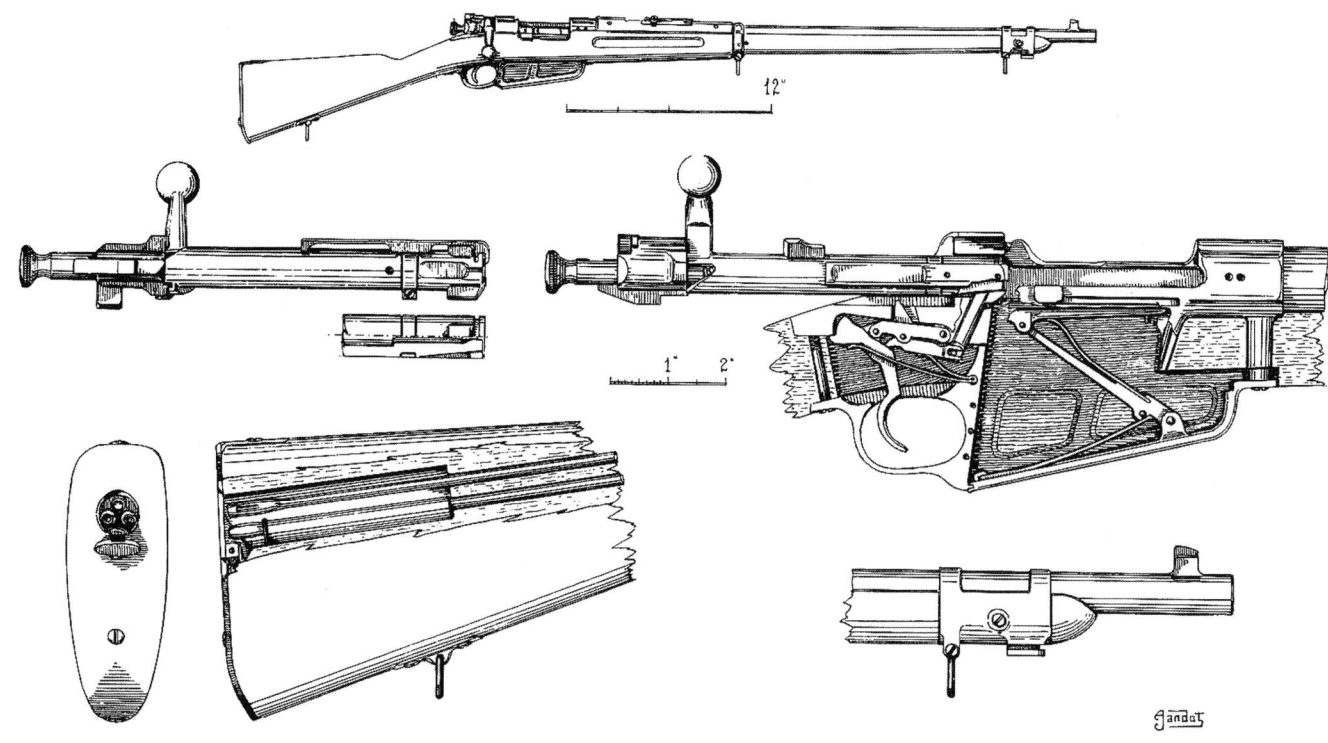

Line drawings of 1900 Prototype Rifle. *(U.S. Military Firearms)*

Close-up of open bolt on 1900 Prototype Rifle.
(Springfield Armory Museum collection. Courtesy Stuart C. Mowbray)

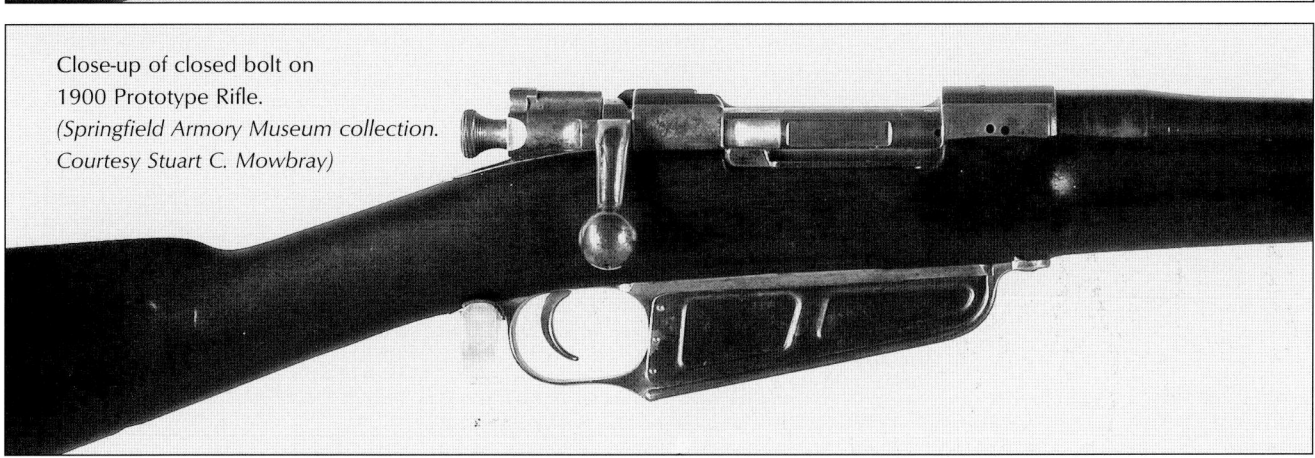

Close-up of closed bolt on 1900 Prototype Rifle.
(Springfield Armory Museum collection. Courtesy Stuart C. Mowbray)

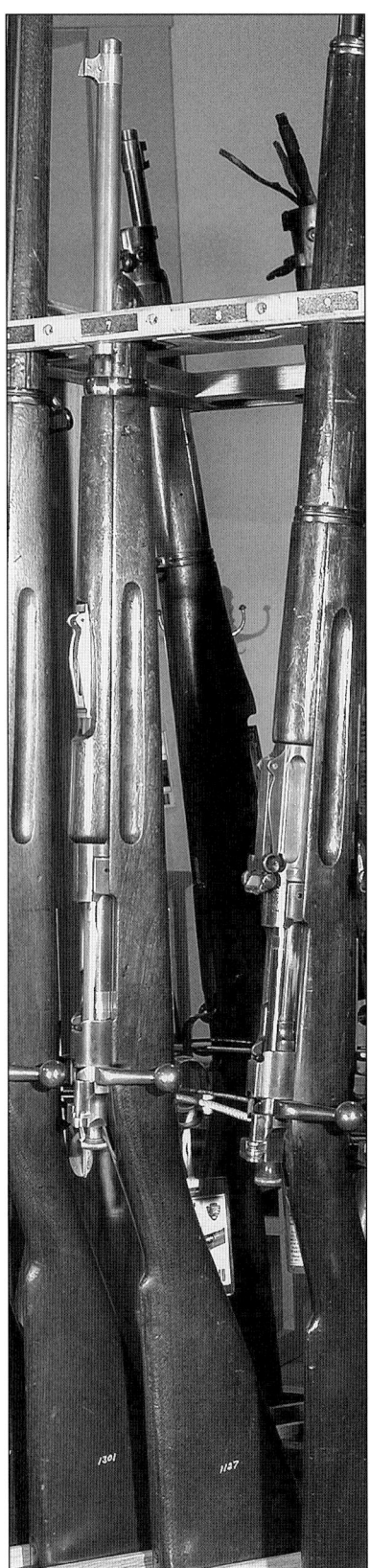

Experimental Springfield '03 carbine. (Springfield Armory Museum collection. Courtesy of Stuart C. Mowbray)

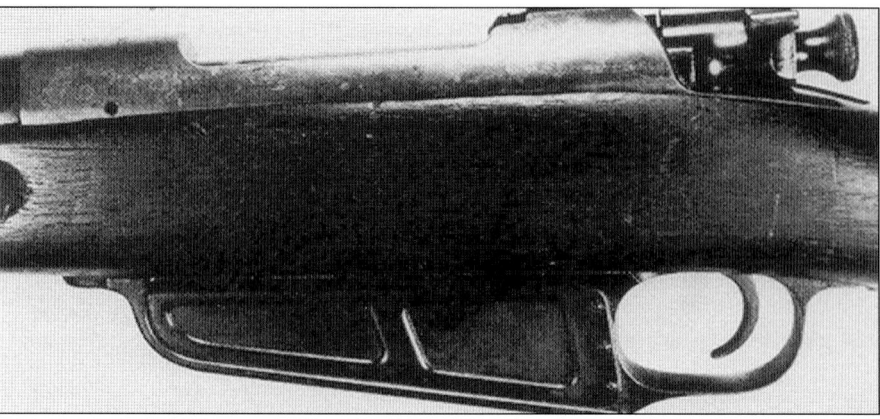

Close-up views of Experimental 1900 and 1901 protype rifles.
(Springfield Armory Museum collection. Courtesy Stuart C. Mowbray)

1901 Prototype

An improved design incorporating the changes recommended by the Ordnance Board was fabricated by Springfield Armory. In addition to being chambered for the cannelured cartridge, the new prototype rifle incorporated a five-round staggered-row integral magazine with clip-loading capability, an improved magazine cut-off, and, except for the first few examples, an integral rod bayonet. The rod bayonet was intended to replace the standard knife bayonet as used with the Krag. The rod bayonet concept had previously been utilized with various types of U.S. military weapons including the final production version of the .45-70 Trapdoor Springfield rifle, the Model of 1888. Reintroduction of the rod bayonet for the new service rifle was precipitated by the desires of the Chief of Ordnance as reflected in his 1901 Fiscal Report:

"The present service rifle (Krag-Jorgenson) has met with approval by the Army at large. The sword bayonet with which it is equipped is considered by the Chief of Ordnance as imperfect and antiquated. It is heavy and, with its scabbard, a costly part of the soldier's equipment, and is a needless impediment to his freedom of action and comfort on the march, and as an intrenching tool, it is a poor substitute. The bayonet has now only a very rare use and may well be dispensed with, relieving the soldier of considerable weight and inconvenience and saving the very considerable cost."

Similar negative comments against the standard bayonet by the U.S. Army Ordnance Department can be traced back for several decades. The fact that the rod bayonet had never worked out well in service was apparently ignored or forgotten. In any event, preliminary testing of the 1901 prototype resulted in approval to manufacture 5,000 rifles for troop trial, and limited issue. Although some components of the prototype rifle were similar to those used with the Krag, which was still in production at Springfield Armory, it was determined that tooling up for the new weapon would be a lengthy and time-consuming process. It was therefore decided to fabricate a small number of essentially hand-made examples for further testing and evaluation while production was being set up and an Ordnance Board convened to conduct additional tests.

The exact number of 1901 prototype rifles fabricated is not known, but examples with serial numbers as high as 36 have been observed, so it can be assumed that at least this

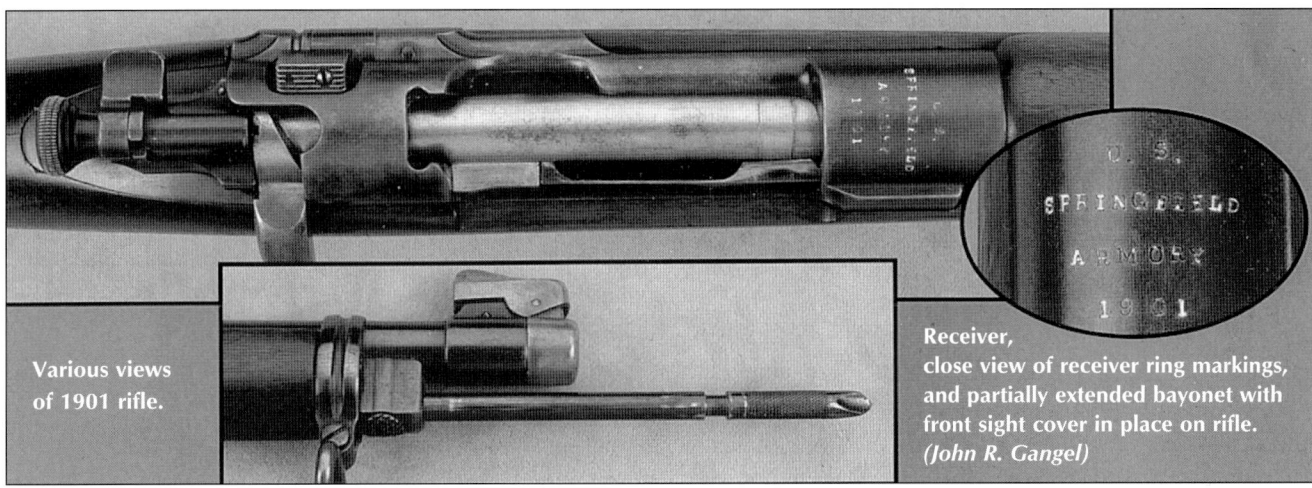

Various views of 1901 rifle.

Receiver, close view of receiver ring markings, and partially extended bayonet with front sight cover in place on rifle. *(John R. Gangel)*

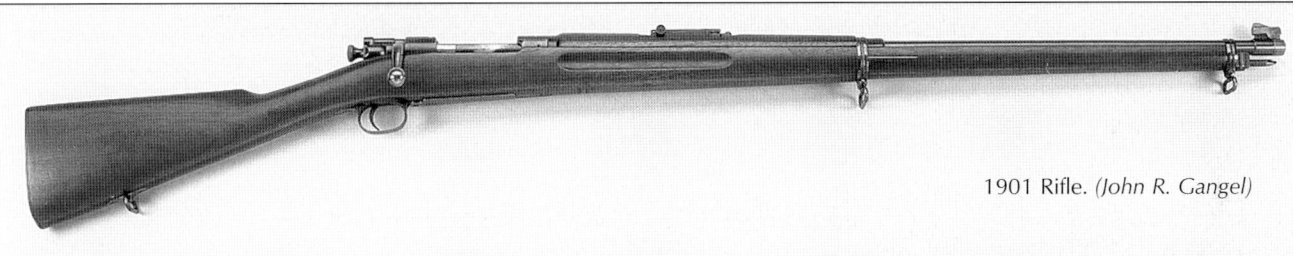

1901 Rifle. *(John R. Gangel)*

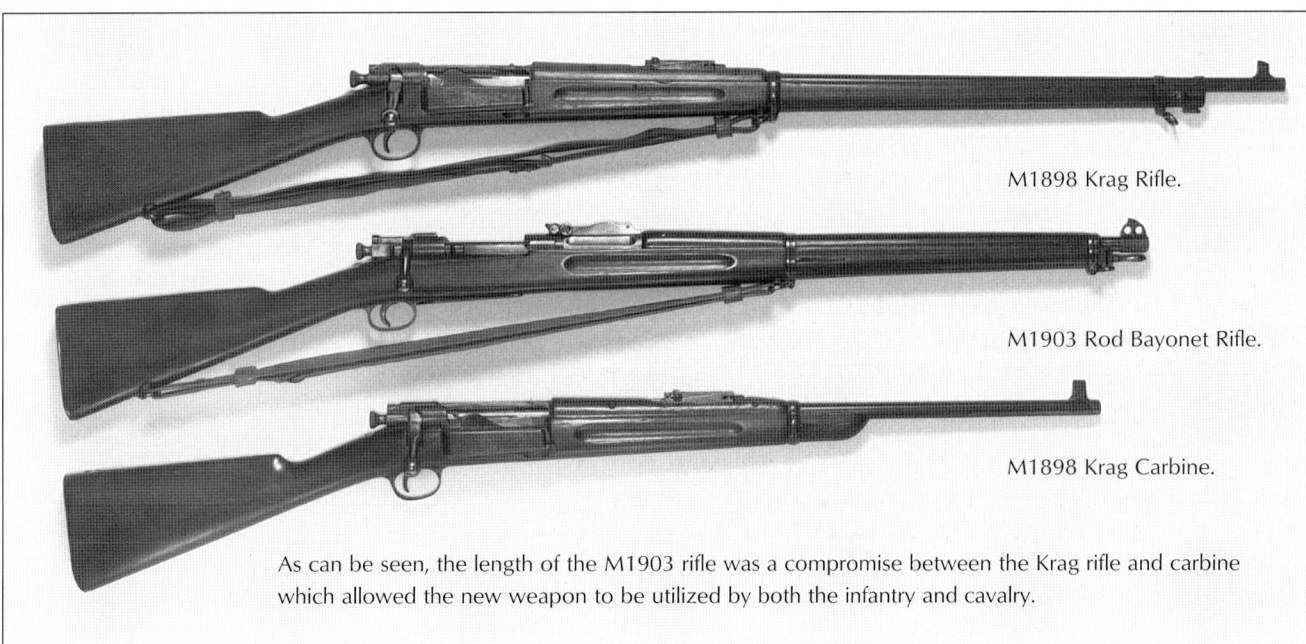

M1898 Krag Rifle.

M1903 Rod Bayonet Rifle.

M1898 Krag Carbine.

As can be seen, the length of the M1903 rifle was a compromise between the Krag rifle and carbine which allowed the new weapon to be utilized by both the infantry and cavalry.

number were made, far from the 5,000 for which funds were appropriated. The receivers had hand-stamped markings, including serial numbers, although some examples without serial numbers have been noted. Some 1901 prototype rifles marked "Model of 1902" as well as "1901" may be encountered. The 1902 rifles are identical to those of 1901 and were most likely marked in this manner because production was in 1902 instead of signifying another model of experimental rifle. Most of the 1901 rifles were produced with the same 30-inch barrel length of the Krag, however, a few were also fabricated in the 22-inch carbine length. Roy Dunlap, in one of his hand-loading books from the early 1950s, mentioned conducting velocity tests by installing a 1901 barrel in a receiver, and cutting off one inch at a time to take chronographic measurements.

On January 23, 1903, the final Ordnance Board was convened to test and evaluate the latest 1901 prototype rifle, to make recommendations regarding the weapon's performance, and to ascertain if it was enough of an improvement over the Krag to warrant adoption as the new U.S. service rifle. Ten of the 1901 prototype rifles were tested at Springfield Armory and the Sandy Hook Proving Ground in New Jersey. The control rifle was a standard M1898 Krag, which was tested along with the prototype rifles.

The extensive testing revealed that the prototype rifle performed satisfactorily but several changes were suggested. Except for the suggestion that the barrel be reduced from 30 inches to 24 inches, most of the changes were relatively minor in nature. The Krag had been manufactured in rifle configuration (30-inch barrel) for the infantry and carbine configuration (22-inch barrel) for the cavalry. It was realized that by compromising on a barrel length of 24 inches, one weapon could serve the needs of both branches of the army. Although not needed for cavalry use, it was recommended that the rod bayonet be retained, but reduced in length and changed in configuration to prevent its use as a cleaning rod, presumably to mitigate damage to the bore. A subsequent Ordnance Board report stated:

"In recommending the adoption of the rod bayonet, the board was influenced by the weight saved, the unsatisfactory means provided for carrying the knife bayonet, the unavoidable noise made by the bayonet in its scabbard, the frequent loss of the bayonet in the field, that the use of the bayonet with the clip-loading magazine arm will be very limited, and that, as a matter of fact, the muzzle of a military rifle carries with it a well-known moral effect regardless of the presence of a bayonet.

"The Ordnance Department was of the opinion that a new rapid-firing clip-loaded magazine rifle would render a bayonet essentially superfluous. It was undoubtedly believed that any token need for a bayonet would be met by the rod bayonet which was lighter in weight and cheaper to produce than a traditional knife bayonet and scabbard."

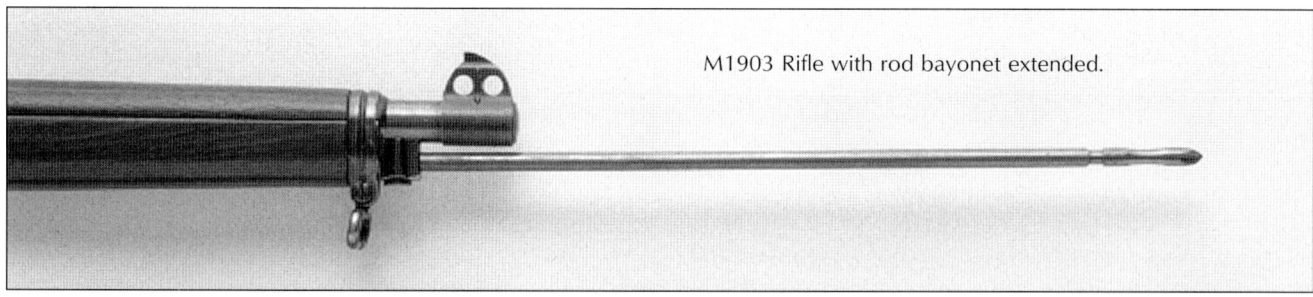

M1903 Rifle with rod bayonet extended.

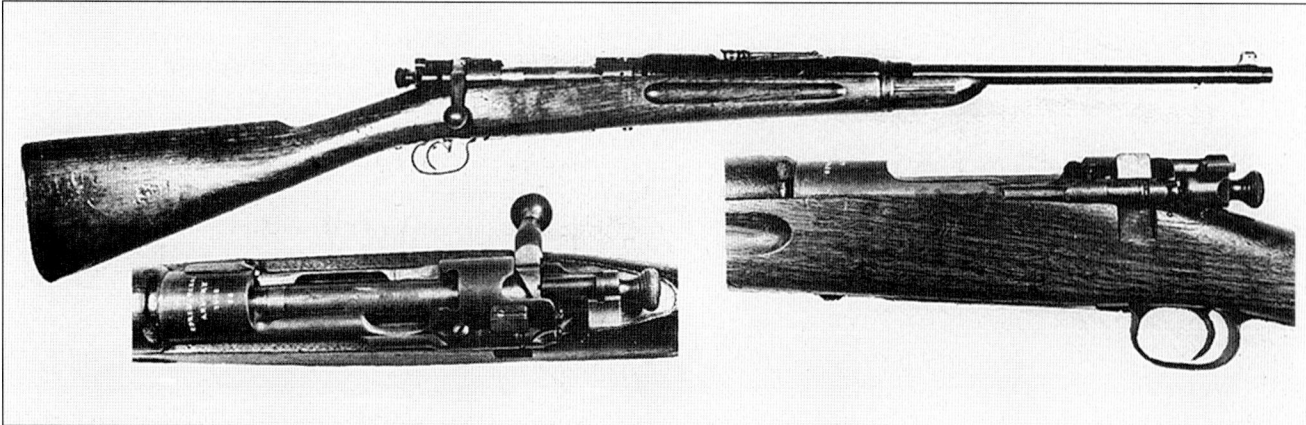

1901 Prototype Carbine. *(Bob Hill collection)*

The final conclusion of the Ordnance Board was to recommend the adoption of a slightly modified version of the 1901 prototype rifle with a 24-inch barrel chambered for a rimless .30 caliber cartridge and fitted with a rod bayonet. The decision to have a single weapon with which to arm both the infantry and the cavalry made a lot of sense from an economic standpoint, as Springfield Armory did not have to change tooling back and forth from rifle to carbine as had been done when manufacturing the Krag. Manufacturing one standard pattern rifle allowed economies of scale that were not possible with a separate standardized rifle and carbine, and also reduced logistical problems.

Despite some initial misgivings, the decision eventually proved to be a popular choice with most of what would now be called the using services, even though the new rifle had more recoil and muzzle blast than the Krag rifle. Compared to the previous Krag carbine, most of the cavalrymen did not view the new rifle's longer barrel and slightly greater weight as serious disadvantages. The average infantryman, on the other hand, likely found the Krag rifle's 30-inch barrel an unnecessary and somewhat unwieldy encumbrance and was generally pleased with the handier and lighter new rifle with its 24-inch barrel.

Very few of the 1900, 1901 or 1902 prototype rifles were manufactured, making the likelihood that a collector might find one in an out-of-the-way gun shop or flea market remote. There are a few in private hands but most reside in the Springfield Armory Museum. One example of a 1902-dated prototype in carbine configuration, serial number 29, has been in a major private collection since at least the early 1970s. A very nice 1901-dated, 30-inch barrel prototype rifle, not serially numbered, sold at auction in 2002 for an impressive sum. Otherwise, there has been very little market activity for these weapons.

A number of unfinished 1901-vintage receivers exist and are encountered from time to time. A collector should be aware of the possibility of a counterfeit rifle being made from one of these unfinished receivers. The fact that the original receivers had hand-stamped markings only simplifies the fakery. Anyone offered a weapon of this type purported to be original should be wary and consult someone knowledgeable in the field, especially given the hefty price tag that will undoubtedly be involved. No two of the extant 1901/1902 prototype rifles are exactly the same. Markings and some other small features vary from example to example, so it is difficult to make a useful comparison when attempting to judge authenticity. This makes positive identification problematical for even experienced collectors. It would be wise to deal with a recognized dealer or auction house and to insist upon some form of guarantee of authenticity. Even so, a guarantee of authenticity is only worth the reliability and net worth of the person or entity issuing it. If faced with the opportunity to purchase one of these elusive arms, the well-known phrase *Caveat Emptor* certainly applies.

The M1903 Rod Bayonet Rifle (1903–1905)

On June 19, 1903, the recommendations of the Ordnance Board were formally approved and the new rifle was adopted as the United States Magazine Rifle, Caliber .30, Model of 1903. The rifle was chambered for the Cartridge, Ball, Caliber .30, Model of 1903 (.30-03). The following day, Springfield Armory was directed to begin the production and acquisition of the tools, fixtures and other implements necessary to begin manufacture of the M1903 rifle, with an initial target goal of 125 rifles per day. In order to have a secondary production source, Rock Island Arsenal was also mandated to establish a M1903 rifle production line, with the same daily quota as Springfield. In July 1903, the target production goals were modified to increase Springfield's daily production rate to 400, with Rock Island's quota to remain at 125 rifles per day.

The first pattern M1903 is widely referred to as a rod bayonet rifle. This designation is strictly unofficial collector shorthand, but is a handy way to differentiate the first pattern of the M1903 rifle from the later variants, and the term will be used in this book.

The change-over from the Krag to the new M1903 rifle proceeded somewhat faster and smoother than initially anticipated. Springfield Armory was able to get underway with production of the new rifle in November 1903, even though the M1898 Krag was still being manufactured. While the first examples of the new rifle were coming off the assembly line, Ordnance Department engineers continued refining the design, and a number of relatively minor changes were incorporated. These changes included the previously suggested decrease of the rifling twist from 8 inches to 10 inches in order to reduce erosion caused by the hot burning gun powder used in the cartridge, the redesigning of the safety, bolt sleeve and cocking piece, the slight modification of the rear sight and the lengthening of the magazine follower. The change in rifling twist did not sufficiently reduce the severe bore erosion, and the muzzle velocity of the .30-03 cartridge was reduced from 2,300 f.p.s. to 2,200 f.p.s., in an attempt to improve the situation. It was determined that this decrease in muzzle velocity of 100 f.p.s. did not materially affect the accuracy or power of the rifle, yet allowed double the number of rounds to be fired before severe bore erosion was experienced.

The stock and handguard were made from an excellent grade of black walnut and extended closer to the end of the muzzle than subsequent variants of the '03 rifle. Unlike later handguards, the rod bayonet rifle's handguard did not have the familiar hump in front of the rear sight that was later incorporated as a protective feature for the sight. The stock was stamped on the left side, below and behind the magazine cutoff recess, with a rectangular cartouche, usually consisting of script inspector initials and the date of production ("1903", "1904" or "1905").

As originally adopted, the safety lever was unmarked and was similar to the earlier Mauser safeties. This design proved to be insufficiently strong and the safety was modified to a more robust design, with the now-familiar lever with "Ready" and "Safe" designations on either side. This change was due, in large measure, to revisions in the infantry drill regulations that called for the rifle to be carried, loaded and cocked. The constant locking and unlocking of the safety lever resulted in rapid wear on the component that was corrected by the stronger design.

The rear sight of the rod bayonet rifle was similar to the previous M1902 sight as used with the final production version of the M1898 Krag rifle. The original '03 rear sight was referred to in some Ordnance Department documents as the Dickson sight. The sight was modified in 1904 by the adoption of a sliding plate with peep sight aperture.

The front sight differed from the previous Krag front sight in that it consisted of a separate band assembly, while the Krag front sight was attached to the barrel by brazing. The original pattern '03 front sight had a distinctive appearance compared to the later sights, and can be easily identified by the two holes below the blade. In 1904, the rear face of the front sight stud was serrated to reduce light reflection when aiming the rifle.

ABOVE – Receiver markings on early Rock Island Arsenal '03.
BELOW – Inspection stamp on rod bayonet rifle stock. Note the 1904 date.

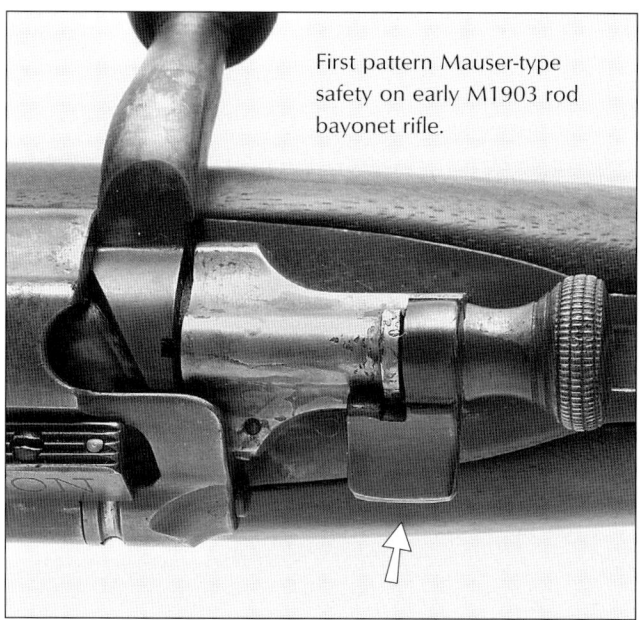

First pattern Mauser-type safety on early M1903 rod bayonet rifle.

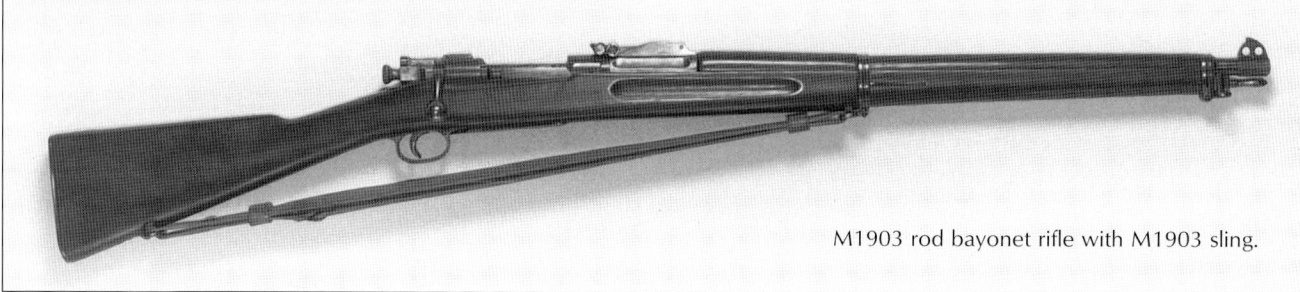

M1903 rod bayonet rifle with M1903 sling.

Unlike the later '03 rifles, the rod bayonet rifle barrels were not marked with the initials of the manufacturer, date of production, or the Ordnance Department's flaming bomb insignia behind the front sight. The barrels had a script "P" (proof) mark on the bottom of the chamber area, which is only visible with the stock removed. This marking signified that the barrel had been successfully fired with a heavy test cartridge, called a proof load, as part of the factory inspection procedure. The rifles were issued with an easily removable sheet metal cover, which protected the front sight when the rifle was not in use, and also served as a muzzle cover.

The barrel and most of the furniture of the new M1903 rifle were finished during this period in the typical high-quality Springfield Armory rust blue called *browning*. Rust bluing was a time-consuming process that involved coating the metal parts with a chemical solution and placing them in a special chamber. The parts were exposed to high humidity inside the chamber, which caused them to rust. The rust was then removed with a fine wire brush. This process was called "carding," and the procedure was repeated (rusting and carding) several times until the part was properly finished. Oil was then applied to stop the rusting process, and the resulting part had an attractive and distinctive blued finish.

U.S. Army soldier with rod bayonet '03 rifle.

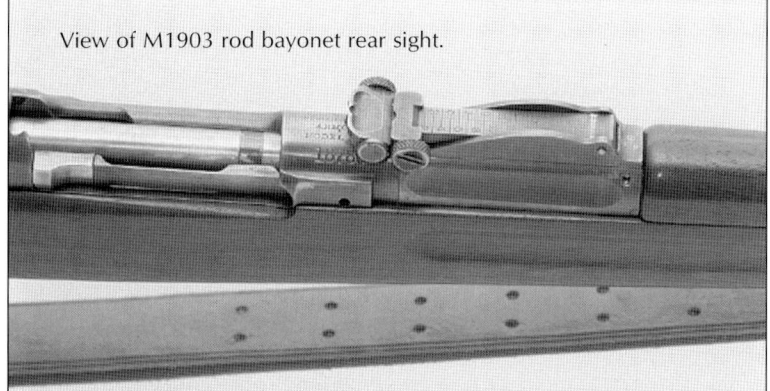

View of M1903 rod bayonet rear sight.

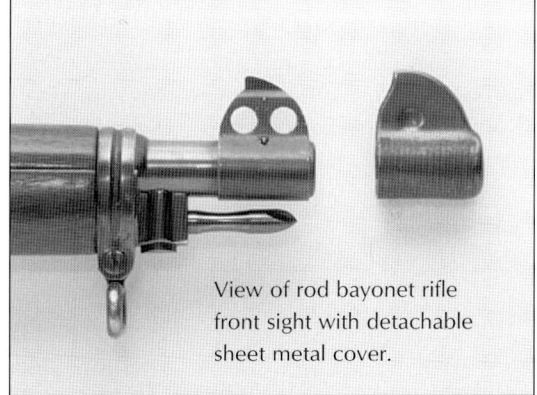

View of rod bayonet rifle front sight with detachable sheet metal cover.

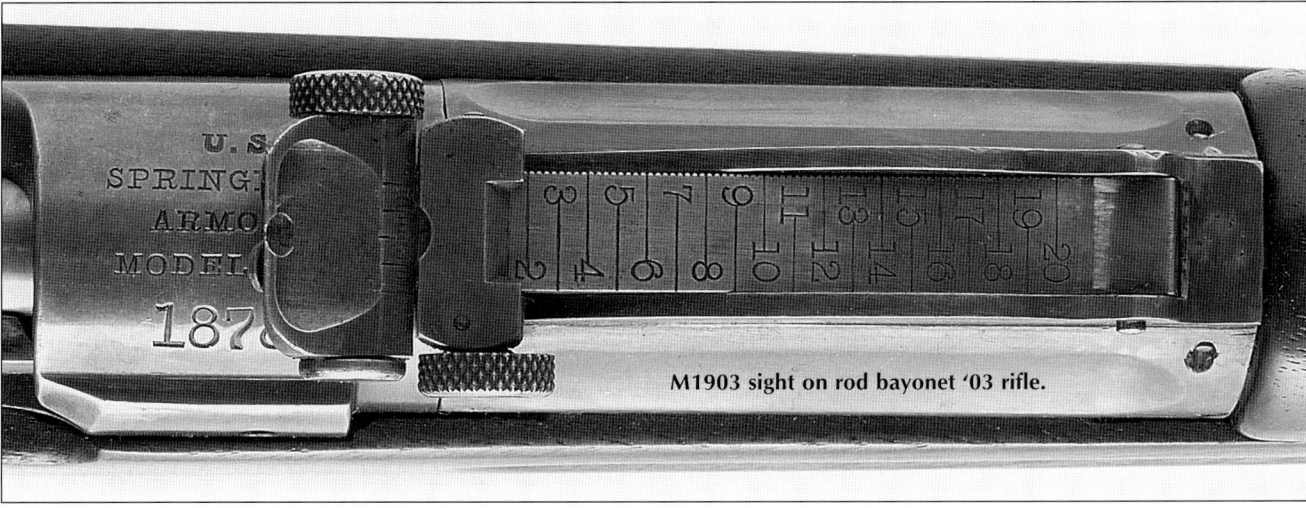

M1903 sight on rod bayonet '03 rifle.

Some smaller parts, such as the rear sight leaf face and magazine cutoff lever, were rust blued in this manner, and then polished. The polishing allowed the graduations of the sight and letters on the cutoff to be more easily defined than if the parts were left with a dark blued finish. Only the "ON" side of the cutoff lever was polished in order to make it readily apparent that the magazine cutoff was engaged. Early bolt bodies were polished, and the handles were blued. The finish on the extractors left a subtle purplish tint. By 1906, the entire bolt body was blued rather than left bright. The receiver of the rifle was case hardened and oil quenched. The quenching process involved quickly cooling off the hot receiver in an oil bath which resulted in a durable, if somewhat mottled, grayish finish.

The trigger had a slim profile, similar to the Krag trigger, and was not grooved. One defect of the rod bayonet rifle was the fact that, in addition to firing the weapon in the normal manner by pulling the trigger, it could also be fired by pushing forward on the trigger. When these early rifles were later modified, a metal pin was added to the forward portion of the trigger slot to rectify the problem.

Another problem that was discovered was that the sliding rod bayonet could not be easily extended or retracted if the stacking swivel was rotated forward. To correct this problem, the stacking swivel of the rod bayonet '03 rifle was milled flat on one section to provide the necessary clearance. There were also several minor changes made to the design of the bayonet locking mechanism to more securely latch the bayonet in the open position.

Another distinctive feature of the rod bayonet rifle was the lower barrel band which was solid and not split as were subsequent barrel bands. This type of barrel band could be difficult to remove without marring the stock, and the later split band, introduced in 1906, could be more easily removed or installed by loosening the retaining screw. The magazine follower was shorter and had a square-profile front end as compared to the later followers which were longer and had a tapered front end.

The new rifle's buttplate was smooth (non-checkered), with a hinged cap to access a recess in the butt. Initially, the recess was supposed to be designed to contain a small oiler and a cleaning rod head that could be screwed to the end of the rod bayonet to form a cleaning rod. This was similar to detachable cleaning rod heads carried in the butt trap recesses of later model .45-70 Trapdoor Springfield rifles equipped with rod bayonets. Likely, before the first '03 rifles got into quantity production, this concept was discarded, and a combination oiler and thong case replaced the smaller oiler and cleaning rod head. Surviving examples of the small oiler or the cleaning rod head are rare.

Some buttplates had a smaller diameter opening which indicates that they were converted Krag buttplates. These Krag buttplates were modified by grinding down the lower toe. They usually had Krag assembly numbers stamped inside of the buttplate and the hinged trapdoor. The majority of later production rifles utilized newly made buttplates with slightly larger recesses, although the modified Krag buttplates continued to be used until the supply was exhausted. Springfield Armory's production proceeded relatively smoothly, but Rock Island Arsenal was plagued by difficulties and delays, and it was not until May 1904 that RIA began manufacture of parts for the M1903 rifle. It is interesting to note that Rock Island Arsenal M1903 rifle, serial number 1, was not assembled until December 1904. Although Rock Island Arsenal was able to produce sufficient parts for 125 rifles per day by January 1905, there is some question whether the Arsenal produced any completed rod bayonet rifles, other than a handful of prototypes. Some sources have stated that as many as 1,500 may have been completed. In any event, few, if any, of the Rock Island rod bayonet rifles were issued, and virtually all were retained at RIA and subsequently converted to later specifications.

Springfield Armory, on the other hand, continued to turn out fair numbers of complete rod bayonet rifles. As the new rifles came off Springfield's assembly line, the War Department decided to withhold the weapons from widespread general issue until sufficient numbers were on hand to equip the majority of the regular U.S. Army units. A number of VIPs, including some state governors, were presented with standard issue M1903 rod bayonet rifles by the Ordnance Department or War Department, presumably for P.R. (Public Relations) purposes. A few of these rifles have surfaced and are obviously valuable and desirable weapons. In addition to these VIP rifles, just over 30,000 of the rifles were issued, based on Ordnance Department records. Among the first units to receive the rod bayonet rifle was the Corps of Cadets at West Point, which received the new weapon in March 1904. Limited numbers of U.S. Army infantry units are confirmed to have received the new rifles, including at least one unit based in Alaska. Some U.S. Army units in China and the Philippines were also slated to receive the weapon.

Users of the new rifle initially had mixed feelings about the weapon as compared to the Krag. The Krag rifle was a much milder weapon to shoot, given the longer barrel and less powerful cartridge. The new '03, on the other hand, while shorter and handier, had a greater muzzle blast and recoil than did its predecessor. Also, as is typical with any new weapon introduced into military service, some complaints were lodged against the '03 that can be primarily attributed to reluctance to change. Eventually, the accuracy, handling characteristics, and performance of the '03 won over most of its detractors.

As was the case with most products of the national armories, Springfield and Rock Island, the M1903 rod bayonet rifle was a very attractive weapon that exhibited

ABOVE – M1903 rifle production machinery at Rock Island Arsenal. *(Rock Island Arsenal Museum)*
BELOW – U.S. Army unit armed with M1903 rod bayonet rifles. A faint hand-written inscription "Alaska, 1905" was on the original print. Few Regular Army units were issued rod bayonet rifles.

LEFT – Stacking swivel on rod bayonet rifle rotated to show the portion that was milled flat to permit the bayonet to be easily extended or retracted.
BELOW – U.S. Army soldier sighting early rod bayonet rifle.
(Rock Island Arsenal Museum)
BELOW, LEFT – U.S. Army soldier posing with early production M1903 rod bayonet rifle. *(Rock Island Arsenal Museum)*

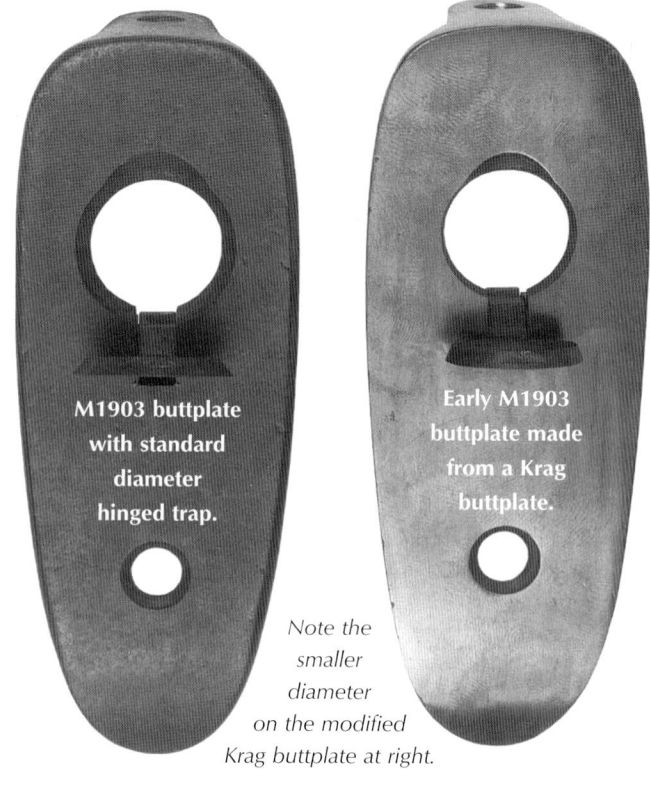

M1903 buttplate with standard diameter hinged trap.

Early M1903 buttplate made from a Krag buttplate.

Note the smaller diameter on the modified Krag buttplate at right.

top-quality workmanship. The attractive rust bluing, stocks and handguards made from a high grade of walnut, and a superb wood-to-metal fit resulted in a weapon that rivaled many high-grade sporting rifles in quality. Infantry and cavalry drill regulations had to be updated for the new rifle that was slated to come into service, and some of the above-referenced modifications were due to defects, or other unanticipated problems, encountered in the field. **Table 3** on page 211 in this book is a 1914 Ordnance Department synopsis of the various changes made in the components of the M1903 rifle from the time of its adoption in 1903 through early 1914.

West Point cadets in dress formation with rod bayonet '03 rifles. *(West Point Museum)*

West Point cadets on the range firing rod bayonet '03 rifles. *(West Point Museum)*

M1903 rod bayonet rifle and accessories including wooden ammo crate, cartridge belt, ammunition, saddle scabbard and manual.

German Patent Infringement Claims

The fact that the design of the M1903 rifle and its stripper clip were clearly based on the Mauser resulted in concerns about possible patent infringements. On March 15, 1904, General William Crozier wrote a letter to the Mauser firm raising this possibility and suggesting consultation to look into the issue. Further investigation determined that the new American service rifle and the stripper clip violated five of the Mauser rifle patents and two of the clip patents. Eventually, an agreement was reached for the U.S. government to pay royalties of 75 cents per rifle and 50 cents per thousand stripper clips, until a total of $200,000 had been paid. The final installment was paid in July 1909.

Soon after the agreed-upon royalty to Mauser had been paid, another German firm, Duetsch Waffen-und-Munitionsfabriken, filed a claim against the American government for patent infringement regarding the spitzer bullet used with the M1906 cartridge. The United States responded that no patents were violated, as the Army Ordnance Department had conducted experiments with such bullets at least as early as 1894. The German company disagreed, and filed suit demanding payment of a royalty of $1.00 per thousand for 250,000,000 M1906 cartridges. Before the suit could go to trial, the First World War intervened, and the German bullet patent was seized by the American government under the Alien Property Custody Act. This action, for the moment, rendered the entire claim moot. However, in 1921, an international tribunal found that, although the initial German claim was without merit, the American seizure of the German patent was a violation of existing treaties and awarded damages in the amount of $300,000. By the time all appeals were exhausted and accrued interest assessed, the American government eventually paid over $400,000 to settle the claim. It is ironic that the amount paid to settle a groundless bullet claim was more than double that paid to satisfy the clear patent violations that were amicably settled between the U.S. government and the Mauser firm. Any doubt that the design of the '03 was based on the Mauser can be easily put to rest by looking at the royalty settlement mutually agreed to by the United States and Waffenfabrik Mauser. In hindsight, that may have been the best $200,000 we ever spent!

By January of 1905, there was a sufficient quantity of the new rod bayonet rifles on hand to begin general issue to the regular Army. However, before this could be accomplished, the proverbial monkey wrench was thrown into the works. President Theodore Roosevelt, an ardent rifle enthusiast, was not at all enamored with the concept of the flimsy rod bayonet on the U.S. new service rifle. There is an oft-repeated story about how Roosevelt demonstrated the unsuitability of the rod bayonet by means of a hands-on demonstration in the Oval Office, where he succeeded in snapping a rod bayonet in two with a single well-placed

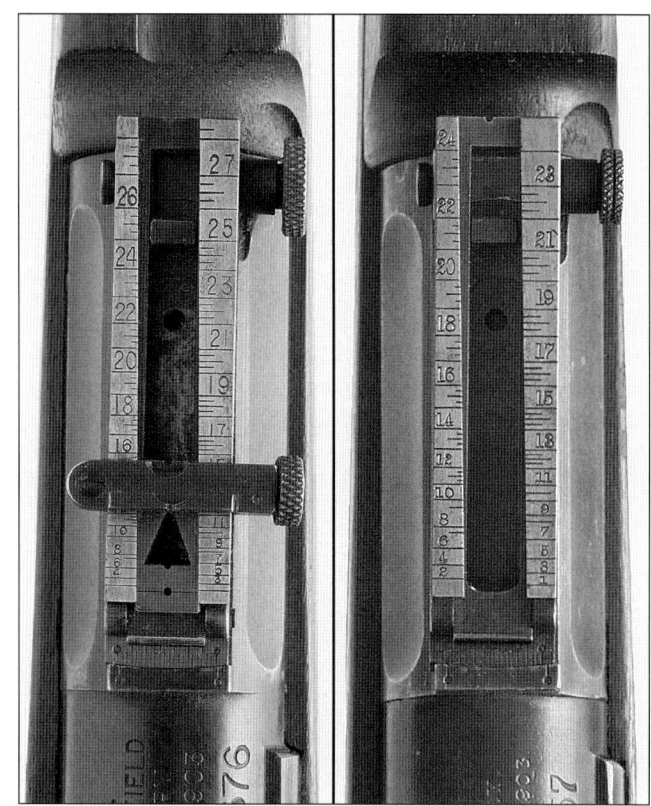

ABOVE, LEFT – M1905 sight leaf-graduated for .30-06 cartridge. Note the differences in the style of numerals as compared to .30-03 sight leaf. ABOVE, RIGHT — M1905 sight leaf-graduated for .30-03 cartridge. Note that the slide has been removed.

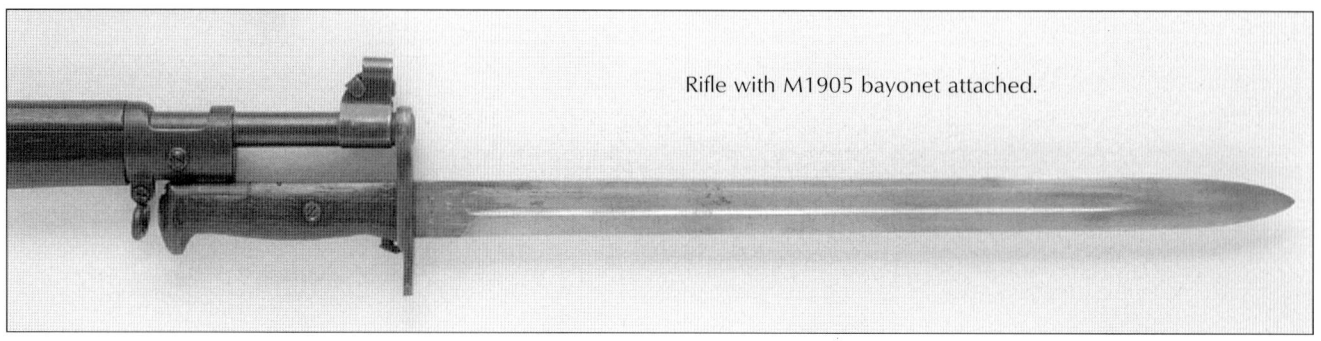

Rifle with M1905 bayonet attached.

blow from a Krag rifle, with attached knife bayonet. Shortly after this incident, Roosevelt stated in a letter to the Secretary of War dated January 4, 1905:

> "I must say that I think the ramrod bayonet is about as poor an invention as I ever saw."

Of course, such high-level displeasure was not lost on the Secretary of War, and a week later, January 11, 1905, production of the M1903 rifle was ordered to be halted pending a review of the suitability of the rod bayonet. It has been stated that the Russo-Japanese War raging at this time had revived the flagging popularity of the knife bayonet, which resulted in a reconsideration of the suitability of the rod bayonet vis-à-vis the knife bayonet.

In hindsight, Roosevelt and the other detractors of the rod bayonet were clearly correct. When the '03 was initially adopted, the bayonet had fallen from favor in the eyes of many military experts, and the new weapon's clip-loading capability was believed to render moot the necessity for a bayonet. The rod bayonet was incorporated primarily to satisfy the wishes of the old die-hards in the Ordnance Department and the War Department, who were reluctant to give up the concept of massed bayonet charges. In actuality, the rod bayonet was really nothing more than a vestigial bayonet. It should be remembered that bayonets were used much more often as camp tools, for opening ration cans and sharpening tent pegs, than for hand-to-hand combat. Unlike the knife bayonet, the rod bayonet had little utility as a weapon and even less as a tool.

M1905 Bayonet

An Ordnance committee was appointed to evaluate various types of bayonets and make recommendations regarding which pattern should be adopted to replace the unsatisfactory rod bayonet. Several types of bayonets were evaluated, but the committee eventually selected a conventional knife bayonet that was similar to the Krag bayonet but with a 16-inch blade in order to compensate for the reduced length of the '03 rifle. On April 3, 1905, the Bayonet Model of 1905, was standardized.

M1905 Sights

While rifle production was suspended pending evaluation of the bayonet, the Ordnance Department revisited the issue of the rod bayonet rifle's sights, as there had been some criticism of the original sights. The Ordnance Department developed a rear sight that combined some features of the M1884 Buffington Trapdoor Springfield and the M1901 Krag sights. The new sight featured a folding leaf and an improved peep and offered better adjustment capability than the original M1903 sight. The new rear sight was adopted and also given the Model of 1905 designation. Concurrently, the configuration of the front sight was changed to a more simplified pattern.

The leaf of the new M1905 rear sight was graduated to 2,400 yards on the face with a small notch at the top of the slide for 2,500 yards. The battle range, with the leaf in folded position, was 441 yards and was sighted by means of a U-shaped notch in the slide cap. The face of the leaf was blued and then polished bright.

M1903 Rifle with the Modifications of 1905

With the adoption of the M1905 bayonet and M1905 sights, production resumed at Springfield Armory in November 1905 on M1903 rifles incorporating these changes. Rock Island Arsenal did not begin assembly of the modified rifles until after April 1906. The rod bayonet rifles still in store were ordered to be modified to the specifications of 1905, and the rifles already issued were recalled for conversion as well.

The changes required to convert the rifles to the specifications of 1905 included removing the rod bayonet mechanism, modifying the stock accordingly, scrapping the original sights, and replacing them with the new M1905 sights. The original pattern handguard was replaced with a handguard having a prominent hump to protect the rear sight. The barrels made after incorporation of the modifications of 1905 were stamped with the year of production "05", the initials of the maker "S.A." or "R.I.A", and the Ordnance Department's flaming bomb insignia.

In 1906, the barrels were marked with both the month and year of production. After conversion to .30-06, most

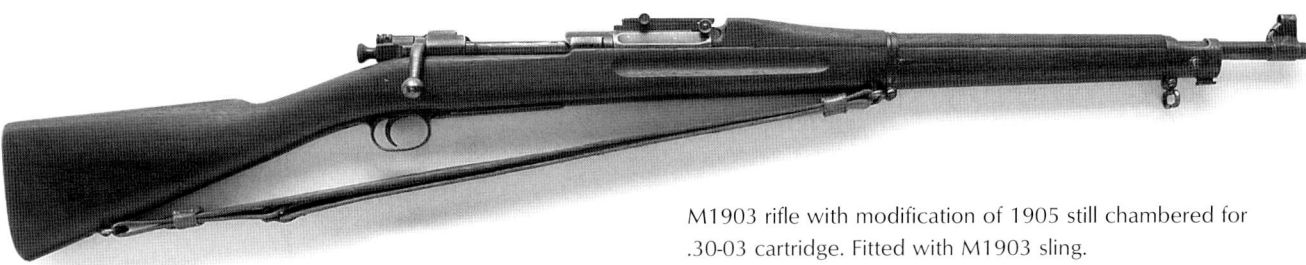

M1903 rifle with modification of 1905 still chambered for .30-03 cartridge. Fitted with M1903 sling.

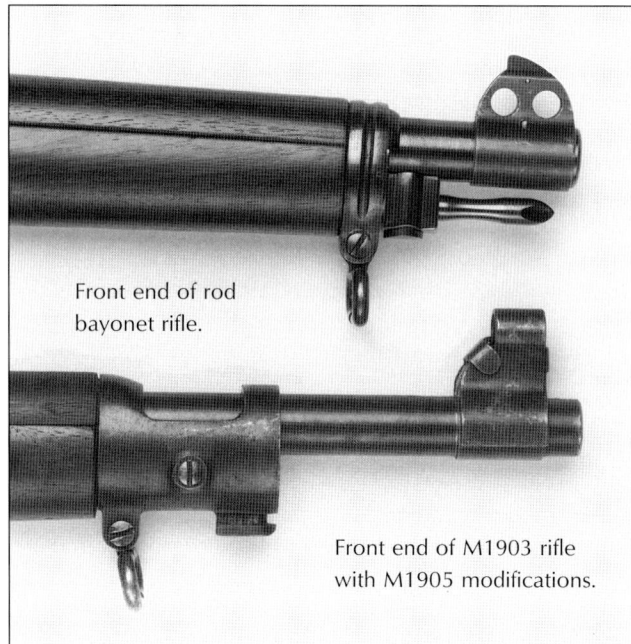

Front end of rod bayonet rifle.

Front end of M1903 rifle with M1905 modifications.

 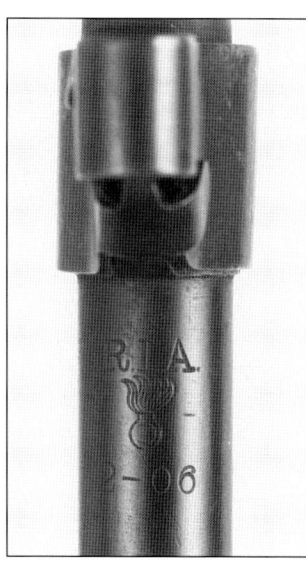

ABOVE, LEFT — Markings on Springfield Armory barrel made in 1905. ABOVE, RIGHT – Early Rock Island Arsenal barrel dated February 1906.

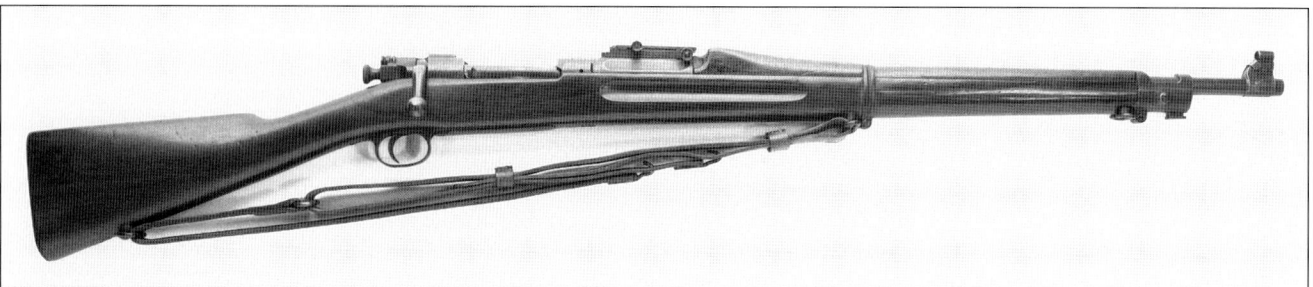

Right view of early M1903 with M1905 modifications. Note the *high hump* handguard and the lack of recoil screws in the stock. This rifle is fitted with a M1907 leather sling.

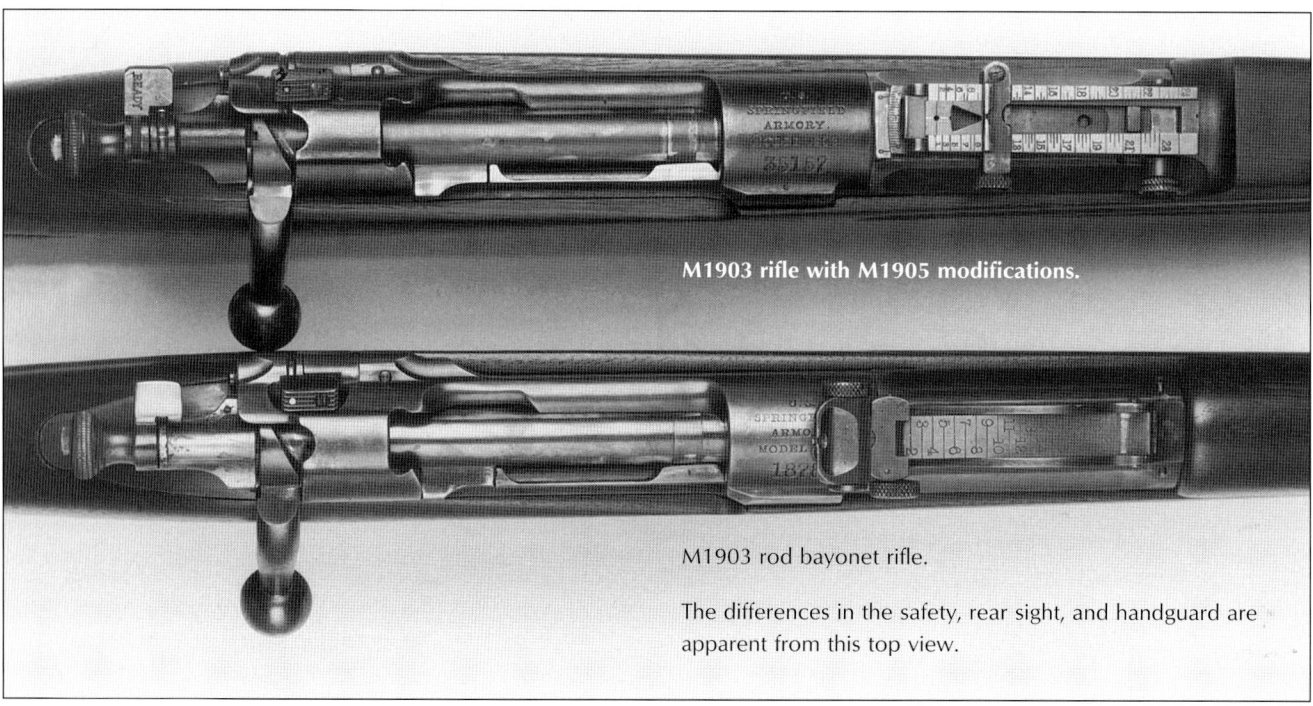

M1903 rifle with M1905 modifications.

M1903 rod bayonet rifle.

The differences in the safety, rear sight, and handguard are apparent from this top view.

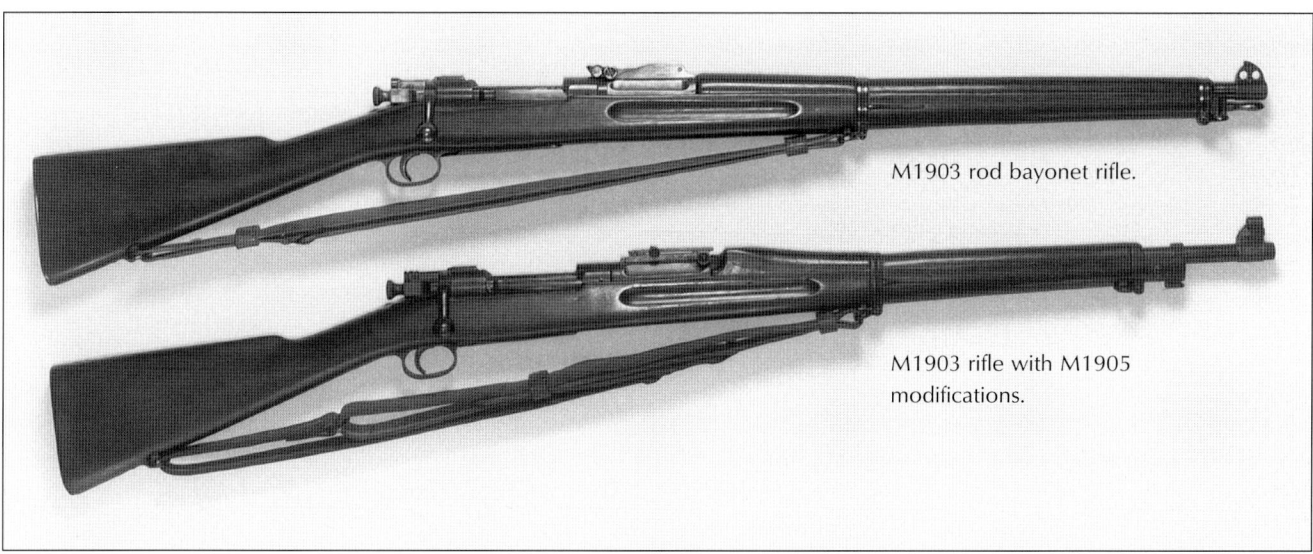

M1903 rod bayonet rifle.

M1903 rifle with M1905 modifications.

M1903 rifle chambered for .30-06 cartridge fitted with M1907 sling.

of the rod bayonet rifle barrels were believed to have been stamped with dates as well.

Rock Island Arsenal had assembled some 5,000 rifles by June of 1906, but there were shortages of the new M1905 rear sight leaves, which resulted in many rifles not being issued until new sight components became available. From all indications, Springfield Armory was not as handicapped as Rock Island Arsenal by the shortage of the new sight leaves, but also experienced some minor shortages of the component during this period.

There were relatively few new production M1903 rifles manufactured with the modifications of 1905, as most of the rifles of this type assembled from November 1905 until the Fall of 1906 were converted rod bayonet rifles. The altered rod bayonet rifles can be identified by the serial number (under approx. 95000) and the modified stocks which were neatly plugged on the front end when the rod bayonet mechanism was removed. The original rod bayonet stocks also typically had 1903 or 1904-dated cartouches. Newly made M1903 rifles with the modifications of 1905 had serial numbers above approximately 80,000, stocks without the plugged area, undated inspection cartouches and barrels stamped with the date of production ("05"). The newly made M1905 pattern stock was designated as the Type S.

M1906 Cartridge

While Springfield Armory and Rock Island Arsenal were laboring to get the newly modified M1903 rifle back into production, manufacture was again ordered to be halted pending evaluation of the rifle's cartridge. Ongoing testing and evaluation revealed that the sharp-pointed spitzer bullet, recently adopted by Germany, offered significant ballistic advantages over the round-nosed .30-03 M1903 bullet. Advances in the formulation of less erosive smokeless powder resulted in a much more satisfactory composition, which greatly extended the life of the barrel without unduly sacrificing ballistic performance.

A new cartridge incorporating the spitzer bullet and improved powder, was approved on October 15, 1906, by the Secretary of War, and adopted as the Cartridge, Ball, Caliber .30, Model of 1906. Soon after adoption of the *thirty aught six* cartridge, the manufacturing tooling for the M1903 rifle was modified to accommodate the new cartridge. By this time, there had been approximately 200,000 .30-03 barrels manufactured. In order to salvage these barrels, it was necessary to shorten them by 0.200 inches on the chamber end, re-cut the threads and shoulder, and rechamber them for the new .30-06 cartridge. It was also necessary to reduce the length of the rifle's stock and handguard by 0.200 inches to accommodate the shorter barrel. Stocks and handguards manufactured after the change from the .30-03 to the .30-06 cartridge were made in the shorter length. The flatter trajectory of the new .30-06 cartridge, as compared to the .30-03, required modifications to the rifle's rear sight leaf as well as the recalculation of firing tables. The new rear sight leaf was graduated to 2,800 yards, rather than the 2,400 yards for the .30-03 cartridge, and the battle range (sight leaf in folded position) was now 547 yards.

The M1903 rifles chambered for the .30-03 round remained items of issue for a period of time until the supply of the new .30-06 cartridge reached sufficient levels. The .30-03 rifles were recalled to be modified to the new cartridge, and by 1909 the U.S. military was more or less fully equipped with '03 rifles chambered for the .30-06 cartridge. As was the case with the rod bayonet rifles, virtually all of the M1903/M1905/.30-03 rifles were eventually modified to .30-06 but, as is always the case, a handful escaped conversion primarily due to theft or otherwise being unofficially removed from the system. Surviving examples of original M1903 rifles in 1905 configuration, still chambered for the .30-03 round, are rare.

The fact that the vast majority of the .30-03 rifles, both rod bayonet and M1905 pattern, were subsequently converted results in few original specimens available on the market. The few that do change hands typically have a large price tag attached. Unfortunately, there are more fake or restored early '03s of this type around than originals. This makes it mandatory that a potential buyer be wary and consult someone knowledgeable on the subject before a large sum of money is spent on a questionable rifle. Some of the restored rod bayonet and M1905/.30-03 rifles will evidence amateurish workmanship and are easy to spot. Others are remarkably well done and can easily fool many people who fancy themselves experts on the subject. It is often best to buy from an established dealer who has the integrity and financial strength to stand behind his merchandise. Like the old saying goes, "If you don't know your diamonds, you better know your jeweler."

This having been said, there are a number of key things to look for when evaluating an early '03 rifle. There are a few components of rod bayonet '03 rifles still relatively available today including receivers, some furniture (buttplates, etc.) and the rod bayonet itself. Other components such as unmodified rear sight bases and original, unmodified .30-03 barrels are quite rare. Unaltered original stocks, especially with genuine inspector cartouches, are also uncommon. Some rod bayonet '03s have been restored using .30-06 barrels. These can be identified by the slightly shorter overall length as compared to originals, the markings behind the front sight, and the fact that the bolt will not close on a .30-03 cartridge in a .30-06 chamber. Of course, a later barrel could have the markings removed and the chamber opened

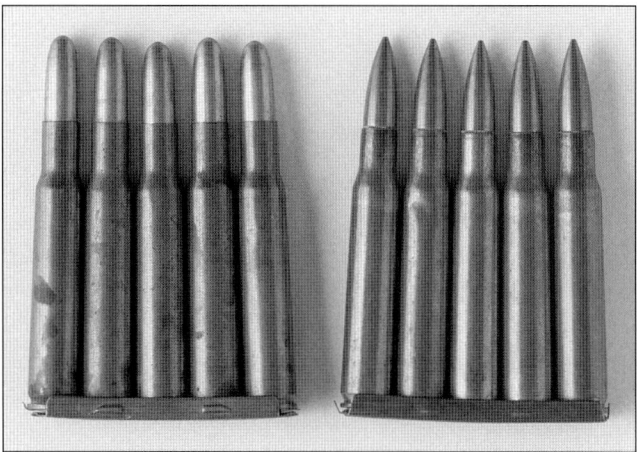

M1903 (.30-03) cartridges on left and clip of M1906 (.30-06) cartridges on right.

up a bit to allow the bolt to close on a .30-03 cartridge, so close observation, especially of the length, is mandatory to be certain that a common .30-06 barrel has not been altered to mimic one of the very rare .30-03 barrels. Likewise, reproduction (fake) rod bayonet stocks are around, some complete with new inspection stamps.

Seemingly small features can be very important in determining the authenticity of a rod bayonet rifle. For example, the lower barrel band which is solid (not split) is a key feature, as original bands of this type are not common. If a rod bayonet '03 rifle has the later split band, the weapon is not all original. The presence of a single incorrect part such as a barrel band does not necessarily rule out the legitimacy of the balance of the rifle, but can be a strong hint that something may be amiss. More obvious features that should cause great concern are barrels that exhibit signs of buffing or lathe turning to remove markings and stocks that look too new or which differ from known originals in overall workmanship.

Unaltered original rifles in M1905 configuration still chambered for the .30-03 cartridge are significantly rarer than original rod bayonet rifles, but prices are often lower due to the visual appeal of the latter. Genuine examples are rare, but there are probably some M1903/1905 rifles around that are not recognized due to the similarity of this variant to the 1905-vintage rifles that were subsequently modified to .30-06. Many of these latter rifles may have 05-dated barrels but were modified to .30-06 and are much infinitely more common than unmodified examples still chambered for the .30-03 cartridge. The easiest way to ascertain if a circa 1905 rifle is an original .30-03 example or has been modified to .30-06 is to observe the overall length. An original .30-03 rifle will be 0.200 inches longer than the same rifle converted to .30-06. While this may not sound like a big difference, side-by-side comparison will make it obvious whether such a rifle remains in its original .30-03 length or has been modified.

There are some rod bayonet and M1905/.30-03 rifles around today that were assembled from original parts. If a rifle is assembled from genuine parts with matching wear patterns, it can be difficult to ascertain such a weapon's originality. Such parts guns are less valuable than totally or substantially original rifles, but are clearly much more desirable than rifles containing bogus and/or incorrect components. An original M1903 .30-03 rifle, either rod bayonet or M1905 pattern, is a valuable and desirable collectible that would be a centerpiece to any M1903, Springfield Armory or 20th-century U.S. martial arm collection.

Springfield Armory and Rock Island Arsenal Rifles – Circa late 1906-1908

With the adoption of the M1906 cartridge, the M1903 rifle was in the basic configuration that would see production for the next thirty-five years. Springfield resumed manufacture of new rifles chambered for the .30-06 round and also began conversion of the older .30-03 rod bayonet and 1905 pattern rifles that had not yet been modified. The converted rod bayonet stocks can be identified by the plugged area at the tip and the older-pattern (script letters and dated) cartouche. The original rod bayonet pattern handguards were discarded and were then replaced with the later M1905-type handguard with the sight-protecting hump. The 1905 Pattern .30-03 length stocks and handguards were modified by shortening them the requisite 0.200 inches, but otherwise they were identical to the newly manufactured stocks and handguards of the period.

Other than the obvious changes due to the elimination of the rod bayonet mechanism, the incorporation of the .30-06 cartridge and the change to the M1905 sights, the post-1905 '03 rifles manufactured by Springfield Armory and Rock Island Arsenal retained most features of the earlier rifles. The specific features found on '03 rifles manufactured by both Springfield Armory and Rock Island Arsenal in the late 1906 to 1908 period included:

Finish

As with the earlier rifles, most external metal parts were finished in the same high-quality rust blue as the original rod bayonet rifles. The case hardening used by Springfield Armory on their receivers did not result in the brilliant colors often associated with this process. There were no parkerized parts utilized on rifles of this vintage.

Receivers

The receivers were marked "U.S., Springfield Armory" or "Rock Island Arsenal, Model 1903" and the serial number. Serial numbers for new production Springfield rifles made during the late 1906 to 1908 timeframe were numbered between circa 270000 to 350000 range, and Rock Island rifles were serially numbered up to about 65000. The first 300,000 (approximately) M1903 rifles had script-style serial numbers. After 1908, the serial numbers were changed to slightly larger block-style digits. All '03 rifles up to this time had case-hardened receivers of uncertain metallurgy which were sometimes dangerously brittle due to faulty heat control during the forging process. These are usually referred to as low-numbered receivers and are generally considered as being unsafe to fire. This topic will be more thoroughly discussed later.

Receiver markings on Rock Island '03.

Receiver markings on Springfield '03. Note early script lettering and numbers on the Springfield receiver.

Barrels

Barrels were marked behind the front sight with the initials of the manufacturer, "SA" or "RIA", the Ordnance Department flaming bomb insignia, and the month and year of production. Barrels made in 1905 were only marked with the year of production "05", while those produced afterward were stamped with both the month and year (i.e., "5-13"). Most barrels had the steel lot identification, typically consisting of a letters and a code number. These identification markings were stamped in front of the sight base on Rock Island barrels and midway down the barrel on Springfield barrels.

Some collectors have proffered the theory that Springfield Armory and Rock Island Arsenal supplied barrels to each other to assist in production. However, there is absolutely no evidence to suggest that any barrels were shared between the two manufacturers during this period, and such statements are usually examples of crafting erroneous theories to explain away nonoriginal rifles with mismatched barrels. During subsequent arsenal rebuilds, a barrel made by one manufacturer was often utilized in a receiver made by another manufacturer, but this was not done at the factories when the rifles were originally produced. Mismatched barrels are an absolute indication that the rifle in question is not all original. An exception to this occurred in the late 1920s when leftover Rock Island '03 components were shipped to Springfield Armory for finishing and assembly. Among these parts were relatively large numbers of unfinished Rock Island Arsenal receivers. Since these receivers were from all stages of manufacture, some already had the Rock Island Arsenal indicia applied on the receiver ring. These were stamped with a Springfield Armory serial number (over 1200000), which was well beyond the highest serial number (approximate 420000) that had actually been used at Rock Island.

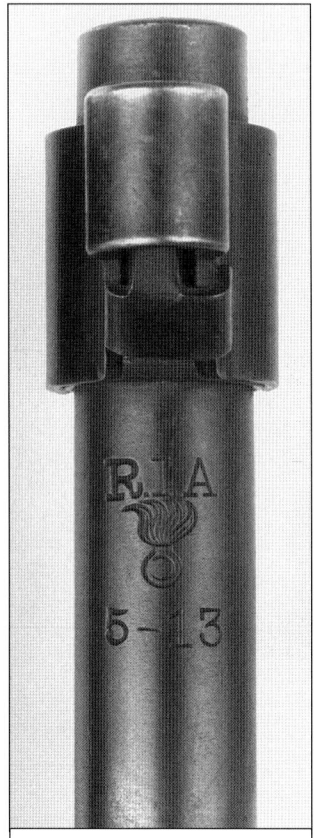

Markings on Rock Island Arsenal barrel made in May 1913. Note also the front sight cover.

Stocks

M1903 rifle stocks of this vintage evidenced a straight-edge configuration on the left side, and the stocks were not sloped on the right side under the receiver gas-escape hole. Stocks made prior to 1908 did not have the transverse reinforcing stock screw, sometimes referred to as a stock bolt. A single reinforcing stock screw was authorized in February of 1908 and was incorporated into production rifles shortly afterward. The screw was added after problems were reported regarding stocks cracking or splitting in this area. The presence, or absence, of stock screws, along with the configuration of the right and left sides, will ascertain the approximate vintage of a stock. It should be noted that some early stocks subsequently had screws retrofitted as part of an overhaul procedure. In any event, an original '03 .30 caliber service rifle stock without reinforcing screws was manufactured prior to 1909.

The inspection stamps used during this period at Springfield Armory generally consisted of the inspector's initials enclosed in a rectangular box and were not typically dated. A number of different Springfield Armory inspector initials will be encountered. Rock Island Arsenal stocks of this vintage were stamped with a stamp consisting of the script initials "C.N." (Conrad Nelson) above the year of assembly enclosed in a box with rounded corners.

It should be noted that the term cartouche is widely used in collecting circles today to denote the various inspection markings stamped on stocks although this was not any sort of official terminology. Such inspector initials are technically the *Final Inspection Stamp*. Some fledging collectors today use the term cartouche to refer to any and every type of stamp found on military stocks but, for the sake of consistency, the term should be reserved to refer to the final inspection stamp, and this term will be so used in this book. The final inspection stamp was applied after the rifle passed all requisite inspections and was accepted by

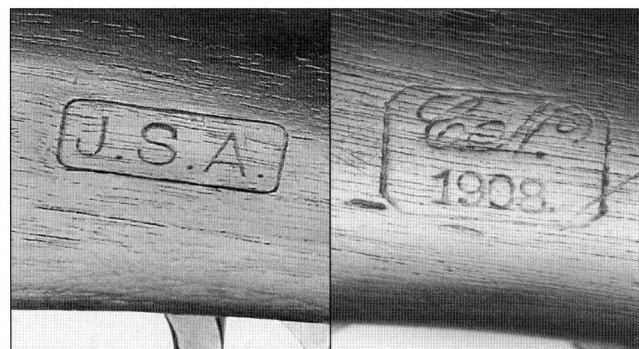

ABOVE, LEFT – Inspection stamp on pre-WWI Springfield M1903 rifle. "J.S.A." is Springfield Armory inspector J. Sumnar Adams. ABOVE, RIGHT – Inspection stamp dated 1908 on Rock Island Arsenal '03. "C.N." represents Conrad Nelson who was Rock Island's chief of small arms inspection prior to WWI.

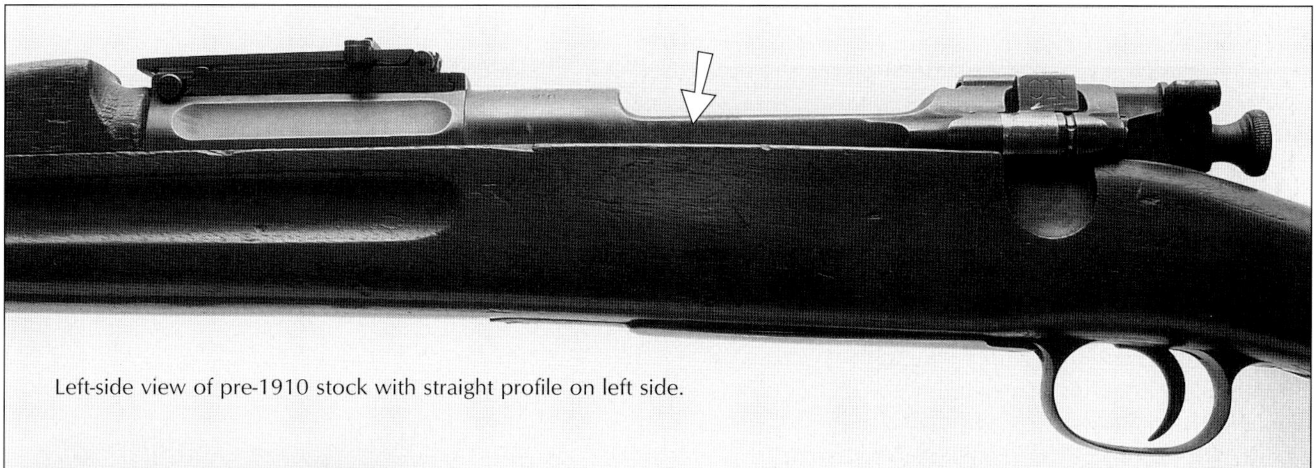

Left-side view of pre-1910 stock with straight profile on left side.

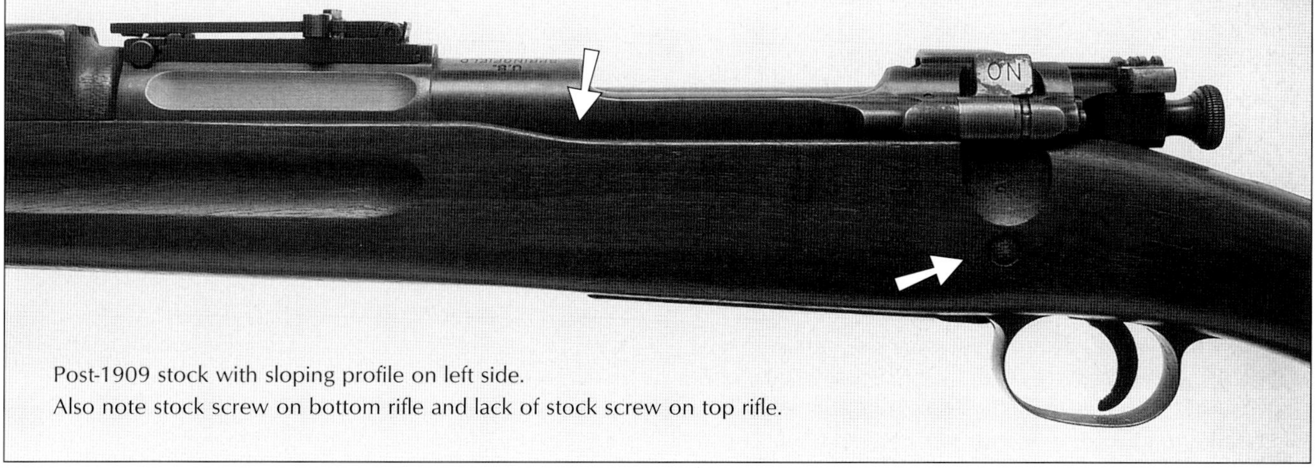

Post-1909 stock with sloping profile on left side.
Also note stock screw on bottom rifle and lack of stock screw on top rifle.

the government. Despite some theories to the contrary, stocks were definitely not pre-stamped with cartouches and set aside for later use. The stocks were stamped behind the triggerguard with a script "P" enclosed in a circle. This signified that the rifle was successfully proof-fired as part of the final inspection process.

Unmodified early stocks are uncommon and are highly sought after by collectors for restoration purposes. Unfortunately, some newly made replica stocks may be encountered, some with new inspector stamps applied. If possible, it is always a good idea to compare a suspect stock with a known original as there are a number of sometimes subtle, but unmistakable differences between the genuine article and the fakes. In addition, the overall condition of the stock should be evaluated. A 95+ year old stock found on the loose today will almost certainly show patina of age and signs of wear, and a stock that looks like it was made yesterday probably was!

Handguards
- Prominent hump in front of the rear sight.
- No sight clearance groove on top as found on later handguards.
- No metal reinforcing clips.

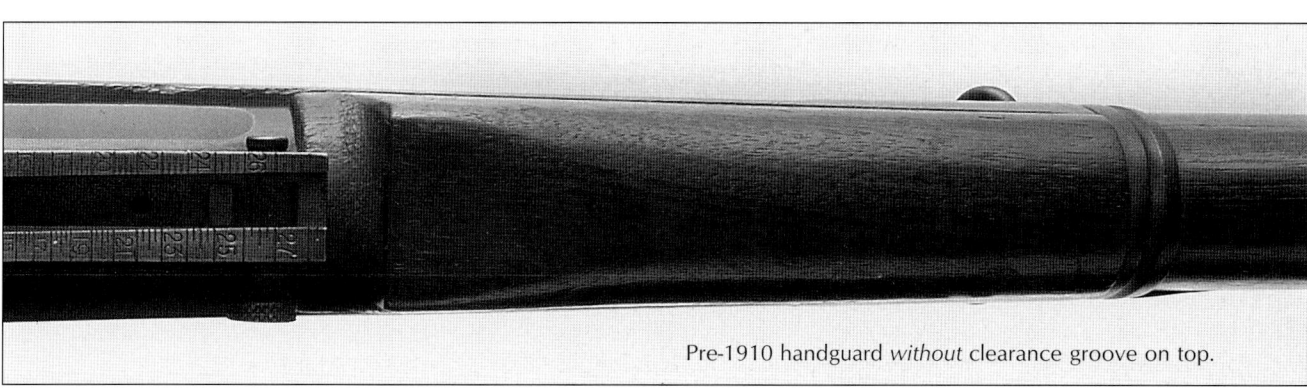

Pre-1910 handguard *without* clearance groove on top.

Rear Sights
- Sight leaf graduated to 2,800 yards plus a 50-yard notch with bright finished face.
- Small windage knobs approximately .45 inches in diameter.

Sight knobs prior to the 1920s were of the dished variety which means the face of the knob had a concave profile. Most pre-WWI knobs also had a groove around the circumference of the knob.

There were some problems encountered in producing new rear sight leaves graduated for the .30-06 cartridge. This resulted in delays in assembling new rifles. Rock Island produced few, if any, of the new sight leaves prior to November 1907 and some shortages of the component existed at Springfield Armory until mid-1908.

Rear Sight Fixed Base

In October 1907, a fixed rear sight base with a solid bottom replaced the earlier fixed sight base that was partially relieved (cut away) on the bottom. The configuration of the new sight base required that the stock be routed out a bit more to provide the necessary clearance.

As the earlier M1903 rifles were sent to Springfield Armory for maintenance and repair, the old pattern fixed sight bases were scrapped and the new model bases were retrofitted to the salvageable barrels. This is confirmed in a 1912 Springfield Armory memorandum signed by Ordnance Department Colonel S.E. Blunt which stated:

"...I would report that all rifles cleaned and repaired at this Armory since October 1907, have the new model fixed base assembled to the barrels...

"...it is recommended that the old model bases not be used when removed from barrels...they are very difficult to properly assemble again and were never suitable for the purpose for which designed as they are easily warped and affect the accurate setting of the rear sight."

View of receiver markings on 1912-vintage rifle used by Capt. F.S. Hird at the 1912 Olympics. Note the grooved elevation and windage adjustment knobs indicative of '03 sights of this period. Also note the *dished* areas.

On the back of this original photograph is written, "Taken 60 miles from camp. You can hardly see me in the back of the bushes. This is the way we was shooting for over a week." *(Courtesy Stuart C. Mowbray collection)*

Front Sight Covers

The M1903 rifles with M1905 pattern front sights were issued with a protective metal cover for protection of the front sight. These covers will be briefly discussed in a subsequent section of this book.

Buttplates and Butt Trap Recess

Buttplates of this vintage were smooth (uncheckered). Some earlier rifles used modified Krag buttplates, identifiable by the smaller diameter trap. Buttplates made afterward all had the larger diameter trap. The buttplate trapdoor provided access for a hole drilled into the butt that accommodated the metal oiler/thong case. A second hole was drilled in the butt below the oiler recess for weight-reduction purposes. Butt trap recesses of this vintage were not grooved on the bottom for the spare parts container that came into use circa 1910.

Triggers

Triggers manufactured from the beginning of production until circa 1910, were smooth and had a thin profile, very much like the earlier Krag triggers. Later triggers were wider and serrated in order to reduce finger slippage when firing the rifle.

Stock Fore-end Tip Markings

A feature of many Springfield and Rock Island rifles manufactured during this period is the presence of an "S" or "s" on the tip of the stock fore-end. This seemingly minor feature is the source of disagreement among some experienced students of the subject today. Several theories have been proffered to explain the real meaning of this marking and at least one demonstrably incorrect theory has been related as factual in one monograph on the subject. This incorrect theory postulates that stocks found with this marking are of the .30-06 length, as opposed to the slightly longer .30-03, length and that the "S" or "s" marking indicates shortened. This erroneous theory can be easily disproved for several reasons, not the least of which is the fact that the marking is often found on stocks that were never shortened. What, then, does the "S" indicate?

Definitive proof is lacking, and there may very well be different meanings for these markings depending on the timeframe in question. For example, for both Rock Island Arsenal and Springfield Armory rifles made from 1905 to

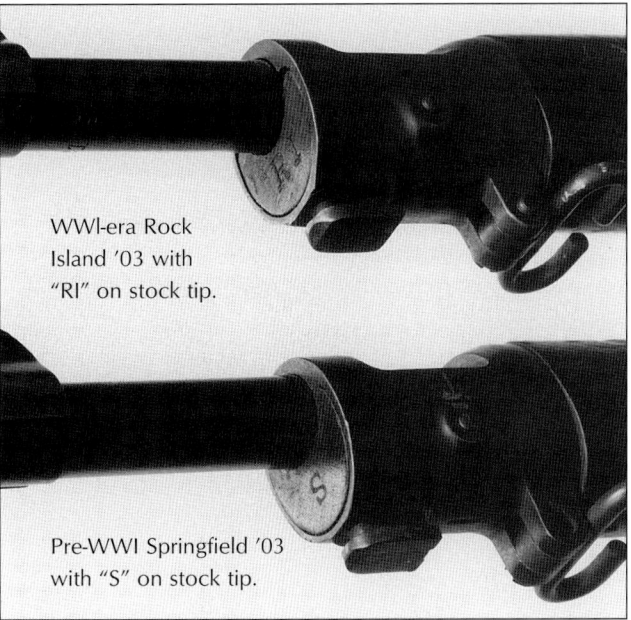

WWI-era Rock Island '03 with "RI" on stock tip.

Pre-WWI Springfield '03 with "S" on stock tip.

circa 1913 with this marking, the most credible theory is that the "S" (or "s") stands for Type S stock. Most of the earlier rod bayonet stocks that were subsequently altered to 1905 specifications were also stamped with an "s" on the tip, which suggests that this was done to denote that the stock was changed from the original rod bayonet pattern to the Type S pattern.

For rifles made in the 1917–1918 period, the marking on the stock tip likely indicates the manufacturer of the stock. Soon after Rock Island resumed rifle production in 1917, Rock Island stocks are found with "RI" on the fore-end tip. Some Springfield Armory '03s had an "s" stamped in the same location. Unlike the pre-1917 rifles, it is reasonable to assume that these markings indicate Rock Island and Springfield, respectively. It must be stressed that this is a theory, but it is hard to dispute that, in this instance, "RI" identifies Rock Island. If so, it logically follows that an "s" stamped in the same location, in the same time period, indicates Springfield (Armory).

There may be some other reason for the fore-end tip markings besides the two theories presented above, but these seem to be the most logical explanations. In any event, such minor mysteries are part of the lure of '03 collecting and can be cause for numerous friendly discussions and disagreements.

Post-1907 Assembly of Rock Island Arsenal Rifles

Relatively few Rock Island Arsenal '03 rifles were assembled prior to 1908. Therefore, it is not unusual to see totally original Rock Island rifles with receivers and barrels of various pre-1908 vintages but with a 1908 dated stock cartouche. Thus, a collector should not assume that such a rifle found today is a non-original assembly of parts. If all the components are of Rock Island Arsenal manufacture and are of 1908 or earlier vintage, the rifle could well be original, even if the 1908-dated cartouche postdates the vintage of the other parts by several years. Springfield

LEFT – Camp photos such as this one showing soldiers posing with their '03 Springfields are quite common and often include an impressive backdrop such as this cannon. In fact, this particular piece of ordnance appears over and over again in surviving photographs from this era. *(Courtesy Stuart C. Mowbray collection)*

RIGHT – Portrait of two soldiers with '03 Springfields at an encampment in Ohio. The man at left is also carrying what appears to be a cleaning rod. *(Stuart C. Mowbray collection)*

Armory rifles of the same vintage also had some inconsistency in this regard, but not to the same extent as may be found on many Rock Island rifles of the period. Ascertaining the specific date of the assembly of the entire rifle is not as clear-cut with Springfield rifles as with Rock Island rifles because the former's stock cartouches were not typically dated after 1904. However, the features of the stock and other components should be consistent with rifles manufactured during the time period of the receiver/barrel combination. In other words, a rifle produced by Springfield Armory prior to 1908 would not, for example, have a stock reinforcing screw if the weapon remains in its as-manufactured condition. Some collectors who have a rifle with a barrel date predating or postdating that of the receiver by several years will sometimes theorize that the barrel was laying around Springfield Armory for more than a year or so and was subsequently used to assemble the rifle. As with most theories of this type, this is a case of crafting a questionable theory with little or no basis in fact in order to justify or explain away a non-original rifle. There are, of course, some exceptions such as the above-discussed 1908-dated Rock Island Arsenal rifles. Otherwise, in almost all cases, all parts should be of the same general vintage if a rifle remains in its original factory configuration.

The period of 1903 to 1915 was a time of relative peace for the United States, and there was no extreme rush to rearm the military with the new service rifle. As production caught up with the relatively modest demand, the '03 began to replace the Krag rifles and carbines in service. Combat use of the new rifle first occurred in the closing stages of the pacification campaigns in the Philippines, although combat action in the islands was winding down by the time of the M1903's introduction into service.

Springfield Armory: 1909-1917/Rock Island Arsenal: 1909-1913

The '03 rifle went through many design changes from the time of its adoption until production ceased. These various changes are important to collectors today in order to determine if a rifle remains in its original configuration for the period in question.

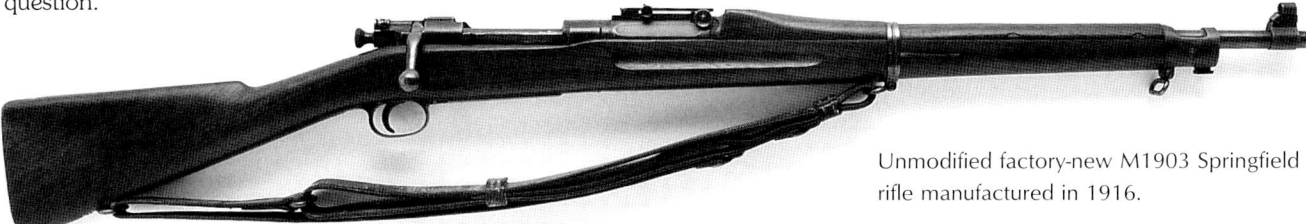

Unmodified factory-new M1903 Springfield rifle manufactured in 1916.

Finish

The type of finish for the rifles of the 1909–1917 period remained unchanged from the earlier vintage '03s.

Receivers

The only discernable change in the receivers beginning after 1908 was the use of slightly larger block-style digits for serial numbers on the receiver ring. *(Note: shown on page 31).*

Barrels

Same as the 1906–1908 barrels including the marking of the initials of the maker, "SA" or "RIA", the Ordnance Department flaming bomb and the month/year of production stamped behind the front sight.

"Part of our squad," dated July 6, 1915, in New York. Below is a close up of the marking on the butt. *(Courtesy Stuart C. Mowbray collection)*

Upper Bands

Beginning circa 1910, the bottom of the bayonet lug on the upper band was stamped with an "H" to denote hardened. This hardening process was instituted to increase the strength of the bayonet lug.

Stocks

Circa 1910 the configuration of the left side of the stock was changed from the earlier straight-sided profile (sometimes called *high wood* by collectors) to a sloping profile (occasionally referred to as *low wood*). The right side of the stock, underneath the receiver gas escape hole, was also changed from a straight variety to a sloping profile. These changes were instituted to reduce splitting or cracking of the stock in this area. Stocks still had a single reinforcing screw.

Stocks were stamped with the final inspector's initials on the left side and a script circled "P" firing proof mark on the bottom behind the triggerguard. As was the case with the rifles manufactured previously, the final inspection stamp (cartouche) for Springfield Armory rifles typically consisted of three initials contained in a rectangular box. Rock Island Arsenal rifles had the script "C.N." (Conrad Nelson) initials enclosed in a box above the date of final inspection. Even though many stocks found today may have missing or illegible markings due to wear or refinishing, the general vintage of the stock, if still in original configuration, can be easily ascertained by the configuration of the stock.

Handguards

Although the handguards produced prior to the First World War still had the prominent sight-protecting hump, two changes to the M1903's handguard occurred during the 1908–1910 period. In 1908 metal clips were added to the handguard to strengthen the component and permit continued use if it became split. The earliest handguards of this type had only one clip near the front for a brief period

1913-dated Rock Island Arsenal inspection stamp.

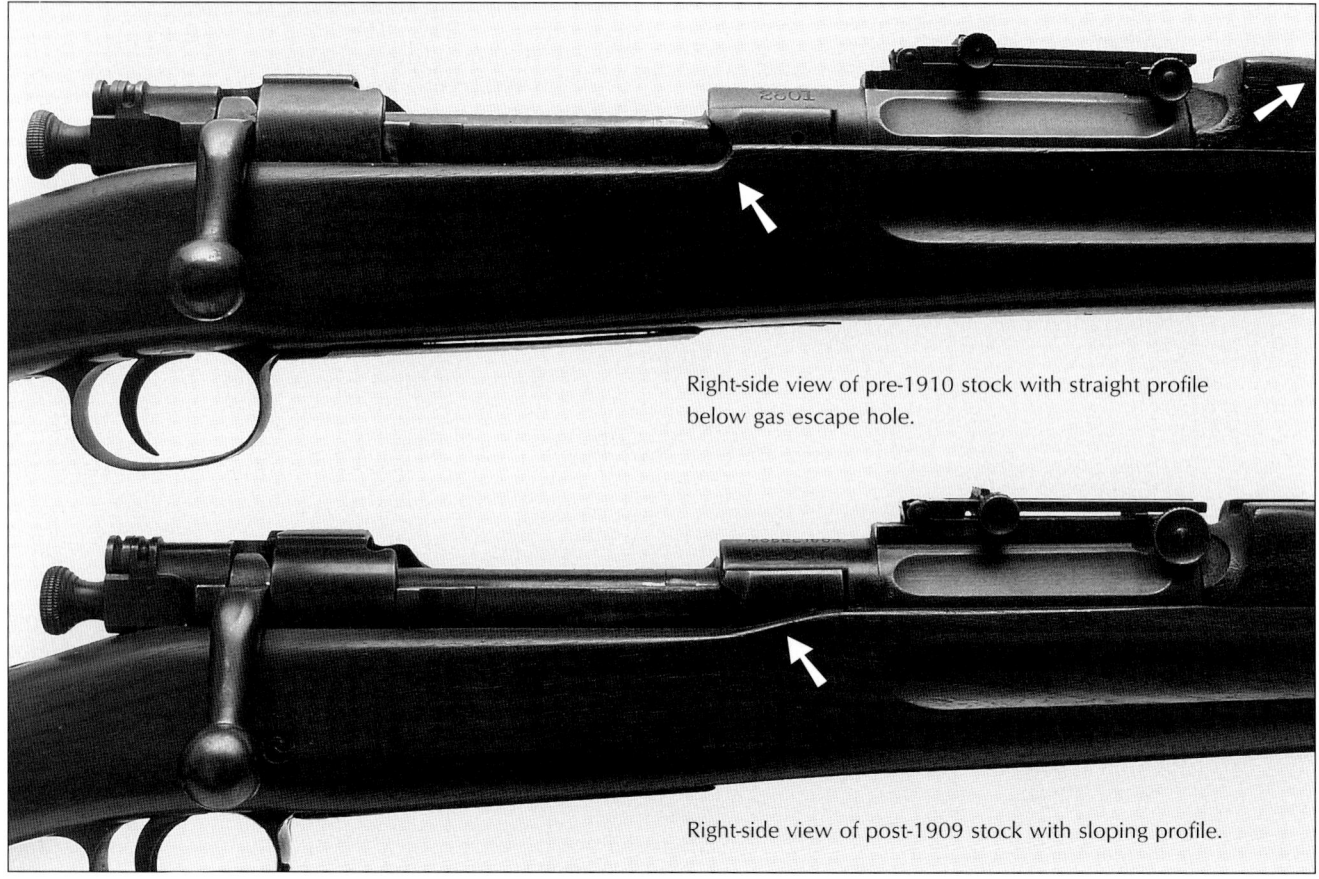

Right-side view of pre-1910 stock with straight profile below gas escape hole.

Right-side view of post-1909 stock with sloping profile.

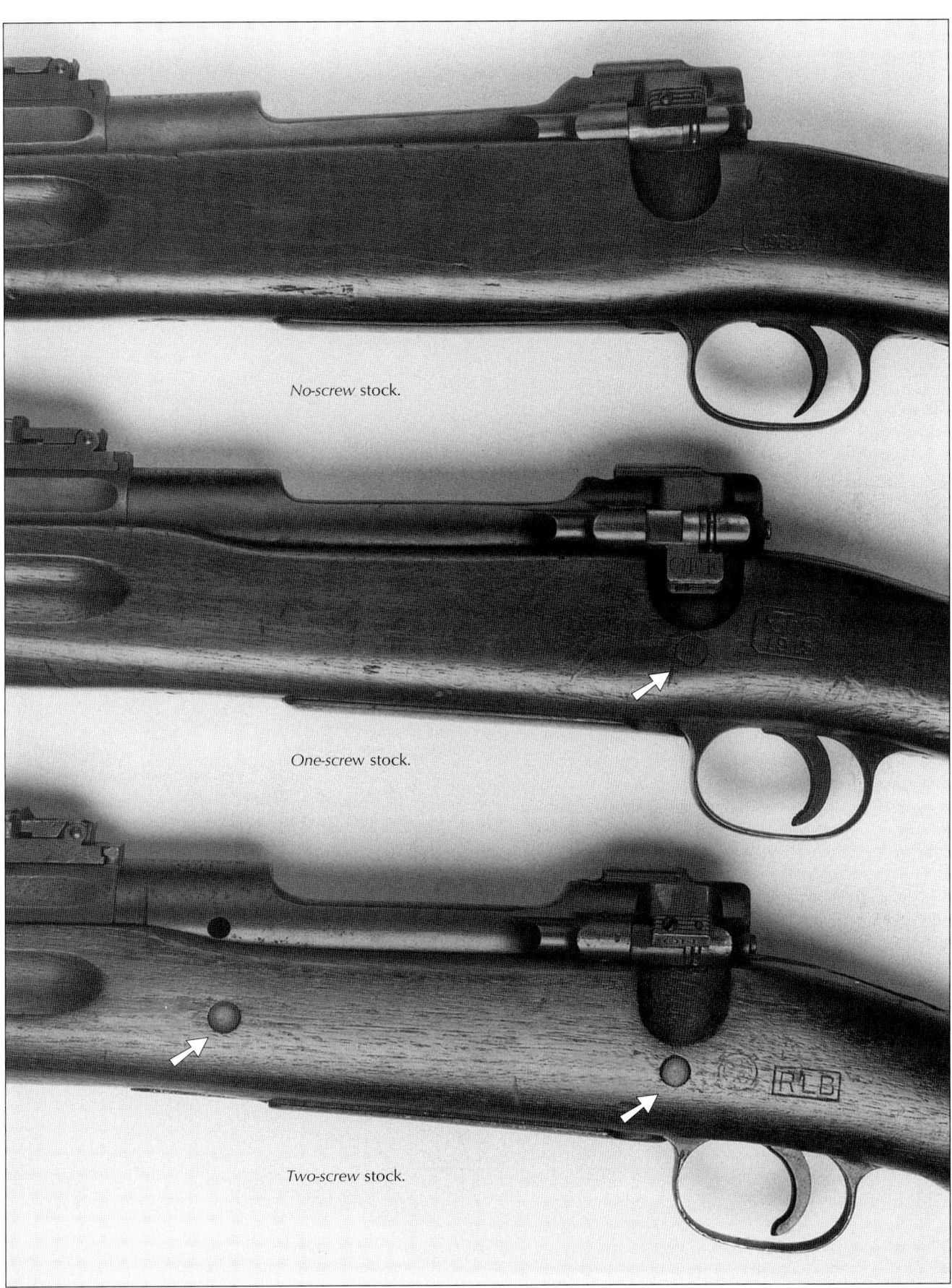

No-screw stock.

One-screw stock.

Two-screw stock.

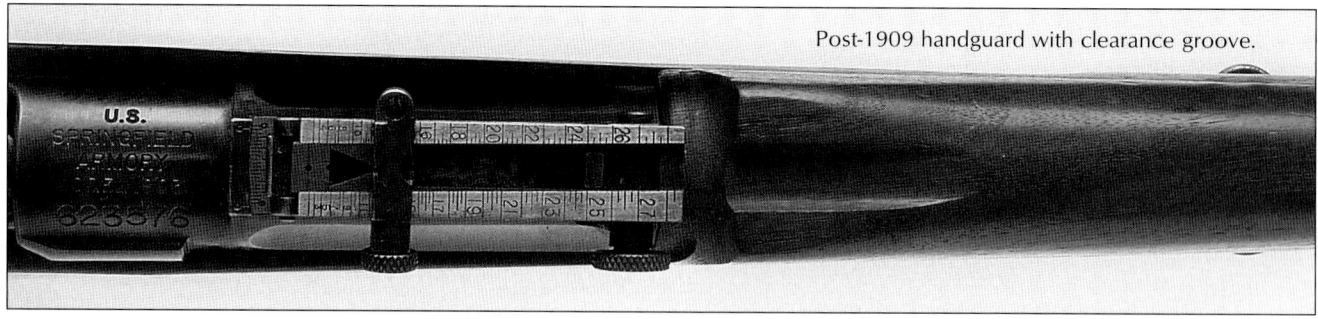

Post-1909 handguard with clearance groove.

of time but a second clip was soon added, about 4.25 inches behind the first clip. In 1909, a sight clearance groove was milled into the top of the handguard in order to prevent interference while sighting the rifle. As is the case with stocks, determining the general vintage of an '03 handguard is not too difficult. Unmodified pre-1908 handguards will not have the metal clips, pre-1909 handguards will not have a sight groove on top, while handguards made from 1910 and afterward will evidence both of these features.

Rear Sights

The windage knob was increased in size from the earlier 0.450 inches in diameter to 0.575 inches, in order to make manipulation easier. The knobs were still of the dished variety, but by 1915 or 1916 the groove around the circumference of the knob was eliminated.

Buttplates and Butt Traps

By 1910, the buttplate was checkered to reduce the tendency of the buttstock to slip off the shoulder when firing. The butt trap recess was also modified slightly by milling a groove in the bottom of the recess in order to accommodate the wooden spare parts container that came into use in 1910. The spare parts container held a spare firing pin, striker and extractor. It was intended to have alternate rifles equipped with the metal oiler/thong case and the spare parts container. Very few original spare parts containers have survived, but some well-made reproductions were fabricated in the early 1980s and are sometimes encountered.

Triggers

In 1910, the thickness of the trigger was increased and the face was grooved. These changes made slippage of the finger less likely as compared to the earlier thin, ungrooved trigger.

Table 3 in this book is a Memorandum of Changes made in the M1903 rifle from the time of adoption until early 1914 as published by the U.S. Army Ordnance Department.

The only significant change in the accessories and accouterments issued with the '03 rifles during the 1909–1916 period was the adoption of 1910 infantry equipment, including new types of Mills cartridge belts and the M1912 cavalry equipage. These will be discussed in the Accessories, Accouterments and Appendages section of this book.

Cessation of M1903 Rifle Production at Rock Island Arsenal

By 1913, the rather small armed forces of the United States were essentially fully equipped with M1903 rifles. Production was halted at Rock Island Arsenal since production at Springfield Armory could keep pace with the limited demand. The last Rock Island '03 rifles during this period came off the assembly line on November 17, 1913.

Adoption of new infantry equipment in 1910 included new types of Mills Cartridge belts and M1910 bayonet scabbard.

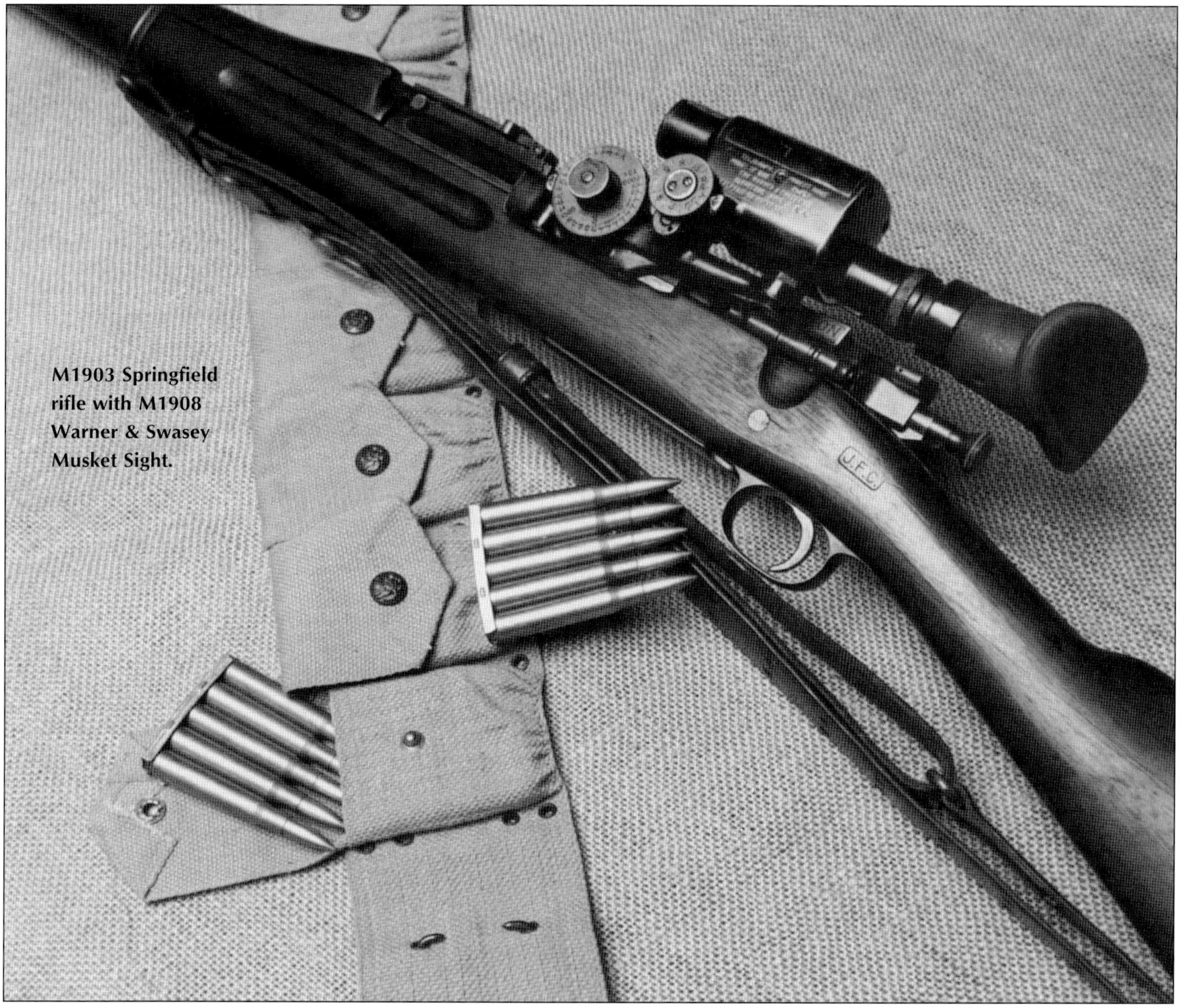

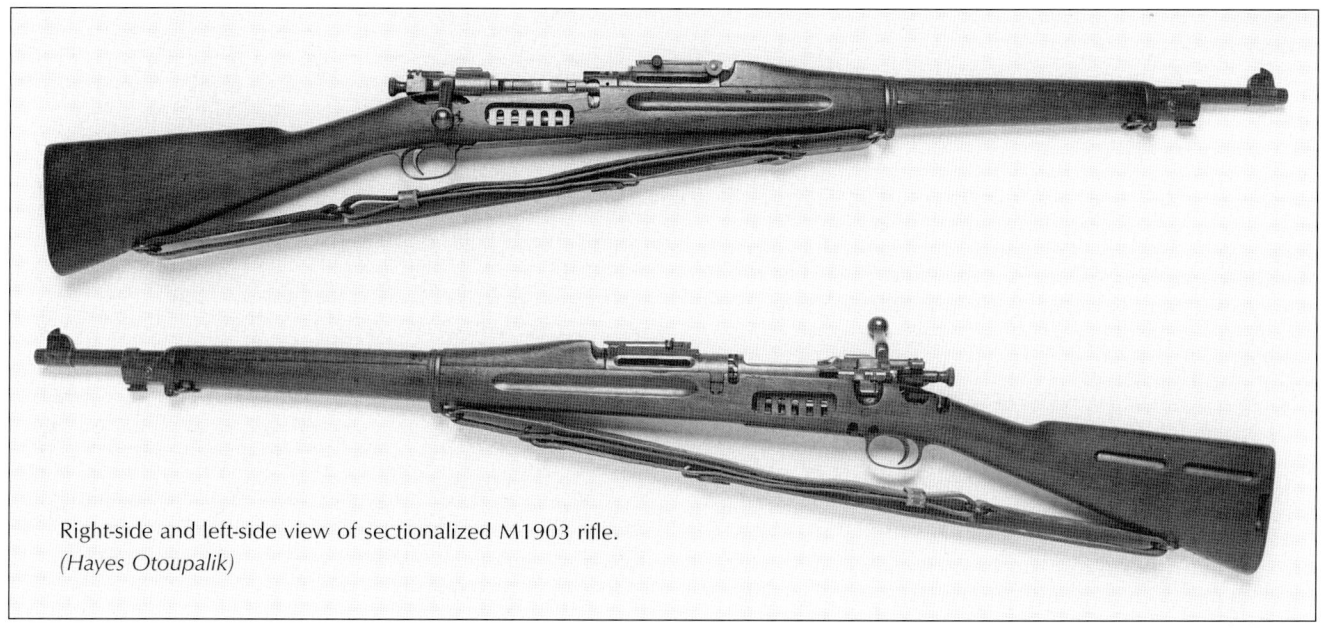

M1903 Springfield rifle with M1908 Warner & Swasey Musket Sight.

Right-side and left-side view of sectionalized M1903 rifle.
(Hayes Otoupalik)

Springfield Armory continued its M1903 rifle production line, albeit at a reduced rate. Sources vary on the number of '03 rifles manufactured at Rock Island Arsenal from the beginning of production until the cessation of manufacture in 1913. Estimates range between just under 235,000 to over 263,000. Analysis of serial number data tends to support the lower estimate.

Sniper Rifles

In 1909, the first standardized U.S. Army sniper rifle was adopted and put into limited production at Springfield Armory. The new sniping arm was a M1903 service rifle fitted with an unusual prismatic telescopic sight designed and produced by the Warner & Swasey Company and given the designation Musket Sight – Model of 1908. The Model of 1908 W&S sight was followed by the slightly improved Model of 1913. The '03 sniper rifles fitted with Warner & Swasey telescopic sights and other '03 sniper rifles of the pre-WWII period will be discussed at some length later in this book.

Springfield Armory Sectionalized Rifles

Springfield Armory produced a number of M1903 rifles that had some of the components, wood and metal, sectionalized (cut-away) to reveal various aspects of the mechanism. This was done primarily as a training aid for armorers and similar personnel to illustrate various internal aspects of the rifle. Some Springfield Armory-made sectionalized rifles may be encountered with receivers marked "U.S. S.A. M.1903" and with barrels marked "S.A." and dated "4-09". Other sectionalized rifles may be seen that were made from standard '03s. These did not have such specially marked receivers. Unlike WWII-vintage Remington factory sectionalized rifles (to be discussed later), both the left and right sides of the Springfield-made rifles were typically sectionalized. It should be noted that a competent machinist can sectionalize a rifle today, so it must not be assumed that any and all examples are the product of Springfield Armory. The Springfield Armory-made sectionalized rifles are uncommon and valuable, but a civilian-sectionalized example has only marginal collector value. Therefore, the sectionalized rifles with specially marked receivers are more avidly sought after by collectors than standard '03s that have been sectionalized, since their provenance can be readily determined. The chambers were also cut away, thus these rifles cannot be fired. Regardless, a sectionalized rifle is an interesting addition to an '03 collection, and original specimens are not very common.

In addition to a modicum of combat action during this period, standard '03 service rifles were used in a number of national and international rifle matches, including the Olympics. At the time, the Olympics featured a Military Rifle competition which required the use of unaltered service rifles of the participating nations. American shooters

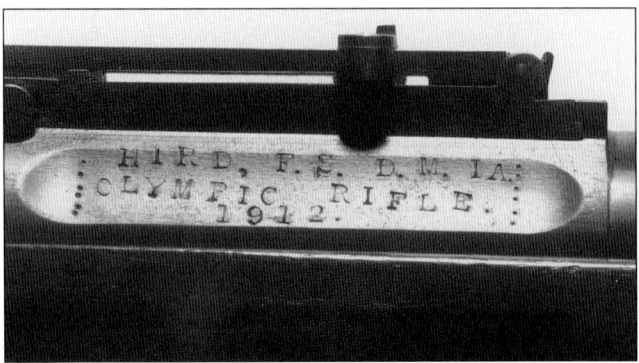

Inscription on 1912-vintage M1903 rifle used by Capt. Fred S. Hird, Iowa National Guard. Captain Hird won a Gold Medal at the 1912 Olympics in Stockholm.

acquitted themselves very well with off-the-shelf M1903 service rifles. The performance of the '03 in such high-level international competition speaks volumes regarding the inherent accuracy of the rifle, the quality of craftsmanship of the government ordnance facilities and, of course, the skill of the American marksmen. This was aptly summed up in a subsequent report by the Assistant Secretary of War:

"There is no questioning the superiority of the Springfield in point of accuracy. Time after time we pitted our Army shooting teams against those of other nations of the earth and won the international competitions with the Springfield... Much is to be said for the men behind those guns, but due credit must be given the rifles that put the bullets where the marksmen aimed..."

NRA-Marked Rifles

By 1910, production had reached a point that allowed limited sales of standard service rifles, as well as some special target rifles, to members of the National Rifle Association (NRA) as permitted by legislation passed several years earlier for the National Board for the Promotion of Rifle Practice. The Board was the forerunner of the Director of Civilian Marksmanship (DCM) and the Civilian Marksmanship Program (CMP). The '03 service rifles sold to NRA members during this period were standard issue military rifles. It is interesting to note that only Life Members of the NRA were permitted to buy Model 1903 rifles and Annual Members could only buy Krags under the program.

Eventually, some of these rifles found their way into the hands of used gun dealers which resulted in some of the rifles being mistaken for stolen government property. It was initially intended to have special markings on the receivers to identify the NRA sales rifles, but it was determined that this would not be feasible. These matters were discussed in two Ordnance Department memorandums dated January 7, 1915 and March 30, 1915, which stated:

"On two different occasions Springfield Rifles Model of 1903 have been found in the hands of dealers in second hand rifles who were offering them for sale. Upon investigation, it was found that these rifles were purchased by members of civilian rifle clubs affiliated with the N.R.A. and had become more or less unserviceable for their purpose and had been sold to the dealers for about one half their original cost. There seems to be no way to prevent this practice. The fact that members of civilian rifle clubs can dispose of ordnance stores in this manner discourages the police authorities in their efforts to assist the State in this regard. It is suggested that some distinguishing mark be placed on rifles sold to members of civilian clubs in order that they may be distinguished when found in the hands of second class dealers thereby relieving the police authorities of the necessity of an investigation.
Adj. Gen. to the Chief,
D.M.A.
January 7, 1915

"It is impracticable for this Department to mark the receivers of rifles sold to members of civilian rifle clubs affiliated with the National Rifle Association, as the receiver of a rifle is case hardened after manufacture and there is not a sufficient number of rifles sold to such persons to warrant such receivers being specially manufactured and stamped before case hardening. It has been decided, however, to stamp on the front tang of the guard of all rifles sold to members of civilian rifle clubs affiliated with the National Rifle Association of America the letters "N.R.A." together with the shell and flame. All guards sold to members of rifle clubs will like wise be so stamped. Steel stamps for this purpose have been directed manufactured and upon completion will be distributed to the various arsenals from which sales to the above described individuals may be made.
William Crozier
Brigadier General
Chief of Ordnance
March 30, 1915"

The practice of stamping the front tang of the triggerguard with a flaming bomb insignia and "N.R.A." continued until the eve of America's entrance into the First World War when the sale of '03s to civilians was suspended due to the pressing need for rifles with which to arm our expanding military. Both Springfield Armory and Rock Island Arsenal M1903 rifles were sold during this period to qualified members of the NRA. The desirability of the NRA-marked '03s is an issue of debate among some collectors. One position holds that such rifles are less valuable as martial collectibles because the "NRA" stamp indicates that rifles marked in this manner were never in the U.S. military's arsenal. On the other hand, some collectors believe that the "NRA"-marked rifles are an interesting and fairly scarce variant in their own right and are worth a bit more than standard '03s of like vintage, condition and degree of originality. Still other collectors consider the markings as being neutral in regard to value and desirability and judge such a weapon solely on its other merits. This is a matter of personal preference. It is true that a high percentage of "NRA"-marked '03s remain in their original factory condition, whereas most service-used rifles of the same vintage were subjected to numerous arsenal rebuilds. It is safe to say that almost any collector would prefer a pre-WWI '03 remaining in its original factory configuration (blued finish, etc.) to one that subsequently went through an arsenal rebuild, even with the presence of the "NRA" marking on the former.

Issuance of M1903 Rifles with Maxim Silencers

In September 1910, orders were given that one standard M1903 rifle fitted with a Maxim silencer and specially modified M1905 bayonet was to be issued to each company of infantry, engineers, coast artillery and Signal Corps.

Each cavalry company was to be issued one silencer-equipped '03 rifle but no bayonet. This practice remained in effect until August 1914 when it was suspended. The Maxim silencer was given the Model of 1910 designation. The issuance of the silencer-equipped rifle was restricted to soldiers who had qualified as Marksmen. Several years later, in the 1918–1919 period, 9,100 Maxim silencers and a like number of specially modified M1905 bayonets were fitted to select '03 rifles, but it is doubtful if any were actually

"NRA" marking on triggerguard front tang as stamped on rifles sold to members of the National Rifle Association prior to the First World War.

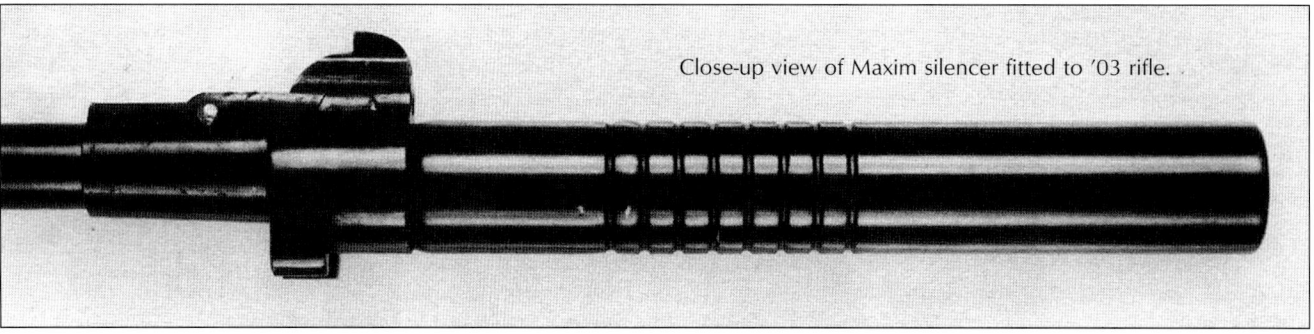

Close-up view of Maxim silencer fitted to '03 rifle.

issued and utilized in overseas combat during WWI. Some of the silencer-equipped '03 rifles were sold as surplus by the Director of Civilian Marksmanship via an ad in the November 1, 1920, issue of *Arms and the Man* magazine. In March 1925, the remaining unsold silencers were declared as obsolete items and were presumably destroyed shortly afterward. The sale of silencers was perfectly legal in the 1920s, although the National Firearms Act of 1934 made such items illegal without going through the same transfer/registration procedure and payment of a $200 tax stamp as required by machine guns and Destructive Devices. Any functional silencer extant must be properly registered with the ATF, or possession is illegal. Registered original Maxim silencers are quite rare on the collector market today.

A later version of the M1910 Maxim silencer was used by a few National Guard units after WWI. These were referred to in a Maxim Company postwar catalog as the Model 15 U.S. Gov. Silencer. The exact reason for the use of such silencers by the National Guard or their ultimate disposition is not known. There have been some reproduction sectionalized Maxim silencers produced over the past couple of decades. Since these replicas are non-functional, they do not require any sort of registration.

Pre-WWI Combat Use of the M1903 Rifle

Prior to the First World War, '03 rifles did not see extensive combat use. The '03's baptism of fire occurred in the Philippines during the closing stages of the pacification campaigns but, by 1912, such actions were drawing to a close. In April of 1914, a force of 800 U.S. Marines and Navy seamen, armed largely with '03 rifles and some M1895 Colt machine guns, landed at Vera Cruz, Mexico, in order to protect American citizens during a time of civil unrest and violence. Smedley Butler, a Marine Corps legend, won the Medal of Honor during the Vera Cruz campaign.

An early photograph showing soldiers relaxing on a porch with their '03 Springfields. The second soldier from the left is sitting on a box marked for the early Texas Company (Texaco) and bears their trademark star. *(Courtesy Stuart C. Mowbray collection)*

M1903 rifles saw additional combat during the U.S. Army's incursion during the 1916 Mexican Punitive Expedition to subdue the bandit Pancho Villa. This campaign also marked the first combat use of M1903 rifles fitted with Warner & Swasey Musket Sights, including some equipped with Maxim silencers which had been issued in limited numbers since 1910. Our troops were also armed with some *M1909 Benét-Mercie Machine Rifles*, which experienced some functioning problems due primarily to inadequate training. A handful of Lewis light machine guns chambered for the British .303 cartridge were also utilized during the campaign. The M1903 rifle performed superbly during the rather short-lived campaign, and the weapon gained an enviable reputation for reliability and accuracy that would continue in the trenches of France a year or so later.

U.S. Navy sailors with '03 rifles and M1895 Colt Machine Gun, Vera Cruz, 1914.

The crew of the *U.S.S. Montana* practicing marksmanship with their '03 Springfield rifles. On the right we see shipboard target practice, presumably aiming at floating targets. Often, a tarp was rigged above the sailors to protect them from the sun, but not in this case. Below, target practice was taken ashore in both prone and kneeling positions. *(Courtesy Stuart C. Mowbray collection)*

First World War: 1917–1918

By 1916, it was apparent to all but the most myopic observer that the United States would be drawn into the war raging in Europe. America was woefully unprepared to fight a modern war and our military had shortages in all types of first-line combat weapons. The United States did have the superb Colt M1911 .45 pistol and the M1903 rifle, but these fine weapons were in short supply. Clearly, additional weapons were needed.

Resumption of Rock Island Arsenal Production

To this end, on September 19, 1916, Rock Island Arsenal was directed to re-establish its M1903 rifle production line. This was easier said than done. Much of Rock Island's talented work force that had successfully produced the M1903 rifle prior to 1914 was gone, and many of the skilled artisans had taken jobs in other industries. In addition, the demands of the war in Europe resulted in shortages of raw materials. Rock Island Arsenal was eventually able to assemble and train a new work force and put the production machinery back in working order. In late February 1917, production resumed on the M1903 rifle at the Arsenal. Apparently RIA began to produce some parts before this time as barrels dated as early as December 1916 have been reported. Prior to the assembly line production of new rifles, Rock Island assembled several thousand rifles from parts remaining on hand from the previous production run that ended in 1913. The M1903 rifles manufactured by Rock Island Arsenal beginning in early 1917 were essentially the same as the rifles being made prior to cessation of production in 1913. The various features found on these WWI-vintage Rock Island '03s will be detailed later.

The United States declared war against the Central Powers on April 6, 1917, and additional suppliers of rifles were sorely needed. Production was ordered to be increased at Springfield Armory and Rock Island Arsenal as quickly as possible. The Ordnance Department consulted with Springfield and Rock Island engineers for ways to reduce production time and cost for '03 manufacture but, without substantially redesigning the rifle, only cosmetic changes could be accomplished. It was apparent that the combined output of these two national arsenals could not meet the burgeoning demand, and large numbers of additional rifles would be needed soon.

Rifle racks in a barracks view from Hawaii. The sign hanging from the ceiling shows a schematic drawing of the rifle and the bold reminder, "AMMUNITION HITS WHERE YOU AIM." *(Courtesy Stuart C. Mowbray collection)*

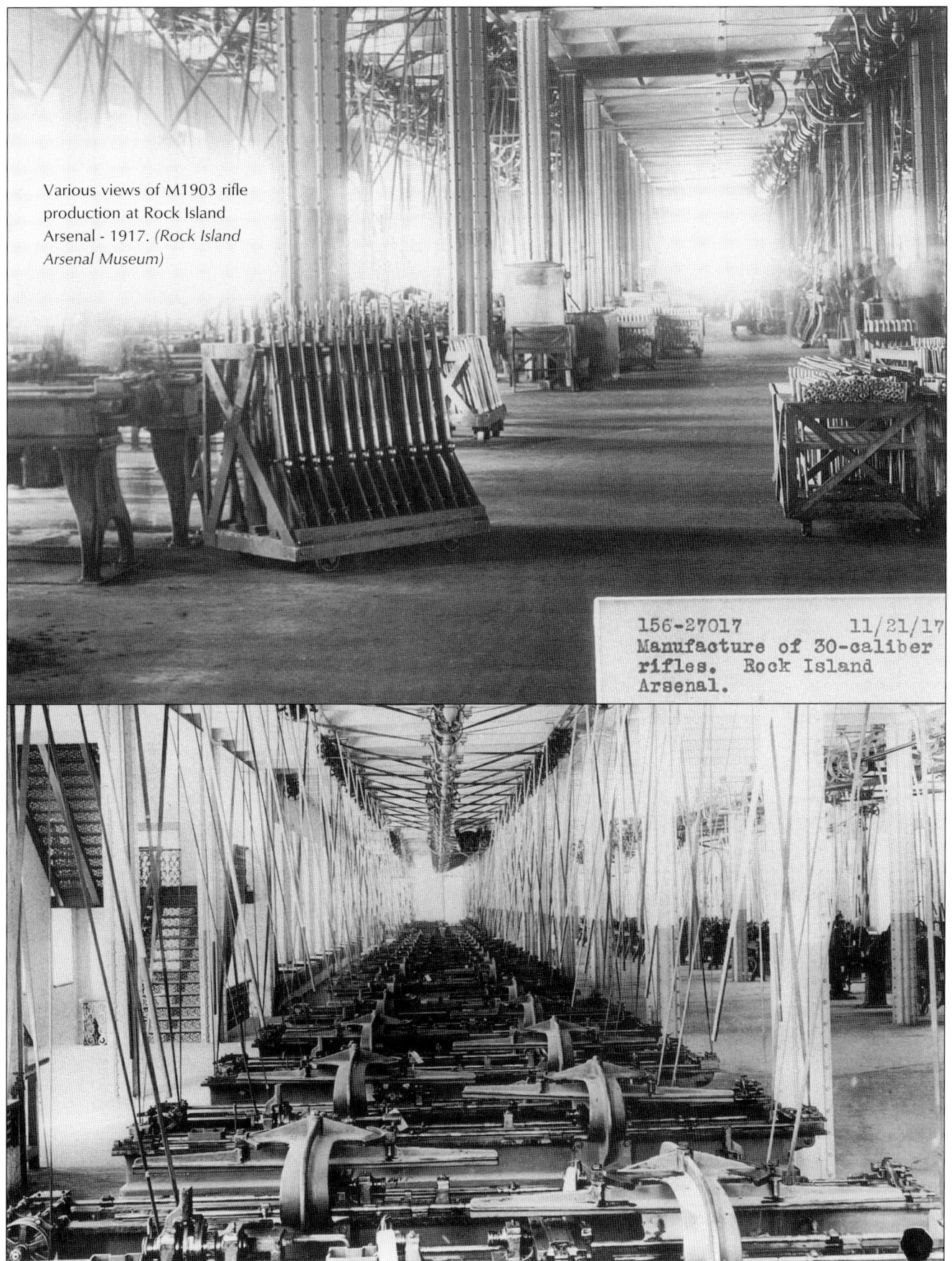

Various views of M1903 rifle production at Rock Island Arsenal - 1917. *(Rock Island Arsenal Museum)*

Various views of M1903 rifle production at Rock Island Arsenal - 1917. *(Rock Island Arsenal Museum)*

ABOVE – Contingent of U.S. Army *Doughboys* disembarking in France in WWI. Note the M1903 rifle with *Type S* stock with grasping grooves. *(National Archives)* BELOW – This 1917 postcard entitled "A Call to Arms" suggests an image of military life that was perhaps a little misleading! *(Courtesy Stuart C. Mowbray collection)*

A typical posed camp scene featuring '03 Springfields with their bayonets fixed. *(Courtesy Stuart C. Mowbray collection)*

Lt. Barnes of Company F giving instruction on hand-to-hand combat. Here he is demonstrating how to strike at an opponent with the butt of the rifle. *(Courtesy Stuart C. Mowbray collection)*

Soldiers were always eager to send photos of themselves in uniform to loved ones back at home. And, of course, the '03 Springfield rifle made the perfect photographer's prop.
(Courtesy Stuart C. Mowbray collection)

WWI Doughboys marching with M1903 rifles. *(National Archives)*

BELOW — U.S. troops in trench position, WWI. Note the soldier armed with M1903 rifle and the damaged. American helmet to his right. (*US. Army Military History Institute*)

U.S. Army patrol returning from front lines. The patrol members are armed with a variety of weapons including M1911 .45 pistols, M1903 rifles and a Chauchat light machine gun. (*US. Army Military History Institute*)

U.S. troops firing M1903 rifles from damaged building in France, WWI. (*National Archives*)

WWI photo depicting U.S. troops firing M1903 rifles from a building in France. *(National Archives)*

M1917 U.S. Enfield

In order to secure the required additional service rifles, the Ordnance Department determined that there were two basic options available:

(1) Seek additional manufacturing sources for the M1903 rifle;
(2) Adopt a second type of service rifle to augment the M1903 rifle.

After some preliminary discussion, it was determined that option #1 would not be viable because the significant lag time required to find suitable manufacturer(s), negotiate contracts, train a qualified work force and procure necessary raw materials and machinery would not alleviate the crippling shortage of rifles. This left option #2, by default, as the only real alternative.

Fortunately, there was a source for the manufacture of suitable service rifles already in existence that could be available in a relatively short period of time. This was due to the fact that three American firms had previously received contracts for the production of the Pattern 1914 rifle for the British government. The Pattern 1914 was a modified Mauser design, chambered for the British .303 cartridge. The British contracts for American-made P14 rifles were nearing their end at the time of the United States' declaration of war, and the work forces and production lines of the manufacturers were still largely intact. Even though the Pattern 1914 rifle was somewhat heavier, longer and bulkier than the M1903 rifle, the weapon possessed a strong action and better battle sights than the Springfield.

This left the United States government with another dilemma. The options available were:

(1) Adopt the British Pattern 1914 rifle *as is*. This would permit the maximum number of rifles to be manufactured in the minimum amount of time. On the other

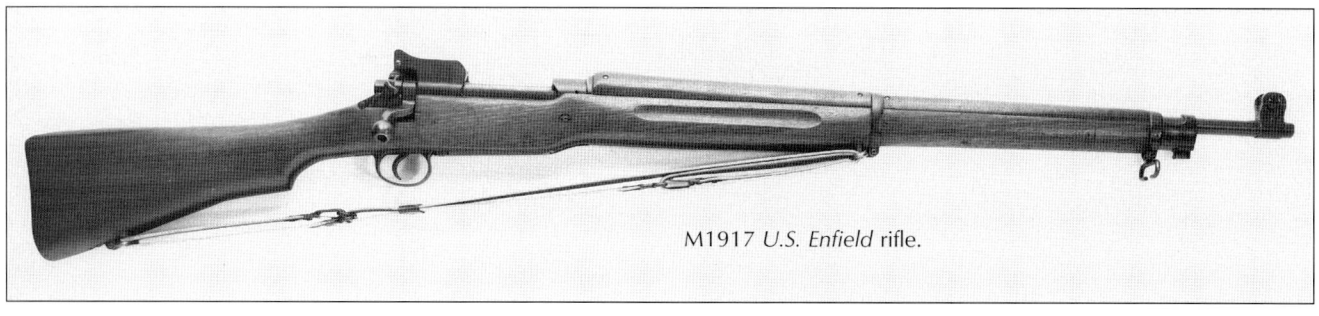

M1917 *U.S. Enfield* rifle.

hand, it would also introduce a non-standard cartridge into the United States' military service which would result in troublesome supply problems. In addition, the British .303 was widely considered as being markedly inferior to the American .30-06 cartridge.

(2) Modify the Pattern 1914 rifle to accept the standard U.S. .30-06 cartridge. This would cause a delay in getting into production but would result in a rifle chambered for the standard, and superior, U.S. cartridge.

The War Department opted for the second option and began plans to modify the British rifle to accept the American service cartridge. Even though the modification was not particularly difficult, the government was roundly criticized in some quarters for unnecessarily delaying the acquisition of badly needed rifles for our military. In retrospect, this was the only logical choice, and a post-WWI Ordnance publication proclaimed that it was "...one of the greatest decisions of the executive prosecution of the war..."

The three American plants, Winchester, Eddystone and Remington, produced well over two million M1917 rifles during the relatively brief period of America's involvement in the war. On March 8, 1918, the War Department directed that M1903 rifles in the hands of rear echelon troops be replaced by M1917 rifles.

The number of M1917 rifles manufactured during this period was substantially greater than the number of M1903 rifles, and by the time of the Armistice, an estimated 75% of the American Expeditionary Force (AEF) was armed with the American Enfield. Nevertheless, the M1903 rifle saw widespread overseas combat duty during the war, and most Doughboys favored it over the more cumbersome M1917.

At the end of the war, some thought was given to making the M1917 the standard U.S. service rifle, and reclassifying the '03 as Substitute Standard. However, the popularity of the '03, its superiority as a match rifle and postwar labor problems in the civilian plants that produced the M1917 all argued in favor of retaining the Springfield as standard. In April 1919, the War Department issued orders that the M1917 rifles in service be withdrawn, placed into storage and replaced by M1903 rifles.

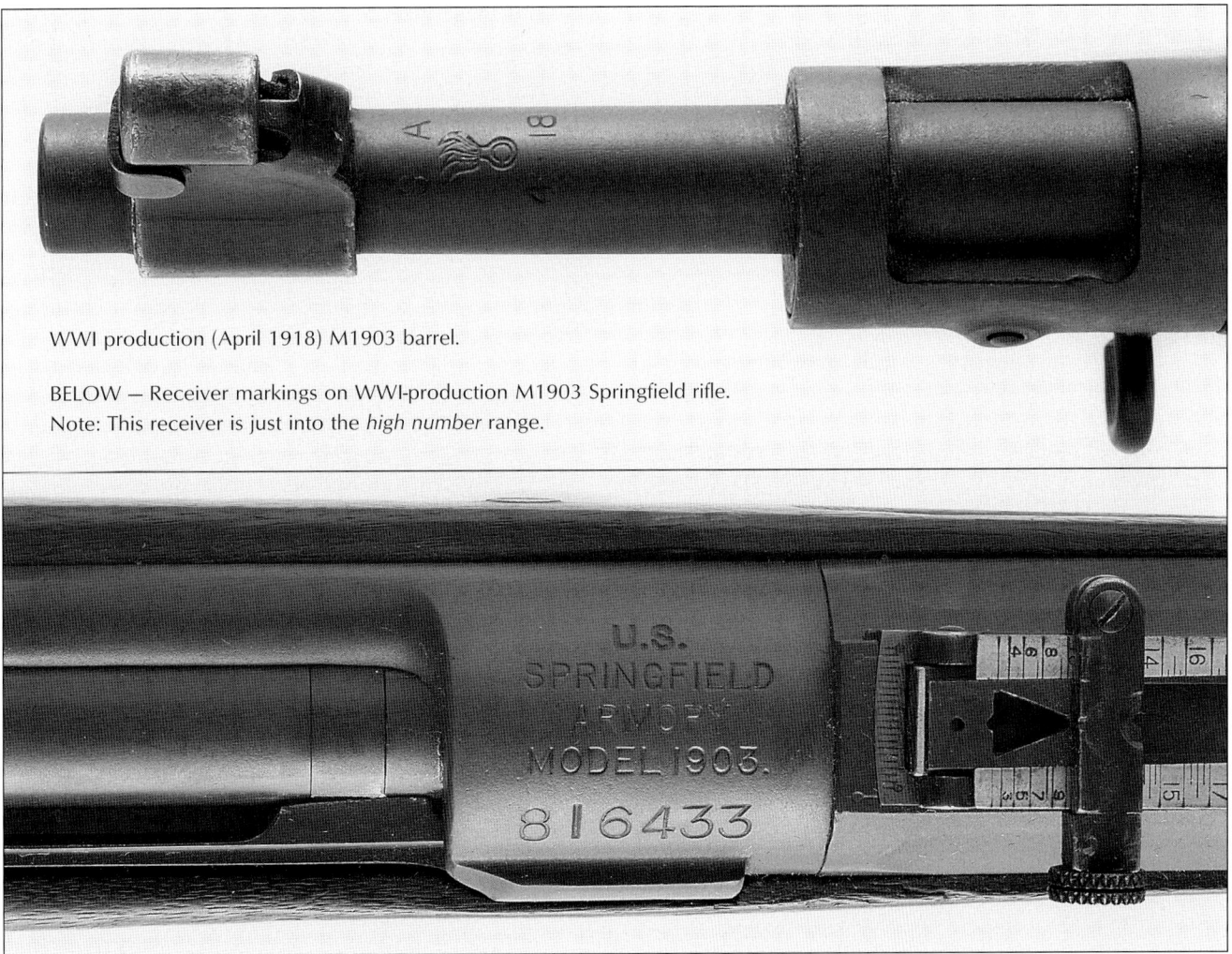

WWI production (April 1918) M1903 barrel.

BELOW – Receiver markings on WWI-production M1903 Springfield rifle. Note: This receiver is just into the *high number* range.

The M1903 and M1917 rifles were issued concurrently throughout the First World War and both weapons provided valuable service to our Doughboys. Technically speaking, any M1903 rifle manufactured prior to December 1918 can be properly classified as a World War I rifle. The rifles made prior to the United States' entrance into the war were the first weapons issued to our troops deploying to Europe, and the first to be used in combat. Many collectors today generally consider a WWI '03 as one that was manufactured during the time that the United States was actually involved in the war (April 1917 to November 1918). Although the M1903 rifles made during this period were essentially the same as those made prior to WWI, some relatively minor changes occurred that decreased production time and/or lowered costs. The most noteworthy were:

(1) Elimination of the checkering on the buttplate in order to save machining time.
(2) The serrated triggers that were incorporated circa 1910 were simplified by elimination of the serrations. The trigger did, however, keep its general outline, which was different than the earlier unserrated trigger used until 1910. The change to the unserrated trigger occurred circa late 1918 and continued until the early 1920s when the supply was exhausted and the serrated triggers were reintroduced.
(3) The addition of a second stock reinforcing screw. This occurred by 1918 and was reportedly done to reduce stock damage caused by severe recoil when firing the V-B rifle grenade launcher. Some of the earlier no-screw and one-screw stocks were subsequently modified by incorporation of additional stock screws to bring the earlier stocks up to current standards.
(4) Springfield Armory stock cartouches typically consisted of three initials, enclosed in a rectangle, as found on most post-1905 SA rifles.

Upon resumption of '03 production in February 1917 until sometime in early 1918, Rock Island's final inspection stamps consisted of a single letter stamped on the left side of the stock. Letters noted include, "A", "F", "H", "J" and "L". In early 1918, the inspection stamp format reverted to a type similar to that used prior to 1914 at RIA, which consisted of two or three initials over the year of assembly, enclosed in a square box. Rock Island inspector cartouches of this period that have been observed are "OEL" (Ora E. Lindsay), "SS" (Samuel Spangler), "ELV" (Edgar L. Vanier) and "OHA" (Otto H. Armstrong), "WHM" (William H. Hilbert) and "JLH" (John L. Hanssen) and dated 1918 or 1919. Rock Island Arsenal began stamping "RI" on the tip of stocks soon after production resumed in 1917.

(5) In very late 1918, the rust bluing previously used was replaced by a phosphate finish developed by the Parker Rust Proofing Company. This finish, known as "parkerizing," produced a dull, non-reflective surface that was more durable than bluing. Even though it was aesthetically less pleasing than the attractive bluing, it was inarguably a superior finish for military weapons. The exact date that Springfield Armory changed to parkerizing is not known, but the best estimate is October or November 1918. It can be safely assumed that no parkerized Springfield '03s were produced in time to be sent to France during the war. There is some evidence that Rock Island Arsenal utilized parkerizing as early as March 1918. All pre-WWII parkerizing used on the '03

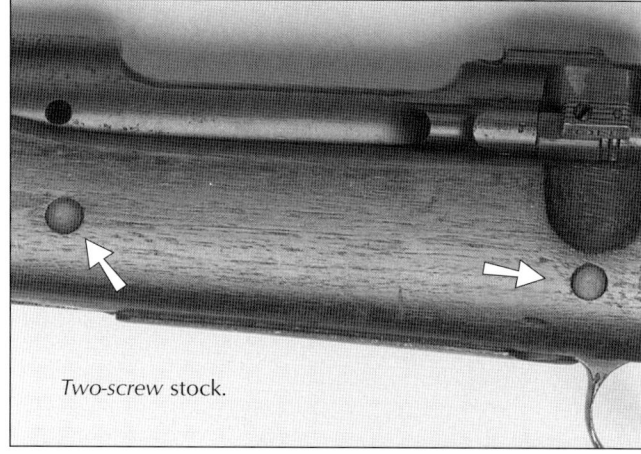

Two-screw stock.

Inspection stamp on Rock Island Arsenal '03. "OEL" represents "RIA" inspector Ora E. Lindsay and "1919" is the date of final inspection.

ABOVE – The kneeling position as executed by R.O.T.C. members at Plattsburg in 1917. BELOW – Referring to the blindfolded recruit, the note attached to this photo reads, "This is what they do on the range at Plattsburg when a recruit cannot close his left eye." Note the instructor's M1905 bayonet and M1910 scabbard. *(Both photos courtesy of Stuart C. Mowbray collection)*

rifle had a noticeable black tint. Despite some theories to the contrary, there was no green or other color tint to the finish. Parkerizing with a greenish tint is of WWII origin. The distinctive black finish is a hallmark of '03 parkerizing from the time of its introduction in late 1918 to the eve of the Second World War. It should be mentioned that parkerizing was originally a copyrighted trade name, but eventually came into the public lexicon as a generic term and is so used today.

(6) The handguard was changed by replacing the prominent sight-protecting hump with a type having a slightly more concave profile. Rock Island handguards were very similar to Springfield's except they generally lack a fixturing slot.

(7) The change in metallurgy heat-treatment process from single heat-treated receivers to double heat-treatment. This occurred in 1918 with Springfield Armory rifles at approximately serial number 800000 and with Rock Island Arsenal rifles at serial number 285507. Rifles below this range are typically referred today as *low numbers* and the rifles above the range are dubbed *high numbers*.

It is interesting to note that Rock Island began the use of nickel steel as early as May 1918, beginning at serial number 285507 according to Crossman, whereas Springfield Armory did not utilize nickel steel receivers until early 1928. Rock Island produced double heat-treated and nickel steel receivers concurrently for a rather brief period of time. Rock Island's use of nickel steel was reportedly due to the influence of a Major Penny who was formerly affiliated with the Winchester Repeating Arms Company. Winchester had long been a proponent of nickel steel for the company's firearms.

(8) In very late 1918 or early 1919, Springfield Armory changed the configuration of the bolt handle from its original straight pattern to a swept-back configuration in order to improve bolt manipulation during rapid fire. All of these swept-back bolts were of the improved double heat-treated variety until the late 1920s, when Springfield Armory began using nickel steel bolts. Rock Island apparently did not change to the swept-back design, but the RIA bolts made after the spring of 1918 were made of nickel steel and stamped "NS" beneath the bolt's safety lug, which identifies them from the earlier single heat-treated bolts.

Otherwise, the M1903 rifles manufactured during the 1917–1918 period were essentially unchanged from those made a few years earlier. In addition to the new rifles manufactured during the war at Springfield and Rock Island, government records reveal that some 30,000 M1903 rifles were assembled from parts in ordnance shops in France, although the source of these parts was not identified.

Mark I Rifle

One notable variant of the M1903 rifle which appeared in late 1918, was the U.S. Rifle, Model of 1903, Mark I. This interesting variant was designed for use with the Pedersen Device. The Mark I rifle and Pedersen Device will be discussed together in a subsequent section of this book.

Low-Numbered *and* High-Numbered *Receivers*

The change in the heat-treatment process cited above is of particular interest to persons today who may be concerned about the safety of firing the older low-numbered, single heat-treated receivers. The problem was primarily due to steel being burned during the forging process. This resulted in a number of receivers being overly brittle, and which could shatter with no prior warning. To correct the problem, pyrometers were installed in December 1917 to accurately measure and monitor the forging temperatures.

In his classic *Hatcher's Notebook*, General Julian C. Hatcher detailed a number of failures of the low-numbered M1903 rifles from 1918 to the late 1920s. The results of these failures ranged from moderately damaged rifles to grave injuries suffered by the shooter. Faulty ammunition proved to be the primary culprit. If a cartridge case failed, gas escaping into the receiver ring could be of sufficient power to cause the receiver to fail. Ammunition with poorly manufactured cases (a common occurrence in wartime), and the occasional use of a German 8mm round, were found to be the most common causes for receiver failures.

In 1918, the method of heat-treating the '03 receivers was changed from single heat-treating to an improved process known as double heat-treating. This resulted in receivers that were stronger and much less likely to shatter in the event of a cartridge case failure. The double heat-treated receivers were followed by still stronger receivers made from nickel steel.

Rock Island Arsenal temporarily ceased production of receivers in early 1918, in the midst of WWI, so that the issue of the low-numbered receivers could be addressed. At that time, there were about 15,000 unfinished receivers on hand at Rock Island. About one third of these had previously been improperly forged and were destroyed. The remaining unfinished receivers had not yet been heat-treated, and when Rock Island resumed '03 production shortly afterward, they were subsequently double heat-treated and used to assemble complete rifles in the approximate 270000 to 285500 serial number range. Therefore, it cannot be assumed that all Rock Island rifles below the generally accepted serial number of 285500 had the inherently unsafe receivers, because some 10,000 rifles of this vintage utilized properly forged double heated-treated receivers.

U.S. Troops taking a break. Note the '03 rifles slung over their shoulders. *(U.S. Army Military History Institute)*

Co. H of the 9th Training Regiment coming in from an eight-mile hike at Plattsburg, NY, August 27, 1916. *(Courtesy Stuart C. Mowbray collection)*

However, there is no sure method to determine which RIA receivers in this serial number range were improperly forged and which were satisfactory, so all are suspect.

It should also be noted that the older bolts were subject to the same metallurgical problems due to improper forging as the low-numbered receivers. Therefore, an early case-hardened bolt used in a later double heat-treated or nickel steel receiver is also inherently unsafe because the strength of the entire action is no greater than the strength of the bolt.

Despite the potential danger, many thousands of low-numbered '03 rifles were used in service and large numbers have been subsequently utilized by civilian sportsmen and hunters. Does this mean that there is no risk in firing such rifles? This is the subject of some disagreement today as it has for many years. Some people believe that all of these old rifles are dangerous and will blow up if fired even once. Others believe that all of these weapons are perfectly safe, and anyone who questions their safety is an uninformed fool who has fallen for some old wives' tale. As is often the

Marines being instructed in marksmanship at Parris Island, South Carolina. Notice the one-on-one instruction and scorekeeping. *(Courtesy Stuart C. Mowbray collection)*

case, the truth is actually somewhere in the middle. It is absolutely certain that some of the low-numbered receivers were produced from the burnt, brittle steel and are subject to failure. On the other hand, many of the receivers of this vintage were properly forged. The problem arises because a dangerous receiver of this type cannot be readily distinguished from one that was not made of burnt steel. A low-numbered receiver could have been fired thousands of times over many decades with no problems. On the other hand, the next shot could cause such a receiver to shatter with no warning, and with possibly catastrophic consequences, especially in the event of a case head separation or other serious problem.

There is a statistically significant risk to firing low-numbered rifles and the risk is avoidable. One person may fire such a rifle many times with no problems, but that is precious little comfort to another person who may lose an eye, or worse, while engaging in the same activity. It is the general consensus among a majority of collectors and students of the subject that early '03s should be withdrawn from active shooting and retired to the rifle rack or gun safe to be enjoyed as historic relics. There are too many later variants available to risk shooting one of the low-numbered rifles.

Because of their inherent potential danger, the older single heat-treated receivers were ordered to be withdrawn from service and scrapped, but budgetary and logistical considerations resulted in many of them remaining in use throughout the Second World War. The possibility of catastrophic failure was judged to be an acceptable risk as compared to the very real problems that would be encountered in the event of a serious shortage of service rifles which would have resulted if all the low-numbered receivers had been scrapped. In other words, the cost/benefit analysis of retaining some potentially dangerous rifles in service was judged to be a better alternative than having our troops train or fight with broomsticks because of a shortage of rifles. Experience with the low-numbered rifles reveals that the vast majority of low-numbered receivers did not cause any problems. Indeed, virtually all of the '03s used in the First World War were of this variety, and any such potential problems did not handicap the rifle's overall utilization as a combat weapon.

The various accessories, accouterments and appendages of the First World War, including rifle grenade launchers and extension magazines, will be profiled in a later section of this book. Whether used for long-range sniper use with a telescopic sight, fitted with a bayonet and wielded in hand-to-hand combat, or as a mini-mortar (grenade launching platform), the '03 was clearly a versatile weapon.

In addition to the standard M1903 service rifle, there were several interesting and historically significant variants of the '03 produced during the Great War. While some of these weapons saw little, if any, use, their inclusion in this book is necessary in order to have a complete picture of the role that the '03 rifle played in U.S. military ordnance history.

M1903 Sniper Rifles: 1908-1918

To digress a bit, rifles equipped with telescopic sights were not unknown previously. The first real combat action of such weapons occurred during the War Between the States when both Union and Confederate sharpshooters made effective use of telescopic-sighted muzzle-loading rifles. These early military snipers inflicted causalities and caused morale problems well out of proportion to the numbers employed. After Appomattox, however, the use of telescopic-sighted rifles by the U.S. military became virtually non-existent. This remained the case for the next 40+ years.

In 1900, three M1898 Krag rifles were fitted with telescopes made by the Cataract Tool & Optical Company for limited testing and evaluation. After reviewing the results, the Chief of Ordnance recommended that the telescopic-sighted Krag rifles should be thoroughly field tested, with a view toward standardization. The decision to pursue adoption of a new service rifle to replace the Krag resulted in this recommendation being put on hold until a new rifle was selected. Just a year after adoption of the M1903 rifle, the Small Arms Firing Regulations for 1904 and the subsequent Small Arms Firing Regulations of 1906 were revised to include the authorization of telescopic-sighted rifles to selected marksmen. As published in Chapter II, Section 235 of the Regulations:

"Telescopic Sight — To encourage efforts, to award efficiency, and to properly equip a special class of shots who shall not only be designated as expert, but who, in action, shall be employed as such, the telescopic sight is adopted. These sights will be supplied by the Ordnance Department and assigned to enlisted men who have qualified under these regulations as expert riflemen. They will be issued to and accounted for by the company commander and, under his discretion, may be carried by the men at inspection under arms."

It is interesting to note that even though the Small Arms Firing Regulations for 1904 and 1906 stated that "...the telescope is adopted..." there were no telescopes in inventory for issue with the new service rifle.

Warner & Swasey Musket Sights

In order to procure the required telescopes, twenty-five optical sights designed and manufactured by the Cleveland, Ohio-based firm of Warner & Swasey were purchased by the Ordnance Department. This firm was a well-known entity to the War Department, as it had supplied various types of optical artillery fire-control instruments for a number of years and enjoyed a good reputation within ordnance circles. The experimental Warner & Swasey telescopic sight, invented by company co-founder Ambrose Swasey, was a somewhat unconventional design that featured prismatic construction. The prismatic design permitted an unusually wide field of view given the relatively high 6X magnification.

The telescope, termed Musket Sight, was attached to the M1903 rifle by means of a dovetail bracket fastened to the left side of the rifle's receiver. Very early test rifles reportedly had the bracket attached by soft solder, but this proved to be insufficiently strong, and the method of attachment was soon changed to three screws. The sight had a corresponding dovetail mount with a spring-loaded locking plunger. The bracket was machined with two slots to receive the mount's retaining plunger. With this system, the sight could be removed or replaced on the rifle, without (theoretically) affecting the zero.

The offset location of the scope also allowed the rifle to be clip-loaded in the normal manner, and permitted the use of the iron sights. On the other hand, the location of the scope made for a relatively awkward shooting position, and the short eye-relief required a rubber eyepiece to properly position and protect the shooter's eye.

After preliminary testing, the W&S design was found to be satisfactory, but the price of about $80 per unit, several times the cost of an entire '03 rifle, was deemed excessive. After some minor modifications and negotiations, the price was reduced to an acceptable figure, and approval was given for adoption of the United States military's first standardized telescopic rifle sight.

Model of 1908 Warner & Swasey Musket Sight

The new sight was standardized as the Telescopic Musket Sight, Model of 1908. The sight was constructed of black painted steel and bronze, and weighed a hefty $2\frac{1}{4}$ pounds. The sight had Warner & Swasey Company markings stamped into the left side of the body. Two brass plates containing firing and adjustment data were screwed onto the top of the sight and a stadia plate was fastened to the rear. There were three stadia lines inscribed on the reticle for use in estimating distances. A factory serial number was stamped into the left side of the body which was unrelated to the rifle's serial number. W&S sight serial numbers are known to range from as low as 40 to as high as 998 as evidenced by government documents. This is not an all-inclusive range, and W&S sight serial numbers that are slightly out of this range may be encountered.

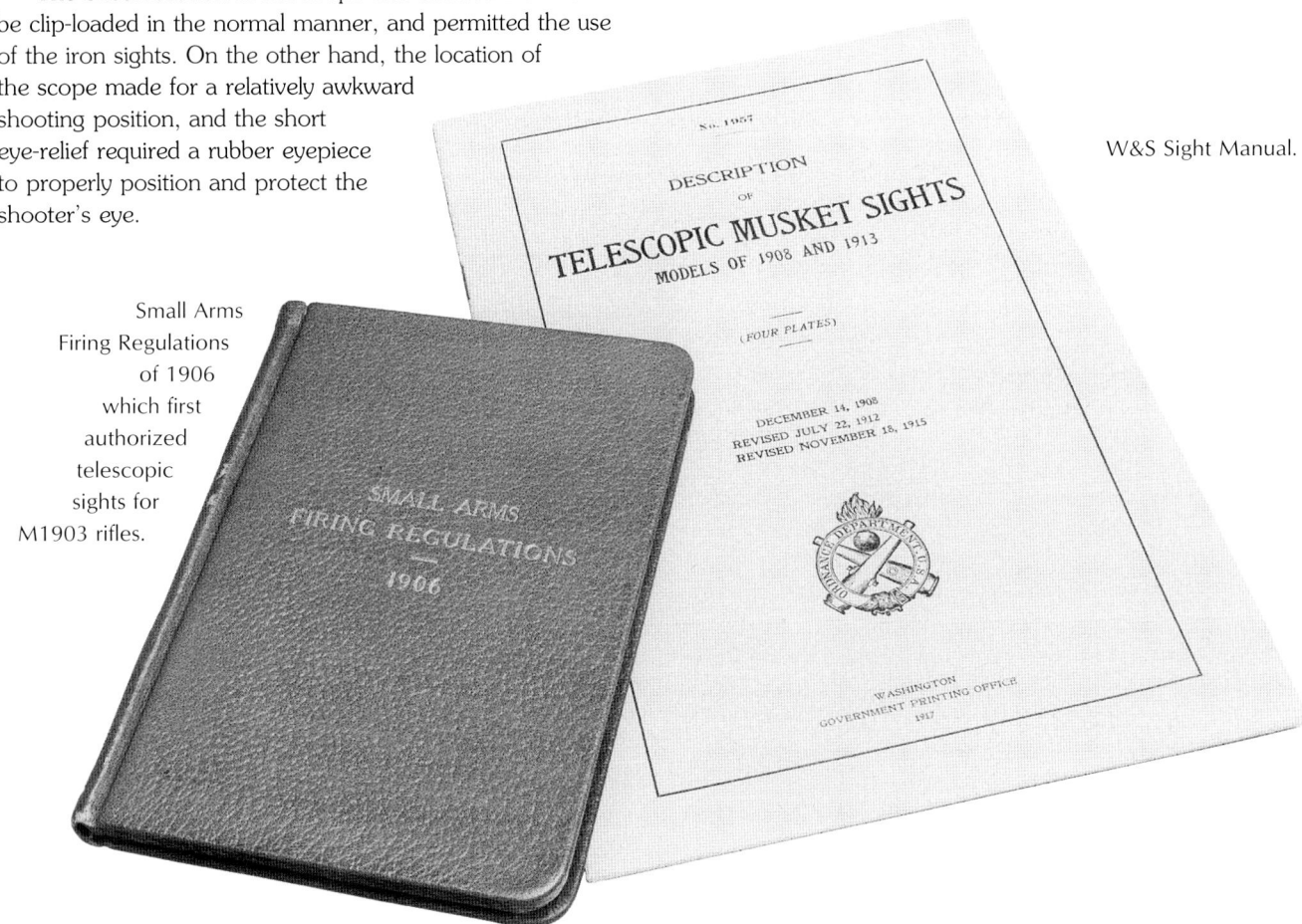

Small Arms Firing Regulations of 1906 which first authorized telescopic sights for M1903 rifles.

W&S Sight Manual.

A total of 2,075 M1908 W&S sights were procured as follows:

1909–1,000
1910–10
1912–1,065

The Warner & Swasey telescopic sights were mounted to M1903 rifles at Springfield Armory. Although the rifles were standard '03 service rifles, they were selected for their fit and finish and most, if not all, of the barrels were star-gauged. Neither the use of a star-like stamp on the barrel's crown, nor the star-gauge record number, were stamped into the barrel to denote star-gauging. These marks were not instituted until the early 1920s, so there is no way to positively ascertain whether or not a particular barrel of this vintage was, in fact, star-gauged. It should be noted that there was nothing magical about star-gauging a barrel. The star-gauge was simply a measuring instrument that ascertained whether or not the barrel's lands and grooves were within specifications. Star-gauging, in and of itself, did not somehow make a barrel more accurate.

The only modifications performed at Springfield Armory to the rifles fitted with W&S sights were the attach-

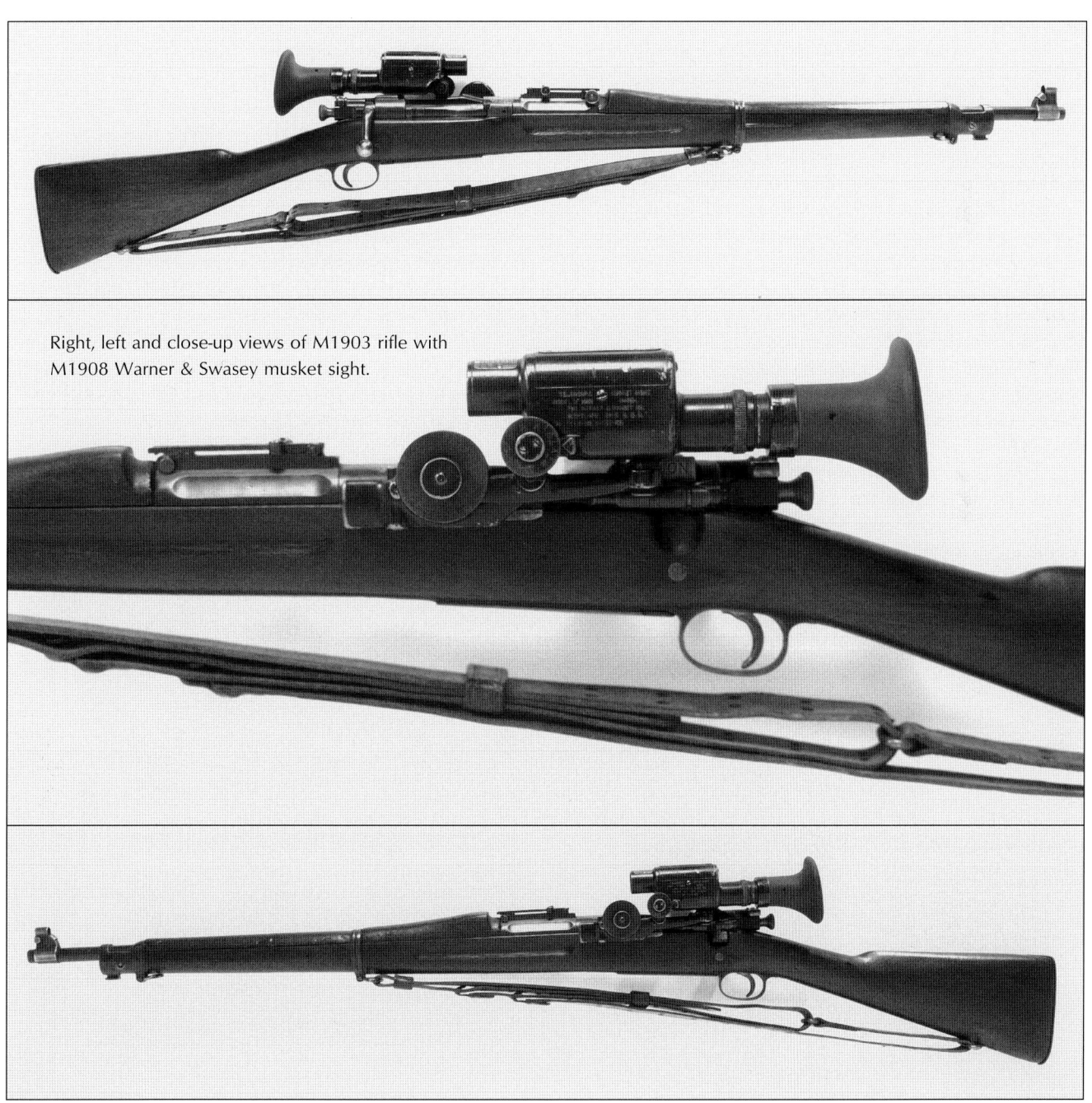

Right, left and close-up views of M1903 rifle with M1908 Warner & Swasey musket sight.

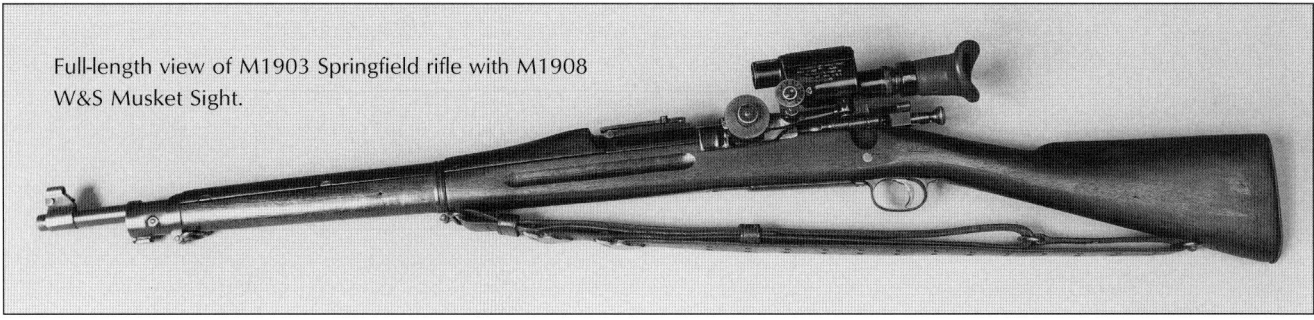

Full-length view of M1903 Springfield rifle with M1908 W&S Musket Sight.

ment of the dovetail mounting bracket to the left side of the receiver after drilling and tapping the three screw holes, staking the screws in place, and beveling of the inside of the left side of the stock to provide clearance for the bracket. Otherwise, the configuration of the rifles was identical to the standard '03 service rifles of the same vintage. The serial number of the rifle to which a particular M1908 W&S sight was mated was stamped inside of the sight's dovetail recess. Regulations called for matched rifles and sights to be kept together at all times but, in actual practice, the rifles and sights were soon mixed up, and non-matching numbers are the norm for most surviving examples. A matching rig would be exceptionally rare and desirable. In addition to being used on M1903 rifles, some M1908 W&S Musket Sights were fitted to *M1909 Benét-Mercie Machine Rifles*. These can be easily identified because of the one to three-digit number stamped inside of the sight's dovetail recess, as opposed to the six-digit '03 rifle serial numbers.

There are some serial numbers cited in government records of M1903 rifles fitted with M1908 W&S sights. The earliest serial number cited, 155268, was likely a prototype example that was fitted with a W&S sight and sent to the Office of the Chief of Ordnance for evaluation. M1903 rifle, serial number 207211, was tested at Springfield Armory. The earliest '03 rifle with a W&S M1908 sight reflected in government records as actually being in the hands of troops is serial number 207213, which was issued to Troop G, 5th Cavalry. The highest number cited in government records is rifle #468504, although original examples up to at least the #483000 serial number range are known. See **Table 4** on page 213 for a list of the serial numbers of the M1903 rifles fitted with W&S M1908 sights as reflected in government records. As can be seen from this table, the W&S sight serial numbers stamped on the left side of the body bear no correlation to the serial number of the rifles to which the sights were mated.

The W&S sights were fitted with a rubber eyepiece and issued with a leather carrying case (with shoulder strap and cartridge belt hooks) and adjustment wrench. The leather cases were used to carry and protect the telescopic sights when they were removed from the rifle. The adjustment wrench for the M1908 scope was carried in a pocket inside of the case's cover flap. All M1908 leather carrying cases are believed to have been manufactured by Rock Island Arsenal.

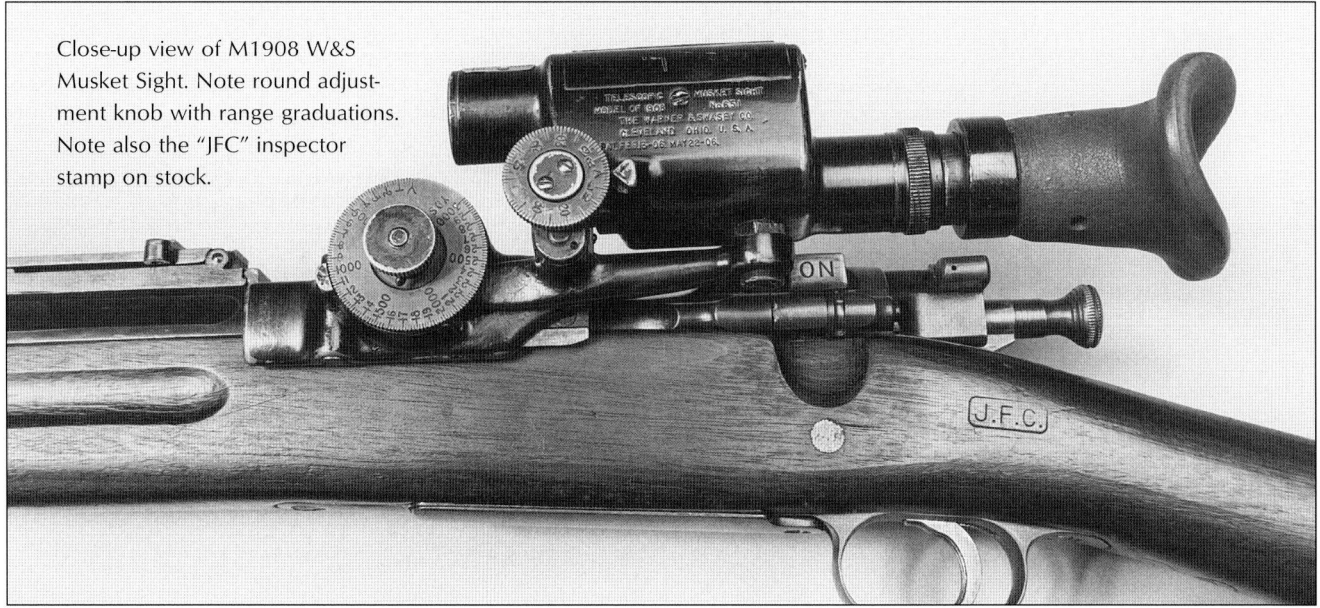

Close-up view of M1908 W&S Musket Sight. Note round adjustment knob with range graduations. Note also the "JFC" inspector stamp on stock.

M1908 W&S Musket sight with serial number matching rifle receiver. Matched rifle/scope rigs are rare.

Warner & Swasey Musket Sight Carrying cases: (Left) Case for M1908 sight, (Right) Case for M1913 sight. Note the stamped metal adjustment wrench in the pocket located on front of the latter case.

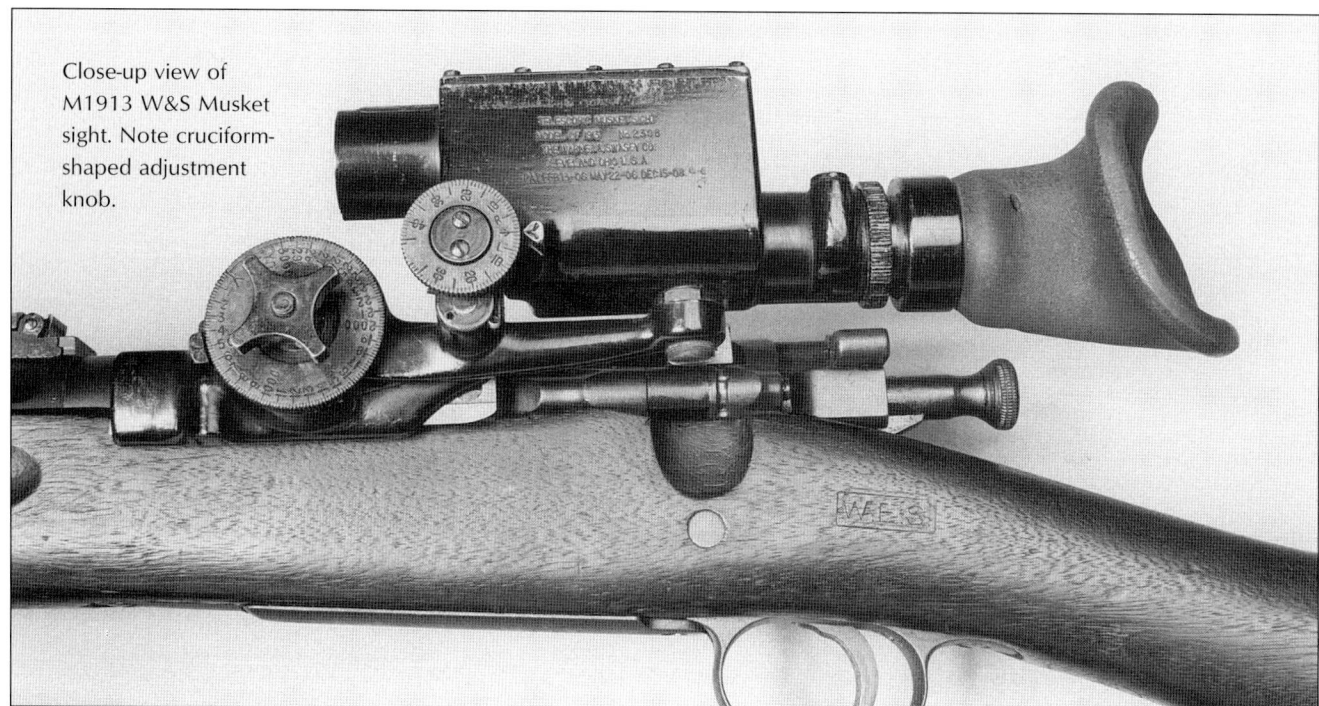

Close-up view of M1913 W&S Musket sight. Note cruciform-shaped adjustment knob.

To the military marksmen who had never before used a telescopic rifle sight, the W&S sight was likely something of a novelty, but the deficiencies of the sight soon became apparent. The heavy scope mounted on the left of the receiver tended to make the rifle somewhat unwieldy and unbalanced, and the short eye-relief (about 1½ inches), required that the shooter place his eye firmly against the rubber eyepiece. The offset location of the scope and the minimal eye relief resulted in an awkward shooting position, which made good marksmanship problematic. Perhaps it was best stated by E.C. Crossman in his classic *Book of the Springfield*, when he opined that the Warner & Swasey musket sight could "...make a flincher out of a cigar store Indian." There were also reportedly some problems experienced when the rubber eyepiece was shoved back against the shooter's face by recoil, and was stuck in place by suction. Crossman stated, with tongue firmly in cheek, that it could sometimes take "... several strong men to pull the sight off the shooter's face."

In addition to the position of the sight, there were problems encountered with moisture clouding the internal prisms and the fact that any specks of dirt or paint that worked their way inside the scope were magnified six times in the sight picture. Crossman stated, once again half-jokingly, that a grain of sand would look very much like a brick in such instances! The suction problem of the eyepiece and the magnification of foreign objects in the sight picture were, hyperbole aside, among several problems encountered with the M1908 Warner & Swasey musket sight that needed to be addressed in order to improve the telescope.

U.S. Marine Corps Match Use of the M1908 Warner & Swasey Sight

It has been documented in government records that ten M1903 rifles with star-gauged barrels and fitted with M1908 W&S sights and Maxim silencers, were acquired for use with the U.S.M.C. rifle team at Camp Perry in 1910. This is the only known procurement of W&S sights by the Marine Corps. The effectiveness of the W&S sights (and Maxim silencers) for such exacting match competition has not been recorded.

M1903 Springfield rifle with M1913 W&S Musket sight and Maxim silencer. *(Springfield Armory)*

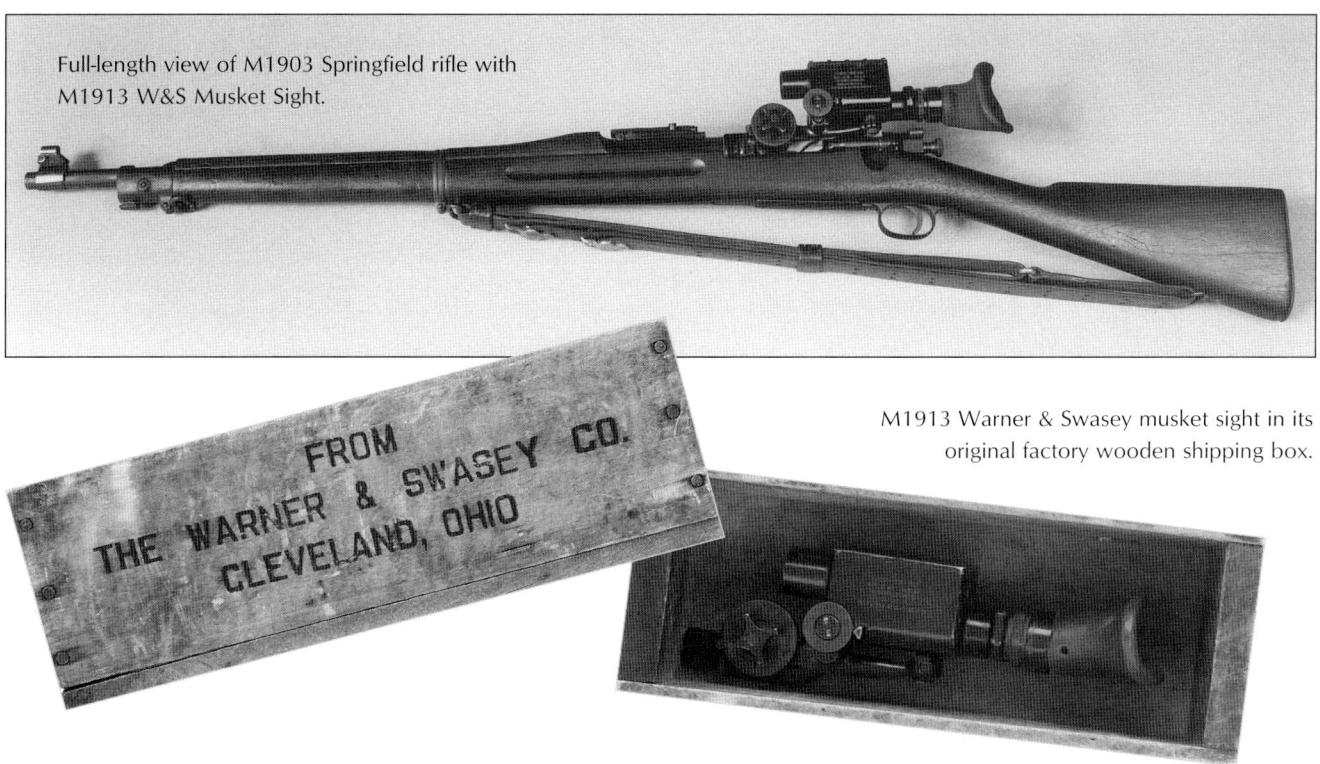

Full-length view of M1903 Springfield rifle with M1913 W&S Musket Sight.

M1913 Warner & Swasey musket sight in its original factory wooden shipping box.

Model of 1913 Warner & Swasey Musket Sight

To this end, the Warner & Swasey Musket Sight, Model of 1913 was adopted. The M1913 had a slightly different external profile than the M1908, and the power was reduced to 5.2X in order to improve its light-gathering characteristics. Most production M1908 sights had three holes in the rubber eyepiece to alleviate the suction problem, and this feature was retained on the later M1913 W&S sights. The method of mounting the M1913 sight on the rifle was the same as for the M1908 sight, and it used the same type of dovetail receiver bracket. The M1913 sight was issued with a leather carrying case similar to the previous model, along with a simplified stamped sheet metal adjustment wrench carried in a pocket on the outside of the case body. Initially, the M1913 leather carrying cases were made by Rock Island Arsenal, but some WWI-vintage cases were procured under contract from the Diamond D Company. Like the M1908 W&S sight, the M1913 sight was stamped with a serial number on the left side of the body.

The improvements of the M1913 were, in reality, more perceived than real, and there was little actual difference in performance and utility between the two models. Some Model of 1913 W&S sights were fitted to select M1903 rifles at Springfield Armory in Fiscal Year 1916. In Fiscal Year 1917, a total of 503 M1903 rifles were fitted with M1913 W&S sights at Springfield Armory and another 1,041 M1913 W&S sights were installed on '03 rifles at Springfield in FY 1918. According to an August 20, 1919, Springfield Armory report by Lt. Col. Lindley D. Hubbell, a total of 3,014 M1903 rifles had been fitted with telescopic sights at the Armory through that date. While not spelled out in the report, this number likely included only M1913 W&S sights. Despite some published information to the contrary, no W&S sights were installed at Rock Island Arsenal. Although some examples may be encountered today, any RIA '03 fitted with a W&S sight is not a genuine sniper rifle and is a non-original assembly.

As was the case with the M1908 W&S sights, the serial number to which a particular scope was mated was stamped inside of the sight dovetail recess. Government records reflect M1903 rifles fitted with M1913 W&S sights had serial numbers ranging from 577890 to 936527. See **Table 5** on page 218.

Combat Use of the Warner & Swasey Sights

The first combat use of M1903 rifles fitted with W&S sights, primarily the M1908 variant, was during the Mexican Punitive Expedition in 1916. There has been little recorded regarding these early sniper rifles, but anecdotal information indicates that they were at least marginally satisfactory. Some of the rifles were also equipped with Maxim silencers. **Table 4** reflects a few of the serial numbers of the rifles fitted with W&S sights and Maxim silencers.

The United States' entry into the First World War resulted in a number of M1903/W&S sniper rifles being sent to France. War Department records reflect that the 1st Army's allowance of M1903 rifles with W&S sights was 96 per division. It was also recorded that some of the W&S

sights were sent to France without rifles, presumably for replacement purposes.

The M1903/Warner & Swasey sniper rifles saw rather widespread issue in World War I, and a number of the weapons were utilized in front-line combat. From all indications, these sniper rifles were adequate within the limitations of the W&S sight. A number of Ross rifles were equipped with M1913 W&S sights for use by Canadian snipers, and the sights were apparently held in higher esteem by the Canadians than the Americans. The interesting book *A Rifleman Went to War* by H.W. McBride details the Canadians' use of the W&S-sighted Ross rifles during World War I.

A couple of recurring problems were encountered with the W&S sights. One was interference of the rubber eyepiece with a soldier's helmet and/or damage to the fragile eyepiece. In order to reduce or prevent these occurrences, a common field-expedient measure was for the eyepiece to be either removed or cut-down. A number of WWI-vintage combat photos reflect M1903/W&S sniper rifles in front-line use with altered or removed rubber eyepieces.

Another problem was a less-than-secure attachment of the W&S sight to the receiver's telescope bracket. A common fix was to fashion shims from razor blades, wedging the shims between the sight and the bracket, and rusting them in place. While some soldiers were on the receiving end of the First Sergeant's wrath for such an unauthorized modification, it was reportedly an effective procedure. A later authorized modification to alleviate this problem was the addition of one or two screws that could be tightened to better secure the W&S sight to the bracket. Apparently, this modification was not performed at Springfield Armory or the Warner & Swasey factory, but on the ordnance depot or field maintenance level.

A number of standard M1903s, as well as some M1903/W&S sniper rifles (rifles and scopes), were painted with camouflage colors to help conceal the weapons while in the trenches. Such *pattern painting* was rather common on helmets as well. A M1903/W&S sniper rifle, serial no. 689442, documented as having been used by a U.S. sniper in the Argonne campaign, resides in the Springfield Armory Museum collection today. The rifle still has traces of the camouflage paint on the receiver.

Although the M1903 fitted with M1913 Warner &

Solider displaying M1903 rifle with M1913 W&S sight that has been *pattern painted* for camouflage. *(U.S. Army Military History Institute)*

ABOVE — Group of four *Doughboys*, three of them are armed with M1903 sniper rifles with M1913 Warner & Swasey sights.
BELOW — Same group examining their W&S M1913 sniper scopes. *(Both from the U.S. Army Military History Institute)*

Doughboy firing M1903 rifle with a Warner & Swasey M1913 sight from trench position. Note the cut-down rubber eyepiece which was a common *field expedient* modification. *(U.S. Army Military History Institute)*

Swasey musket sights, was the standard U.S. Army sniping rifle of the First World War, the majority of the M1913 W&S sights purchased by Uncle Sam were never fitted to rifles or issued. These unissued sights can be identified by the absence of an '03 rifle serial number inside of the dovetail recess. Since an example with an '03 serial number in this location can be assumed to have been issued, it is a more desirable item for most martial collectors. The same can be said of the sights modified by the addition of a locking screw (or occasionally two), and most collectors will accept modified examples, as long as the '03 serial number is stamped inside of the dovetail. An example with a missing or damaged rubber eyepiece usually diminishes the value to some extent, even though this modification may have been done in the field. Some reproduction rubber eyepieces have been produced, and the tint and texture of the rubber generally makes it easy to identify them. The original eyepieces were made of rubber with a grayish-green tint while the reproductions are black.

Unfortunately, the majority of M1903 rifles fitted with W&S sights encountered today are non-original assemblies of parts. Surplus sights and receiver brackets were fairly common until just a few years ago, and many were attached to standard '03 rifles in order to create an ersatz W&S sniper rifle. There are several things to look for when evaluating a rifle of this type to help determine its authenticity, including the method of modifying the stock to provide the necessary clearance for the receiver base (the inside of the stock should be professionally beveled), and whether or not the W&S sight has a rifle serial number stamped inside of the dovetail. While an unnumbered sight is not proof positive of a bogus assembly of parts, it is a clue that at least the sight was not originally issued. This makes the entire rifle suspect. It should be recognized that some previously unnumbered surplus M1913 W&S sights have been stamped with '03 rifle serial numbers inside of the dovetail recess. Most of these fake numbers were applied with hand-stamped characters and can be identified due to misalignment of the digits and/or use of the wrong font.

Doughboys at entrance to dugout. The soldier at left has a M1903 sniper rifle with M1913 W&S sight. *(U.S. Army Military History Institute)*

The Warner & Swasey M1903 sniper rifles were withdrawn from service in the 1920s as confirmed in an April 14, 1925, report from the Chief of Ordnance that stated:

"The existing models of telescopic musket sights, viz., M1908, M1913 and Winchester Type 5-A, have been declared unsatisfactory and their issue discontinued."

Government records further reflect that many of these M1903/W&S sniper rifles were sent to Rock Island Arsenal in 1925, reportedly for destruction or conversion to service rifle configuration. Some of these sniper rifles were scrapped and others had the receiver holes plugged and were subsequently rebuilt as standard service rifles. A plugged '03 receiver will occasionally surface on a rebuilt '03 today, and such examples are desired by some collectors for restoration purposes. A genuine plugged receiver is certainly better for this purpose than drilling holes in a standard '03 receiver in order to create a fake M1903/W&S sniper rifle. The last date noted for a M1903/W&S sniper rifle still in the hands of the U.S. Army is 1926, although the use of such rifles may have lingered a bit longer.

Like the rifles, some of the W&S sights were scrapped after the weapons were withdrawn from service and some were sold as surplus. The majority of the M1913 W&S sights were never installed on rifles, and virtually all were sold on the civilian market. These are the most commonly encountered W&S sights and can be identified by the lack of a rifle serial number in the dovetail recess. Unlike the M1913 sights, all of the M1908 Warner & Swasey musket sights are believed to have been issued. It is unlikely that an unnumbered sight of this type will be encountered, so there is little likelihood that fake serial numbers will be found on M1908 W&S sights. In addition to reproduction rubber eyepieces, some reproduction W&S receiver brackets are around.

Due to the fact that there are many fake M1903/W&S sniper rifles extant today, any potential buyer should proceed with the utmost caution when considering a purchase. In spite of the problems inherent in the W&S sight, these early U.S. sniper rifles are visually impressive and historic U.S. military weapons. Original examples are always sought-after additions to any collection.

M1903 Rifle with Winchester A5 Telescope

While the U.S. Army settled on the Warner & Swasey musket sight for use on its sniper rifles, the U.S. Marine Corps did not initially develop a sniper rifle of its own. Although the Marines weren't looking for a sniper rifle *per se*, they were interested in a telescope for use with their match rifles. Soon after its introduction in 1910, the Marines procured a quantity of Winchester Model A5 telescopes for this purpose. Unlike the unusual prismatic Warner & Swasey sight, the A5 was a conventional design with a long metal tube and windage and elevation adjustments located on an external mount. Beginning shortly after 1910, the Marines mounted some Winchester telescopes on a number of their rifle team '03s. Several different types of civilian scope mounts were utilized for this purpose.

The U.S.M.C. rifle team '03s were fitted with A5 tele-

U.S. Marine sighting a M1903 rifle with Winchester A5 telescope, circa WWI. *(National Archives)*

scopes, on a more or less individual basis, and the method of modifying the rifles could, literally, vary from example to example. Some of the rear mounts were screwed directly to the receiver ring, and others were attached to the rear sight base, which required removal of the rear sight. The front mount was screwed to the barrel which required that a hole be cut into the handguard and a portion of the handguard's hump be relieved. The fact that each rifle was essentially modified to suit the desires and whims of the armorer or Marine marksman makes it difficult to ascertain the originality of a particular example encountered today. Some contemporary Marine Corps documents referred to the weapons as Sniper and Rifle Team Rifles. Government records dating from February of 1914 reveal that at least twelve M1903 rifles were fitted with A5 telescopes by the Winchester Repeating Arms Company. (See **Table 6**).

The purpose and disposition of these rifles is not known. America's active involvement in the First World War and deployment of a contingent of the U.S. Marine Corps to France resulted in some of the telescopic-sighted rifle team '03s being pressed into service as sniping weapons. In order to increase the supply of available sniping rifles, the Marine Corps procured a quantity of specially made tapered Mann-Niedner mounts. There was a bit more conformity in the '03 rifles converted to sniper configuration by means of the Mann-Niedner type mounts than the commercial mounts used previously but there was still some variance from rifle to rifle.

The Winchester A5 scopes were issued with leather carrying cases (with web shoulder straps) that were used to carry and store the scopes. Little has been written regarding use of their A5-sighted '03 rifles, but the weapons were

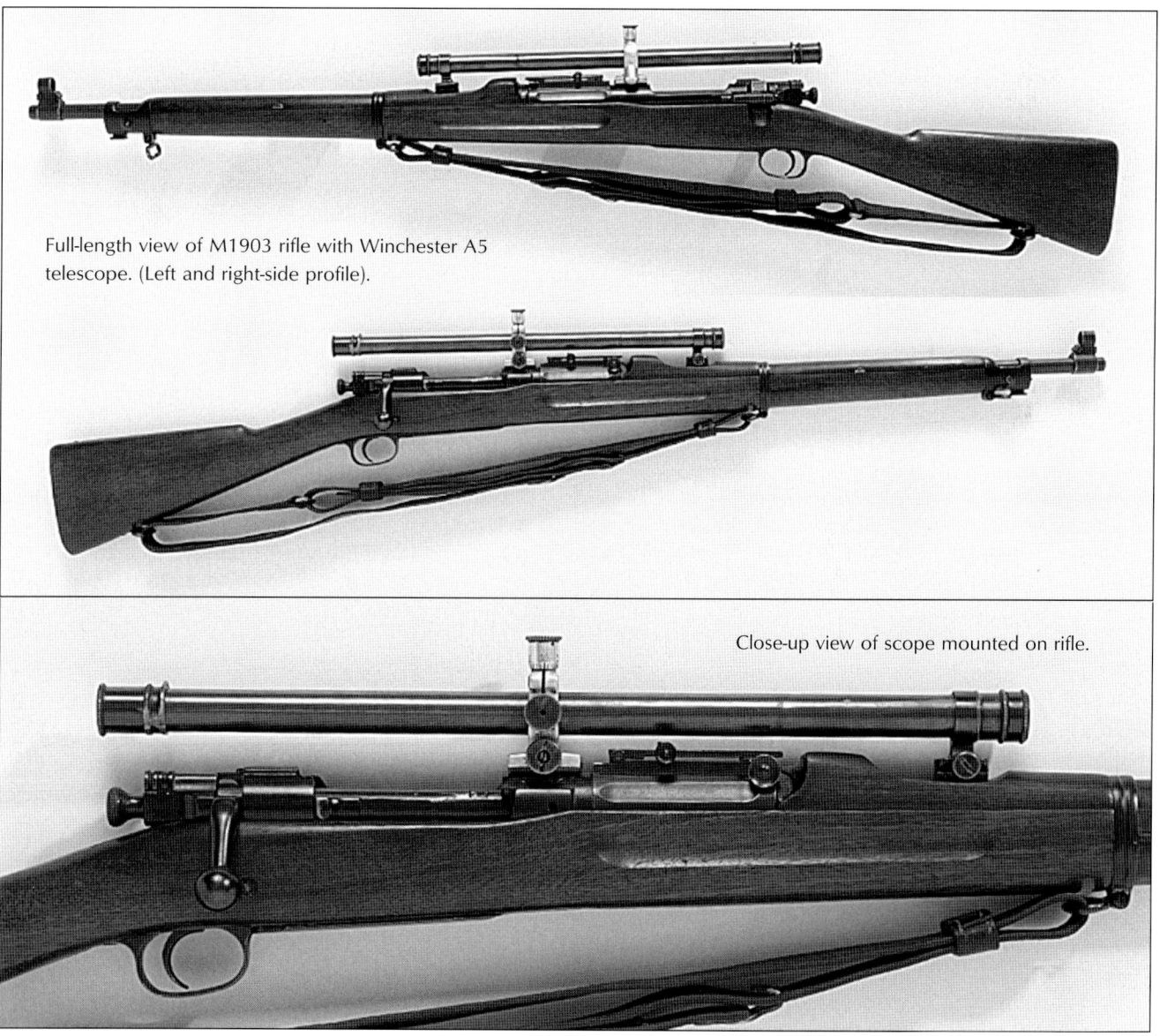

Full-length view of M1903 rifle with Winchester A5 telescope. (Left and right-side profile).

Close-up view of scope mounted on rifle.

undoubtedly put to good use by the skilled Marine marksmen, even if the number of '03/A5 sniper rifles employed in WWI was rather small. Unlike the '03 rifles with Warner & Swasey and Winchester A5 scopes that were withdrawn from service by the U.S. Army beginning in the mid-1920s, the Marine Corps retained their '03/A5 sniper/match rigs after the war. Some of these weapons remained in use during World War II, although some of the A5 scopes were replaced by the Lyman 5A telescope. Lyman purchased production rights for the A5 telescope from Winchester. The Lyman 5A was a slightly improved version of the Winchester A5 scope. In addition to the Winchester A5 scopes used by the Marines, government documents reflect that the U.S. Army Ordnance Department was directed to purchase 500 of the scopes in March 1918 from Winchester. The scopes were referred to in the Ordnance Department documents as the Marine Corps Model.

Reports indicate that some target grade M1903 rifles fitted with A5 scopes were sent to France with AEF U.S. Army National Guard units, but it is uncertain if any were actually employed in combat. There are few details available regarding these U.S. Army '03/A5 rifles, and it can be assumed that at least some were fitted with commercial type mounts as were the earlier U.S.M.C. rifles, rather than the later Mann-Niedner tapered mounts. However, some of the mounts may have been the tapered variety, as one ordnance document cited *Marine Corps mountings* in reference to these rifles. There were also at least two M1903 rifles fitted with Winchester A5 scopes issued to Troop E, 5th U.S. Cavalry, as reflected in a Ordnance Department report dated 1923. These exceptions notwithstanding, use of the '03 rifles with A5 scopes was much more common in U.S. Marine Corps service than U.S. Army service during this period. While better than the W&S sight for general use, there were still some problems encountered in combat with the Winchester A5 scope. These problems were mainly due to the rather fragile nature of the scope, since it was designed for civilian sporting and match purposes rather than as a durable combat telescope. This was addressed by E.C. Crossman in *The Book of the Springfield*:

"The Winchester A5 represents a fine composite of things we don't want in the sniper glass, length, fragility, unsubstantial construction, sliding mounts, delicate micrometer, hard to read and easily confused readings. I watched them to the number of nearly 100 take themselves apart at the Small Arms Firing School in the hands of presumably intelligent student officers from the division of our Army. In service they would make metallic sights popular."

Evaluating an '03 rifle fitted with an A5 scope for the purpose of determining originality is difficult due to the fact that even the genuine U.S.M.C. rifle team weapons were converted on an individual basis, with a great deal of variance between examples. It is important to ascertain that the features of the rifle in question are consistent with service rifles of the same period. This is not definitive either, because numbers of the rifles were fitted with replacement barrels and stocks under U.S.M.C. auspices. The '03 rifles fitted with the special tapered Mann-Niedner mounts should not generally be found on rifles manufactured earlier than circa 1917–1918. As long as the general features are consistent with '03 rifles issued prior to WWI, including the original blued finish, it is often very difficult to state one way or the other whether or not a particular example is legitimate. The overwhelming majority of examples seen for sale today are fakes, and very few specimens can be documented as original. There are no specific serial number ranges for the rifles fitted with A5 scopes, which makes positive identification even harder. A few serial numbers of M1903/A5 sniper rifles are listed in the government records **(Table 6)** and these range from 468493 to 785424. A potential purchaser should not pay a premium for an undocumented rifle of this type due to the uncertainty involved in evaluating such a weapon. A good rule of thumb is not to pay more for such a rifle than the value of the sum of the parts.

In addition to the sniper rifles, there were several other types of specialized variants '03 rifles that were developed for use during the World War I period, which will now be discussed but, almost without exception, none were actually issued or used for combat prior to the end of World War I.

The Winchester A5 scopes were issued with leather carrying cases (with web shoulder straps) that were used to carry and store the scopes.

Pedersen Device and the M1903 Mark I Rifle

At the time of the United States' declaration of war, our military immediately searched for effective weapons with which to wage trench warfare. A number of ideas were forthcoming, some valuable and some worthless. One of the most interesting and innovative weapons of this type was conceived in the fertile mind of John D. Pedersen. Pedersen was a noted designer of firearms and was affiliated with the Remington Arms Company. He was previously responsible for the design of several noteworthy weapons including the Model 10 slide-action shotgun and the Model 51 semi-automatic pistol. In the late 1920s and early 1930s, Pedersen designed a semi-automatic military rifle that was a serious competitor to the rifle which was later adopted as the M1 Garand.

Pedersen's idea was to address and correct two fundamental problems inherent in all military service rifles of the time, including the M1903. The manual bolt-action mechanism resulted in a relatively slow rate of fire, and the typical service cartridge, such as the U.S. .30-06, was overly powerful for some applications. These problems were discussed in an article published in *Army Ordnance* magazine:

"It may seem at first glance that the military rifle cartridge is unduly powerful but it must be remembered that this cartridge is intended to be used against various targets such as airplanes, armored cars, tanks, etc... These same bullets are used by machine guns for laying out barrages at long distances or for shooting at high flying aircraft.

"Thus a soldier in firing his army rifle is frequently in a situation where he has more power in his bullets than he needs for a particular job in hand; moreover for each shot he must open the bolt of his gun and throw out the empty cartridge and then close the bolt and lock it before he can shoot another shot."

Obviously, the full-power service cartridge was overly powerful for some tasks, but such power was needed for other applications. Also, a semi-automatic rifle would be quite valuable, but no satisfactory rifles of this type had yet been developed that were capable of handling full-power service cartridges. Finding a solution to these rather contradictory issues seemed beyond reach, but John D. Pedersen believed otherwise, and he began working on a very imaginative concept.

Pedersen labored on his project until he believed he was ready to demonstrate it to the U.S. Army Ordnance Department. In the summer of 1917, Pedersen requested a secret demonstration of his new weapon, and given the inventor's reputation within ordnance circles, this request was immediately granted. On October 8, 1917, a number of select individuals, including General William Crozier (Chief of Ordnance) and a few Congressmen who were all sworn to secrecy, gathered at the Congress Heights Rifle Range in Washington, D.C. The results of this demonstration were related in a subsequent article in *Army Ordnance* magazine:

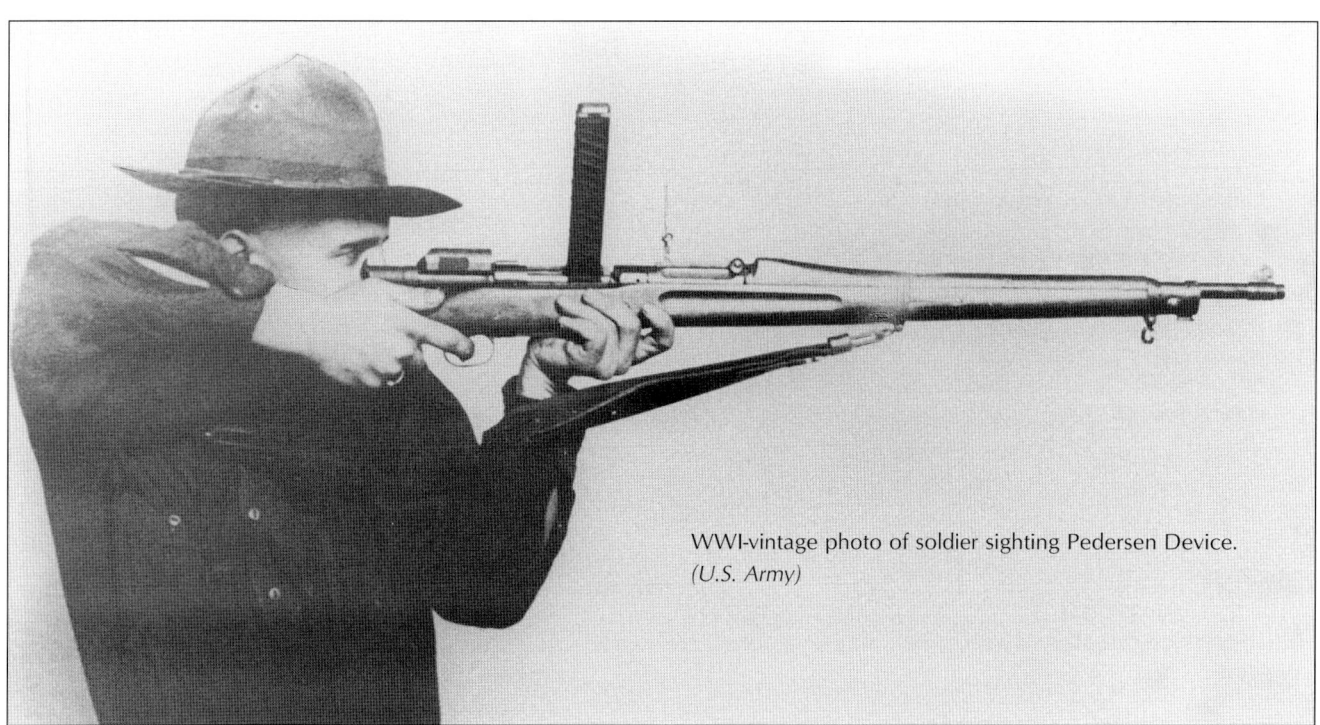

WWI-vintage photo of soldier sighting Pedersen Device. *(U.S. Army)*

"Mr. Pedersen started his demonstration by firing the Springfield rifle which he brought with him. After firing a few shots in the ordinary way he suddenly jerked the bolt out of the rifle and dropped it in a pouch which he had with him, and from a long scabbard which was on his belt he produced a mysterious looking piece of mechanism which he quickly slid into the rifle in place of the bolt, locking the device to the rifle by turning a catch provided for the purpose. Then he snapped into place a long black magazine containing forty small pistol size cartridges whose bullets were, however, of the right diameter to fit the barrel of the rifle. All this was done in an instant and in another instant Mr. Pedersen was pulling the trigger of the rifle time after time as fast as he could work his finger and each time the pulled the trigger the rifle fired a shot, threw out the empty cartridge and reloaded itself."

Pedersen's demonstration amazed the witnesses who eagerly examined the mechanism afterward. The device was termed an automatic bolt by Pedersen but was capable of only semi-automatic operation. The mechanism soon became widely known as the Pedersen Device. The device operated in the same manner as a semi-automatic blow back pistol. The barrel of the device was the same configuration as a .30-06 cartridge and was rifled with shallow lands and grooves which enabled the bullet to start spinning before it reached the barrel of the rifle. With the standard bolt removed, the device was inserted into the rifle and locked in place by a modified magazine cutoff lever.

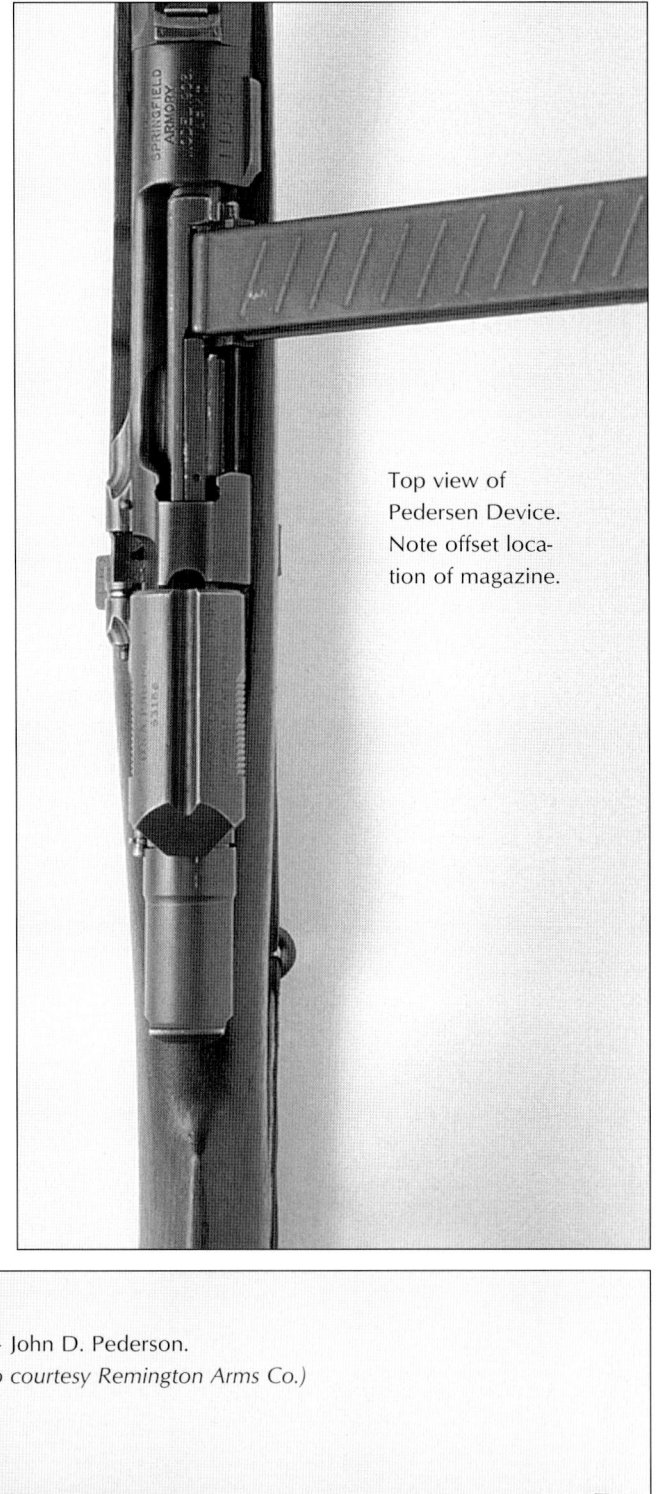

Top view of Pedersen Device. Note offset location of magazine.

LEFT – John D. Pederson. *(Photo courtesy Remington Arms Co.)*

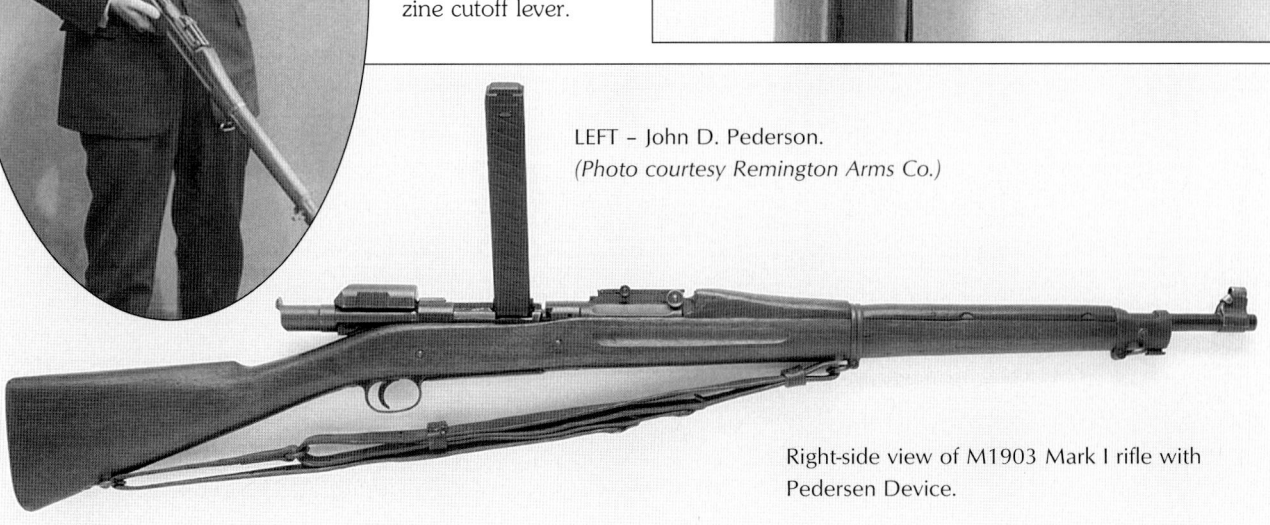

Right-side view of M1903 Mark I rifle with Pedersen Device.

M1903 Mark I rifle receiver markings.

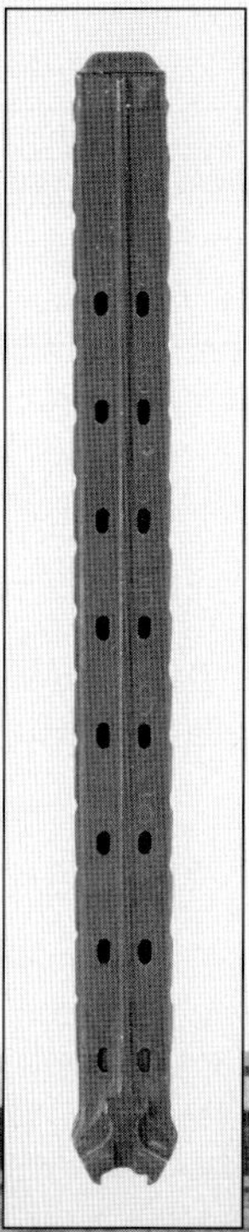

Pedersen Device magazine with view of slots on back.

Right side of M1903 Mark I rifle with M1918 Pedersen Device and magazine. The two spring-loaded catches are visible behind the magazine.

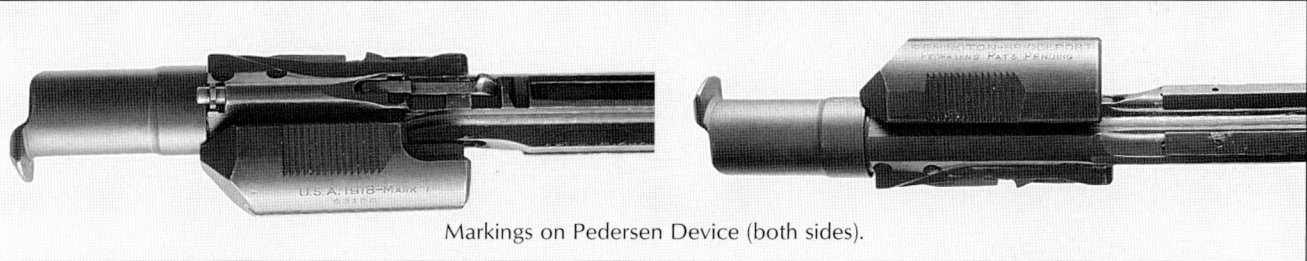

Markings on Pedersen Device (both sides).

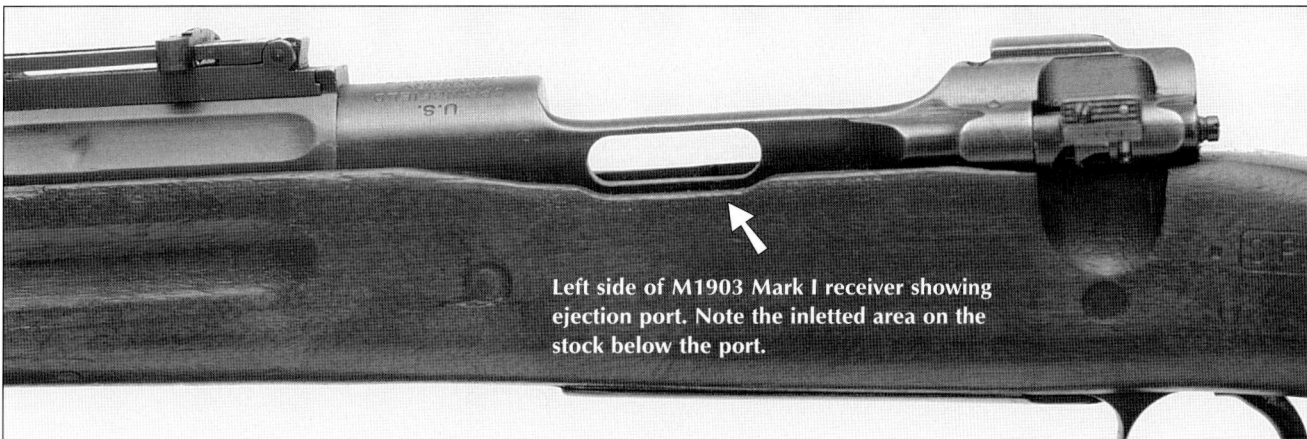

Left side of M1903 Mark I receiver showing ejection port. Note the inletted area on the stock below the port.

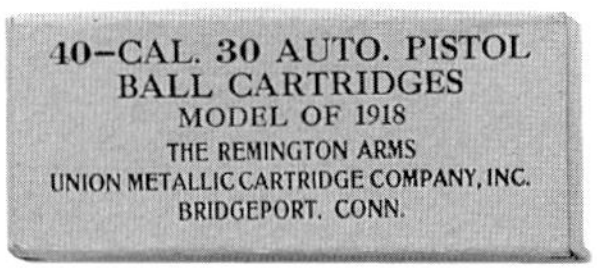

Pedersen Device ammunition.
LEFT – 40-round box.

BELOW – 200-round carton.

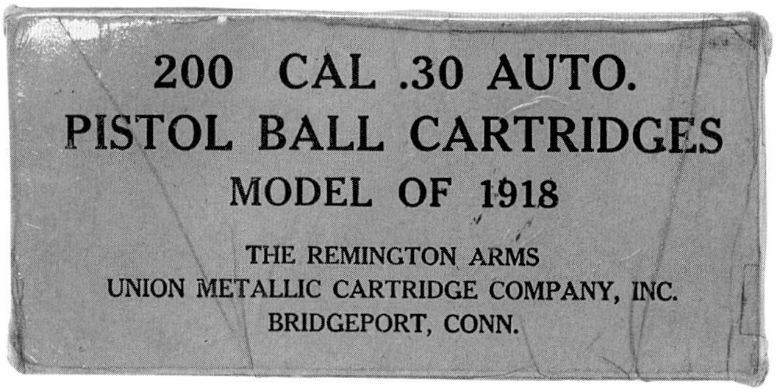

Adjustment wrench.

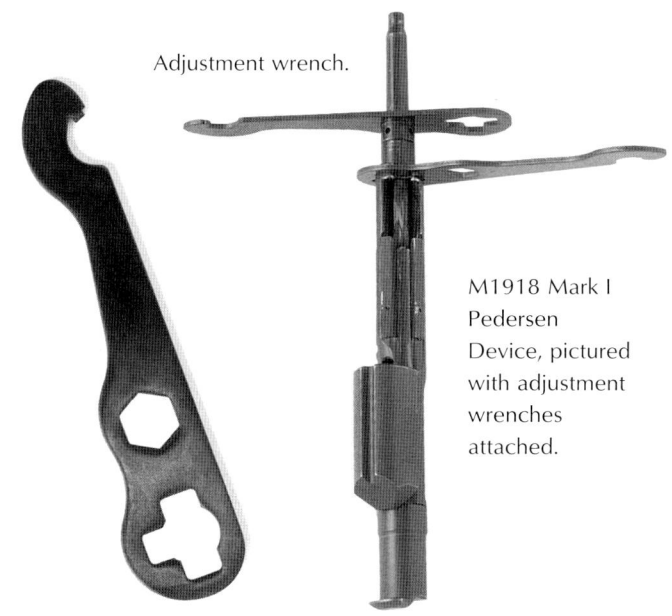

M1918 Mark I Pedersen Device, pictured with adjustment wrenches attached.

BELOW – M1918 Mark I Pedersen Drive, bolt and bolt carrying case, 40-round box of ammunition, loose cartridges, magazine and magazine carrying case.

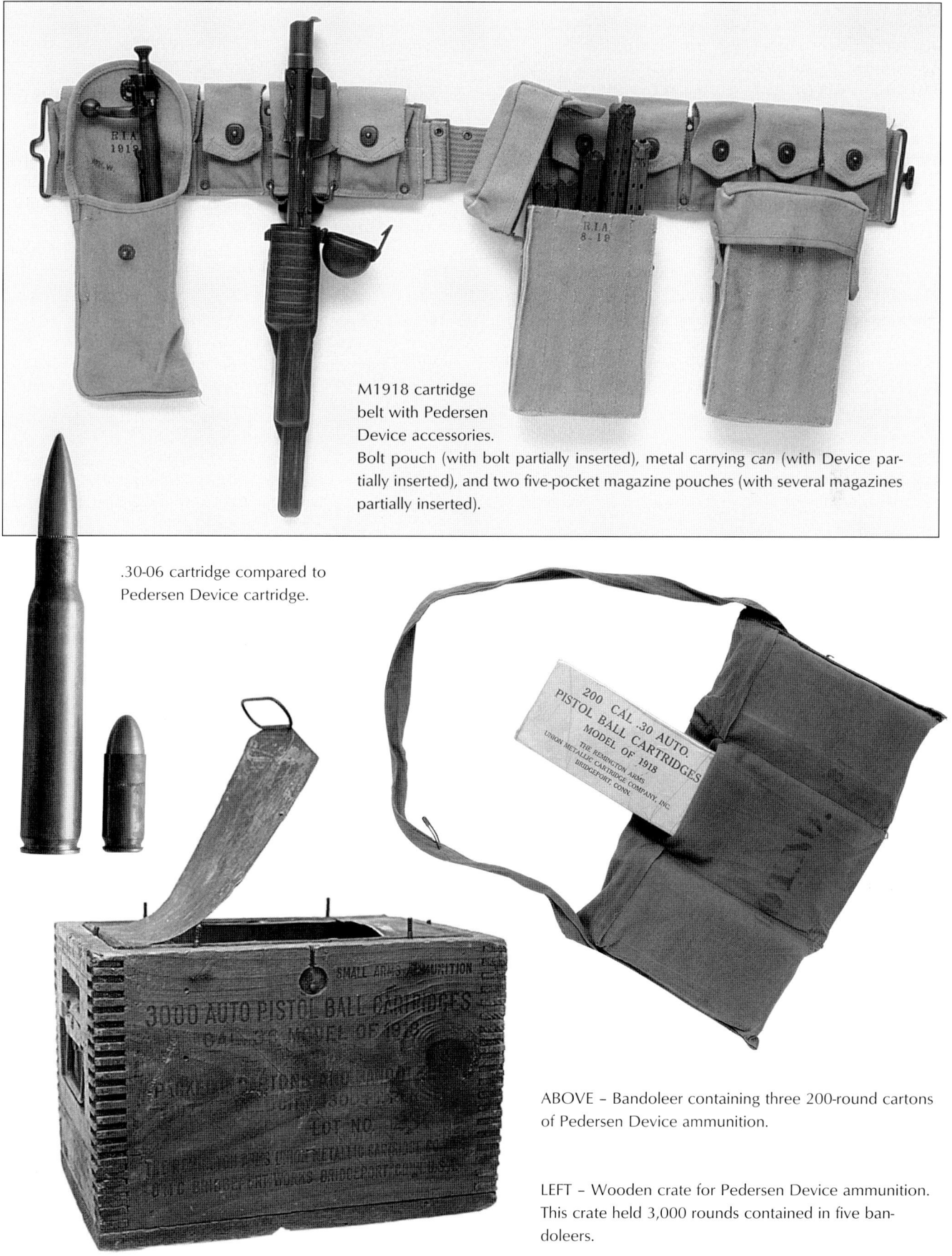

M1918 cartridge belt with Pedersen Device accessories.
Bolt pouch (with bolt partially inserted), metal carrying *can* (with Device partially inserted), and two five-pocket magazine pouches (with several magazines partially inserted).

.30-06 cartridge compared to Pedersen Device cartridge.

ABOVE – Bandoleer containing three 200-round cartons of Pedersen Device ammunition.

LEFT – Wooden crate for Pedersen Device ammunition. This crate held 3,000 rounds contained in five bandoleers.

The trigger and sear were modified by the addition of a series of levers to enable the rifle to fire the standard .30-06 cartridge, as well as the device. The trigger was modified with a relief cut on its rear surface which allowed it to impinge on a small lever, known as a fly, attached to the modified sear. The fly moved forward when the trigger was pulled, disengaging the separate sear of the device.

The Pedersen Device utilized a forty-round detachable box magazine that was inserted into the right side of the mechanism at about a 45-degree angle and was secured in place by two spring-loaded catches. The offset location of the magazine enabled the standard rifle sights to be used. Fired cartridge cases were ejected through an elongated oval-shaped port milled into the left side of the receiver.

The Pedersen Device cartridge was similar to the Colt .32 ACP pistol cartridge, but the 80-grain bullet was .30 caliber to be compatible with the '03's barrel. The Pedersen Device cartridge was loaded with $3\frac{1}{2}$ grains of smokeless power, which resulted in a muzzle velocity of approximately 1,300 feet per second and a muzzle energy of about 300 foot pounds. While the muzzle velocity does not sound very impressive as compared to the standard .30-06 service cartridge, it was about 50% greater than comparable rounds fired through a handgun.

The device was carried on the cartridge belt in a stamped sheet metal scabbard with a hinged lid and wire cartridge belt hooks. When removed from the rifle, the '03 bolt was stowed in a canvas pouch suspended from the cartridge belt by a belt hook. Five 40-round Pedersen Device magazines were carried in a canvas pouch with cartridge belt hooks. Two of the magazine pouches were to be carried on the cartridge belt. Each loaded magazine weighed approximately one pound, and the Pedersen Device, complete with metal scabbard, weighed about two pounds, two ounces.

The military observers who witnessed Pedersen's demonstration that October morning in Washington quickly grasped the potential significance of his invention for both offensive and defensive trench warfare. One of the Ordnance Department observers summed up the defensive usefulness of the Pedersen Device as follows:

"As the enemy came charging across No Man's Land each of our soldiers would start firing with this miniature machine gun and the entire zone in front of the trenches would be covered with such a whirlwind of fire that no attack could survive…"

The same observer held equally optimistic views about the usefulness of the Pedersen Device for offensive operations:

"…a line of soldiers advancing across No Man's Land firing this device at the enemy trenches as they ran would make it extremely difficult for anyone in the trenches to show his head or any part of his body. Of course, fire while running or walking would not be so accurate, but the tremendous number of shots would more than make up for any inaccuracies and the whole enemy trench system would presumably be smothered in a storm of bullets."

This assessment is possibly the first example of the *spray and pray* doctrine of firepower! In any event, the War Department was suitably impressed with the Pedersen Device, and in November 1917 ordered Captain J.C. Beatty to deliver a Pedersen Device to General Pershing in France. Capt. Beatty was sworn to secrecy and the entire project was cloaked in a Top Secret designation.

On December 9, 1917, General Pershing convened a board in France to test and evaluate the Pedersen Device. The board, consisting of Captain Beatty and four high-ranking ordnance officers, tested the device for rapidity of fire, accuracy, penetration and endurance. The Board concurred with the prior assessment in Washington that the Pedersen Device could be of great value for trench warfare. Pershing was sufficiently impressed with the weapon as well and sent the following confidential memo on December 11, 1917:

"For the Chief of Staff and Chief of Ordnance -
…Board recommends adoption of Pedersen attachment for rifle and the initial purchase of 100,000 of same. Great secrecy urged in connection with this device. Initial supply of ammunition 5,000 rounds per gun with daily supply of 100 rounds per gun. Strongly approve of device and believe it will materially increase efficiency of our infantry. Pershing."

General Pershing followed up with another memo that stated:

"Desire 25,000 Pedersen attachments be held in reserve. Replacements 50% per year on devices and 200% on magazines. Request 40 magazines be shipped with each device. When will shipments be made? Pershing."

Pershing's clear desire to procure a large number of Pedersen Devices, and his seeming impatience about shipments, make it apparent that he considered the weapon as a potentially valuable tool. He was likely envisioning the Pedersen Device's role in the planned *Grand Offensive*, scheduled for the spring of 1919.

The Top Secret status of the Pedersen Device project was maintained and the weapon was given the purposely misleading name of Automatic Pistol, Caliber .30, Model of 1918, Mark I when it was adopted. When word of a new weapon leaked out, the War Department was roundly criticized in some contemporary magazine and newspaper articles for the adoption of a puny .30 caliber pistol when the superb .45 caliber M1911 pistol was already in production!

On March 26, 1918, Remington Arms Company was given an order for 100,000 Pedersen Devices. John Pedersen was to receive a lump sum payment of $50,000 for the rights to his invention and a royalty of fifty cents for each device manufactured. Remington received a net profit of $2.00 per device and 3 cents per magazine. The government paid for all necessary machinery and equipment needed by Remington for production of the device.

The original order for 100,000 was soon increased to 133,450. On May 24, 1918, Remington received a contract for the production of 800 million .30 caliber Pedersen Device cartridges. These had RA (Remington Arms) or RAH (Remington Arms – Hoboken, New Jersey, plant) head stamps and were marked with the last two digits of the year of production. Examples dated "18", "19" or "20" may be encountered. The cartridges were packed in 40-round boxes, thus each box would fill one magazine. Five boxes were packed in a 200-round carton and three cartons were carried in a light canvas bandolier. Five bandoliers were shipped in a metal-lined wooden crate.

The Pedersen Device magazines were reportedly manufactured by Mt. Vernon Silversmiths, with some parts being fabricated under subcontract by the Gorham Manufacturing Company. The Gorham Company also produced the stamped sheet metal scabbards. The web bolt and magazine pouches were produced by Rock Island Arsenal, and were normally stamped inside the cover flap with the date of production (1919 is the most commonly encountered date).

M1903 Mark I Rifle

While Remington Arms was laboring to get production of the Pedersen Device underway, Springfield Armory began manufacture of a 1903 rifle modified for use with the device. The variant was standardized as the U.S. Rifle, Caliber .30, Model of 1903, Mark I. Externally, the Mark I's most obvious difference from standard '03s was the ejection port, which was milled into the left receiver rail, through which the fired Pedersen Device cartridge cases were ejected. A portion of the stock was slightly relieved under the port to provide the necessary clearance. The Mark I designation was added to the standard markings on the receiver ring. The special Mark I components unique to this rifle included a modified magazine cutoff, cutoff spindle, cutoff spindle screw, sear, trigger, receiver and stock. Assembly of the Mark I rifle began in December 1918 and continued until March 1920 when production was cancelled. A total of 97,520 Mark I rifles were produced and serial numbers ranged from 933045 to 1186358.

The M1903 Mark I rifle began production at about the same time that Springfield Armory instituted parkerizing. Mark I rifles utilized many components finished in the black-tinted parkerizing of the era, including receivers. Some original Mark I rifles may be found with blued barrels and other blued components, so a mixture of parkerized and blued parts are not uncommon on original examples.

The planned widespread use of the Pedersen Device resulted in a version for the M1917 U.S. Enfield rifle being adopted as the Mark II. In September 1918, Remington Arms Company was granted a contract for the production of 500,000 Mark II Pedersen Devices for the U.S. M1917 rifle. A device for the Russian Mosin-Nagant rifle was also planned but only a small prototype number were made for this weapon. It has also been rumored that a version of the device was contemplated for the French Berthier rifle, but none are believed to have actually been fabricated.

The Armistice of November 11, 1918, resulted in cancellation of the Mark II Pedersen Device and only a handful of prototypes, likely no more than a half dozen, had been fabricated. Production of the Mark I device for the M1903 rifle continued after the Armistice but at a reduced rate. Approximately 65,000 Mark I Pedersen Devices had been manufactured by Remington by the time production was cancelled on March 1, 1919. Springfield continued production of the M1903 Mark I rifle a bit longer, and examples dated as late as 1920 may be encountered. Production also continued on Pedersen Device ammunition and magazine pouches until at least 1920.

Even though the Mark I rifle was intended to function as a service rifle, with the standard bolt installed, the special magazine cutoff apparently caused some problems. A memo dated January 10, 1919, from the Commanding Officer of Springfield Armory to the Ordnance Engineering Division opined that the Mark I rifle, "...is not a serviceable rifle and should not be issued to the troops." During testing at Springfield, it was discovered that the design of the cutoff was faulty, and the component was easily broken after as few as ten manipulations of the bolt. The Mark I cutoff was redesigned to eliminate the flaw, but the M1903 Mark I rifles were withheld from issue pending a decision on the disposition of the Pedersen Devices.

After the conclusion of WWI, the U.S. Army conducted testing in France and at several stateside army bases to determine what role, if any, the Pedersen Devices would play in the postwar military arsenal. In a November 1919 memo, the Secretary of War ordered the Chief of Ordnance to send 50 Mark I rifles and Pedersen Devices to the Infantry and Cavalry School for training purposes. In 1920, 3,998 Mark I rifles, with Pedersen Devices, were sent to the Panama Canal Zone where they remained until early 1928, when they were returned to Springfield Armory. In 1927, 20 rifles and devices were shipped to Fort Benjamin Harrison and 20 to Fort Thomas for testing.

These tests revealed that the trigger pull was unacceptably heavy. Springfield Armory attempted to rectify the problem, but eventually determined that the pull could not be safely reduced to less than 11 pounds. As of September 1930, there were 4,387 Pedersen Devices in storage at Springfield Armory (which likely included the 3,998 returned from Panama), and these were directed to be maintained there until storage space became critical. The production tooling for the Pedersen Device had previously been shipped from Remington to Springfield Armory in 1921. **Table 7** on page 221 is a list of Pedersen Device serial numbers reported in ordnance records.

A critical, but objective, evaluation of the device revealed that the advantages were outweighed by the disadvantages. While capable of a much more rapid rate of fire than a bolt-action rifle, the Pedersen Device's cartridge was woefully underpowered and was of little use beyond a couple of hundred yards. Also, the added weight of the device, ammunition and related accessories added a significant burden to the soldier's load. In the heat of battle, the changing back and forth between the rifle's bolt and the device could easily result in the loss of one or both items. The U.S. Army explored several potential uses for the Pedersen Devices, including consideration as riot control weapons as related in an Ordnance Department memo which stated:

"It is probable that in case of any extended riot duty, the Device may be issued to troops."

Issuance of the Pedersen Device for riot control purposes apparently never materialized. In 1928, approval was granted for the 26th Infantry at Plattsburg Barracks to use Pedersen Devices for gallery practice (marksmanship training), and some devices remained in use there for the next three years. As something of a last-ditch measure, in 1930 the Pedersen Device was tested for possible use as a subcaliber device for the 75mm pack Howitzer. The Artillery Board turned down the idea, as it became apparent that there was no real need to retain the Pedersen Devices any longer given the general lack of interest.

To this end, an order was given in April 1931 to destroy all of the devices, magazines, metal carrying scabbards and ammunition. The most common method of destruction was to throw the crated devices, magazines and metal carrying scabbards into bonfires. Since the devices were heavily coated in cosmoline, they burned readily. Much of the ammunition was destroyed as well. The canvas bolt pouches and magazine pouches were sold as surplus. Only a few devices and magazines were *unofficially appropriated* (stolen) or otherwise salvaged from the destruction fires, and surviving examples are rare today. The metal carrying scabbards are even rarer than the devices and magazines. However, the canvas magazine pouches are still commonly encountered.

After the decision was made to destroy the Pedersen Devices, the M1903 Mark I rifles were sent to ordnance facilities for removal of the special Mark I components, which were replaced by standard parts. The modified Mark I rifles were then issued as standard service rifles. Even after the secret status was lifted, the existence of the Pedersen Device was not widely known, and some soldiers issued refurbished M1903 Mark I rifles likely wondered why their rifles had a hole in the left side of the receiver! Most Mark I rifles were subsequently overhauled and examples are still rather common today. In most cases, the only surviving Mark I component is the receiver, and even that part has likely been refinished one or more times. A rebuilt Mark I rifle typically has only a slight premium over a standard '03 of like condition and vintage. Unmodified original Mark I rifles are scarce and are prized Springfield collectibles. The Mark I rifle receiver was of the double heat-treated variety, and even with the unsightly hole in the left receiver rail, the rifles are fine for shooting purposes.

Some of the surviving Pedersen Devices show evidence of burning, which means they were likely salvaged from the fringes of the destruction bonfires. Original Pedersen Devices are very valuable collectibles, and the few that sell from time to time typically change hands for quite impressive sums. While a few fake Pedersen Devices have been reported, this is not yet a real problem. Regardless, one should examine very carefully any device offered for sale before paying a lot of money for what may be a questionable item. The number of surviving Pedersen Devices is not known, and estimates range from a few dozen to perhaps a hundred. Condition can range from pristine examples to burnt-out relics. Mark II Pedersen Devices for the M1917 rifle are very rare, with less than six complete examples known. While the Pedersen Device was never fired in anger, it was nevertheless a very innovative, ingenious concept, and is a most interesting footnote to U.S. ordnance history.

Cameron-Yaggi Trench Periscope M1903 Rifle

The Pedersen Device was not the only modification of the '03 that was intended to make the rifle more useful for trench warfare. When the United States entered WWI, there was much concern over the horrendous casualties suffered by both sides during the first three years of the war. A number of suggestions for ways to reduce the exposure of our troops in the trenches to enemy fire were evaluated. Myriad types of periscopes that allowed observation over the top of the trenches were issued, and protective devices such as metal sniper shields, various types of special helmets, and body armor were tested in limited numbers. While useful in varying degrees, none of these implements permitted a rifleman to fire above the top of the trench while remaining concealed below.

Even before America's declaration of war, two inventors from Cleveland, Ohio, James L. Cameron and Lawrence E. Yaggi, developed a concept that allowed a rifle to be fastened into a metal framework that rested on the shooter's shoulder and held above the head in order to fire over the top of a trench parapet. The bolt and trigger were manipulated by extension levers, and sighting was done by means of periscopic sight. The two inventors fabricated a working prototype and went to France to demonstrate it to our allies and to solicit suggestions for improvement. The British and French had experimented with similar designs, but no weapons of this type had been manufactured in quantity.

Cameron and Yaggi returned from Europe and developed a refined version of their *trench periscope rifle*.

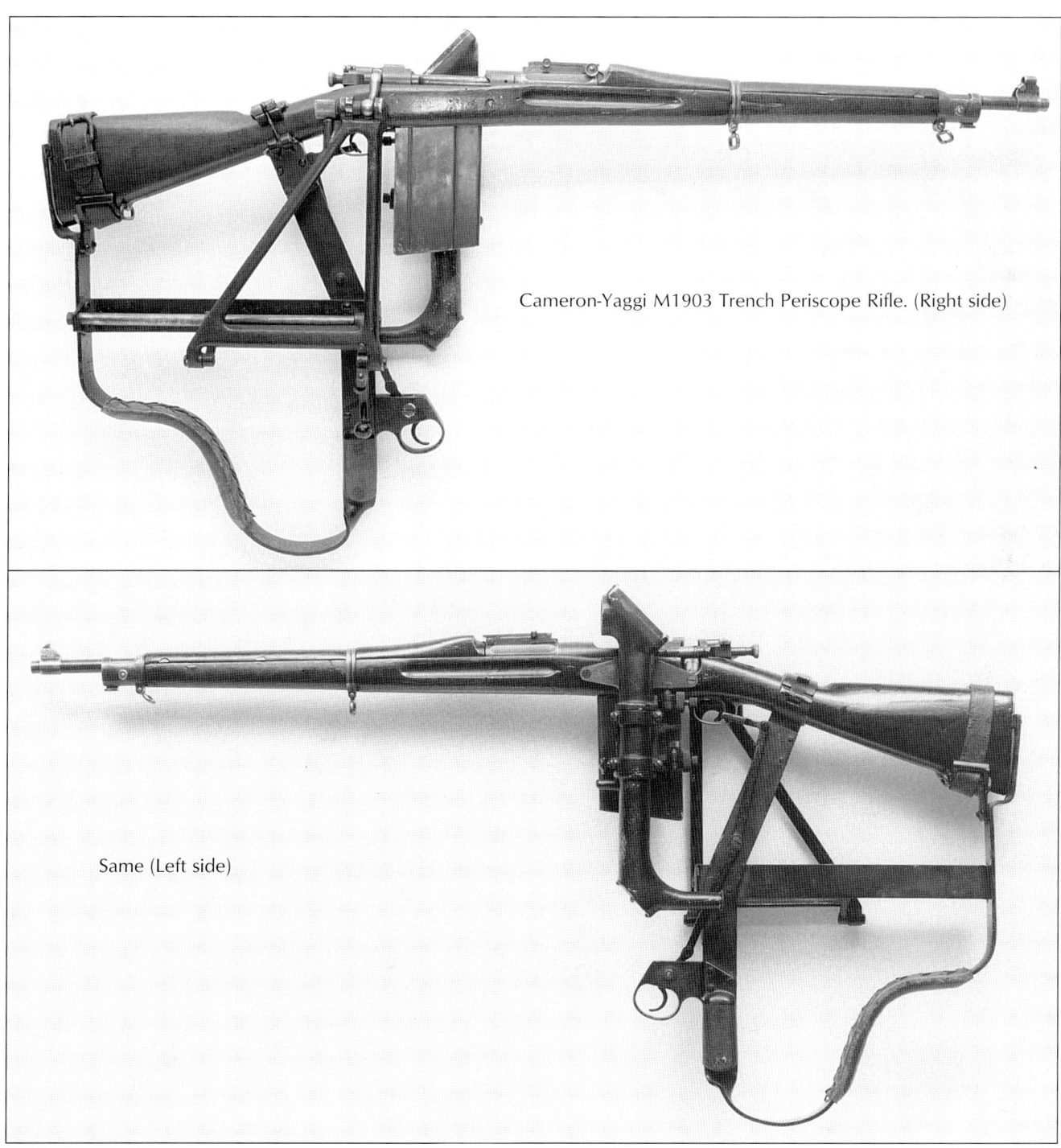

Cameron-Yaggi M1903 Trench Periscope Rifle. (Right side)

Same (Left side)

The inventors held preliminary discussions with representatives of the U.S. Army Ordnance Department. Cameron and Yaggi were informed that the Army would desire that such a weapon utilize the standard M1903 service rifle with no permanent or substantial alterations.

The refined prototype of the Cameron-Yaggi Trench Periscope Rifle utilized a standard M1903 rifle. The only modification was the removal of the stock reinforcement screw in order to affix a dovetail mount on the left side for attachment of the periscope sight, termed *sitascope* by the inventors. The rifle was held in the metal framework by a metal clamp that attached to the small of the stock. The butt rested in a metal cup at the rear. A thin leather pad was laced to the shoulder support of the framework. The trigger was attached to a wooden handgrip that was connected to the rifle's trigger by means of a hinged extension. The remote bolt handle was located in close proximity to the wooden handgrip and was attached to the rifle's bolt by another extension lever that slid back and forth on a metal rod to operate the '03's bolt. The bolt knob was secured in a concave metal socket that was adjustable for the proper tension. A 25-round extension magazine was fitted so that the rifle could be fired for an extended period of time without having to remove it from the shoulder for reloading.

The sitascope allowed the rifle to be sighted and fired with a surprising degree of accuracy. During preliminary testing, the weapon fired ten rounds at 200 yards with a maximum spread of only 1.3 inches. The periscope sight had no internal adjustments, and windage and elevation were changed with two external knobs. There were several different magnifications tested with the Cameron-Yaggi sitascopes, including a 1X sight (no magnification) to 4X. Some had double stadia reticles. The periscope lenses were recessed so as to reduce glint in the sunlight, which was in response to a suggestion previously offered by our allies.

The Cameron-Yaggi rifle appeared to be cumbersome and heavy, but the apparatus only added about six pounds to the weight of the rifle. The weapon could be slung over the shoulder and carried but was designed to remain in a static trench environment. With the barrel resting on the top of the parapet, the rifle could be fired for an extended period of time with no undue discomfort to the shooter.

View showing dovetail mounting base and left side of 25-round extension magazine.

LEFT — Close-up view of the extension lever which controlled the rifle's bolt mechanism. The knurled thumbscrew was tightened enough to securely hold the bolt handle yet enable it to rotate sufficiently to operate the action. The metal clamp which held the small of the stock is also visible in this view.

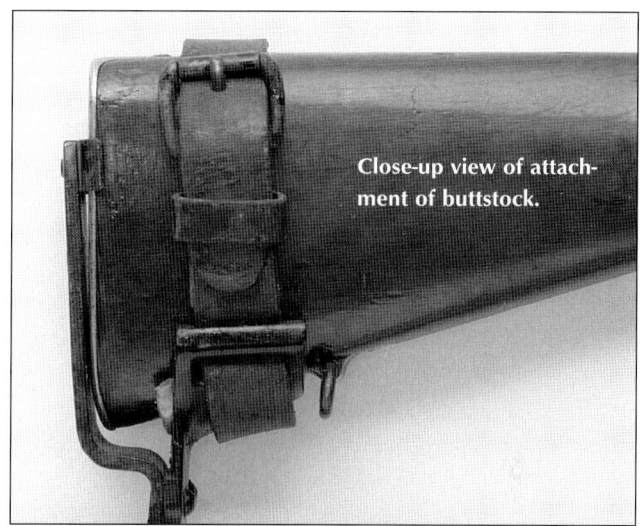

Close-up view of attachment of buttstock.

Left-side view showing periscope sight (*sitascope*) attached to rifle.

Cameron-Yaggi hand grip. Note the trigger assembly in front of the grip and the extension bolt handle just above it.

Bolt in closed position. Note lever arrangement and leather strap on stock.

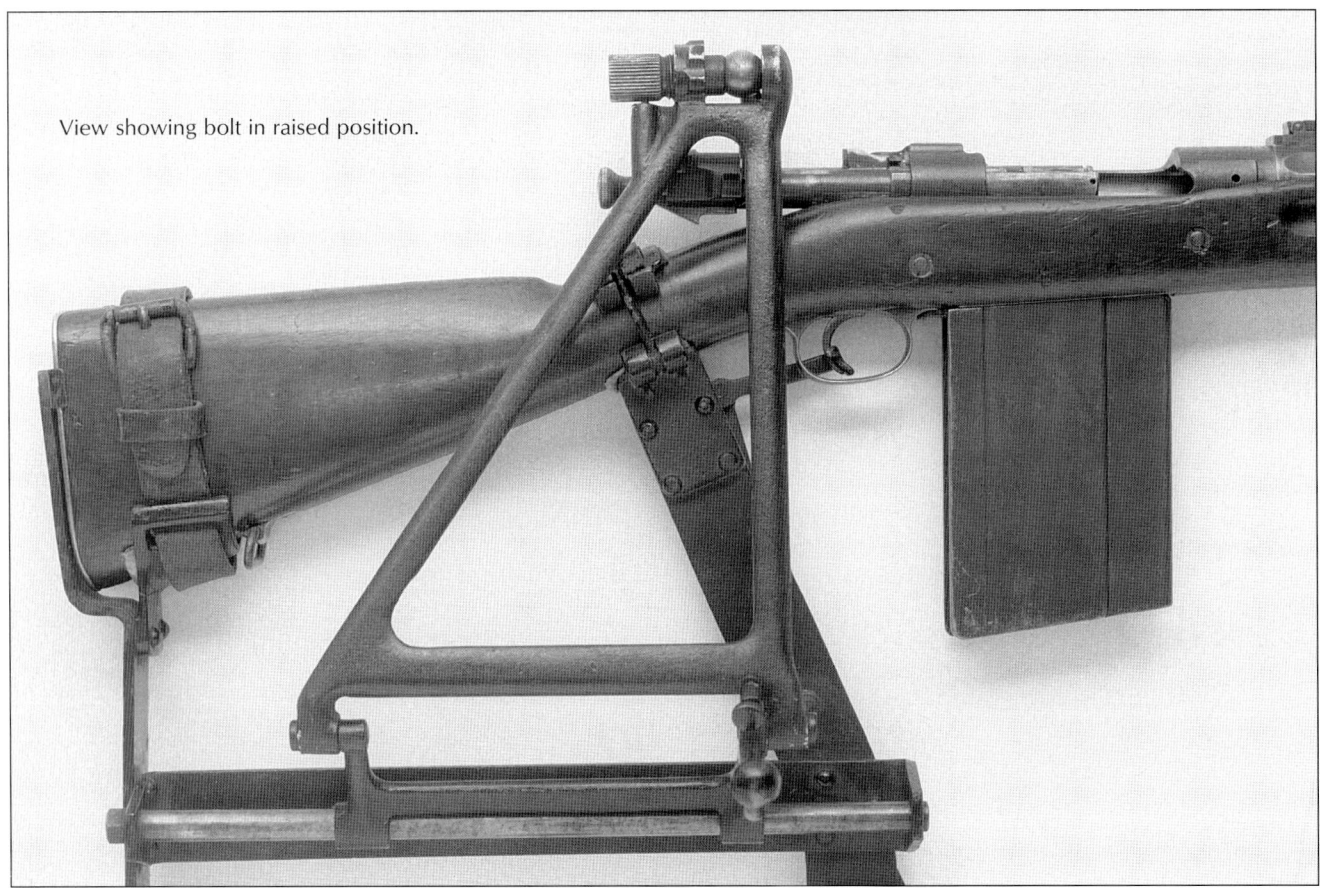
View showing bolt in raised position.

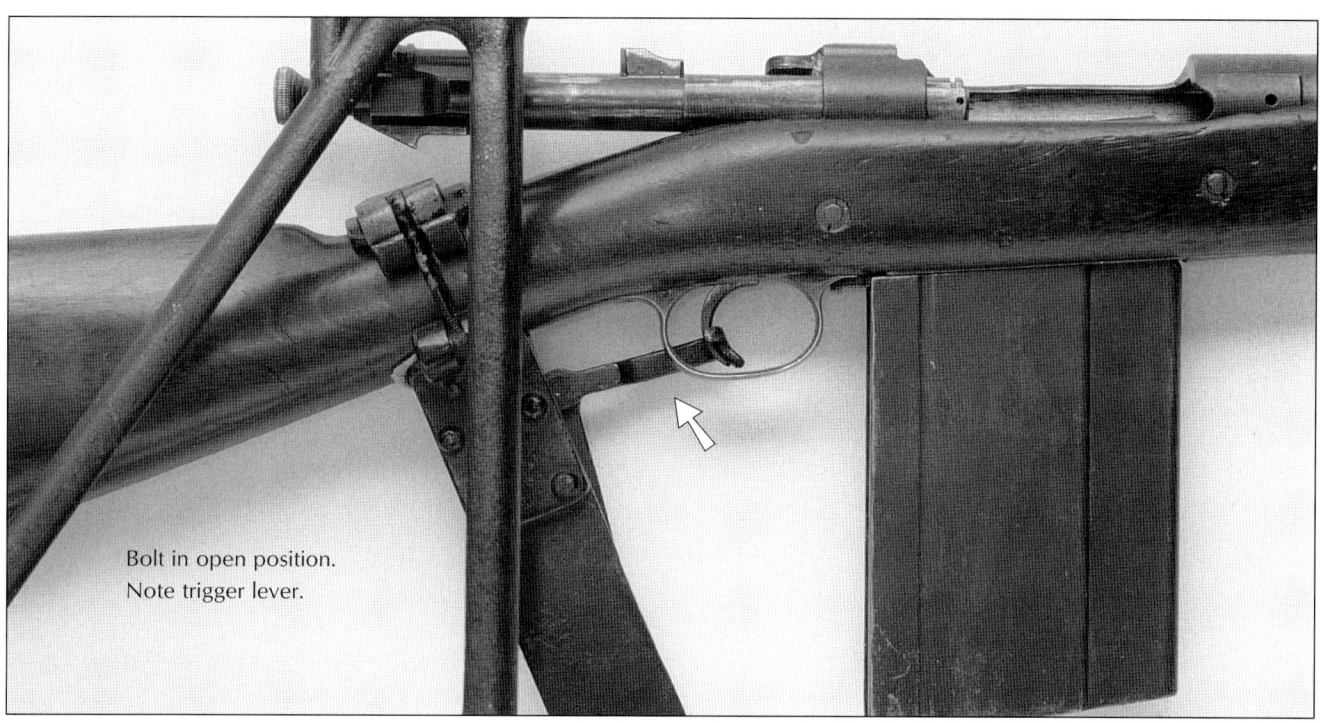

Bolt in open position. Note trigger lever.

From 1917 *Arms and the Man* article demonstrating how the Cameron-Yaggi rifle can be carried. This individual may be one of the inventors. *(American Rifleman)*

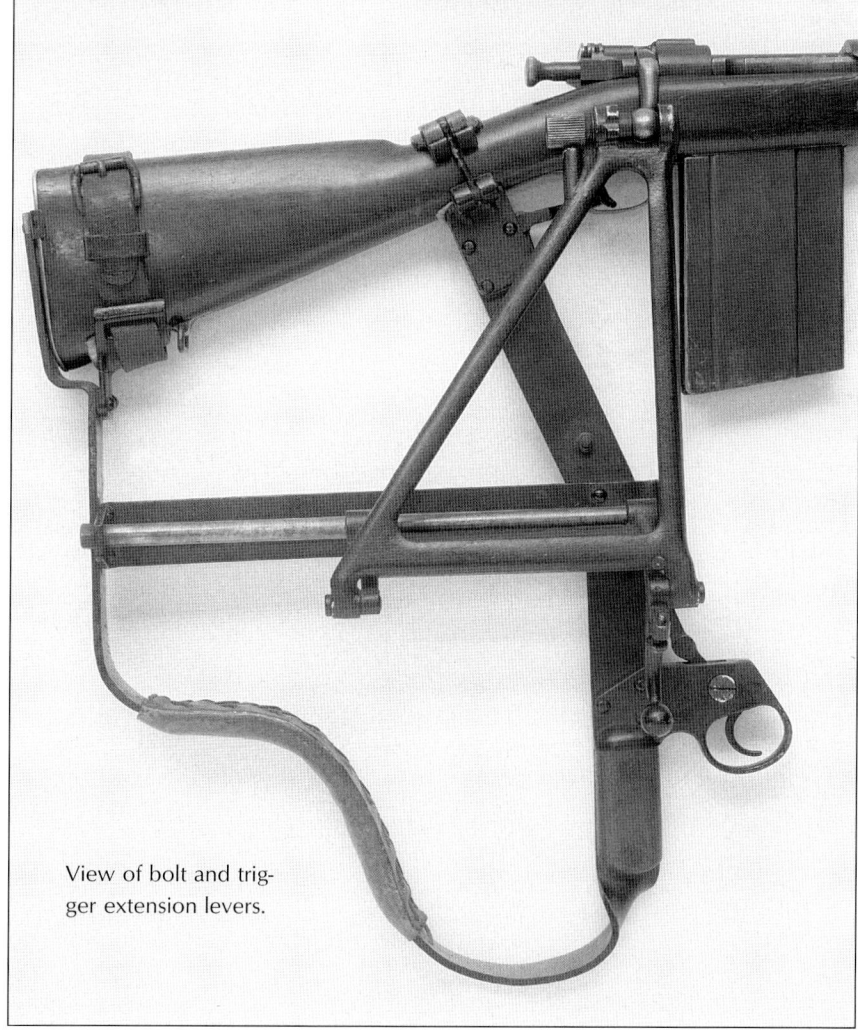

View of bolt and trigger extension levers.

One of the demonstrations of the Cameron-Yaggi rifle was in the summer of 1917 at a Winthrop, Maryland, rifle range. Among the spectators was a noted writer and marksmanship proponent of the day, Col. C.B. Winder, who requested permission to fire the weapon. Col. Winder's experiences were related in a subsequent article in *Arms and the Man* magazine, forerunner of *American Rifleman*:

"...About the first thing the peculiar framework suggested to the Colonel was KICK! But when Yaggi fired the rifle he seemed to experience no inconvenience. Afterwards, describing the effect of the heavy service charge on the weapon held in the light framework (Winder) said: "There was a lot less kick to it than the rifle ordinarily gives. The whole framework, rifle and all, just seemed to rock back a little."

The added weight and design of the apparatus substantially mitigated the recoil. Even though the eyepiece of the periscope sight was very close to the shooter's eye, the effect of recoil rocked the sight away from the eye. Cameron and Yaggi formally submitted their weapon to the Ordnance Department in late 1917. It is recorded that the Ordnance Engineering Department tested the weapon and requested that the design be revised to reduce the weight, simplify the periscope sight, and improve the balance and "...functional arrangement." There were several prototypes fabricated, presumably in response to the Engineering Department's requests. It is interesting to note that most of the prototypes differed in various aspects, including the configuration and placement of the shoulder supports and extension levers. The exact number of prototypes made is not known, but likely numbered no more than a dozen or so. There is some suggestion in ordnance documents that production of 100 was contemplated, but it is doubtful if anywhere near this number were actually fabricated. While referred to as a Cameron-Yaggi Trench Periscope Rifle, it should be noted that the weapon was, in reality, a standard M1903 Springfield rifle affixed to the special apparatus, and periscopic sight, developed by Cameron and Yaggi.

Table 8 on page 222 cites the serial numbers of eight Cameron-Yaggi rifles with serial numbers between 247954 and 266635. The rifles were apparently retained until December 1925 when they were shipped to Rock Island Arsenal, presumably for destruction or conversion to standard service rifles. There are several Cameron-Yaggi rifles on hand today in the Springfield Armory Museum and a handful of specimens (in varying degrees of completeness) in private collections. Surviving examples are extremely rare. Some original examples have serial numbers substantially higher than the few rifles cited in **Table 8**.

The Cameron-Yaggi rifle was never formally adopted by the U.S. military, and testing was still in progress at the time of the Armistice. Apparently, the government thought the apparatus had some promise, but the fact that it was not immediately adopted and put into production would suggest that there were questions about the suitability of the weapon as well. Cameron and Yaggi had plans to produce a similar contrivance for the M1917 rifle and Lewis machine gun, but there is no indication that either type was fabricated. Similar ideas were explored by other inventors during this period including the Guilderson rifle, which featured a specially made collapsible stock that could be unfolded to fire over an embankment or folded and utilized as a service rifle. Apparently, the Guilderson rifle did not elicit the same degree of interest by the government as the Cameron-Yaggi, possibly because it required substantial modification of the standard rifle and was likely less effective. Another roughly similar weapon tested by the

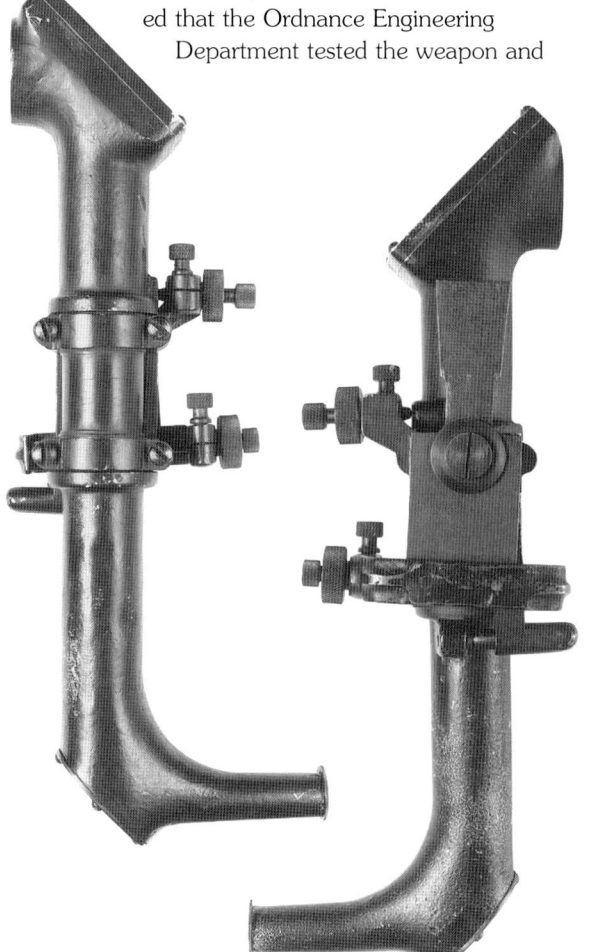

FAR LEFT — Left side of Cameron-Yaggi periscope sight, called a *sitascope* by the inventors. The two knobs visible in the middle of the periscope tube are windage and elevation adjustments. The periscope has a cross-hair reticle.
LEFT — Right side of the periscope sight. This view clearly shows the dovetail mount which attached to the dovetail base fastened to the rifle's stock.

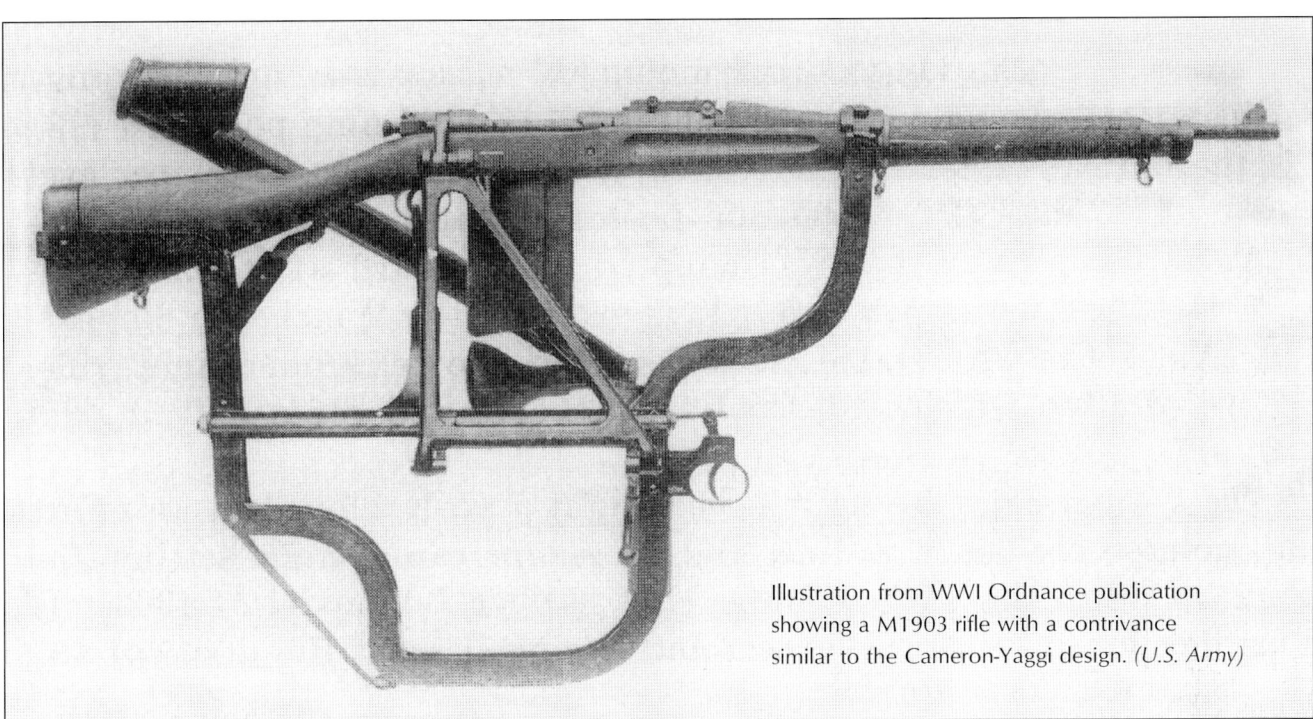

Illustration from WWI Ordnance publication showing a M1903 rifle with a contrivance similar to the Cameron-Yaggi design. *(U.S. Army)*

Photo from 1917 *Arms and the Man* article showing Cameron-Yaggi rifle being fired over a trench parapet. *(American Rifleman)*

Ordnance Department was designed by Major E.H. Eider. Based on photos, the Eider apparatus would likely have been more cumbersome, and even less effective, than the Cameron-Yaggi rifle.

The end of the First World War resulted in little perceived need for special trench warfare weapons, and the Cameron-Yaggi Trench Periscope Rifle soon dropped out of sight. The weapon is now an all-but-forgotten variant of the M1903 rifle. Like the Pedersen Device, this was an idea that may have looked good on the drawing board but which had less utility than envisioned. Nevertheless, the Cameron-Yaggi trench periscope rifle further illustrates the versatility of the M1903, and the numerous modes in which it could have been employed.

M1903 Air Service Rifle

Another modification to the M1903 rifle during World War I was the Air Service Rifle. This was a standard '03 service rifle with a shortened stock and handguard, simplified rear sight, and fitted with the same type of 25-round extension magazine as used with the Cameron-Yaggi trench periscope rifle. The weapon was not equipped with sling swivels.

The rifle was not intended for infantry use. It was described in a 1918 Ordnance Department Report as *Stripped for Air Service*. While the existence of these rifles has been well established, the intended use for which the weapon was designed remains the subject of some conjecture even today. There are several theories regarding the intended purpose of these arms. One theory postulates that the Air Service rifles were to be utilized as a form of rudimentary armament for observers in observation balloons

1918 vintage 1903 Service rifle

Air Service M1903.

Left-side profile of M1903 Air Service rifle.

BELOW – Top view of special air service rifle handguard.

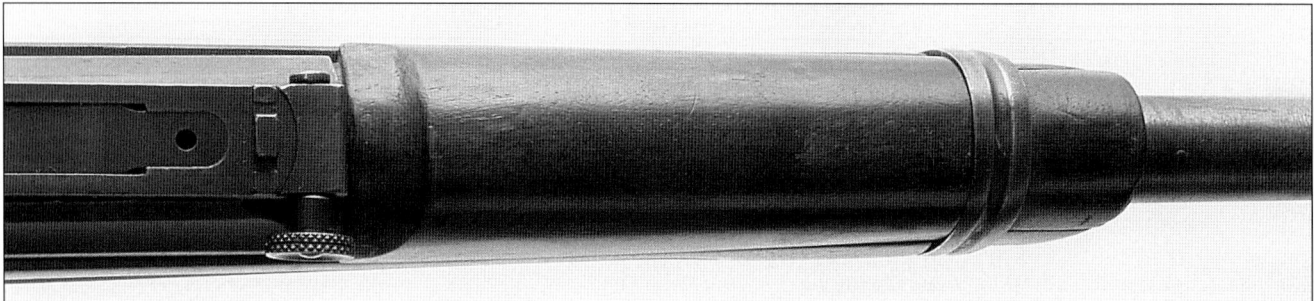

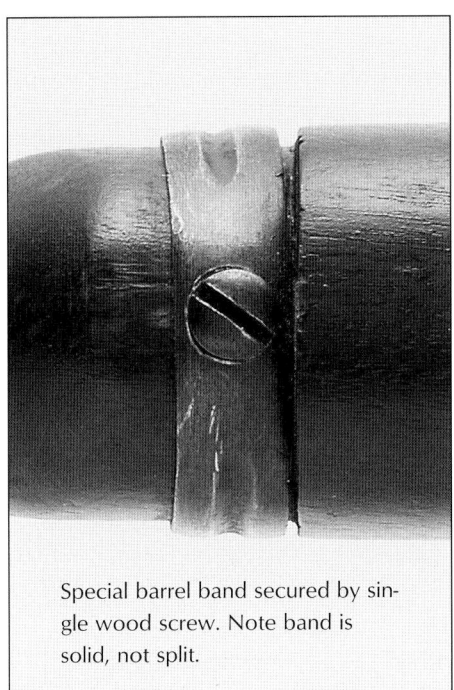

Special barrel band secured by single wood screw. Note band is solid, not split.

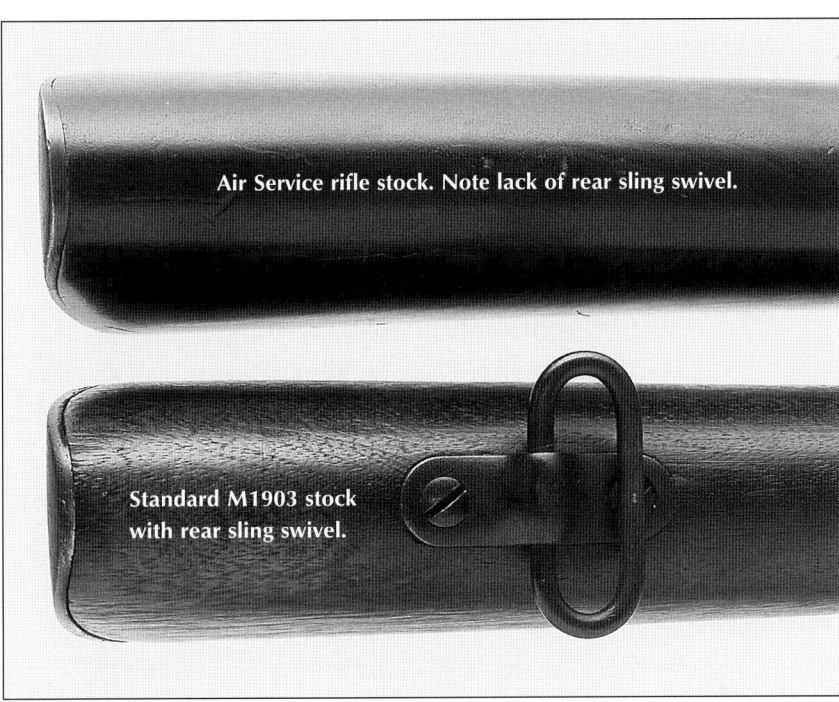

Air Service rifle stock. Note lack of rear sling swivel.

Standard M1903 stock with rear sling swivel.

which were widely used in the First World War. It has also been suggested that the rifles were to be used as defensive armament for a two-man fighter and/or observation airplanes. Yet another theory is that the rifles were intended to be carried in airplanes, to be used for personal defense in the event an aviator was forced down behind enemy lines.

Frankly, the latter application clearly makes the most sense. The usefulness of a bolt-action rifle against an enemy fighter airplane while in the swaying confines of an observation balloon basket, is certainly open to question. Also, the use of machine guns on fighter and observation aircraft was well established several years before development of the Air Service Rifle. A bolt-action rifle would have been of only marginal use, at best, against an enemy aircraft armed with machine guns. On the other hand, a full-power service-type rifle with which a downed aviator could defend himself seems logical. The fact that a pilot would not likely be wearing a cartridge belt would argue in favor of the 25-round extension magazine in order to have a supply of ammunition already in the rifle and ready for immediate use. The weight savings of the shortened stock and elimination of unnecessary sling swivels also point to aircraft use where any sort of weight reduction, slight as it may have been, would have been viewed as an asset. This theory is further bolstered by several Ordnance Department documents, including the original Springfield Armory blueprints, which identify the weapon as *U.S. Rifle, Model of 1903, Altered for Aircraft Use*. Balloons were seldom referred to as aircraft. In this same vein, an early 1918 Springfield Armory report on the 25-round extension magazine stated that the item was expected to be adopted "...for aeroplane...use."

A March 20, 1918, Ordnance Department memo requested permission from the Chief of Ordnance to ship a prototype Air Service rifle to Washington, D.C., and subsequently to France, for testing under combat conditions. A memo the following day requested that Springfield Armory prepare an evaluation of the time required for production of 2,000 rifles of this type. A memo dated April 29, 1918, confirmed that the prototype Air Service rifle was delivered to Col. H.H. Arnold (Hap Arnold who later gained fame as a general in WWII), along with a request by General Pershing that 825 of the rifles be supplied to the AEF by June 1, 1918. The Control Board of the Signal Corps met the same month to evaluate the Air Service Rifle and suggest modifications. At this time, the Signal Corps was the branch of the U.S. Army responsible for aircraft procurement and related equipment. The modifications suggested by the Control Board were primarily related to minor changes in the rear sight and were agreed to by Springfield Armory prior to production of the 825 rifles ordered by General Pershing.

The Air Service Rifles used the same receivers, barrels and front sights as standard service rifles. The barrel bands, stocks and handguards were specially made for this weapon and were not modified standard components. The barrel band was secured to the stock by a single screw. The standard M1905 rear sight was modified by cutting down the sight leaf, altering the sighting notch and fixing the drift slide at the 100-yard increment by means of a machine screw through the peephole. The 25-round magazines used with the prototype rifles were reportedly made by the National Blank Book Company.

Original specimens that have been noted range from serial number 856709 to 862069, and barrel dates generally early to mid-1918. According to Ordnance Department documents, 908 Air Service rifles were completed and sent from Springfield Armory for shipment to France on June 25, 1918. The date of the rifles' arrival in France, or their initial disposition, is not known. On November 5, 1918, there were 680 Air Service rifles in storage at Issur-Tille, France, according to a report by H.J. Malony, now promoted to Lt. Col. and named Head of the Aircraft Armament Service Headquarters. The reason for the difference between the 908 rifles shipped, and the 680 in storage, was not revealed. Lt. Col. Malony's report stated that the rifles, "...were definitely not needed as armament for observers in aircraft..." It was suggested that the Air Service rifles could perhaps be used as personal armament for couriers and similar personnel, but it is not known whether the rifles saw any such use. There is also some indication that a total of 25 Air Service rifles were employed for testing purposes by the infantry to ascertain the suitability of the 25-round extension magazine with which they were equipped. The Fiscal Year 1920 report by Springfield Armory indicates that 910 rifles "...stripped for Air Service" had been manufactured which likely represented the total production.

After the war, the Air Service rifles that had been sent to France were apparently returned, and placed in storage until their final fate could be determined. By the mid-1920s, it was decided to either destroy the inventory of Air Service rifles, or convert some to standard service rifle configuration. According to a June 19, 1925, Ordnance Department memorandum, 139 Air Service rifles were converted to service rifle configuration at the Raritan (N.J.) Arsenal. The memo stated:

"...information is furnished that the modification of the caliber .30 Rifles, altered for aircraft use...required re-stocking, substituting lower band complete, assembling upper band complete, and substituting movable stud and front sight leaf, U.S. Rifle cal. .30, M'03 for the movable stud and front sight leaf, for aircraft use. One hundred and thirty-nine (139) of these Rifles have been modified as stated above and are now available for issue as U.S. Rifles, caliber .30, M-1903, at a cost of $168.38."

The other Air Service rifles were likely either destroyed or converted at other ordnance facilities. The stock, handguard and lower band of the Air Service Rifle were used to assemble the first experimental rifles tested with a proposed Winchester sniper telescope. This scope was eventually adopted as the Model of 1918 and was eventually slated for use with a modified M1917 rifle. It has been sug-

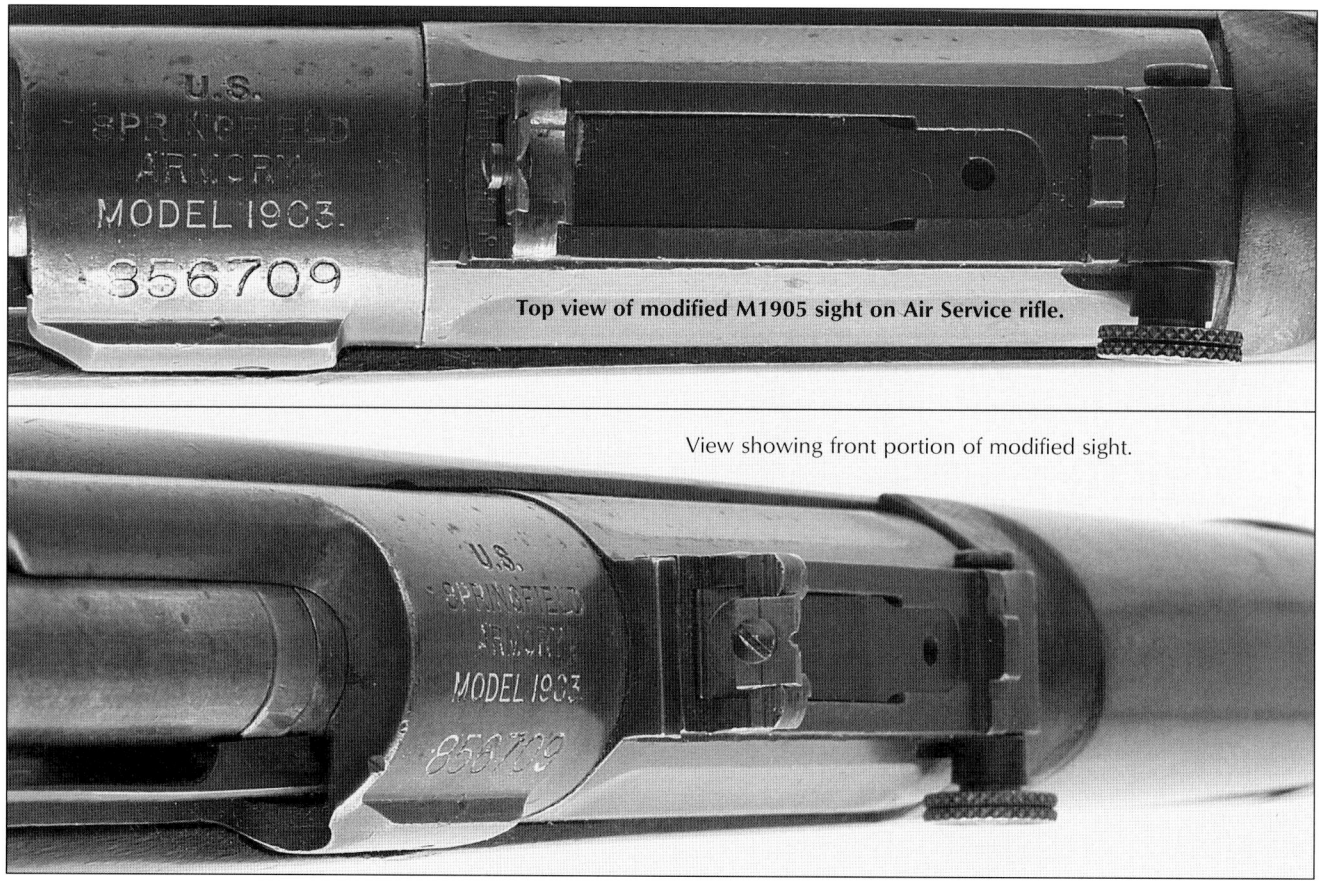

Top view of modified M1905 sight on Air Service rifle.

View showing front portion of modified sight.

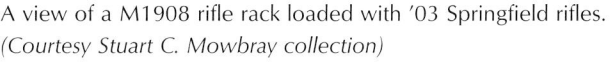

Doughboy cleaning his M1903 rifle in the correct method (from breech). *(National Archives)*

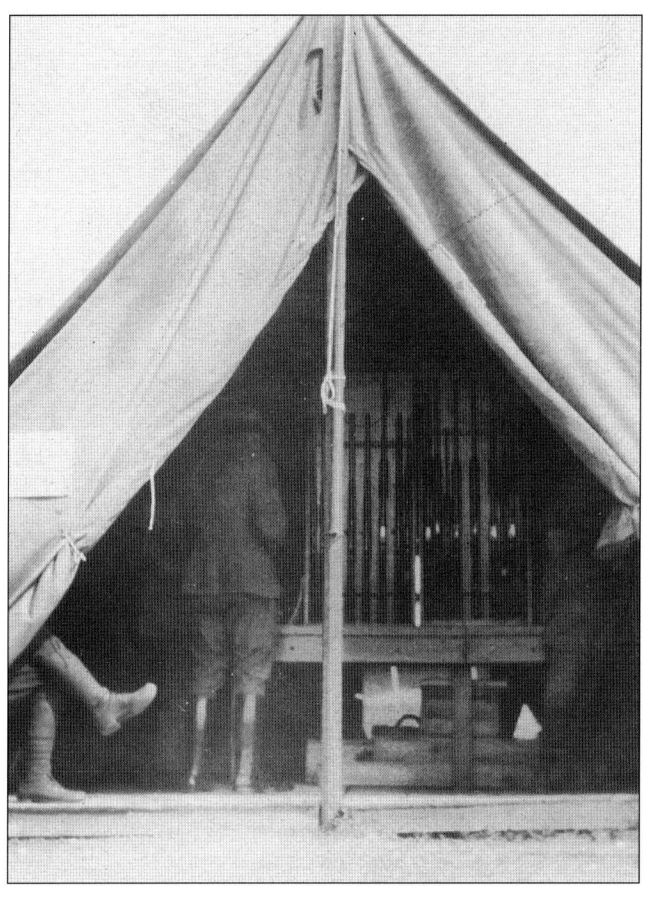

Racks of '03 Springfield rifles as they were stored in tents. *(Courtesy Stuart C. Mowbray collection)*

A view of a M1908 rifle rack loaded with '03 Springfield rifles. *(Courtesy Stuart C. Mowbray collection)*

gested that some of the Air Service rifles were utilized in Navy dirigibles in the 1920s and 1930s, but documentation to verify this has not been discovered.

Surviving examples of original Air Service rifles are extremely rare. Very few are in museums, and even fewer in private hands. Even though the weapon gives the appearance of a cut-down or sporterized '03, so far, fake Air Service rifles have not been a problem. The stock and handguard were special for this weapon. If someone attempted to simply shorten a service stock and handguard to create a bogus Air Service rifle, the lightening cuts in the stock, the band spring recess, and the rear sling swivel recess would be immediate tip-offs that something was amiss. Of course, the possibility of newly made wooden components in the proper configuration should not be dismissed, and any example of an Air Service rifle offered for sale as the real thing should be examined very closely for either signs of alteration, or wood that appears too new for a 90 year old weapon. There have not been enough original Air Service rifles sold to establish a general price range, but examples are much rarer than either original rod bayonet rifles or Pedersen Devices. While never used in combat, the M1903 Air Service rifle, like the Pedersen Device and the Cameron-Yaggi Periscope rifle, are examples of how the basic '03 rifle was modified to meet a specific application that was never envisioned when the rifle was originally adopted in 1903.

WWI Combat Use of the '03 Rifle

Though overshadowed in terms of sheer numbers by the M1917 rifle, the '03 was favored by the majority of Doughboys, and the rifle performed superbly in combat during the First World War. There are numerous contemporary references, extolling the excellence of the '03 during WWI, that vividly illustrate the esteem in which the weapon was held by many of our troops. As an example, a passage in the book *The Marine from Manatee* stated:

"... in the matter of defeating machine gun nest, two U.S. Army General Staff officers who had been in the thick of fighting reported the value of accurate rifle fire. They said that in some cases American riflemen had been able to get on one or more flanks or to the rear of machine gun nests at some distance and had been able to fire their Springfields with such accuracy that the machine gunners were often shot through the head or vital part of the body..."

First Lt. Samuel W. Meek of the 6th Marines, 2nd Division, saw extensive combat in the First World War and he went on to sum up his feelings about the '03 rifle as follows:

"Let me say something right now about the Springfield. It was a great weapon. Not only was it accurate, but it rarely jammed...it seemed to absorb the dirt and still work...and dirt was something we were always living in."

Even though many Doughboys were issued M1917 rifles, rather than '03s, the Springfield was the preferred weapon in the eyes of a majority of the AEF. This feeling was aptly stated by Corporal Mike Shelton, "L" Company, 308th Infantry, 77th Division:

"...what we really wanted were Springfields. They were the best rifles in the war."

The First World War ended with the '03 rifle's legacy as a superb military rifle firmly ensconced. Germany's Mauser and Great Britain's Lee-Enfield rifles proved to be serviceable military weapons but neither garnered the '03's reputation for reliability, accuracy, overall craftsmanship and general excellence.

WWI U.S. troops firing M1903 rifles from a foxhole position. Note the fixed M1905 bayonets. *(U.S. Army)*

ABOVE – That's one popular nurse! The Marines and Doughboys surrounding her are all carrying '03 Springfields. *(Courtesy Stuart C. Mowbray collection)*

BELOW – American soldiers upon their arrival in France, ready to turn the tide of WWI with their '03 Springfield rifles. *(Courtesy Stuart C. Mowbray collection)*

Doughboy of the 33rd Division on guard duty in France during WWI. Note the M1903 Rifle and M1905 bayonet. *(U.S. Army)*

WWI soldier on guard duty with M1903 rifle and M1905 bayonet affixed. *(U.S. Army)*

BELOW, LEFT – Doughboy lighting lantern in trench, WWI. Note the M1903 rifle with M1907 leather sling close by. *(National Archives)*
BELOW, RIGHT – WWI soldier in dugout opening with M1903 rifle close at hand. *(National Archives)*

WWI U.S. Army snipers with camouflage and *pattern painted* M1903 rifles. Not all snipers were armed with telescopic rifles. *(U.S. Army Military History Institute)*

M1903 rifles with M1905 bayonets firing from trench position in WWI. *(National Archives)*

WWI U.S. *Doughboys*. Note M1903 rifle with M1907 sling and fixed M1905 bayonet. *(National Archives)*

Post-WWI

The conclusion of the First World War resulted in the M1903 remaining firmly entrenched as the standard United States military service rifle, even though larger numbers of M1917 rifles were on hand. The coming of the Armistice resulted in greatly reduced demand for rifles, and production schedules at Springfield Armory and Rock Island Arsenal were drastically curtailed. At the conclusion of the First World War, just over 8,000 complete sets of M1903 rifle parts manufactured by Rock Island Arsenal were sent to Springfield Armory where they were assembled into rifles. Upon assembly, the stocks were stamped with the typical Springfield Armory Final Inspection Stamp, but all other parts were of Rock Island origin, and so marked, which occasionally causes confusion among collectors.

Springfield Armory remained in production after 1918, albeit at significantly lower levels than during the war. Rock Island continued to manufacture some complete rifles into Fiscal Year 1920 (July 1, 1919 to June 30, 1920), primarily from receivers and other components that had been made circa 1918 and which remained in inventory. Rock Island continued making barrels until mid-1922. After cessation of the '03 production program, a number of unfinished receivers remained in storage at RIA for potential future use, and a number of the barrels made after the war were utilized for subsequent rebuild/overhaul purposes.

After the war, Springfield Armory's primary mission shifted from manufacture of new rifles to overhaul. Most of the rifles that were manufactured during the war, or previously, and which had seen heavy use over the last few years, were in need of some form of refurbishment. M1903 rifles that were sent to Springfield Armory, as well as other ordnance facilities, were inspected and repaired as necessary. As part of the overhaul procedure, most of the rifles were subsequently parkerized, and new barrels were fitted when required. Existing barrels that proved to be salvageable were typically stamped with an "A" below the original markings behind the front sight. This had been the practice for a number of years and is confirmed in a Springfield Armory memorandum dated August 5, 1912, which stated:

> "All rifles cleaned and repaired at this Armory have been packed in chests so marked as to distinguish between rifles which have been provided with new barrels and those which have had the old barrel retained. In the latter case, the barrel is marked with the letter "A" just below the Ordnance escutcheon near the muzzle and the chests are distinctly marked "C.&R." In the case a new barrel has been inserted in the rifle the remaining parts of the rifle are repaired so that the rifle is in as good condition as if it was a new one and the chests are then marked with a letter "C" which indicates the rifles have been cleaned but are serviceable and available for any issues."

It is interesting to note that unmodified M1903 rifles manufactured in the 1917–1918 period are relatively scarce today, and they may be even more difficult to find than rifles made between 1906 and 1916. The fact that '03 rifles made between 1910 and 1916 turn up in unaltered and sometimes extremely nice condition is due to the fact that a number were sold to NRA members and were not subjected to the extensive postwar arsenal overhaul programs. This is bolstered by the fact that pre-1910 '03s remaining in their original configuration are scarcer than the 1910–1916-vintage rifles, since such rifles were not sold via the NRA. The primary reason for the rarity of unmodified M1903 rifles made circa 1917–1918 is that most went directly from the factory to the training camps or front lines. They saw immediate and extensive use, and most were subsequently overhauled one or more times over the years.

Avis Barrels

In order to procure a sufficient supply of barrels for the extensive postwar rebuild program at Springfield, fairly large numbers of '03 rifle barrels were purchased from the Avis Rifle Barrel Company of West Haven, Connecticut. These were marked "AV" behind the front sight and dated. The most commonly encountered dates are 1919 and 1920. There are some reports that partially finished barrels were procured from Avis and used by Springfield Armory for assembly into newly made rifles near the end of WWI and for a couple of years afterward. Some unfinished Avis barrel blanks, marked "AV", are believed to have been stamped with Springfield Armory markings. Such use of the Avis barrels by Springfield Armory is the subject of some disagreement among students of the subject. In any event, such use would have been limited.

In virtually all cases, '03 rifles with "AV" barrels seen today are clearly arsenal rebuilt weapons. Some of the Avis barrels show evidence of less-than-arsenal-quality workmanship, and the safety of some of these barrels has been questioned. However, any barrels of this type used by Springfield Armory presumably passed all requisite inspections, and were considered as safe at the time. Avis barrels are still commonly encountered, and most have proven to be acceptable for use. A 1920s-vintage arsenal rebuilt '03 with an Avis replacement barrel can be an interesting and sometimes overlooked collector variant in its own right.

Post-WWI Overhaul of M1903 Rifles

Parkerizing and replaced barrels were not the only modifications to the '03 rifles overhauled in the immediate post-WWI period. Indeed, every component of the '03 was inspected by ordnance technicians to determine if replacement or repair was needed. A 1928 issue of *Army Ordnance* magazine contained an article that detailed the procedure used by Springfield Armory for overhauling '03 rifles during this period. It is too lengthy to reproduce in its entirety, but the most pertinent aspects of the piece will be presented. One page of the article includes the following:

"...The general procedure in overhauling the rifle may be divided into the following seven groups of operations: Disassembly and separation of components, repair and refinish of components; reassembly of rifle; proof firing and function firing; bore sighting; final inspection."

The following procedures as detailed in the article are especially interesting and help explain why pre-WWII rifles remaining in their original factory configuration are so scarce today:

"All service rifles sent to Springfield Armory to be cleaned and repaired are put through the same process and it has been found necessary to disassemble completely all these rifles, which because of some major defect have become unserviceable. Before being taken down, the rifles must first be cleaned of the heavy coating of grease. This is just a rough cleaning and is done because it makes the disassembly easier. The bolts are removed from the rifles, washed separately and the stock, barrel and action assembly are cleaned as a unit. The cleaning consists of immersing the parts in a tank of gasoline and scrubbing with a bristle brush. The bolt is stripped leaving the sleeve as an assembly. The handguard and stock are removed from the barrel, the handguard clips removed from the handguard and all metal parts, except the stock screws and guard screw bushings, are removed from the stock, the butt plate and cap remaining as an assembly. The remainder of the rifle is torn down, leaving the following as assemblies: upper band, lower band, rear sight, front sight movable stud and front sight, trigger and sear, and windage screw. The barrel is not removed from the receiver. The rear sight is partly disassembled leaving the following parts as an assembly: base spring, movable base, joint pin and leaf. All the metal parts are then washed in a hot solution of soda and are in a condition to be inspected.

"In the operation described above all the different components and assemblies are kept separated upon

A ship's Marine Guard assembled on deck with their rifles stacked for review.
(Courtesy Stuart C. Mowbray collection)

being disassembled, so that after being washed they are counted and are ready to be inspected."

The article described all of the various gauges used to inspect the components, including the maximum and minimum headspace and other tolerances. The overhaul process continued as follows:

"All parts which are found to be defective and which cannot be repaired as well as all parts which are so badly rust-pitted as to affect the appearance of the rifle are rejected. Screws are condemned if the slot is badly upset or if the threads are stripped or otherwise damaged. Springs which have lost their tension are not used again. All components which are rejected are considered unserviceable and are scrapped. Fig. 2 gives some idea of the number of principal parts which are replaced. These figures have been taken from a lot of 10,000 rifles which have been cleaned and repaired. The reason for the high percentage of receivers which are replaced will be explained later. It will be seen that 91 percent of the barrels are found unserviceable. This figure is not high when it is realized that all rifles which come to an arsenal for repair have been carefully inspected and rejected in the field and that most of the rifles have been found unserviceable because of defective barrels. Also many barrels which might be considered as serviceable by an inspector in the field are rejected when the rifle is overhauled at an arsenal. The standards of arsenal inspection are necessarily higher than those of the field. In the field an inspector might say that the bore of a barrel was pitted but that the rifle could be used another year, whereas, at an arsenal the same barrel would have to be condemned on the grounds that it would not be worth assembling it to serviceable parts to be returned again in a year for complete overhaul. When a rifle has been overhauled at an arsenal it should be in such a condition that it can be stored for many years and still be serviceable. It is well known that the corrosive action in pitted barrels will continue even though the bore is heavily coated with grease. It is therefore readily seen that the standard of inspection for the barrel must be high."

The overhaul procedure for receivers is interesting, as it discussed the low-numbered issue as follows:

"The barrel and receiver are inspected in the assembled condition. All Springfield Armory receivers with numbers under 800,000 and Rock Island Arsenal receivers with numbers under 285,507 are removed from the barrels and scrapped. This accounts for the high percentage of rejected receivers as shown in Fig. 2."

The reasons for the withdrawal of low-numbered receivers from service due to improper forging temperatures were also disclosed. Although Ordnance Department regulations clearly called for these receivers to be withdrawn from service and scrapped, a number of the early receivers remained in service well into the World War II period. The Marine Corps was more lenient than the Army concerning the use of the low-numbered receivers, and rebuilt U.S.M.C. rifles utilizing these receivers are common.

As explained in the *Army Ordnance* article, the barrels removed from the low-numbered receivers were carefully inspected and, if found satisfactory, were put into parts bins for subsequent use.

The bolts, sights and trigger assemblies were also inspected and repaired or replaced as necessary. The overhaul standards for stocks and handguards are of particular interest to today's collectors. As stated in the *Army Ordnance* piece:

"Stocks having splits or cracks of such a nature as to render them unserviceable are rejected. Some of the defects found in the stocks which are not due to fair wear and tear are as follows: initials cut in the stock; company numbers stamped in stock; small metal tags tacked on stock and alterations such as marking stock similar to sporting stocks. All stocks must be equipped with front and rear stock screws which have been added to the stock to strengthen it in front and rear of the guard. Stocks are tested to see whether they are warped. Under service conditions the stock due to its shape will warp and under extreme weather conditions this warping is aggravated.

"Handguards are easily damaged in the service. As is indicated in Fig. 2, over 50 percent of the handguards must be replaced on the rifles which are overhauled. Those which are cracked, bruised or in any way damaged are rejected. All handguards must be equipped with two handguard clips."

The following occurred after the parts had been inspected:

"After inspection components are divided into three groups, those parts which are rejected and are recommended to be scrapped, those parts which are in good condition and those parts which are in need of repairs. Parts in need of repair are repaired and then grouped with those parts in good condition, and all are refinished."

After the specific repair procedures were detailed, the type of finish applied to the metal parts was discussed.

"...the most rust-resisting finish is that applied by the Parker Process. This consists of forming on the surface of the metal a coating of phosphates which are insoluble in water. A parkerized finish is highly resistant to corrosion. It is not a superficial coating but is formed by the chemical reaction between the metal parts and the bath in which they are immersed. The following parts are parkerized: barrel and receiver, butt plate assembly, bolt, extractor, floor plate, guard and upper band.

"The oil black finish is somewhat more smooth than that obtained by the Parker process but is not as resistant to corrosion. However, it does give sufficient protection to the parts on which it is applied. The parts to be reblacked are dipped in oil, placed in a rotary finance at 600 to 650 degrees F and held for approximately one-half hour and then removed and quenched in oil. The following parts are oil blacked: handguard clips, lower band, spring and swivel, rear sight parts, sleeve assembly and stacking swivel.

"The firing pin is browned (what would be referred to as "blued" today). A parkerized finish would not give the smooth finish which is required for the functioning of this parts, and it cannot be oiled blacked because the temperature to which it would have to be heated would draw the temper on the cocking piece.

"The stocks and handguards which have been accepted after the necessary machining operations haven been performed are scraped, sanded and immersed in raw linseed oil and allowed to remain in the oil about five minutes after which they are removed and allowed to dry."

The various components were then "...sent to the component room from which they are drawn in small lots for the reassembly of the rifle." The various assembly steps were presented in some detail including the firing of two proof rounds which generated a chamber pressure of 75,000 p.s.i. Rifles that were successfully proof fired were stamped with a punch mark underneath the bolt handle and a "P" on the bottom of the stock behind the triggerguard (in the same location as the original factory proof circled "P" proof mark). All rifles were then function fired, bore sighted and carefully cleaned before final inspection. The final step in the overhaul procedure was as follows:

"When the rifle is finally accepted it is covered with a rust preventative compound, packed ten rifles to a chest, and the chest marked "A.O." to indicate that the rifle has been overhauled at an arsenal. The rifles then start on their varied careers again, some to be used and some to be abused. After serving their purposes, being worn out and fatigued, they are again declared unserviceable and are again returned to be overhauled."

The term A.O., for Arsenal Overhauled, was a departure from the earlier term C&R (Cleaned and Repaired) for similar procedures. Fig. 2, cited several times in the foregoing piece, reveals the percentage that various components were found to be unserviceable in a lot of 10,000 M1903 rifles sent to Springfield Armory for overhaul. Fig. 2 as reproduced in the original 1928 article, consists of a rather crudely drawn bar chart. **Table 9** on page 222 reflects the percentages gleaned from the diagram in the article. As can be seen from the table, virtually none of the M1903 rifles of the First World War and earlier eras that were subjected to arsenal overhaul survived with all their original factory components intact. Replaced barrels, handguards and any number of other parts were the norm. In addition, many of the rifles were subsequently subjected to other additional overhauls over the next twenty or thirty years. In almost all cases, only those rifles that were somehow removed from the system through legitimate sales or some other means (such as theft), escaped arsenal overhaul. These examples include the NRA sales rifles from the pre-WWI period.

The parkerizing used on these post-WWI arsenal overhauls had a distinctive black dye added to the solution, which was very similar to the parkerizing used on the M1903 rifles manufactured at Springfield Armory and Rock Island Arsenal beginning in late 1918.

Springfield Armory Assembly of Rifles with Rock Island Receivers, circa 1927

A number of semi-finished receivers remained on hand at Rock Island after the Arsenal ceased production of '03 components in the early 1920s. In 1927, some 25,600 of these unfinished receivers were sent to Springfield Armory, to be assembled into complete rifles. Many of the receivers had been marked "Rock Island Arsenal" but had not been serially numbered. Springfield Armory finished the receivers, stamped serial numbers, and assembled them into complete rifles. Published sources vary somewhat regarding the serial numbers used by Springfield on these receivers, and estimates range from as low as 1275767 to as high as 1293000.

Original examples of the RIA/SA rifles of this vintage represent an interesting collector variant. Barrels should be marked "SA" and dated circa 1927, with other features of late-1920s-vintage Springfield rifles, including stocks with grasping grooves and two reinforcing screws. No one should infer from this that Springfield Armory and Rock Island Arsenal routinely swapped components when both entities were involved in '03 rifle production. Other than this exception, Rock Island receivers with Springfield barrels are a sign of a mismatch and do not represent an original production combination.

Marines being trained at Parris Island, South Carolina. Notice the posture of the instructors, indicative of the attention the Marines paid to marksmanship.
(Courtesy Stuart C. Mowbray collection)

The M1903 Experimental Cavalry Carbine

In 1920, a prototype cavalry carbine based on the M1903 rifle was fabricated by Springfield Armory's Experimental Department. The weapon utilized a M1903 receiver and was fitted with a 20-inch barrel, correspondingly shortened stock and handguard, and a Lyman #48 receiver sight. Sling swivels were fitted to the left side of the stock rather than on the bottom as with the service rifle. It was initially envisioned that 75 of the carbines would be fabricated for testing purposes with an estimated conversion cost of $24 per unit, which was slightly more than the $23.80 that a standard '03 cost at the time. In order to reduce costs, it was suggested that unused Air Service rifle stocks and handguards be utilized if the cavalry carbine was to be adopted.

Two prototypes are believed to have been fabricated. One was made using a standard service rifle receiver, serial number 1204591, and sent to Fort Riley, Kansas, for testing and evaluation. The other was apparently a presentation piece and utilized a receiver marked simply "No. 2." The floor plate was engraved, "By Order of/ Col. T.L. Ames/May 1921." The purpose or initial disposition of this second example is not known. The weapon was listed for sale in a militaria dealer's catalog in 2003 for a tidy sum.

Subsequent testing determined that the '03 carbine had a noticeable muzzle flash, but recoil was within acceptable limits. The testing was suspended on November 22, 1922. Apparently, the carbine was not sufficiently superior for cavalry use to justify replacing the standard '03 rifle. Also, the Army was looking at the development of a semi-automatic rifle and did not wish to expend any unnecessary funds in a very tight budgetary environment. Except for the two known prototypes, the handy and attractive '03 cavalry carbine was never put into production and is a little-known footnote to U.S. Ordnance history.

1920s Production M1903 Service Rifles

The reduced demand by the military and the availability of large numbers of refurbished rifles resulted in relatively few new service rifles being manufactured in the 1920s. The rifles produced during this period were substantially similar to the very late WWI production Springfield '03s:

Finish

Springfield Armory continued use of the same variety of black-tinted parkerizing as was used with the '03 rifles manufactured since late 1918. Some collectors have stated that parkerizing of this era sometimes has a very dark olive green tint if examined in direct sunlight. While parkerizing can often have subtle differences, any greenish tint found on 1920s or 1930s parkerizing would be extremely slight and likely due to the effects of cosmoline. WWII parkerizing, on the other hand, typically has a very noticeable greenish cast.

Receivers

Rock Island Arsenal utilized nickel steel receivers as early as the summer of 1918, but Springfield Armory continued the use of double heat-treated receivers until circa

1927, when nickel steel receivers were introduced. According to Crossman, the changeover to nickel steel receivers was at serial number 1275767. The reason for Springfield Armory not changing to nickel steel until the late 1920s, while Rock Island utilized the material during World War I, was due primarily to budgetary considerations. There was a large quantity of *Class A* steel left over at Springfield Armory after the First World War. Since the double-heat-treated receivers made from this steel were safe, and since military appropriations were very tight during this period, it was obligatory to use the existing supply before the change to nickel steel could be justified.

Barrels

The same marking format was used on Springfield M1903 rifles during the 1920s as was used on all post-1905 rifles (e.g. "SA", *flaming bomb* insignia, and month/year of production). The date on the barrels represented the date that the barrel was manufactured and was not necessarily the date that the rifle was assembled. The correlation of the receiver date to the barrel date from the 1920s until the end of production varied more than in previous years. A barrel made a year before, or after, the receiver could conceivably be the original barrel.

Bolts

Springfield Armory bolts produced after late 1918 were of the swept back handle variety and all were double heat-treated. Most bolts of the immediate post-WWI period through the early 1920s were stamped with a letter "J" followed by a single digit. The most common number was "J5", but "J6" and "J7" numbers have been observed as well. After 1924, a new set of letters replaced the "J" number. A complete marking includes "WKL3", however these markings were not made at the same time and are therefore stamped to different depths. During later machining operations, some of the numbers were obliterated and often the "3" is usually the last digit visible.

When the nickel steel bolts were introduced by Springfield, they were stamped "NS" (or "N.S.") on the root of the bolt handle. The use of the nickel steel bolts by Springfield seemed to lag behind production of the nickel steel receivers by a year or two, as some original rifles with nickel steel receivers, but "WKL3" bolts may be noted. After their introduction, nickel steel bolts were used until the end of M1903 production at Springfield Armory. Unfortunately, some earlier bolts have been stamped "NS" by dishonest individuals in order to fool unsuspecting buyers into believing they are acquiring one of the stronger nickel

Sailors of the U.S.S. Texas drilling with their '03 rifles. Notice that they are dry firing, not live firing in this drill. (Courtesy Stuart C. Mowbray collection)

RIGHT – Yet another photograph from Parris Island, South Carolina. This one showing shooting in the prone postion. *(Courtesy Stuart C. Mowbray collection)*

BELOW – A rare photograph of sailors training with their '03 Springfields aboard ship, presumably aiming at floating targets. *(Courtesy Stuart C. Mowbray collection)*

steel bolts. A straight handle bolt stamped "NS" on top of the handle is an obvious fake, and a swept-back handle bolt with crude or indistinct "NS" markings is also quite suspect. Rock Island Arsenal's first nickel steel bolts were manufactured in the summer of 1918, before the introduction of the swept-back bolt handle. Unlike Springfield that marked "NS" on the bolt handle root, Rock Island marked the lower side of the safety lug. The same admonition about fake markings should be noted for Rock Island bolts as well.

Stocks

The 1920s-vintage stocks were essentially identical to the late-WWI stocks including grasping grooves and two reinforcing stock screws. Inspector cartouches usually consisted of three initials enclosed in a rectangle. The firing proof mark was a circled "P", located on the bottom of the stock behind the triggerguard. This was typically a block variety (sans serif), but some of the earlier script-style stamps (with serifs) may occasionally be found on these later rifles.

This vintage photograph of troops resting on their backpacks is marked "105 H.C.-102nd Med. Regt., Pine Camp (later known as Fort Drum, N.Y.), 1935". *(Courtesy Stuart C. Mowbray collection)*

Handguards

Handguards of the 1920s and later period did not have as prominent a sight-protecting hump as the WWI and earlier handguards.

Buttplates

The smooth buttplates, utilized in the WWI-production rifles, were replaced by 1910-style finely checkered variety, beginning circa 1920. The later coarsely checkered variety was introduced circa 1924. Leftover WWI-production buttplates were utilized until the supply was exhausted.

Rear Sights

By the mid-1920s, the dished rear sight knobs were replaced by the non-dished variety that had a simple flat profile on the face of the knob. Knobs of this type have been reported as appearing on National Match rifles as early as 1923. As was the case with the checkered buttplates, earlier vintage knobs that were still serviceable, and on hand, were used even after the official adoption of later pattern knob.

U.S.M.C. "No. 10" Sights

The U.S. Marines were a strong proponent of the '03 rifle but, by necessity, procured a quantity of M1917 rifles during WWI. While the Marines still preferred the Springfield to the Enfield, the latter's sights were seen as markedly superior to the former in many ways, and there was a desire to improve the '03's sights. It was determined that a front sight blade that was wider and higher than the standard '03 blade, coupled with a rear sight having a larger diameter aperture (0.10 inches), would be better suited for marksmanship purposes. To the end, in October 1918, the U.S. Marine Corps ordered 10,000 sets of such sights from Springfield Armory. The sights, known as *No. 10* sights, due to the 0.10-inch diameter of the aperture, were first manufactured in 1919, and a number were fitted to '03 rifles. A special sheet metal front sight cover was produced for use with the No. 10 sights.

The sights were not universally popular with the Marine marksmen and many were removed and replaced with the standard Springfield Armory style. The No. 10 sights remained in service through at least 1936 and were utilized on some WWII-vintage Marine Corps M1903A1/Unertl sniper rifles (discussed later in this book).

Triggers

The smooth triggers, adopted during the First World War, were replaced by serrated triggers which were reintroduced in the mid-1920s when the supply of the unserrated triggers was depleted.

Other Springfield Armory Production

Springfield Armory overhauled thousands of older rifles during this period. Most new manufacture was devoted to limited production rifles, such as National Match, and special target and gallery rifles in .22 and .30 caliber. The rifles of this type made during the 1920s and 1930s are extremely interesting arms, and there are a number of rare and valuable variants that are highly prized collectibles. Since the focus of this book is on the M1903 service rifle, these special rifles, interesting and valuable as they are, will not be profiled. Persons interested in learning more about such arms should consult Brophy's and Crossman's books as listed in the Bibliography.

Although the primary mission of Springfield Armory during this period was the overhaul of older rifles and manufacture of match/target rifles, there was limited production of service rifles as well. Some people have stated that no service rifles were made at Springfield Armory in the 1920s or 1930s, but this is incorrect, as limited numbers of service rifles were manufactured during this period. Few of the service rifles made by Springfield Armory in the 1920s and 1930s were procured by the U.S. Army, as that entity had a sufficient number of overhauled WWI and earlier vintage '03s on hand to meet its needs. Also, by the early 1930s, the Army was firmly focused on development of a semiautomatic rifle which culminated with the adoption of the M1 Garand rifle in 1936. The Army did not wish to expend limited funds for the purchase of new bolt-action rifles at the expense of jeopardizing future procurement of the desired semiautomatic service rifle.

Even though few if any new M1903 service rifles were procured by the U.S. Army during this period, it is known that some of the newly manufactured service rifles were purchased by the U.S. Coast Guard, Navy and Marine Corps as these branches were not focused on acquiring new semiautomatic rifles in the foreseeable future. Other non-military entities that acquired limited numbers of '03 service rifles included the Federal Prison system, National Park Service, Department of Justice and the Bureau of Indian Affairs.

M1903A1 Rifle

In 1929, the Type C stock was adopted for use with the M1903 rifle. This stock differed from the Type S stock used on the M1903 service rifles up to this time primarily in the fact that the stock had a pistol grip and the grasping grooves were eliminated. The configuration and dimensions of the Type C stock were also improvements over the Type S stock for most shooters. The Type C stock was initially utilized on National Match rifles beginning in 1929 and was so favorably received that the stock was approved for use with service rifles when the supply of available Type S stocks became exhausted.

Upon adoption of the Type C stock, the designation of the service rifle became Model of 1903A1. As discussed, production of service rifles during the 1920s and 1930s was limited, and relatively few pure M1903A1 rifles were manufactured. To qualify as such, in addition to the stock, a rifle would have to be of 1929 or later Springfield Armory production (in the corresponding serial number range) with an appropriately dated barrel. Original M1903A1 rifles were finished in the distinctive 1930's-vintage black-tinted parkerizing. The original Springfield Armory Type C stocks were finely crafted and were stamped with a circled "P" proof mark on the grip and a final inspection stamp (cartouche) on the left side, slightly below the magazine cutoff recess. Several final inspection stamps may be encountered, including "DAL" (for Springfield inspector Daniel A. Leary) and later, "SA/SPG" (Springfield Armory/Stanley P. Gibbs). Both Leary and Gibbs were civilian inspectors who worked for Springfield Armory. Gibbs had been employed at Springfield since the First World War. A similar "SA/SPG" inspection stamp will be found on early Springfield Armory M1 Garand rifles made prior to 1941.

Type C stocks were also made under subcontract during WWII, but these differed in several respects from the 1930's-vintage Type C stocks, primarily in the overall configuration. The finely crafted prewar Type C stocks were noticeably slimmer in profile than the WWII-vintage stocks

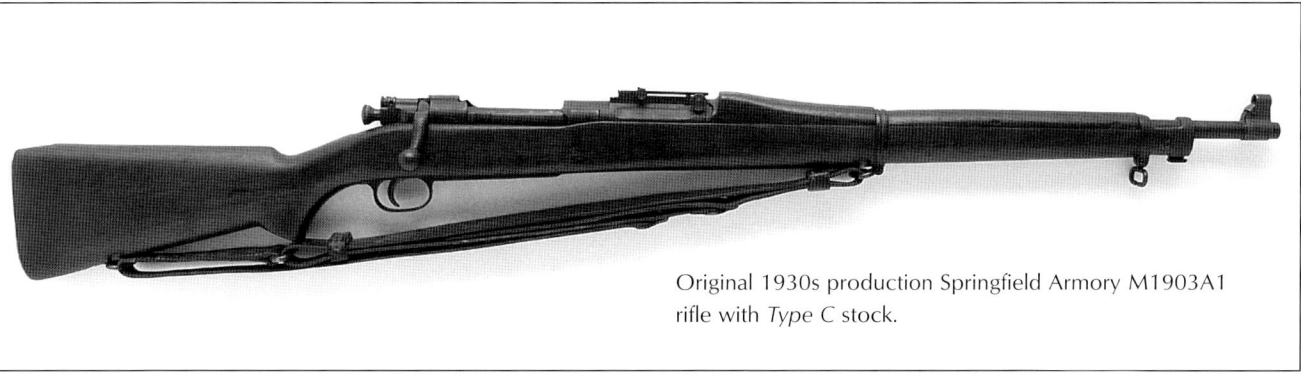

Original 1930s production Springfield Armory M1903A1 rifle with *Type* C stock.

of this type. The inspection stamping format will also help identify the earlier prewar Type C stocks from the later WWII contract variety. It should be noted that the standard Model of 1903 nomenclature on the receiver ring was retained on the M1903A1 variant, and the only substantive difference between the post-1929 rifles of this type and earlier M1903 rifles was the type of stock.

There is some controversy today over exactly what constitutes a M1903A1 rifle. Apparently, the military considered any M1903 rifle fitted, even retrofitted, with a Type C stock as a M1903A1. Therefore, technically speaking, any M1903 rifle of any vintage fitted with a Type C stock can be classified as a M1903A1. On the other hand, many collectors and students of the subject tend to take a more dogmatic approach and classify only those rifles made at Springfield Armory from 1929 until production ceased in the late 1930s, and equipped with the appropriate Type C stock, as true M1903A1s. For the sake of clarity, the latter definition will be used throughout this book, even though the official distinction may not be as clear-cut.

A true 1930's production M1903A1 service rifle is one of the rarest variants of the '03 genre, and original examples are quite elusive. Many M1903 rifles of all vintages have subsequently been fitted with replacement Type C stocks during WWII (and later), but such assembled weapons are infinitely more common and much less valuable than an original 1930's production M1903A1 service rifle.

The Hatcher Hole

In July 1935, the U.S. Army Ordnance Department mandated that an additional gas escape hole be added to the left side of the receiver in order to increase the margin of safety in the event of a cartridge case failure. Around this time, the bolt was also altered by enlarging the gas escape hole. This modification was incorporated in new production rifles shortly afterward and will be found on rifles made from 1936 until the end of production.

The U.S. Marine Corps followed a short time later and added the hole to the '03 receivers in inventory. The extra hole was added to many earlier receivers during arsenal overhaul. Any '03 receiver manufactured prior to 1935 with the additional gas escape hole on the left side of the receiver has been modified from its original factory configuration. This modification is known among some collectors today as the *Hatcher Hole*, in recognition of Gen. Julian S. Hatcher, an early proponent of the feature.

Rifle Bolts Marked with Serial Numbers

Except for National Match rifles and other special rifles, the U.S. military did not typically mark serial numbers on '03 bolts. There were, however, exceptions to this policy. These exceptions included a number of '03s overhauled by the U.S. Marine Corps prior to and during the early stages of World War II. Many of these rifles had bolts that were hand-etched with the serial number. In addition, a report from Fort Riley, Kansas, dated December 1930, stated that it was the practice of the U.S. Army's 2nd Cavalry to stamp the last four digits of the serial number on the rear face of the bolt handle. It should also be mentioned that many of the M1903 rifles sold by the Civilian Marksmanship Program beginning in 2002 will be found with serial numbers stamped or engraved on the bolts and stocks. This was not done under U.S. military auspices but, rather, by the foreign country to which the rifles were originally supplied under post-WWII military foreign aid assistance programs. Unlike the United States, it was the practice of many European nations to stamp serial numbers on many parts of military rifles, especially bolts and stocks.

Use of the M1903 Rifle *Between the Wars*

Even though the United States was not involved in any truly large-scale military actions *between the wars*, a number of our soldiers, sailors and marines were deployed to various and sundry locations around the world to protect our nation's interests. The '03 rifle was in the forefront during virtually all of these actions. However, use of the

M1903 Rifle with *Type S* stock.

1930s production M1903A1 rifle with *Type C* stock. Note the differences in the two stocks including the pistol grip and lack of grasping grooves on the *Type C*.

Springfield during this period was not limited to overseas destinations. While not widely known today, there was a rash of postal robberies in the United States after WWI. The situation became so serious in the early 1920s that a number of U.S. Marines were dispatched as guards at postal facilities and on mail trains and mail delivery trucks. The mail guard Marines were armed with a variety of weapons, including M1911 pistols, M1917 revolvers, 12-gauge shotguns and '03 rifles. The utilization of armed Marines eventually ended the problem. Other domestic military use of the '03 during this period occurred during racial and labor disturbances that cropped up from time to time, including the Chicago Race Riots in 1919 and the unseemly suppression of the *Bonus Marchers* in Washington, D.C., in 1932.

Overseas, M1903 rifles saw widespread issue to our troops in China and combat duty in the numerous hotspots of the Caribbean Basin and Central America, such as Haiti and Nicaragua. As was the case in the trenches of France, the '03 performed superbly and was very popular with the majority of the troops to whom the weapon was issued. The stellar performance of the various National Match and special target '03s on the rifle ranges during the 1920s and 1930s further cemented the rifle's reputation for accuracy and reliability.

The rapid demobilization of our armed forces after the Armistice, the huge amount of surplus war material on hand, and the relative lack of demand resulted in very little procurement of new accessories and accouterments for the '03 rifle. There were ample stocks of cartridge belts, bayonet scabbards, slings and most other items left over from the WWI surplus inventories to meet the needs of our armed forces until the eve of the Second World War. These items will be discussed subsequently in the Accessories, Accouterments and Appendages section of this book.

U.S. Marines firing M1917 Lewis machine gun. Note the '03 rifle slung over the shoulder of the Marine in the foreground. *(National Archives)*

U.S. Marines in the Caribbean, 1920s, firing M1903 rifles. *(National Archives)*

ABOVE – A U.S. soldier on duty during the 1919 Chicago Race Riots. *(Courtesy Chicago Historical Society)*
ABOVE, RIGHT – The U.S. Marine Mail Guard detail in 1921. *(Courtesy Chicago Historical Society)*
RIGHT – The U.S. Marine Rifle Team in 1929. *(Courtesy Chicago Historical Society)*
BELOW – U.S. Marine *Mail Guards* at a Chicago mail facility circa 1921. Three of the Marines are armed with M1903 rifles and one is armed with a Remington Model 10 shotgun. All are armed with M1917 revolvers. *(Courtesy Chicago Historical Society)*

U.S. Marine Patrol, Nicaragua circa late 1920s. The Marines are armed with a variety of weapons including M1921 Thompson submachine guns, M1918 Browning Automatic Rifles, and M1903 Springfield rifles.

The 105 H.C. - 102nd Med. Regt., Pine Camp (later known as Fort Drum, N.Y.), 1935. *(Courtesy Stuart C. Mowbray collection)*

World War II

Even though the dark clouds of war began to gather over Europe and Asia in the late 1930s, the United States public retained a strong and well-established isolationist sentiment. Politicians vowed not to send our boys to spill their blood in another European conflagration as was the case in 1917. Consequently, our military was woefully underfunded and unprepared to fight a modern war overseas.

While relatively little new material was procured for our armed forces during this period, many of the nation's manufacturing firms soon became the financial beneficiaries of the war that broke out in Europe in 1939. Our European allies, primarily Great Britain, looked to the United States for the acquisition of all sorts of badly need war material, ranging from rifles to aircraft. Most American firms capable of handling such work were soon swamped with Allied orders, and a number of companies, still languishing from the effects of the Depression, were flush with lucrative European contracts.

Remington M1903 Rifles

Following the disaster at Dunkirk, the British were in dire need of a source of new service rifles to replace those lost on the Continent, and to arm the expanding Commonwealth armed forces. The British government contracted with the Savage Arms Company in the United States for production of the No. 4, Mark I service rifle. In the course of manufacturing the British rifle, representatives of His Majesty's government made inquiries to the Remington Arms Company to ascertain if a version of the M1903 rifle, modified for use with the British .303 cartridge, would be feasible. It was known that the '03 rifle production machinery, still in storage at Rock Island Arsenal, might be available for such use. To this end, Remington negotiated with the American government for acquisition of the Rock Island '03 tooling and equipment in order to meet the requirements of a British contract for rifles. In March 1941, Remington entered into an agreement with the Ordnance Department to lease the '03 manufacturing equipment. A few months later, Remington agreed to procure some 600,000 sets of walnut blanks for rifle stocks and handguards that were also in storage at RIA, in exchange for military ammunition to be manufactured on future contracts by the company. With the machinery acquired and ample supplies of wood on hand, Remington engineers conferred with representatives from the British government regarding the modifications of the M1903 rifle that would be required to adapt the weapon to the British .303 cartridge.

However, Pearl Harbor changed the nation's mood for war, literally overnight, and plans were quickly formulated to arm the vast number of American troops needed to fight a global war. It was apparent that there would soon be a shortage of service rifles. Contracts were given for the increased production of M1 rifles to Springfield Armory and Winchester Repeating Arms Company. Even with greatly accelerated production of the Garand rifle, supplies of service rifles would be outpaced by the huge demand. The supply of existing M1903 rifles helped fill some of the void. In addition, large numbers of M1917 rifles were taken from the war reserve stockpile and refurbished for issue as training weapons and supplemental service rifles. Even with these additional weapons, a new source of service rifles was sorely needed.

Fortunately, the United States did not have to search very far for a source. The British cancelled their rifle production contract with Remington in September 1941 as they had secured other sources for the production of additional SMLE rifles. The United States War Department was only too happy to enter into negotiations with Remington for renewed production of the '03 rifle to arm the soon-to-be-burgeoning American armed forces.

M1903 Remington Rifle - circa October 1941 to December 1941

Remington submitted ten sample rifles to the Ordnance Department in September 1941, and another 1,273 rifles were produced the following month. The new Remington rifles resembled the late-production M1903 rifles made by Rock Island before the Arsenal ceased production in 1920. The rifles were marked "Model 1903" even though the last standardized variant of the Springfield rifle was the M1903A1. The reason for this apparent anomaly can be attributed primarily to economic reasons. The 600,000 sets of walnut stock blanks, previously procured from Rock Island Arsenal, were not suitable for construction of the full pistol grip Type C stock used with the M1903A1 rifle. Therefore, the new rifle was designated as the Model 1903, since it was to be equipped with the Type S stock.

It is interesting to note that a number of Remington and Ordnance Department documents of this period refer

While this may appear to be a photograph of Doughboys leaving for France in 1917, it is actually a group of American reservists being called to active duty early in World War II. They have WWI-vintage equipment, including M1903 Springfield rifles. (Courtesy of V for Victory)

to the new rifle as the Model 1903 *Modified*. This terminology is rather curious, as the rifles weren't actually modified but were essentially the same type of weapon as made by Rock Island Arsenal between 1918 and 1919. It has been postulated that the term was a hold-over from the proposed British .303 M1903 pattern rifle that was never manufactured. In any event, the term Modified has been the cause for some misunderstanding and confusion among present-day collectors and students of the subject. Some have stated that Remington never actually produced any M1903 rifles because of the use of the term M1903 Modified in company documents. This may be true, but only in a hypertechnical sense. For the sake of simplicity and clarity, these weapons will be referred to as Remington M1903 rifles.

Receivers

The rifles were marked on the receiver ring, "U.S./Remington/Model 1903/Serial #". The company was initially assigned the serial number block beginning with serial number 3000000. As production continued, subsequent serial number blocks were assigned. **(Table 10).**

Soon after production was underway, a gas escape hole, dubbed the Hatcher Hole by collectors, was added to the left side of the receiver rail. All but the first 2,000 Remington M1903 rifles (approximately) had the Hatcher Hole in the receiver.

Barrels

Barrels were marked "RA" (Remington Arms) above the Ordnance Department flaming bomb insignia, and the

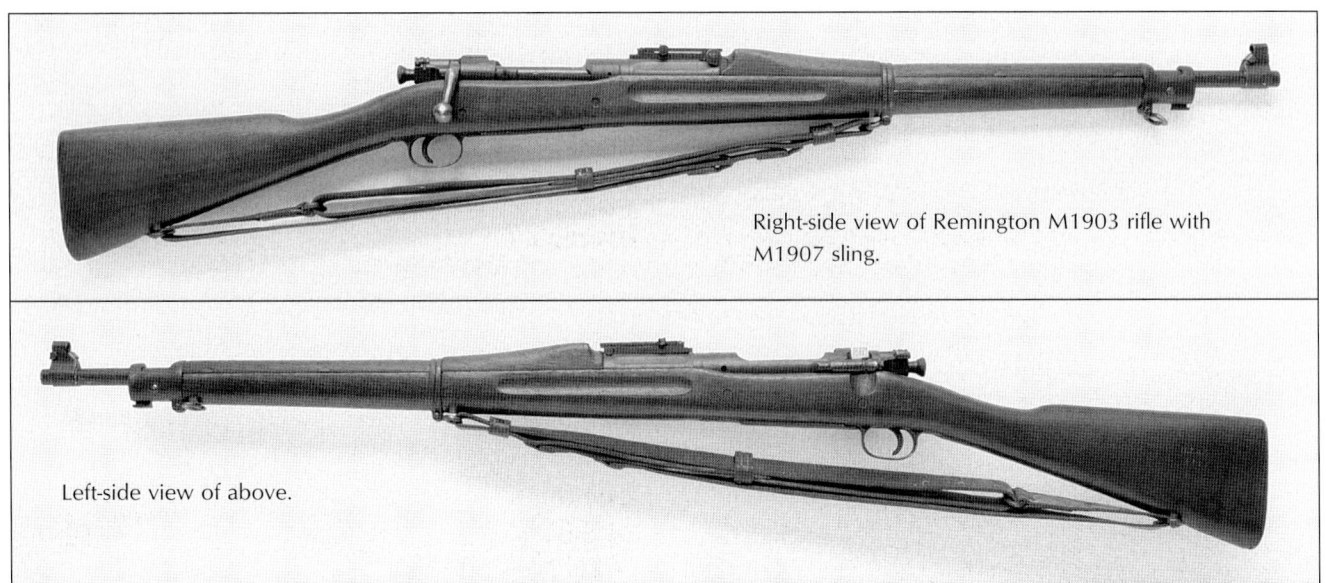

Right-side view of Remington M1903 rifle with M1907 sling.

Left-side view of above.

month/year of manufacture. The earliest barrel date reported on production rifles is 10-41. Unlike most WWI and earlier Springfield Armory and Rock Island Arsenal rifles, barrel dates and receiver vintages did not always track very closely, and there can sometimes be a wide variance. This makes attempts to ascertain the assembly date of a rifle by observation of the barrel date unreliable in many instances.

Stocks

The stocks were very similar to the late WWI Type S with grasping grooves and two reinforcing screws. A cartouche consisting of "RLB" (enclosed in a box) and an Ordnance Department (crossed cannons) escutcheon was stamped on the left side of the stock. "RLB" represents Col. Roy L. Bowlin, head of the Rochester Ordnance District. Col. Bowlin did not actually inspect the rifles, but rather, the weapons were inspected by ordnance personnel operating under his authority. The stocks were stamped with a circled "P" proof stamp (without serifs). Features found on Remington M1903 rifles and its variants are a number geometric symbols, some containing numbers or letters, stamped in front of the floorplate. Remington stocks have been observed with as few as four, to as many as a dozen, such symbols. These markings are believed to have been internal Remington factory sub-inspection stamps. These stocks were comparable in quality to the finely crafted armory stocks made by Springfield and Rock Island during the First World War. Remington did not make any M1903 rifles with Type C stocks.

Handguards

Early production Remington M1903 handguards were of the humped variety as previously used by Rock Island. It is believed that at least some of the handguards used on early Remington '03 rifles were left over from WWI production.

Receiver ring markings on early Remington M1903 rifle.

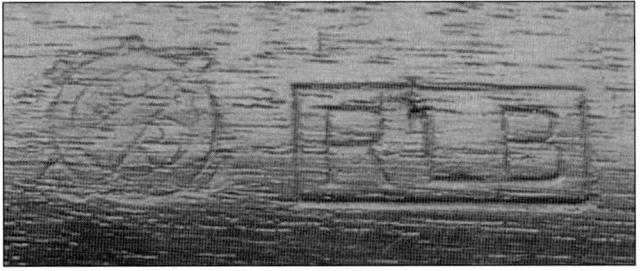

Early production Remington M1903 rifle stock inspection markings. Note the "RLB" (Col. Roy L. Bowlin) initials enclosed in a *box* and the Ordnance *crossed cannons* escutcheon.

Bottom of Remington stock. Note the configuration of the sub-inspection stamps in front of the floorplate. Remington stocks had between 4 and 12 such markings.

Rear Sights

Remington M1903 rifles utilized the M1905 pattern rear sight. The rear sight fixed base was beveled on both sides. Windage and elevation adjustment knobs were of the flat profile variety. The face of the sight leaf was polished bright.

Finish

Production rifles were finished in black-tinted parkerizing similar to that utilized since late WWI.

Furniture

These rifles were fitted with milled furniture including buttplates, bands, band springs, triggerguards and floorplates. Many of the components were marked with an "R" to denote production by Remington. There were no stamped parts found on these early production rifles.

A sheet metal front sight cover was also produced by Remington. These differed from the pre-WWII covers as they were blued and stamped with an "R", "US", and flaming bomb insignia. These and other accessories used with all variants of the Remington M1903 rifles such as slings, bayonets and cartridge belts will be covered in the Accessories, Accouterments and Appendages section.

A U.S. Army soldier (circa late 1941 or early 1942) firing a M1903 rifle. This photo is unusual in that the soldier is wearing an early issue camouflage uniform including a cover for the pre-1941-style helmet.

An unmodified early production Remington M1903 rifle is a rare weapon today and original examples are prized collectibles. The vast majority were subsequently overhauled and fitted with later vintage parts. Relatively few of these very early Remington rifles were issued to United States armed forces. Until the spring of 1942, most of the weapons were diverted to British Commonwealth nations

American troops firing on Japanese aircraft with their '03 Springfields during the December 7, 1941, raid on Pearl Harbor. *(U.S. Navy)*

Remington bolt showing "R" markings.

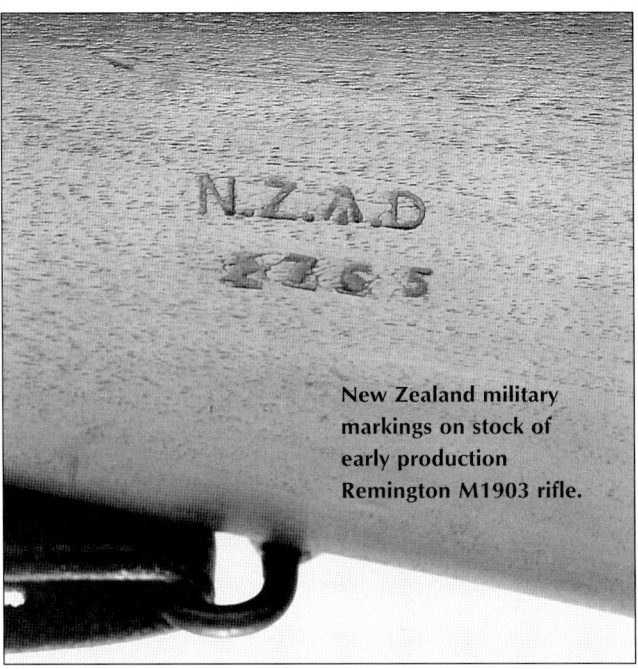

New Zealand military markings on stock of early production Remington M1903 rifle.

Second World War army troops practicing the manual of arms with M1903 rifles. The venerable '03 gave valuable service as a training rifle during WWII but also saw wide use in combat as well. *(National Archives)*

under Lend-Lease and similar military aid programs. New Zealand, in particular, was supplied a number of early production Remington M1903 rifles, and examples may be encountered with "N.Z.A.D." military property markings stamped on the stock. It has been stated that about 22,000 such rifles were supplied to New Zealand during this period. Large numbers of the new Remington M1903 rifles, reportedly as many as 64,000, slated for delivery to the Commonwealth Forces, were on ships sunk by U-Boats while on their way to Great Britain. These losses partially account for the relative scarcity of early production Remington M1903 rifles.

Despite some delays and difficulties in getting production underway, these early Remington M1903 rifles were very similar to the immediate post-WWI Rock Island rifles in quality, craftsmanship and configuration. As the Remington rifles began to flow from the assembly line, Ordnance Department requested ever-increasing numbers of rifles. The company agreed to accept these additional contracts only if it was permitted to implement manufacturing changes designed to increase production rate and decrease costs. The company was spending an inordinate amount of time on cosmetic features, such as final polishing of the metal, which slowed the rate of production and increased costs. Despite some initial reservations from the Ordnance people, Remington was allowed to disregard some noncritical aspects of the rifle's design, such as the requirement for automatic ejection of the cartridge clip when the bolt was moved forward. Certain machining operations were eliminated, and a number of minor machining tolerances were relaxed, as long as they did not negatively affect functioning of the rifle. In the month of November 1941 alone, some 649 such changes were instituted during the course of production. Such changes certainly reduced production time and costs but resulted in a number of parts not being interchangeable with '03 parts of earlier vintage. This was apparently deemed an acceptable trade-off in order to boost production.

M1903 Modified Rifles - circa January 1942 to March 1943

Reducing machining operations and relaxing tolerances were steps in the right direction, but they were only marginally helpful. In order to significantly boost production rate and lower costs, it was necessary to redesign certain components. One such change, approved on December 19, 1941, was the elimination of the lightening cuts on both sides of the rear sight fixed base and on the forward tang of the triggerguard. On February 19, 1942, the rear guard screw hole was completely drilled through to further speed production. The following month, other changes were instituted including elimination of the bolt stop. In order to further reduce production time and costs, some stamped metal parts were designed to replace the costly and time-consuming milled parts. The armory-quality Type S stock, used with initial production rifles, was redesigned to eliminate the grasping grooves and to make the stock easier to manufacture. These stocks were not as well finished and were noticeably fatter than the earlier variety.

The substantial differences between the early Remington M1903 rifles, and the rifles made after the incorporation of the above-enumerated changes resulted in a distinct and identifiable variation of the Remington M1903 rifle. The use of the term M1903 Modified, cited in Remington documents, has resulted in some writers and many collectors assuming that the term pertained to the rifles made after incorporation of the various redesigned parts. This is a logical assumption because the rifles were, indeed, modified in many respects from the initial production Remington rifles, and the term Modified is a handy way to differentiate these rifles from the earlier rifles. Collectors tend to assign types or categories in order to differentiate distinct or sometimes not so distinct variants of the same arm, even though such categories may never have been official nomenclature. The use of the term M1903 Modified for these rifles is an excellent example of such categorization. Even though it may not have been an official designation, this term will be used in this book to distinguish the rifles having these changes from the earlier examples.

As production of the M1903 Modified rifle continued, the Remington engineers searched for additional methods to speed up production and/or decrease costs. The black dye added to the parkerizing solution was eliminated which resulted in a gray finish. Application of cosmoline or oil often resulted in a greenish tint to the parkerizing, which was common to many WWII military weapons including M1 rifles and carbines.

D-Day on Omaha Beach. Note M1903 rifle stacked on top of M1 rifle. *(U.S. Army)*

The following characteristics may be found on Remington M1903 Modified rifles:

Receivers

Receivers had the same marking format as the earlier Remington M1903 rifles. All of the M1903 Modified receivers had the Hatcher Hole on the left side of the receiver rail. The small gas escape hole on the right side was eliminated.

Serial numbers used by Remington for M1903 Modified rifle production ranged from approximately 3020000 to the mid-3380000 range. The last M1903 Modified serial number is reported to be 3386616. (See **Table 10** on page 223).

Barrels

The same barrel marking format was also continued with dates ranging from 12-41 to circa 3-43.

Stocks

Stocks were of the modified Type S variety without grasping grooves. Markings continued to consist of "RLB" and the Ordnance Department's crossed cannons escutcheon stamped on the left side of the stock. The box around the "RLB" cartouche was eliminated. Relatively late in the M1903 Modified rifle's production run, Col. Bowlin was replaced as head of the Rochester Ordnance District by Col. Frank J. Atwood and, shortly afterward, the "RLB" stamp was changed to "FJA". Otherwise, the marking format on the stock remained the same, including the sub-inspection stamps in front of the floorplate and the block letter (no serifs) circle "P" firing proof. As was the case with the earlier Remington Type S stocks, these modified stocks were initially made with two reinforcing screws, but beginning around October 1942, the screws began to be replaced by stock pins.

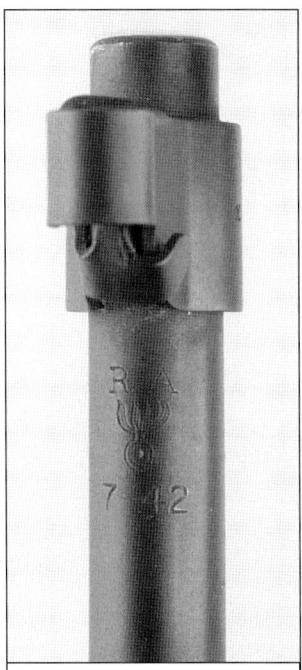

Barrel markings on Remington M1903 Modified rifle. Note front sight cover.

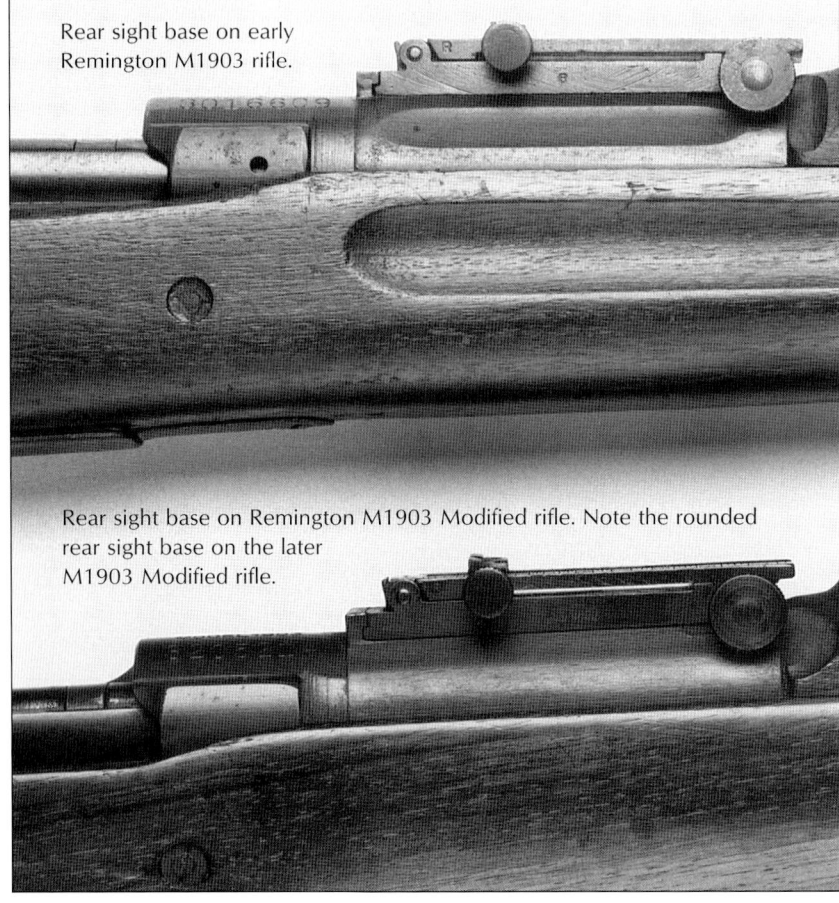

Rear sight base on early Remington M1903 rifle.

Rear sight base on Remington M1903 Modified rifle. Note the rounded rear sight base on the later M1903 Modified rifle.

Stock inspection markings on Remington M1903 Modified rifle. Note the different marking format for the "RLB" cartouche.

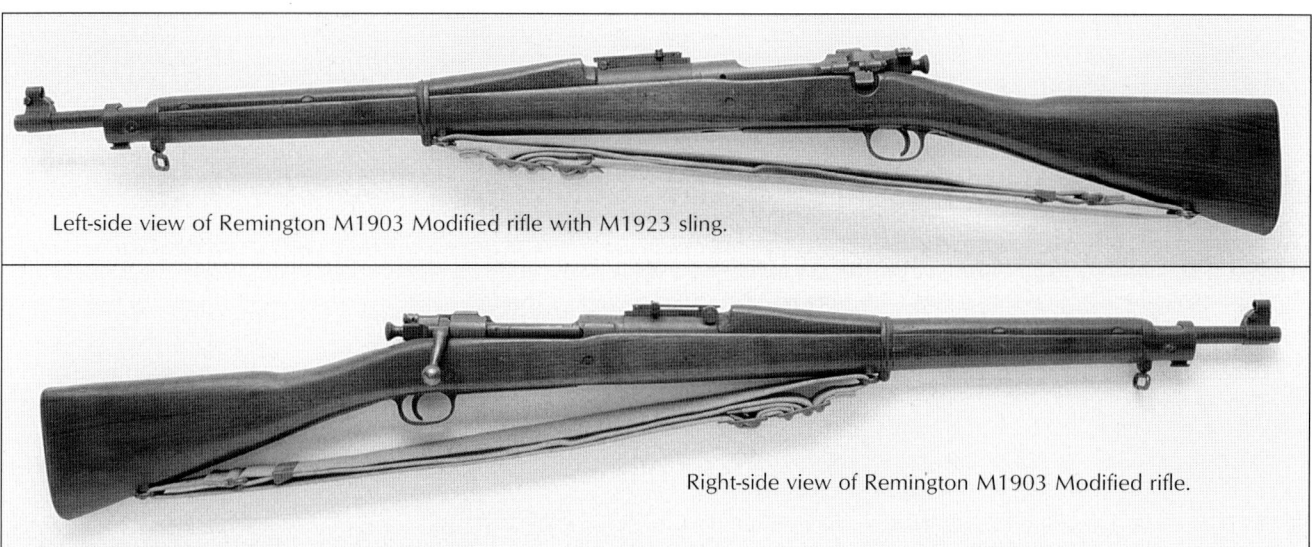

Left-side view of Remington M1903 Modified rifle with M1923 sling.

Right-side view of Remington M1903 Modified rifle.

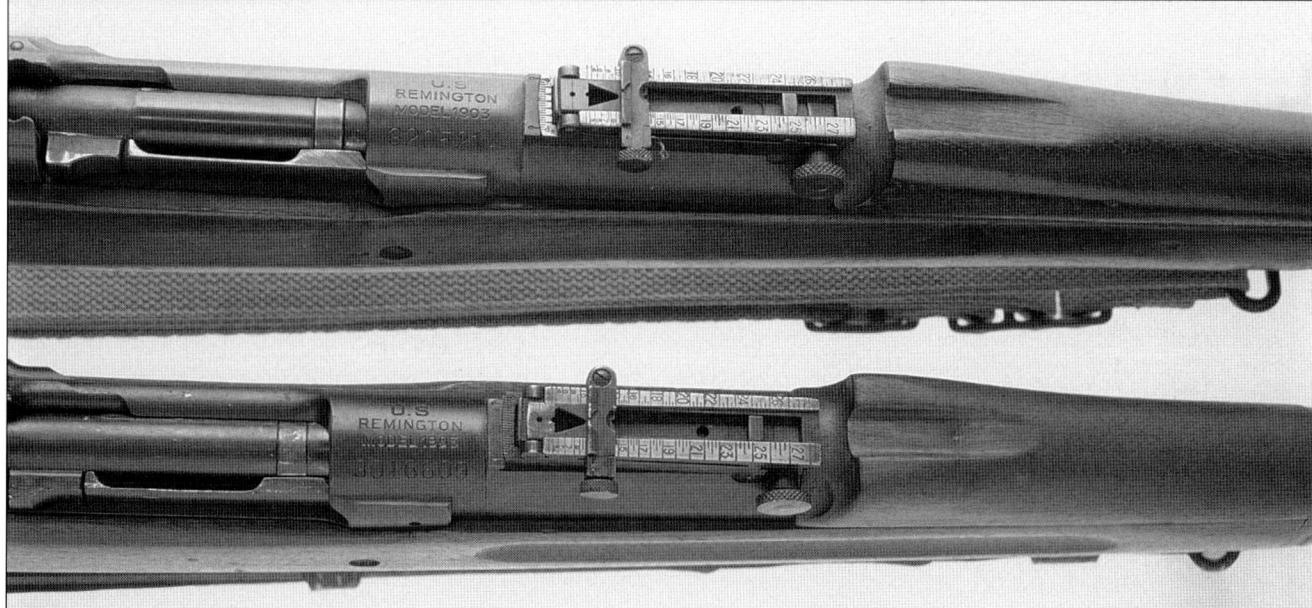

(Top) Remington M1903 Modified rifle (Bottom) Remington M1903 rifle. Note the rounded rear sight base on the M1903 Modified rifle as well as the lack of the gas escape hole on the right side of the receiver ring.

Receiver ring markings on Remington M1903 Modified rifle.

Handguards

The handguards had a less prominent hump than found on the earlier variety. Fairly late in production, the windage knob recess was changed from the semicircular type to a straight-cut profile. This later pattern handguard was also used on a number of M1903 rifles (of all vintages) overhauled during the late-WWII period and afterward.

Finish

Except for relatively early production, most M1903 Modified rifles had gray or grayish/green parkerizing rather than the black-tinted variety as found on the first pattern Remington M1903 rifles.

Rear Sights

Use of the M1905 rear sight continued, but the bevels on both sides of the fixed base were eliminated. Windage and elevation knobs were of the flat profile type.

Furniture

Rifles manufactured soon after the change from M1903 to M1903 Modified configuration still had milled furniture. As with the earlier M1903 Remington rifles, many parts were marked "R". As production continued, more and more milled parts were replaced by stamped components. Among the first stamped parts to appear, circa April 1942, were the lower band, lower band retaining spring, upper sling swivel, magazine follower and extractor collar. A stamped and welded combination triggerguard/magazine assembly was also developed to replace the separate milled triggerguard and floorplate. Unlike the earlier components, which were parkerized, the stamped sheet metal parts were blued. As with the preceding parts, many were marked "R".

Not all the changes found in the M1903 Modified rifles occurred at once but were phased in over time. A number of M1903 Modified rifles had no stamped parts, others contained only one or two, and still others contained several stamped components. As a rule, the later the vintage of the rifle, the more stamped components will be found.

Scant Grip Stock

In mid-1942, the Ordnance Department sought to standardize all rifle stocks to incorporate pistol grips. The Remington M1903 Modified rifles in production at the time utilized a simplified Type S straight-grip stock. Remington had a large number of stock blanks on hand from the aborted British contracts. These blanks were not suitable for finishing into the full pistol grip (Type C) stock configuration, but could be used to fabricate a stock having semi-pistol grip configuration. This stock was soon dubbed the scant grip. It was eventually given the less-appealing moniker of *wart hog stock*. Before Remington could change its tooling to make this pattern stock, the M1903A3 rifle was adopted. Any plans to use the scant grip stock for the manufacture of new rifles were shelved in the interest of getting the new '03A3 rifle into production as soon as possible.

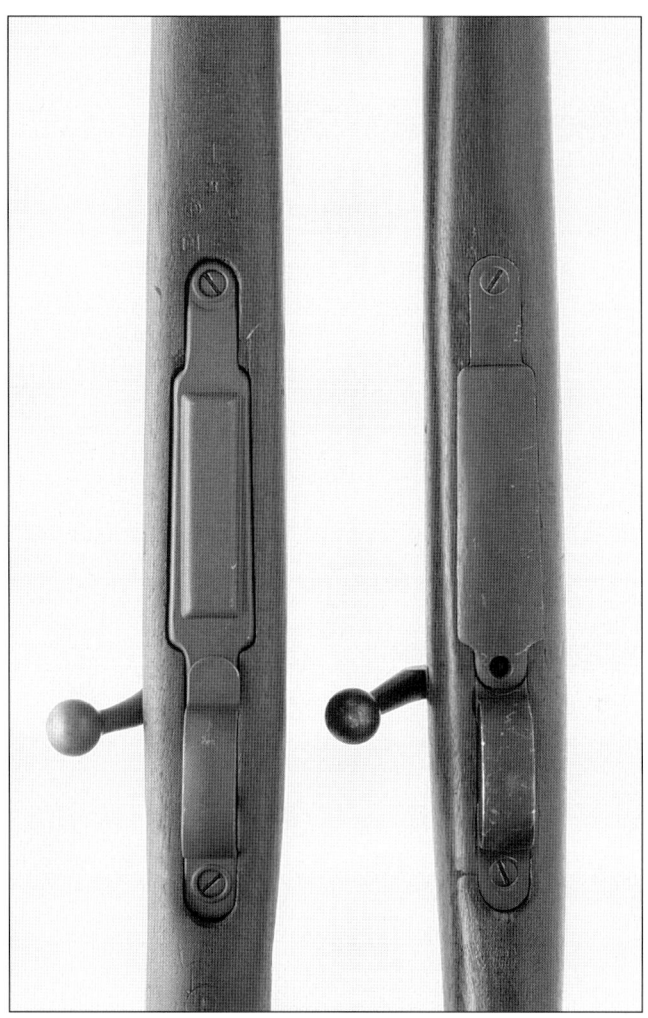

(Left) Stamped/welded sheet metal triggerguard/magazine assembly. (Right) Milled floor plate and triggerguard.

Although the scant grip stock was not used to assemble any new production M1903 Modified or M1903A3 rifles, some were used by Remington for the manufacture of later production M1903A4 Sniper rifles. This weapon will be discussed in the World War II Sniper Rifle section of this book. Large numbers of scant grip stocks were used after WWII for overhaul and replacement purposes, and examples are commonly encountered.

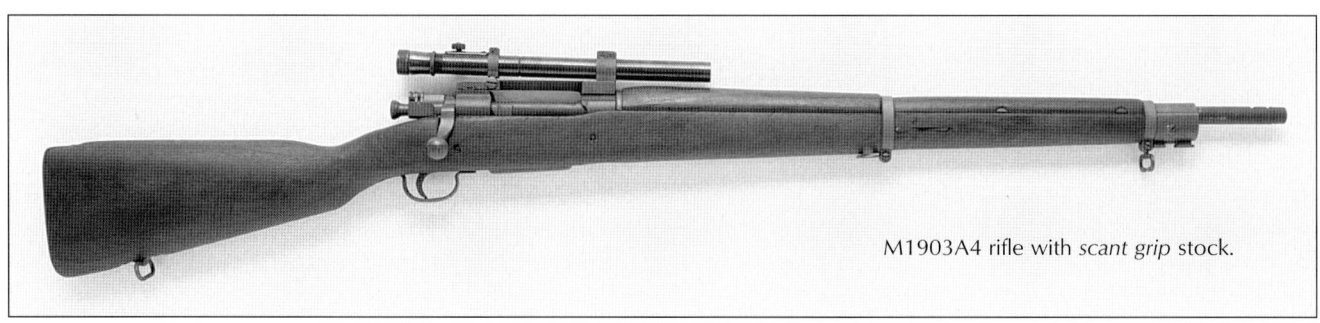

M1903A4 rifle with *scant grip* stock.

Remington Factory Sectionalized M1903 Modified Rifles

Remington produced a relatively small number of factory sectionalized M1903 Modified rifles in 1942. The receivers of these rifles were totally devoid of markings. The barrels were stamped with the same "RA"/date/ flaming bomb format as standard production rifles of the period, but a grinding mark partially obliterated the markings. Most of these rifles were assembled using rejected stocks and other parts as evidenced by the *Scrap* marking stamped on many examples. Unlike the pre-WWI Springfield Armory sectionalized rifles, with the exception of the extractor, the Remington factory rifles were sectionalized only on the left side and appear unmodified when viewed from the right side. Some may even be found with sectionalized metal oiler and thong cases. Some factory sectionalized Remington M1903A3 rifles have also been reported.

Original Remington factory sectionalized rifles are uncommon and are marvelous martial collectibles. The receiver, devoid of markings, is the key identification for these rifles, as any good machinist could sectionalize a standard Remington M1903 rifle today. It is conceivable that the markings on a receiver could be buffed out to mimic one of the unmarked factory receivers, but a large amount of metal would have to be removed and this could be determined by even a cursory examination. An original

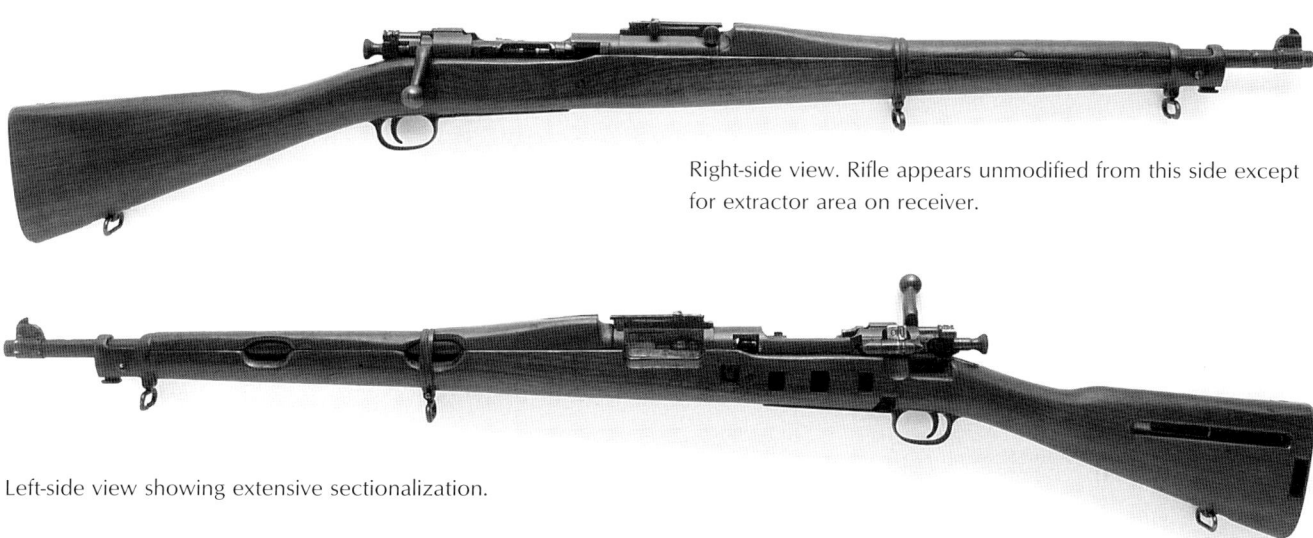

Right-side view. Rifle appears unmodified from this side except for extractor area on receiver.

Left-side view showing extensive sectionalization.

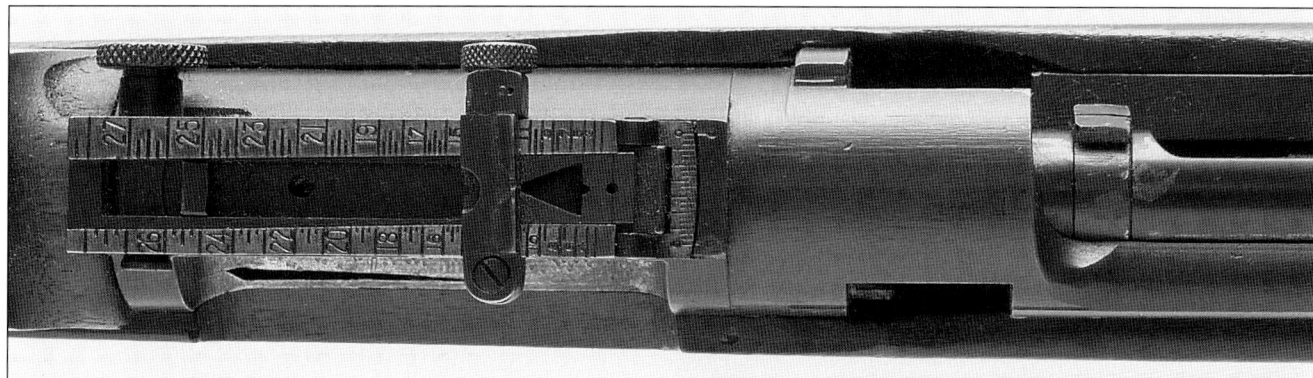

ABOVE – Receiver area. Note the receiver is devoid of markings. Also note the sectionalized areas on the left, right and behind the receiver ring.
RIGHT – "SCRAP" marking on stock indicates that an unserviceable stock was used to assemble the factory sectionalized rifle. Interestingly, the stock has been stamped with a proof mark, indicating it was originally on a rifle that was proof fired.

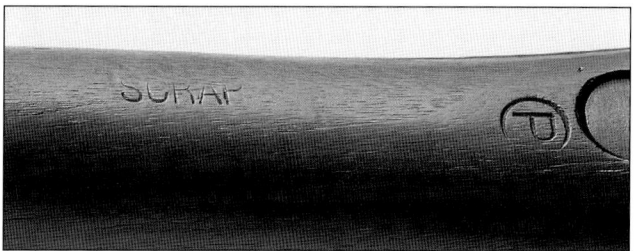

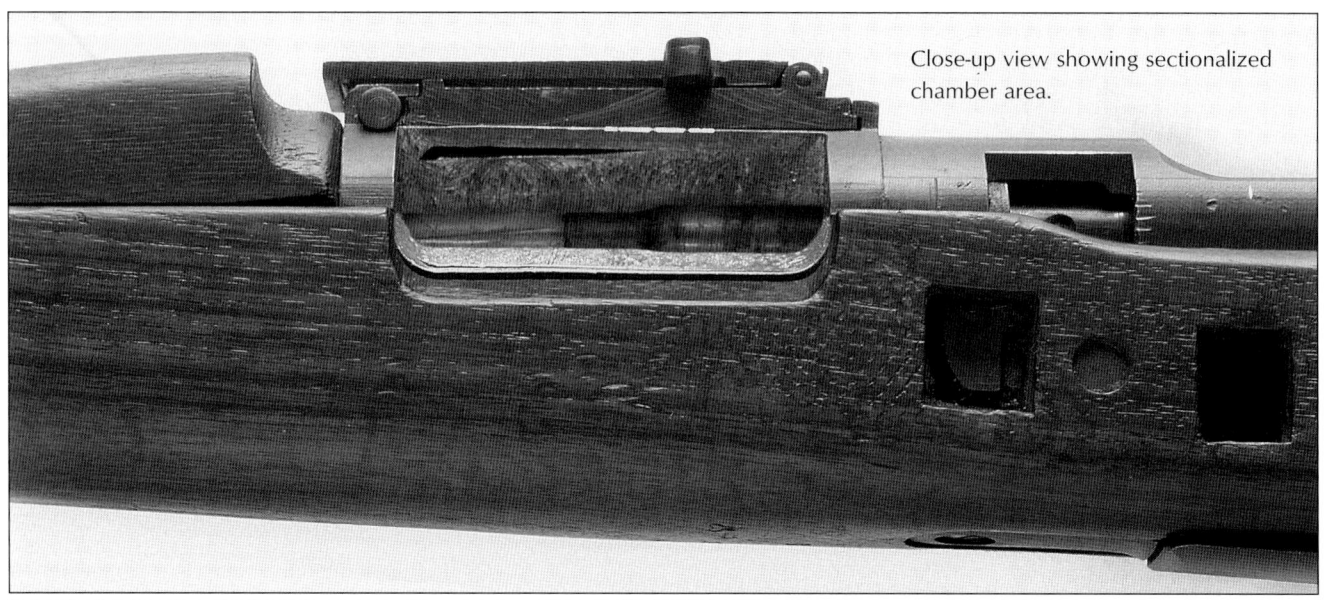

Close-up view showing sectionalized chamber area.

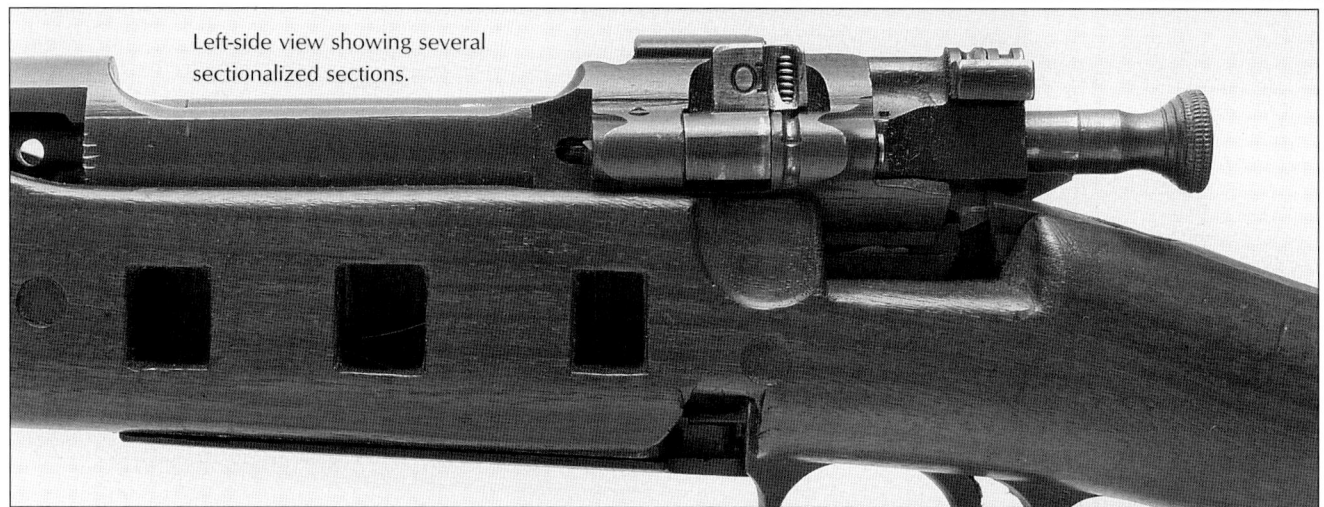

Left-side view showing several sectionalized sections.

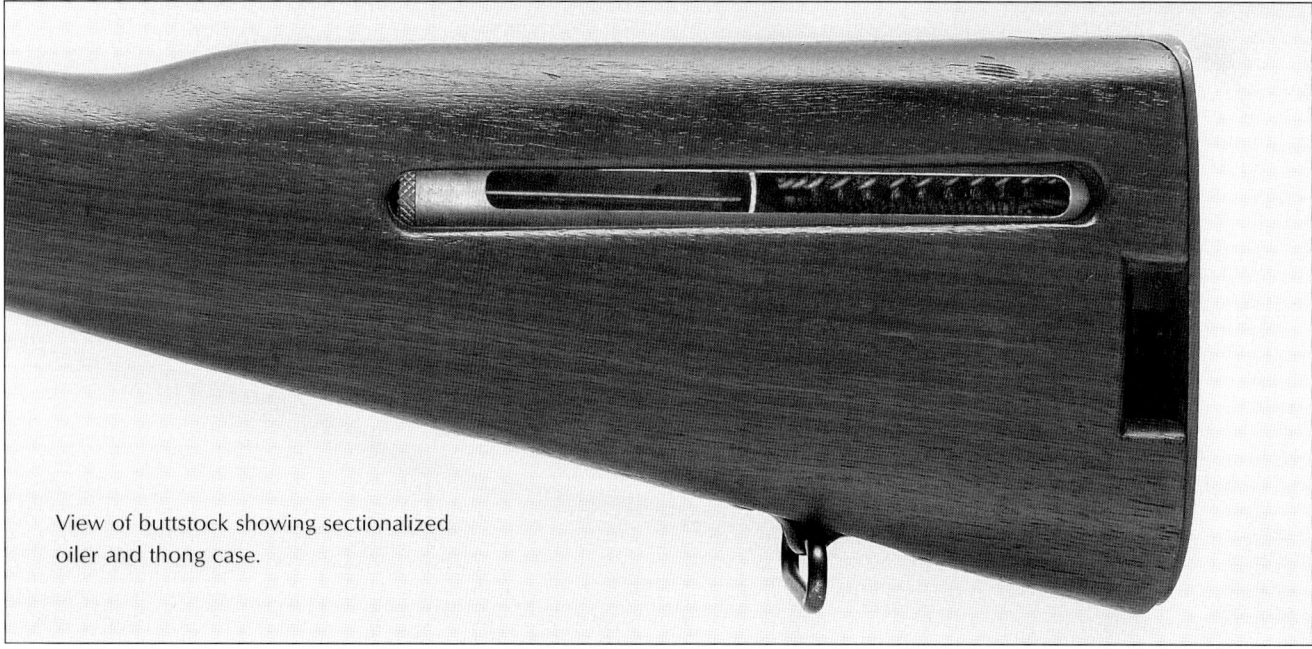

View of buttstock showing sectionalized oiler and thong case.

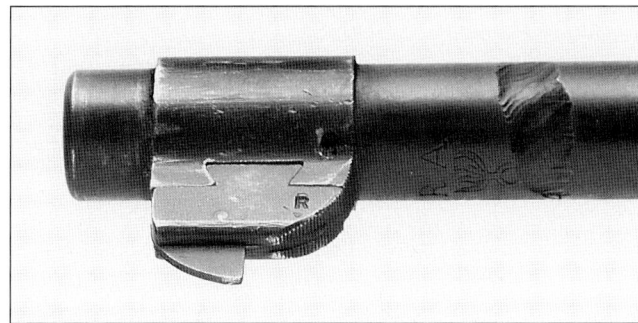

LEFT – Grinding mark on barrel which defaces the date. Note the "R" marking on the sight.
BELOW – World War II photograph of a typical arsenal rebuilt M1903 rifle. This weapon has a combination of early and late pattern parts typically found in such rifles refurbished during the Second World War. *(U.S. Army)*

Remington factory sectionalized rifle is a scarce item and a great addition to a collection.

The Remington M1903 and M1903 Modified rifles were urgently needed by the U.S. military to help arm our rapidly expanding forces. A relatively large number of these rifles were supplied to the U.S. Navy and Marine Corps and were soon in the thick of fighting in the Pacific. The Marines didn't officially adopt the M1 rifle until late 1941, and the Garands were in short supply in the U.S.M.C. larder until well into 1943. The Marines fought most of the early Pacific battles with M1903 rifles, both new-production Remingtons and the older Springfield or Rock Island rifles already in inventory. Many of these latter rifles were rebuilt by the Marines for use in WWII. Unlike the rifles rebuilt under U.S. Army Ordnance auspices, the Marine Corps rebuilds were not generally marked to indicate overhaul. Many of the new-production Remington '03s were also used as supplementary service rifles by the U.S. Army for training and for military aid requirements. A large number of these weapons were deployed to overseas combat zones in all theaters and saw action throughout the war. Remington received additional contracts from the Ordnance Department for rifle production, and the company searched for additional ways to speed production in order to meet the ever-increasing demand.

Remington Model 1903A3 Rifle

By spring 1942, Remington engineers had looked at every part of the rifle with an eye towards reducing production time and expense still further. The M1905 pattern rear sight was the only significant component that remained, more or less, unmodified from the pre-WWII M1903 rifle. Since the M1905 sight required a great deal of machining, especially the fixed base, a simplified sight would be of enormous benefit in Remington's quest to decrease production time and cost. It was recognized that a peep sight mounted on the rear of the receiver, thus closer to the eye, would offer advantages over the M1905 barrel-mounted sight. A simple rear sight with a sliding aperture was developed. The receiver was modified to incorporate a dovetail base for mounting the new sight.

The configuration of the new rear sight required that the rifle's front sight blade be increased in height from .477 inches to .537 inches. The new rear sight was somewhat similar to the adjustable sights used on later production M1 carbines.

Elimination of the barrel-mounted M1905 sight resulted in the handguard being replaced by a longer barrel guard which bridged the gap between the receiver ring and lower band that was previously occupied by the M1905 pattern rear sight base. The rear of the barrel guard was secured to the receiver ring by a sheet metal flange referred to as the barrel guard ring.

With the incorporation of the new sight and other alterations, the configuration of the rifle was sufficiently

Remington M1903A3 rifle with M1907 sling. (Right side)

Remington M1903A3 rifle. (Left side)

Remington M1903 rifle.

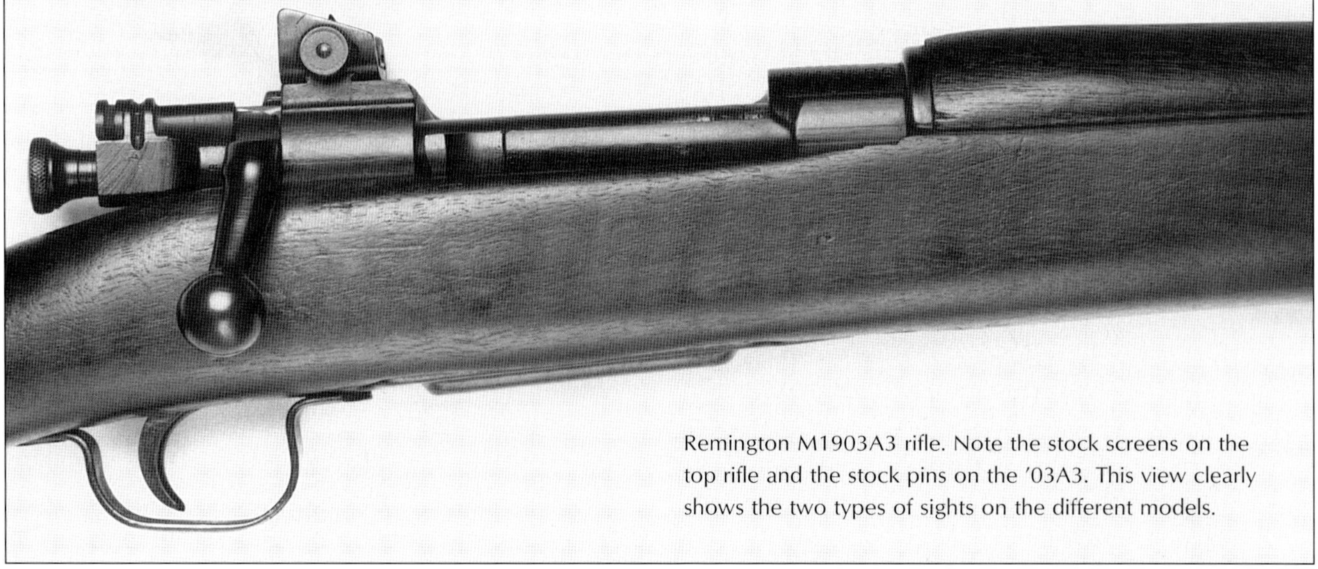

Remington M1903A3 rifle. Note the stock screens on the top rifle and the stock pins on the '03A3. This view clearly shows the two types of sights on the different models.

changed to require a new model designation, and the U.S. Rifle, Caliber .30, Model of 1903A3, was standardized on May 21, 1942. Remington received approval to convert production from the M1903 Modified to the M1903A3 a few weeks later. As Remington labored to switch manufacture to M1903A3, production of the M1903 Modified rifle continued. There were some delays in obtaining the new receiver-mounted M1903A3 rear sight from subcontractors, which delayed assembly of the new rifle. In order to continue production, some unfinished '03A3 receivers were modified by milling down the section of the bridge containing the dovetail sight base. The rifles can be easily identified because a vestige of the 'A3 dovetail base remained on the receiver bridge. Since the receivers had not yet been marked, they were roll-stamped with the same Model 1903 markings as the earlier M1903 Modified rifles. Such rifles are an interesting but relatively minor collector variant.

From December 1942 until March 1943, both M1903 Modified and M1903A3 rifles were manufactured concurrently by Remington (See **Table 10** on page 223). The first M1903A3 rifles were completed in December 1942. The final production of M1903 Modified rifles consisted of 105 rifles shipped from the factory in March 1943. There were 58,960 M1903A3 rifles made the same month.

The following characteristics will be found on Remington M1903A3 rifles:

Receivers

The most obvious difference between the M1903A3 receiver and the previous M1903 receivers was the modification of the receiver bridge for the rear sight base. The receiver ring was marked: "U.S./Remington/Model 03-A3/Serial number". The "03-A3" marking on the receiver is rather unusual as this is a colloquial term and not official nomenclature.

Receiver ring markings on Remington M1903A3 rifle.

The following blocks of serial numbers were eventually assigned to Remington:

3000000–3607999*
3708000–4707999** and
4992001–5784000***

* Remington M1903A3 production is estimated to have begun with serial number 3227503. Due to the overlap in production, M1903 Modified rifles will be encountered with higher serial numbers as evidenced by the fact that the last M1903 Modified receiver is believed to have been serial number 3386116. M1903 Modified and M1903A3 serial numbers were intermixed between 3222503 and 3386116 during this period. This includes the unfinished M1903A3 receivers with the dovetail base milled down for use in completing the M1903 Modified contracts. Initial production M1903A4 sniper rifles were also from this first block of serial numbers.

** Only a portion of this block was used for production and the highest serial number utilized is estimated to be approximately 4208782.

*** The only serial numbers used from this block were for the production of approximately 7,000 M1903A4 sniper rifles.

Note: The highest and lowest approximate serial numbers for each block are based on Campbell's estimates.

There were some receivers made by Remington with duplicate serial numbers. To distinguish these duplicate serial numbers, they were given a "Z" prefix. (See **Table 11**).

Barrels

Barrels had the same marking format applied behind the front sight as the M1903 Modified rifles; "RA/flaming bomb/month and year". The lack of polishing prior to parkerizing was even more pronounced than with the earlier Remington rifles, and machining chatter marks are common.

Four-groove barrels were used on M1903A3 rifles at the beginning of production. The Ordnance

Remington '03A3 barrel markings.

Department had considered the use of two-groove barrels since late 1941 as a method to further reduce machining time. Extensive testing at Frankford Arsenal and Aberdeen Proving Ground had determined that there was little degradation in accuracy with the two-groove barrels. The Ordnance Department approved the use of two-groove barrels in October 1942. By early 1943, Remington changed its tooling to make the simpler barrel, although both four-groove and two-groove barrels were used concurrently afterward. Two-groove barrels were also utilized for replacement M1917 rifle barrels made by other firms during this period.

Stocks

The M1903A3 stock was of the modified Type S variety without grasping grooves. The stock was inletted to provide clearance for the '03A3's barrel guard ring. It had provision for the M1905 rear sight base, so that this pattern stock could also be used as a replacement for earlier '03s for repair and/or overhaul. This is the only type of stock confirmed to have been used on production M1903A3 rifles. Some WWII-vintage scant grip and Type C stocks inletted for the 'A3 barrel guard ring may be encountered, but it is not believed these were used to assemble '03A3 rifles at the factory.

ABOVE – Stock inspection format as found on Remington M1903A3 and M1903A4 rifles. BELOW – Stock inspection format on Remington M1903 modified rifle.

Early production M1903A3 stocks had reinforcing pins, but stock screws were introduced later in production. There was some overlap in stocks made with pins and those made with screws, which makes it virtually impossible to identify the precise time period that the change took place.

The markings on the '03A3 stocks were similar to those found on late-production M1903 Modified rifles and consisted of "FJA" and the Ordnance Department crossed cannons escutcheon. Circa mid-1943, an "RA" stamp was added to the marking format to indicate Remington Arms. This was presumably done to help distinguish the stocks from Smith-Corona. Circled "P" proof firing marks continued to be stamped behind the triggerguard as were the geometric factory inspection symbols in front of the floorplate.

Handguards

The familiar '03 handguard used with the M1905 rear sight was replaced by a longer barrel guard.

Rear Sights

The receiver-mounted peep sight developed for the '03A3 rifle was adjustable for windage and elevation. The component was less expensive to manufacture than the rather complicated M1905 pattern sight. The placement of the '03A3 sight put it much closer to the eye, which made it a better combat sight than its predecessor.

Furniture

The stamped components of early and mid-production rifles were blued. Such parts including barrel bands, band springs, upper bands, buttplates, floorplate/magazine assemblies, some rear sight parts and other components such as screws and pins. Later in production, some of these parts, especially upper bands, were parkerized. Therefore, early-to-mid-production M1903A3 rifles will have blued furniture, while later-production rifles may have a mixture of blued and parkerized parts. If a rifle was subsequently overhauled, the furniture was typically parkerized. A collector wishing to have a rifle in its WWII configuration will look for blued furniture, since this would likely indicate that such a rifle had not been rebuilt/refinished. Many of the parts were marked "R" to denote manufacture by Remington Arms.

As production continued, the configuration of the triggerguard changed from a smaller opening to a somewhat larger opening. It has been suggested that the latter type of triggerguard was intended to offer greater utility in winter warfare when soldiers were wearing gloves. This is certainly possible, but documentation to suggest that this was the reason has not been discovered. More likely, it was a manufacturing change to simply make manipulation of the trigger easier. The precise time of the change is not known, but it likely occurred in mid-1943. The smaller and larger triggerguards were used concurrently for a period of time.

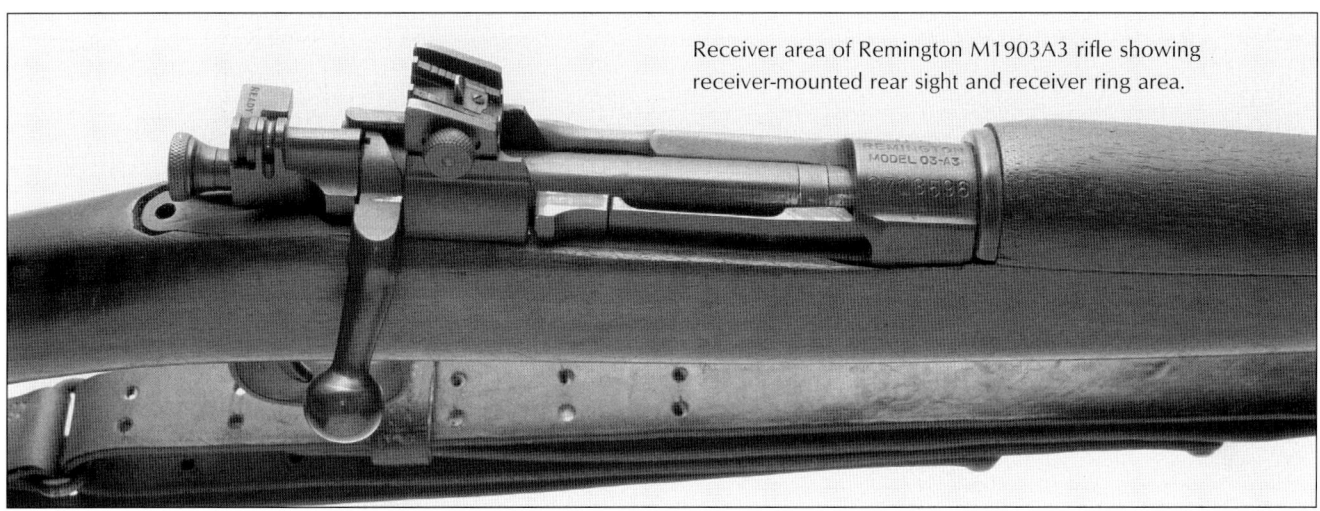

Receiver area of Remington M1903A3 rifle showing receiver-mounted rear sight and receiver ring area.

Finish

The M1903A3 rifles were finished in the same type of gray parkerizing as was used on the later-production M1903 Modified rifles. This finish often had a very distinctive greenish hue, primarily due to the effects of cosmoline or oil. The exact shade of the finish often varied as the parkerizing solution became diluted. When the solution was changed, the tint of the parkerizing could vary noticeably.

The new '03A3 rifle epitomized hasty wartime production, utilizing almost every conceivable manufacturing shortcut, and it showed! Aesthetically, the rough-hewn 'A3 was about as far from the finely crafted pre-WWII Springfield and Rock Island '03s as could be imagined. On the other hand, this was the height of the Second World War, and the nation was literally fighting for its very survival. Cosmetic touches were not as important as shipping as many serviceable rifles out of the plant as fast as possible. The '03A3s may have been rather unattractive and crudely made as compared to the earlier armory-made examples, but they were strong and serviceable rifles that met all requirements. Remington manufactured a total of 707,629 M1903A3 rifles by the time the company's outstanding production contracts were cancelled on February 28, 1944.

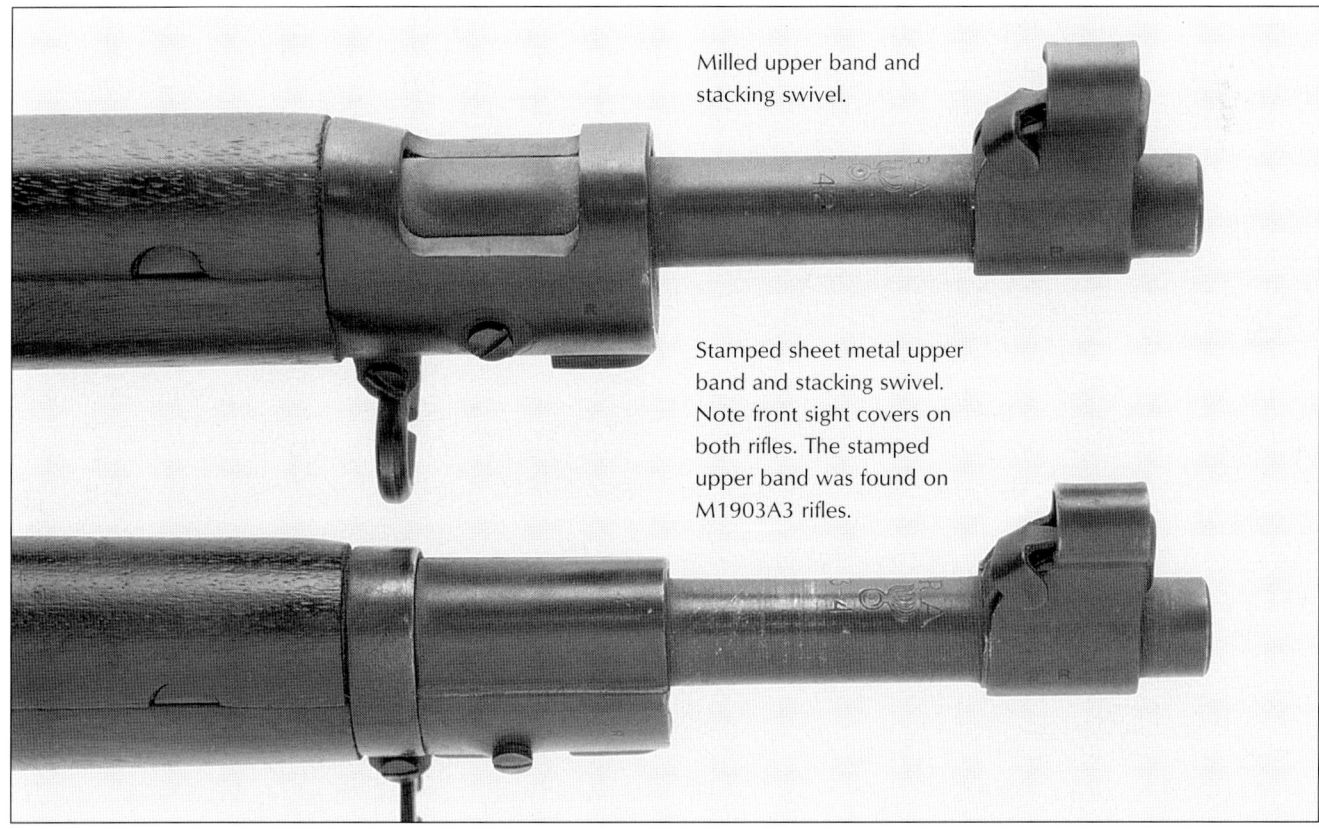

Milled upper band and stacking swivel.

Stamped sheet metal upper band and stacking swivel. Note front sight covers on both rifles. The stamped upper band was found on M1903A3 rifles.

M1903A4 Sniper's Rifle

Remington also manufactured a sniper rifle which was a slightly modified version of the M1903A3 beginning in early 1943. This weapon was standardized as the U.S. Rifle, Caliber .30, Model of 1903A4, Snipers. For the sake of continuity, this weapon will be fully discussed in the subsequent World War II M1903 Sniper Rifle section of this book.

Smith-Corona M1903A3 Rifle

Even with the myriad manufacturing shortcuts incorporated, the demand for additional rifles was outstripping Remington's production capacity. Other manufacturing entities were approached regarding M1903 rifle production. In January 1942, the Ordnance Department contracted with the New Haven, Connecticut, firm of High Standard Manufacturing Company for the production of 100,000 M1903A1 rifles.

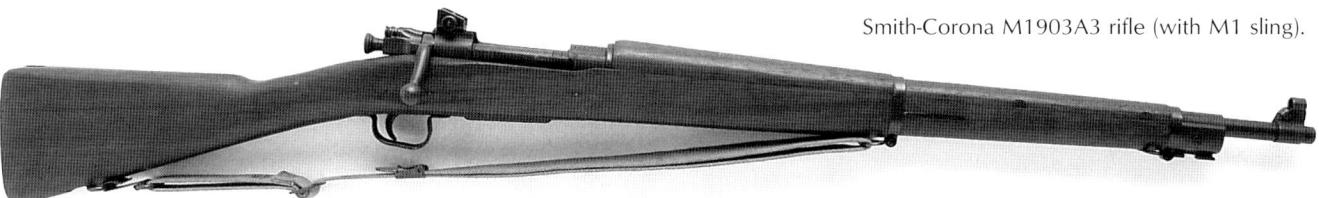

Smith-Corona M1903A3 rifle (with M1 sling).

High Standard was interested in obtaining the contract, but the company was already working at near-peak capacity with existing orders and was unable to serve as prime contractor for the project. The firm offered to accept the contract if it could manufacture only the barrels and then subcontract the remainder of production to the L.C. Smith & Corona Typewriter Company of Syracuse, New York. The Ordnance Department, understandably, believed that Smith-Corona should be named prime contractor of the project since that firm would be producing virtually all components as well as assembling the rifles. It was suggested that High Standard serve as subcontractor for the barrels. The fact that the Smith-Corona plant was located in fairly close geographic proximity to Remington would be conducive to cooperation between the two firms. All parties agreed to the proposal, and on February 25, 1942, Smith-Corona was granted a contract for rifle production. By this time, Remington was manufacturing the M1903 Modified rifle, and the contract specified this variant rather than the M1903A1 as originally intended. While Smith-Corona was in the process of acquiring the necessary equipment to begin production, the M1903 Modified rifle was superseded by the M1903A3. In May 1942, Smith-Corona's contract was changed to substitute the M1903A3 for the M1903 Modified and, subsequently, the initial order for 100,000 rifles was increased to 380,000.

The initial pilot batch of twenty S-C M1903A3 rifles was completed in October 1942, and delivery of completed rifles to the Ordnance Department occurred in November, a month ahead of Remington's delivery of '03A3 rifles. Production slowly increased, and by December some 5,540 rifles had been manufactured. As was the case at Remington, there were some problems encountered with procurement of the rear sights from subcontractors, which delayed initial deliveries. Sufficient quantities of the sights were eventually forthcoming, and soon, increasing numbers of S-C '03A3 rifles were flowing from the Syracuse plant. The Smith-Corona '03A3 rifles were similar to those made by Remington, but differed in some aspects that are mainly of interest to collectors today. The pertinent features of the S-C rifle are as follows:

Receivers

Receivers are marked "U.S./Smith-Corona/Model 03-A3/Serial #". Two serial number blocks were eventually assigned to S-C for '03A3 production:

3608000– 3707999 and 4708000–4992000*

*According to Campbell, the highest serial number used by Smith-Corona was 4845831.

Receiver markings on Smith-Corona M1903A3 rifle.

Apparently, Remington overran their first block of serial numbers and produced and estimated 3,600 '03A3 receivers in Smith-Corona's serial number block. The duplicate Smith-Corona serial numbers were given a "C" prefix for identification and inventory control. (See **Table 12**).

Barrels

Barrels were marked "SC" over a flaming bomb and the month/year of manufacture. Unlike the Remington which only made two- or four-groove '03A3 barrels, the situation with Smith-Corona barrels was not nearly as straightforward. High Standard Manufacturing Company was to furnish barrels to S-C, but was faced with a shortage of barrel blanks. To fulfill its commitments, High Standard procured several thousand unfinished blanks from the Savage Arms Company. The Savage blanks were intended for commercial production rifles and were of the six-groove variety. In order to expedite the delivery of Smith-Corona rifles, the Ordnance Department granted a waiver for the use of such non-standard barrels. High Standard finished the barrels and marked them "SC" to indicate Smith-Corona as the prime contractor. The use of the six-groove barrels permitted High Standard to deliver barrels to S-C much faster than would have been otherwise possible. The number of six-groove barrels used in Smith-Corona '03A3 production is not known, but is estimated to be about 5,000. The utilization of the six-groove barrels allowed High Standard to fulfill contractual commitments, and the firm began production of the standard four-groove barrels for use on subsequent rifles.

The four-groove barrels made by High Standard for Smith-Corona were marked in the same manner as the earlier six-groove barrels. It is a little-known fact that S-C used some two-groove barrels for a brief period of time. All such examples noted have been dated 11-43. The source of these barrels, or the reason for such short-lived use, is not known. For a collector who might choose to specialize in Smith-Corona '03A3 rifles, the three distinct types of barrels; six-groove, four-groove, and two-groove, would make interesting subvariants. The vast majority of S-C rifles will have four-groove barrels. In addition to the M1903A3

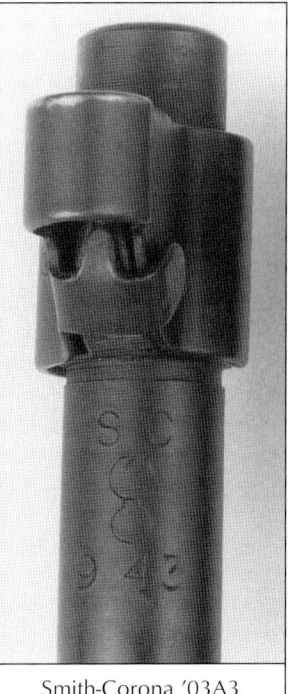

Smith-Corona '03A3 barrel markings

barrels, High Standard also made a number of four-groove M1903 barrels for replacement purposes. These barrels were marked "HS", and most were dated between mid- to late-1944. A number of these High Standard barrels were utilized on M1903 rifles overhauled after WWII.

Stocks

Smith-Corona stocks were primarily of the pinned variety, although stock screws were used on some examples. The inspection marking format on the left side of the stock was the same as found on the Remington '03A3 rifles, except for the lack of the "RA" stamp. Similar sub-inspection markings to those found on Remington rifles were also stamped in front of the floorplate. These typically consisted of four geometric symbols; a triangle, diamond, square, and circle. The symbols will normally contain a one- or two-digit number. Remington stocks usually had between four and twelve such symbols. Some Smith-Corona stocks were also stamped on the bottom, behind the lower barrel band, with a two-digit number.

Stock markings on Smith-Corona M1903A3 rifle. Note the lack of "RA" marking and the configuration of the Frank J. Atwood ("FJA") and Ordnance Dept. escutcheon stamps. Note also the stock *pin* rather than stock screw.

Bottom of Smith-Corona M1903A3 rifle. Note the four sub-inspection symbols and the configuration of the stamped floorplate assembly.

Although similar in configuration, there are several rather subtle differences between the Smith-Corona and Remington stocks. For example, the Remington '03A3 rifles were stamped with a $7/16$-inch circled "P" proof mark, while the S-C rifles had a $1/2$-inch proof stamp. Also, the recess for the lower band spring had a rounded profile on the Smith-Corona stocks, and a square profile on the RA stocks.

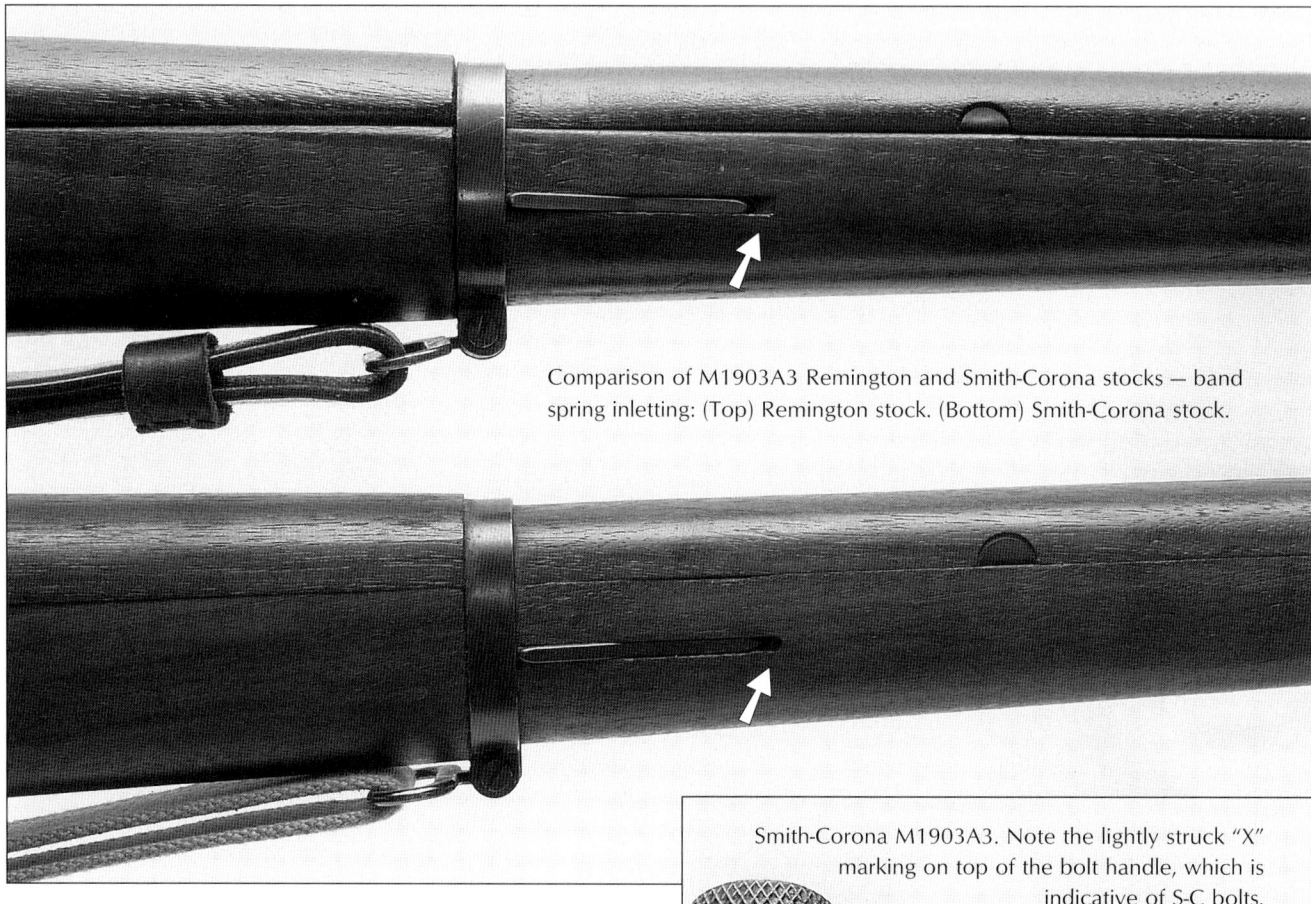

Comparison of M1903A3 Remington and Smith-Corona stocks — band spring inletting: (Top) Remington stock. (Bottom) Smith-Corona stock.

Smith-Corona M1903A3. Note the lightly struck "X" marking on top of the bolt handle, which is indicative of S-C bolts.

Finish

Smith-Corona were parkerized in the same manner as the Remington '03A3 rifles.

Rear Sights

No discernable differences between RA and S-C rear sights.

Bolts

The major difference between Remington and Smith-Corona bolts were the markings. Remington bolts were marked "R" at the root whereas the Smith-Corona bolts were usually marked with an "X" on top of the bolt handle, although some unmarked examples may be found. Some sources have incorrectly stated that original Smith-Corona rifles may be encountered with "CC"-marked bolts (made by Commercial Controls) or "BF"-marked bolts (made by Bonney Forge). Such bolts were used for rebuild purposes or for spare parts but were not utilized on production rifles. Some bolts may also be encountered that are marked "BP".

These were manufactured by the firm of Brown Precision and, like the "CC" and "BF" bolts, were replacement components. There was often a single-digit number stamped on the root of the bolt, below the handle. Any bolt found on a Smith-Corona rifle, other than one marked "X" on top of the bolt handle, or unmarked, is a replacement and not a factory original component. Some extractors found on original Smith-Corona bolts were marked "S" on the bottom. Although it might be a logical assumption, these parts were not made by Springfield Armory. Smith-Corona bolts had a distinctive scalloped profile to the sleeve and safety lug. Some of the bolt sleeves were marked "G". Original bolts were blued and a parkerized bolt, even with proper markings, can be assumed to have been refinished, likely as part of an overhaul procedure.

Furniture

Smith-Corona and Remington rifles used the same type of stamped parts. Unlike some Remington parts, which were stamped "R", the majority of Smith-Corona parts were unmarked. A few Smith-Corona parts were marked "G". It has been theorized that these "G"-marked components were produced by a Smith-Corona-affiliated plant in Groton, Connecticut, but this has not been confirmed. Factory original Smith-Corona rifles will not have any "R"-marked parts. Any such parts found on S-C rifles were installed at some point after the rifle left the factory, usually as part of a rebuild.

Another difference between Remington and Smith-Corona was the checkering pattern on the buttplates. Remington buttplates had 16 squares to the inch while Smith-Corona buttplates had 10 or 11 squares per inch. As was the case with Remington, most of the S-C stamped parts were blued including barrel bands, band springs, screws, pins, floorplate/magazine assemblies and buttplates. Some later production parts, especially upper bands, may have been parkerized. Parkerized furniture is the norm on overhauled rifles. An easy rule of thumb to remember is that an original Smith-Corona '03A3 rifle will not have any "R"-marked parts. **Table 13** details the differences between Remington and Smith-Corona '03A3 rifles.

Another difference between RA and SC M1903A3, albeit rather minor, was the configuration of the stamped and welded triggerguard/magazine assembly behind the front screw hole. The Remington component has a straight profile whereas the Smith-Corona part has a semi-circular indention.

Smith-Corona manufactured a total of 234,580 M1903A3 rifles by the time the firm's contract was cancelled on February 19, 1944. Despite the fact that Remington manufactured over three times the number of '03A3 rifles as Smith-Corona, there is typically not a huge price disparity between examples made by the two firms.

Smith-Corona rifles will often bring a premium over Remington rifles, assuming comparable condition and degree of originality, but the premium is seldom large.

M1903A3 rifles, both Remington and Smith-Corona, are more often found today in excellent or better condition

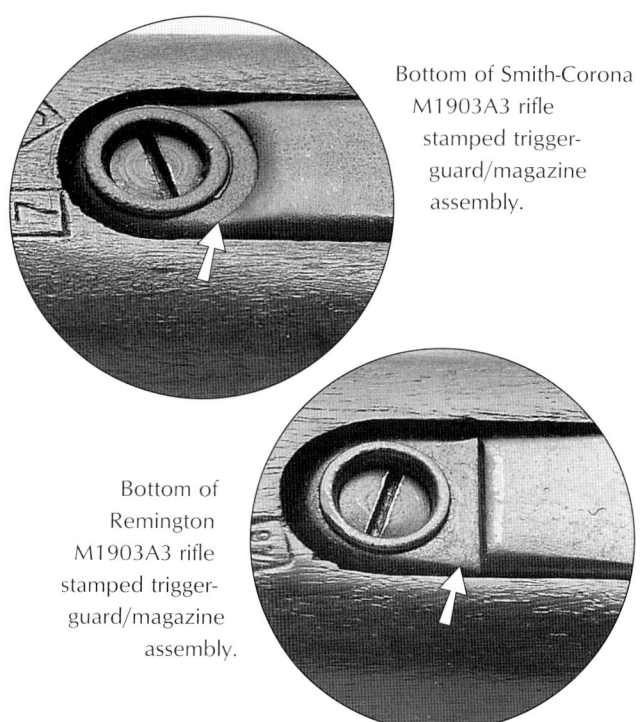

Bottom of Smith-Corona M1903A3 rifle stamped trigger-guard/magazine assembly.

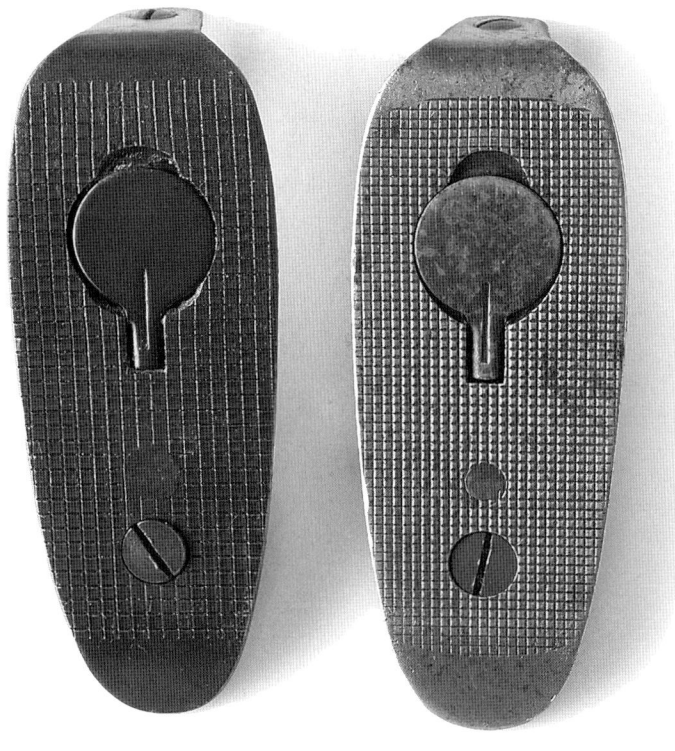

Bottom of Remington M1903A3 rifle stamped trigger-guard/magazine assembly.

Smith-Corona M1903A3 buttplate.

Remington M1903A3 buttplate.

than earlier production M1903 variants. Following WWII, large numbers of these rifles were sent to various ordnance facilities for inspection and overhaul prior to being placed in long-term storage, or offered for sale through the auspices of the DCM (Director of Civilian Marksmanship). Some of these rifles were in new condition when they were received by the ordnance facilities and may have only received an inspection and stamped with the initials of the ordnance facility. Apparently Ogden Arsenal (Utah) performed such inspections on large numbers of new or near-new '03A3 rifles. It is not uncommon to find rifles in pristine condition with an "OG" stamp on the stock, but which, otherwise, remain in their original factory condition. Rifles in similar condition with other arsenal stamps, especially Raritan Arsenal (RA-P), may also be encountered. Some people have acquired M1903A3 rifles that appear to be unfired and covered in cosmoline, and assume these to be factory original rifles. In most cases, such rifles are actually rebuilt examples that have not been used since being overhauled after the war. This can usually be verified by arsenal inspection markings on the stock, the presence of parts with mixed contractor codes, and parkerized furniture. Large number of surplus M1903A3 rifles, and other weapons in all grades of condition, were sold under the auspices of the DCM after WWII.

The Remington and Smith-Corona M1903A3 rifles provided yeoman-like service to our armed forces during the Second World War. There are some misconceptions and erroneous assumptions regarding the utilization of these rifles during WWII.

Ogden Arsenal (Utah) inspection stamp on stock. Some M1903A3 rifles (among other weapons) may be found with this stamp but which otherwise remain in their original factory configuration.

WWII U.S. Army 101st Airborne troops in glider. The soldier in the left foreground is carrying a M1903A3 rifle. Other weapons in the glider include an M1 Thompson submachine gun, M1918A2 BAR, M1A1 bazooka and several M1 rifles. *(U.S. Army)*

U.S. Army troops in Burma, 1945, firing at Japanese from a hill top position. Note the M1903A3 rifle at left and a M1903A4 rifle (with Weaver scope) in center, which illustrates the fact that some M1903A3 rifles were utilized as front line combat weapons. *(U.S. Army)*

Some people have stated that the '03A3 rifles were never issued or were restricted solely to stateside training use. This is incorrect. Although not used for overseas combat duty in the same numbers as M1 rifles, or even the earlier M1903 variants, some M1903A3 rifles did, in fact, see such action. Numerous WWII-vintage photos depict '03A3 rifles employed in overseas combat zones. Military Police (MPs) and other ostensibly noncombat military personnel were issued M1903A3 rifles, but the weapons were also employed by front line combat infantrymen. In virtually all theaters of the war, '03A3 rifles are confirmed to have been used in combat including the European, Mediterranean and C-B-I (China-Burma-India). Large numbers were also utilized for stateside training and for supplementary use by sentries and other personnel. Despite the shortcuts employed in the manufacture, the M1903A3 rifles were every bit as serviceable as the better-finished earlier production rifles. The 'A3s had strong nickel steel receivers, and the rear sights were actually better for combat use than the older M1905 pattern sights. M1903A3 rifles are among the most common variant of the '03 available to collectors, and examples can usually be found without too much difficulty, although prices for pristine examples are steadily rising.

M1903A2

Although outside the scope of this book, brief mention should be made of the M1903A2. Some people have seen this nomenclature and wondered exactly what constitutes an M1903A2, given the fact that the M1903A1 and M1903A3 rifles are so well known. The 'A2 was basically a M1903 barreled action with brass-mounting inserts added, for use as a subcaliber training device for anti-tank guns and/or artillery pieces. It did not have a stock and was not intended for use as a shoulder weapon. Surviving examples are uncommon and do not typically garner a great deal of collector interest.

Other WWII M1903 Procurement

Even with the new production of '03 and '03A3 rifles from Remington and Smith-Corona, there was still a need for additional serviceable weapons during the hectic early days of the Second World War. The M1903 rifles that were overhauled after WWI were taken from storage and issued to help arm our rapidly expanding armed forces. Many of the M1917 rifles left over from the war were refurbished and utilized for military aid purposes and for limited issuance as supplemental service rifles.

World War II-Assembled M1903A1 Rifles

By 1940, Springfield Armory's primary focus was production of the M1 rifle, and much of the overhaul work ceased at the armory. A large supply (estimated to be 200,000) of unused '03 rifle receivers that had been manufactured as spare parts since the late 1920s were still in inventory at Springfield. These receivers, along with various and sundry '03 parts on hand, were shipped to Raritan Arsenal (New Jersey) for assembly into complete rifles, primarily of the M1903A1 pattern. Some leftover Type C stocks were sent from Springfield, and large numbers of new production stocks were procured from contractors. About half of these newly assembled M1903A1 rifles were sent to China immediately after Pearl Harbor, and the remaining rifles were utilized by American armed forces.

Identifying one of these WWII M1903A1 rifles can be tricky, as there was a lot of inconsistency in the type of parts used to assemble the rifles. Receivers were made by Springfield Armory between circa 1927 through the late 1930s. Most barrels were newly made replacement components dated in the very early 1940s, although some earlier barrels were likely used as well. Stocks were of the full pistol grip Type C variety and could be either prewar Armory-made type or early WWII contractor-made stocks. While these M1903A1 rifles assembled from parts marginally helped, the U.S. military was still faced with a potential serious shortage of military rifles in the early days of the war.

U.S. Marine Corps WWII M1903 Rifles

The Marine Corps always believed it was on the short end of the stick regarding the acquisition of weaponry and other material, often with just cause for this belief. Like the other branches of our armed forces, the Marines were faced with shortages of all types of weapons early in the war. Although the Marine Corps had adopted the semi-automatic M1 rifle in late 1941, almost none of the new rifles were in its inventory, and the M1903 was still *the* Marine Corps rifle at the beginning of WWII. Even though some of the early production Remington M1903 and M1903 Modified rifles are believed to have been acquired by the Marines, many of the '03s utilized by the Corps were already in inventory prior to the war. Many of these rifles required varying degrees of refurbishment to put them back into shape for issuance to combat troops.

The '03 rifles refurbished under U.S.M.C. auspices in the early days of WWII can vary from example to example, which makes positive identification of a particular rifle quite problematical. Any weapon with a known or even suspected Marine Corps provenance is very popular with some collectors. Unfortunately, except in rare cases, there is no paperwork extant, such as bills of sale and the like, to confirm that a specific '03 rifle was previously used by the Marines. Having said this, there are some features commonly found on the rifles refurbished under U.S.M.C. auspices in the early part of WWII. These include:

- A smooth buttplate that has been stippled by a punch to help prevent slipping from the shoulder.
- The serial number of the receiver was often engraved on the top of the bolt body by an electric pen. Some of the bolts were polished and subsequently blued.
- A replacement barrel, either made by Sedgley (marked with a circled "S" and "U.S.M.C." and dated 1941, 1942 or possibly 1943) or Springfield Armory. Most of the Springfield barrels used were newly made components, often dated late 1940.
- A Hatcher Hole added to pre-1936-vintage receivers. Receivers can be of any vintage, and many low-numbered examples were retained and used by the Marines.
- The receiver will sometimes evidence a punch mark applied in front of the serial number.
- Some of the rifles were reparkerized. The resulting finish sometimes had an unusual yellowish cast that was noticeably different from the parkerizing normally used on '03s and other U.S. military rifles of the period. Many U.S.M.C.-rebuilt rifles, however, had typical black, gray or gray/green parkerizing.
- Existing stocks were used, if serviceable, or the rifles were fitted with newly made replacement stocks. No special inspection or proof markings were applied. Any stock marked "U.S.M.C." encountered today has almost certainly had a fake stamp applied. Many rifles with the special U.S.M.C. No. 10 sights installed after WWI had the sights removed and replaced by the standard variety, although a few retained the special sights during the Second World War.
- The Sedgley barrels were procured by the Marine Corps for rebuilding purposes, but many were never utilized for this purpose and remained unused until disposed of after WWII. "U.S.M.C."-marked Sedgley barrels dated as late as 1944 have been observed. These late-production examples were not used by the Marines, but some were apparently diverted to U.S. Army Ordnance. Many were demilled after the war by bending the barrels. A late-vin-

tage U.S.M.C. Sedgley barrel should be carefully examined to make sure that it has not been previously de-milled and subsequently straightened. Such reclaimed barrels could be quite dangerous. It should be remembered that the later the vintage of a Sedgley barrel, the less likely it was used by the Marines for rebuild purposes.

The absence of these or any of the above features, with the possible exception of the Hatcher Hole, does not necessarily rule out a specific rifle as being a former U.S.M.C. weapon. By the same token, the presence of one or more of these features does not, by any means, positively identify a particular rifle as being one of the desirable Marine Corps '03s, as it is quite easy for a con artist to stipple a buttplate or engrave a serial number on a bolt.

The Marines made good use of their '03s in the early Pacific battles, such as Guadalcanal. Despite the Marine Corps' legendary fondness for their '03s, and the initial reluctance to adopt a new rifle, the attributes of the semi-automatic M1 were too great to overlook, and a number of Leathernecks desired to get their hands on one of the Garands. One slightly amusing example of this was related in the book by U.S. Army Colonel John George, *Shots Fired in Anger*:

"I saw this Marine, a member of the 2nd Raider Battalion, place and keep himself squarely behind one of the army sergeants in the advance platoon. When the march was well underway the sergeant inquired as to why the leatherneck kept treading on his heels.

The answer came quickly: 'You'll probably get yours on the first burst, Mac. Before you hit the ground I'll throw this damn Springfield away and grab your rifle."

This sentiment was echoed the following narrative:

"...By the time we landed (on Guadalcanal) we had to keep ours (M1s) tied down by wire. Leathernecks were appropriating all they could lay their hands on by 'moonlight requisition.' In daylight, they would come over to our areas and barter souvenirs with freshly landed doughboy units; any crooked supply sergeant who had an extra M1 could get all the loot he wanted.

"When the Marines began to get a few Garands up to the front the demand proportionally increased. They quickly learned that the M1 did not jam any more often than the Springfield, and that it was equally easy to maintain."

Marine cleaning his '03 on Guadalcanal. *(U.S. Marine Corps)*

Three brothers from Glendale, California. (Left to right) Al, John and Walt Madden —South Pacific, 1943 with M1903 rifles. *(U.S.M.C. Photo courtesy Alec Tulkoff)*

Interesting view of M1903 rifles in U.S. Navy arms room. Note how the rifles are placed in the rack to conserve space and the helmets arrayed above. The sailor appears to be checking the barrel with a bore light. *(National Archives - courtesy Martin K.A. Morgan)*

By 1943, the Marine Corps was fairly well equipped with M1 rifles, as evidenced by a Marine Corps memo dated January 26, 1943, which stated:

"M1 rifles are now being received at a rate that will not only permit the equipping of all new Fleet arine Force organizations but the gradual replacement of M1903 rifles now in the hands of other units. M1903 rifles, as received, will be turned over to the Navy."

Even though the M1 was the predominate rifle in Marine Corps service after 1943, a number of the reliable old '03s remained in service through the end of the war. While the majority of combat troops, Army and Marines, wanted the semiautomatic M1, some preferred the '03 for several reasons including familiarity, reliability and accuracy.

Rifle Grenade Launchers

Even though the M1 was clearly a more modern and effective service rifle compared to the '03, there were some problems encountered with developing a satisfactory rifle grenade launcher for the Garand due to its gas system. This was not a problem with the bolt-action '03, and a grenade launcher, standardized as the M1, was developed and issued with the '03 throughout WWII. Even when American infantry units were fully equipped with M1 rifles, an '03 equipped with an M1 launcher was found in most infantry squads. This resulted in a new lease on life for the '03 in its role as a rifle grenade launcher. The M1 launcher used with the '03 rifle will be discussed in the World War II Accessories, Accouterments and Appendages section.

Bushmaster Carbine

A little-known variant of the '03 that saw a modicum of use in WWII was the so-called Bushmaster carbine. This was simply a standard '03 rifle that had the barrel and stock cut-down to make it handier as a jungle warfare weapon. Government records reflect that 4,725 such rifles were converted to this type of carbine configuration under the auspices of the U.S. Army Panama Canal Department in early 1942. These barrels were cut down to 18 inches, and the stocks and handguards shortened correspondingly. Judging from extant photos, the workmanship was a bit on the crude side. The weapons were utilized for training in the Panama Canal Zone by the troops of the Caribbean Defense Combat who called themselves the Bushmasters. These modified rifles have been dubbed *Bushmasters* by collectors because of their utilization by the troops in Panama, but this was never any sort of official nomenclature. The weapons were not used in any other theater and saw no combat use. The weapons remained in use in Panama until replaced by M1 carbines in late 1944.

The Bushmaster rifles on hand were ordered sent to Raritan Arsenal where they were destroyed. According to a War Department memorandum dated May 1945, the weapons were dumped in the ocean.

Surviving examples are rare, and positive identification is virtually impossible. The weapons were not in any particular serial number block, and serial numbers ranged from as low as 6383 to as high as 1467501. The fact that there were no distinguishing features and the fact that even the originals were rather crudely modified, means that it would be quite easy to cutdown a standard M1903 to approximate the configuration of one of these weapons. Therefore, it would be unwise to pay any sort of premium for an example without some sort of convincing documentation to prove or strongly suggest that the weapon is legitimate.

Bushmaster '03 carbine. (U.S. Army)

World War II Sniper Rifles

In addition to its widespread employment as a platform for launching rifle grenades, the '03's effective life during WWII was also extended due to the weapon's utilization as a sniper rifle.

At the time of our entrance into the Second World War, the U.S. Army did not have a telescopic-sighted sniper rifle in its inventory since the M1903/Warner & Swasey sniper rifles had been discarded in the 1920s. This glaring omission was soon recognized early in WWII as requests for sniper rifles came in from all fronts. The Ordnance Department evaluated the various available options and quickly determined that developing a sniper version of the M1 Garand would be a time-consuming proposition due to the top-loading feature of the weapon. Development of a sniping version of the M1 was begun, but there was a clear need for a sniper rifle that could be manufactured, and fielded, in short order. To this end, in January 1943, the War Department negotiated with Remington Arms Company for the diversion of 20,000 M1903 rifles for conversion to sniper configuration. Shortly afterward, the M1903A3 rifle went into production, and the order was changed to specify a sniping version of that weapon instead. In reality, Remington Arms was not overly excited about manufacturing the new sniper rifle, as the company feared it would interfere with existing contractual commitments for production of the M1903A3. Remington proposed to the Ordnance Department that the company's bolt-action Model 720 rifle be considered for the new sniper rifle instead. Remington still had the Model 720 production equipment available, and there were some 4,000 of the rifles on hand at the factory. This proposal was flatly rejected by the Ordnance Department and soon afterward the U.S. Navy purchased the entire stock of Model 720 rifles from Remington. The Ordnance Department wanted the new sniper rifle to be based on the M1903A3, Remington's protestations notwithstanding.

Remington M1903A4 Sniper Rifles

The new sniper rifle was standardized as the *U.S. Rifle, Caliber .30, M1903A4, Snipers*. These rifles retained the "'03-A3" marking, but the marking was applied to the extreme left side of the receiver ring so as to be visible with the scope mount in place. The serial number was applied to the extreme right of the receiver ring for the same reason. The receiver was drilled and tapped so that a telescope mount could be installed. The front sight of the rifle was not fitted, but the milling cuts for the sight were present. It has been stated that the "'03-A3" markings and the milling cuts for the front sight were retained so that any rifles proving insufficiently accurate for sniping use could be easily converted to service rifle configuration by simply removing the telescope mount and installing a front and rear sight. The bolt of the '03A4 sniper rifle was concavely forged to provide clearance for the telescope, and a corresponding notch was cut into the stock so that the bolt could be properly seated. Otherwise, the new sniper rifle was essentially identical to the M1903A3 service rifle.

The Ordnance Department assumed the responsibility of providing telescopes and stocks to Remington for the new sniper rifle. There have been differing opinions on whether or not the M1903A4 rifle had higher manufacturing standards than M1903A3 rifles. As researcher William Hansen relates:

"...there were definitely different performance specifications established for the M1903A4 as opposed to the M1903A3. For example, the original specifications for the 'Snipers' rifle barrel allowed them to be selected from regular barrel production, however they were to be especially chosen '...for any items which would affect shooting, such as smoothness of bore and chamber, correct sizes of bore and chamber, etc.'...

"It is also interesting that the original Remington records estimated the cost variance for furnishing the 'Snipers' rifle to be '...an increase in the net factory cost of the Snipers Rifle of approximately $1.90 per

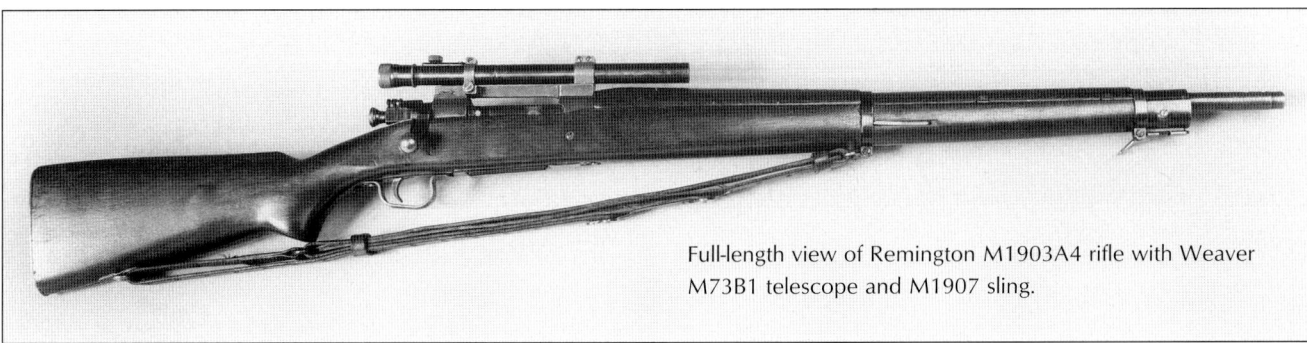

Full-length view of Remington M1903A4 rifle with Weaver M73B1 telescope and M1907 sling.

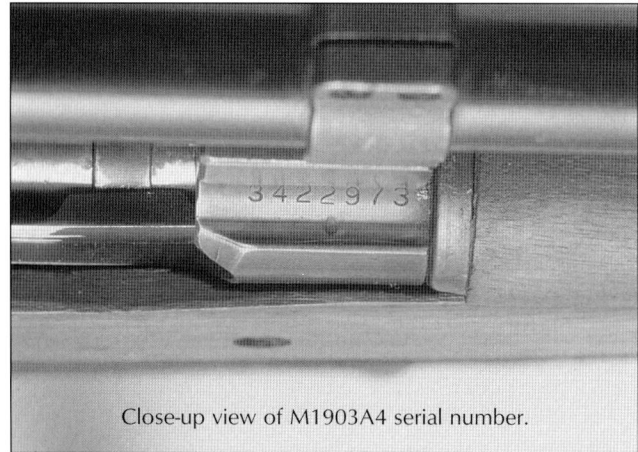
Close-up view of M1903A4 serial number.

ABOVE – Close-up view of M1903A4 receiver ring showing retention of "03-A3" nomenclature. Note how markings are applied to extreme left side of receiver ring.

LEFT – View showing Weaver 330-M8 scope. Note "Redfield" markings on mount and the configuration of the altered bolt handle and "R" marking on bolt sleeve.

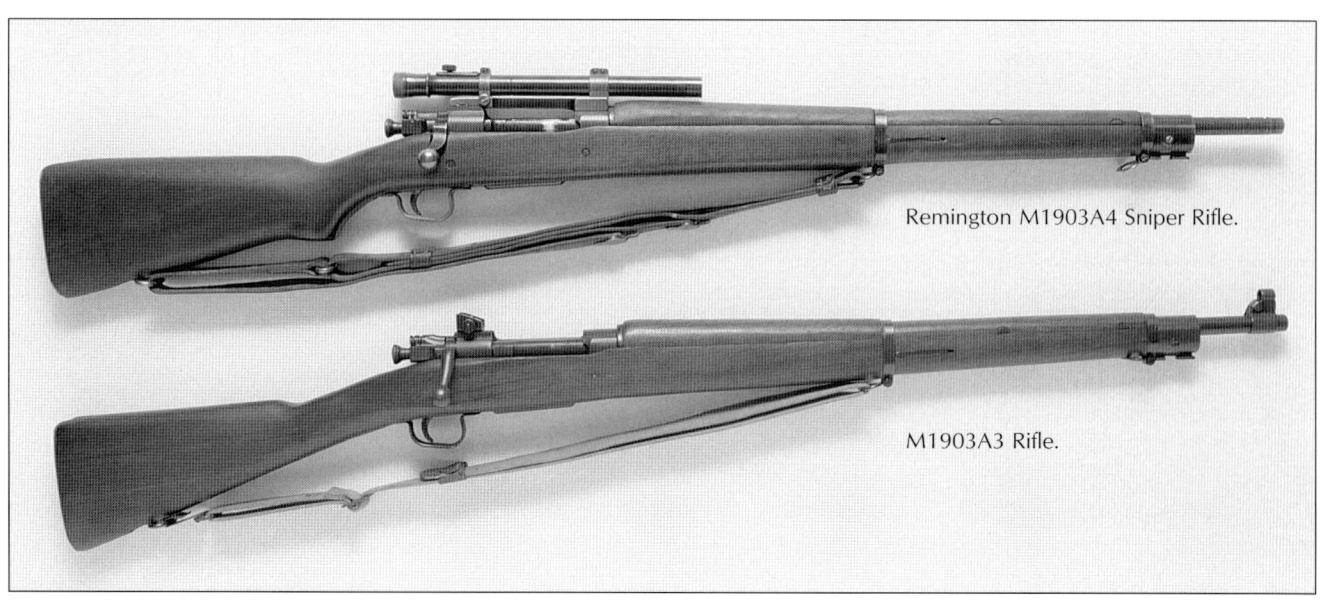

Remington M1903A4 Sniper Rifle.

M1903A3 Rifle.

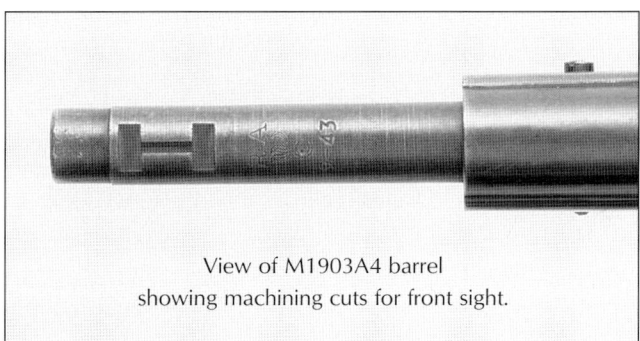

View of M1903A4 barrel showing machining cuts for front sight.

rifle over the regular cost of the M1903A3'. This isn't much of a change by today's prices of course, but you've got to remember that RA (Remington Arms) wasn't responsible for providing either the scopes or the stocks."

Telescopes

Obviously, one of the most crucial components of the new sniper rifle was the telescopic sight. The Infantry Board conducted tests on several types of civilian telescopes and selected the W.R. Weaver Company's 330C and the Lyman Gun Sight Corporation's Alaskan telescopes as the best suited for the new sniper rifle. It was originally envisioned that the readily available Weaver scopes, which could be purchased literally off the shelf, would initially be used with the 'A4 sniper rifle until the Lyman scopes became available in sufficient quantity.

Although the Alaskan was assigned the military designation of M73, Lyman was unable to supply the scope to the government in any meaningful quantity at that time. This was due to prior contractual commitments and a shortage of the special polarized lens supplied by its subcontractor, the Bausch and Lomb Company. Therefore, except for a handful procured for evaluation purposes, none of the Lyman scopes were issued with the 'A4 rifles. The Alaskan telescopes were officially designated as Substitute Standard. Although some WWII ordnance manuals illustrate M1903A4 rifles fitted with Alaskan scopes, and 2,000 sets of Lyman rings were purchased by the government, the Weaver was the only telescope actually issued with the 'A4 rifle during the war.

The Weaver 330C was a popular civilian hunting telescope that was available in sufficient numbers from the Weaver firm, and from commercial wholesalers and other suppliers, to meet the initial demand. The scope was of 2.5X power, with a cross-hair reticle and finger-adjustable windage and elevation knobs. The Weaver firm made several types of similar scopes, but the 330C was the type approved for issue with the '03A4 rifle. The 330C was given the military designation M73B1, and many of these scopes procured by the government had this nomenclature, and a serial number, hand-etched on the tube by an electro-pencil. The government ordered additional scopes from Weaver, and those manufactured directly under government contract had the M73B1 nomenclature stamped on the adjustment knob plate. A serial number was generally

Close-up view of M1903A4 rifle with Weaver M73B1 telescope and Redfield *Junior* mount.

electro-penciled on the tube as well. The serial number applied to the scope had no relation to the rifle serial number and was merely a means of inventory control.

A few M73B1 telescopes were fabricated by Frankford Arsenal and, except for the markings on the tube, the Frankford scopes appear to be identical to the Weaver M73B1s. Original examples of Frankford Arsenal M73B1 scopes are rare. Some Weaver 330-M8 telescopes were also procured for issue with the M1903A4 rifles. The numbers purchased, or the time period they were employed in the war, is not known, but the M8 scopes were certainly procured in much smaller numbers than the 330C/M73B1 scopes. The major difference between the two variants was that the M8 had screwdriver-adjustable knobs. Most M8 scopes originally had a tapered-post reticle rather than cross-hairs.

A leather dust cover (lens cap) was issued with the Weaver scopes. The Ordnance Department contracting officer assigned to the Remington plant requested on March 22, 1943, that the first "...26,000 Leather Telescope Covers be purchased from Lyon and Coulson, Buffalo, New York, at $0.32 each." Perhaps surprisingly, there were contractual difficulties and production delays with this seemingly simple accessory as well. The contractor experienced problems with quality control and many of the leather covers were rejected by inspectors. Acceptable covers were reportedly stamped with a flaming bomb insignia on the connecting strap. Original leather covers are uncommon today but some reproductions may be encountered. Postwar covers consisted of two plastic caps connected by a nylon cord.

The W.R. Weaver Company was never intended to be the sole supplier of telescopes for the M1903A4 rifle, but that turned out to be the case due to the inability of Lyman to provide Alaskan scopes in sufficient numbers. The

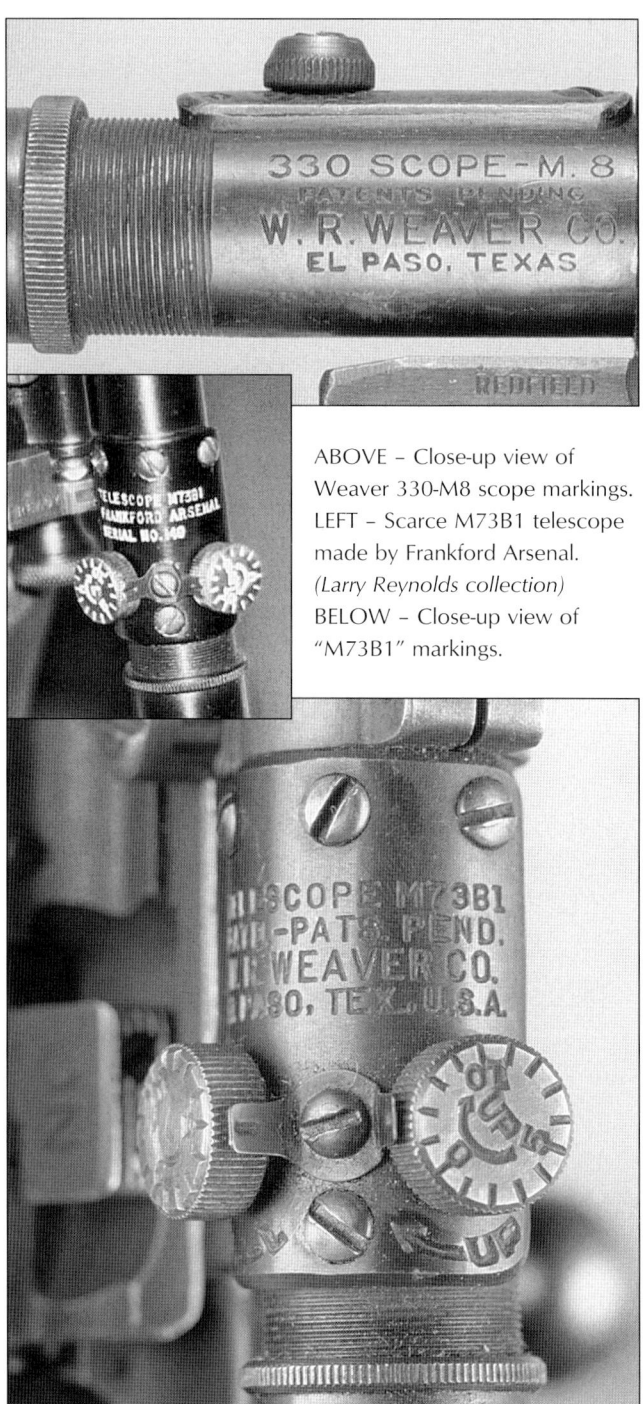

ABOVE – Close-up view of Weaver 330-M8 scope markings. LEFT – Scarce M73B1 telescope made by Frankford Arsenal. *(Larry Reynolds collection)* BELOW – Close-up view of "M73B1" markings.

Advertisement which appeared in the November 1943 issue of *American Rifleman* magazine.

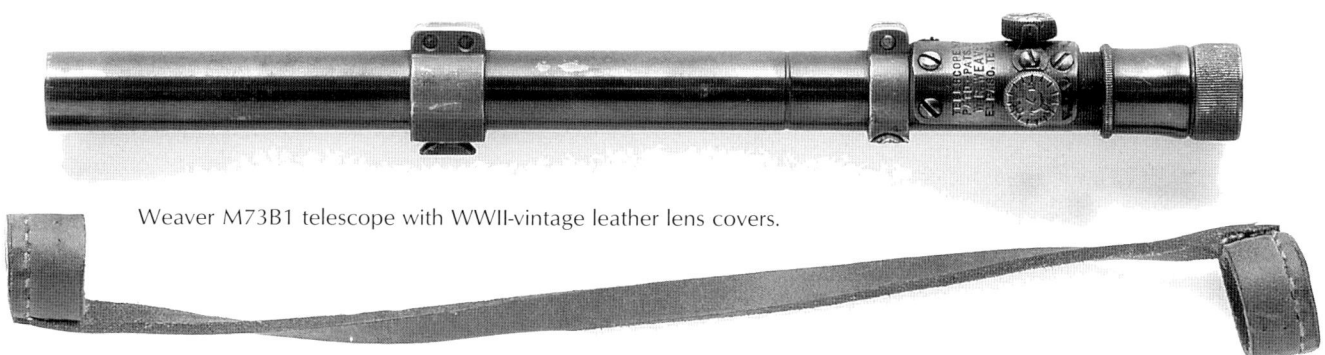
Weaver M73B1 telescope with WWII-vintage leather lens covers.

Weaver firm did not have a large manufacturing capacity which resulted in chronic shortages of scopes. These shortages resulted in many delays in the delivery of M1903A4 sniper rifles by Remington. In some cases, these shortages resulted in completed M1903A4 rifles (sans scopes) languishing in Remington storage facilities for as long as four months until scopes could be delivered. The Ordnance Department had assumed the responsibility of supplying the required telescopes to Remington. This recurring shortage of scopes was a cause of concern for Remington, as the firm struggled to deliver the required number of 'A4 sniper rifles to the government. These concerns resulted in a July 29, 1943, letter to Remington from the Ordnance Department which stated, in part:

"...It is realized that except for the month of June, Remington Arms has never received sufficient telescopic sights to meet its monthly production schedule for the U.S. Rifle, Cal. .30, M1903A4. Also, at this time, it is evident that Remington Arms did not receive sufficient scopes in time to meet its production schedule for July.

"As the A4 rifle is classed as a critical item, Remington Arms can be assured that the Ordnance Department is making every possible effort to supply Remington Arms with as many scopes as possible to insure that every A4 rifle that can be produced is produced.

"The Ordnance Department has estimated that only 2,700 A4 rifles will be accepted from Remington Arms during July. Considering the scopes that Remington Arms has on hand, as of this date, the Ordnance Department is attempting to ship to Remington Arms a total of 3,000 additional scopes prior to 15 August. When Remington Arms has received these 3,000 additional scopes, Remington Arms will have sufficient scopes on hand to produce 3,200 A4 rifles during the month of August.

"Until such time as production of telescopic sights reaches the point where the required quantity of scopes can be supplied to Remington Arms in sufficient time so that Remington Arms can meet its production schedule, it is requested that Remington Arms maintain a bank of approximately 1,000 or more completed rifles, less telescopes, on hand at all times to insure prompt assembly of A4 rifles upon the receipt of telescopic sights. If this is done, Remington Arms will be able to shorten the process time and the result will be faster shipment of A4 rifles to the field.

"With the production of telescopic sights as uncertain as it is at the present time, the Ordnance Department can only ask that Remington Arms continue to cooperate with them in assembling and shipping the A4 Rifles as fast as possible, as the telescopic sights become available."

Shortages of telescopes plagued the 'A4 production program throughout its entirety even with the best efforts of the beleaguered W.R. Weaver Company. The Weaver scope was only intended to be an interim solution, since initial quantities could be obtained in short order from commercial sources while Lyman (and perhaps other manufacturers) got into quantity production to supply the more desirable Alaskan scopes. As events transpired, the short-term quick fix Weaver telescope evolved into the primary U.S. Army sniper rifle telescope of the Second World War.

Mounts

As was the case with the Weaver scope, the mount selected for use with the M1903A4 rifle was a popular and readily available civilian component. Although not ideally suited for use with the Weaver scope, the Redfield Junior mount was a strong and serviceable design. A screw held the rear dovetail ring to the mount, and its removal allowed the scope to be easily installed or taken off the rifle without affecting the zero (at least in theory). This screw could be easily lost, and replacements were reportedly in short supply when the rifles got into the field. Thin metal shims were also utilized to raise the mounts to the proper height as required.

The first M1903A4 rifles were completed by Remington in February 1943, and production continued through June 1944. The following is a synopsis of the characteristics of the M1903A4 sniper rifle:

Receivers

All M1903A4 rifles were made by Remington Arms Company. The nomenclature and serial number was applied to the extreme left and right, respectively, portions of the receiver ring.

Three serial number blocks were assigned to Remington for M1903A4 production:

3407088–3427087
4000001–4015000*
4992001–5784000**

* Only approximately 3,000 serial numbers were used from this block for '03A4 production. Some M1903A3 serial numbers were also taken from this block of numbers. In order to distinguish between the '03A3 and '03A4 serial numbers, "Z" prefix was added to duplicate numbers on the 'A4 receivers.

** This block was initially assigned for both M1903A3 and M1903A4 production. Approximately 6,300 numbers were used for M1903A4 production, and none of the numbers are believed to have been used for M1903A3 production.

The Z-prefix M1903A4 rifles (early 4,000,000 range) are interesting and desirable collector variants. See **Table 11** on page 223 to estimate production date by serial number.

Barrels

M1903A4 rifles were assembled using standard '03A3 barrels without the front sight mounted. The presence of the milling cuts for the sight makes for a rather unusual appearance. The area of the barrel normally occupied by the front sight band should be parkerized on the '03A4 barrels. If this area is bright or has a noticeably different texture to the finish than the rest of the barrel, it is likely that the barrel is a replacement '03A3 barrel to replace a worn or damaged original. It is estimated that the first six or seven thousand M1903A4 rifles had four-groove barrels, and the remainder of production utilized two-groove barrels. There was some overlap in the use of two- and four-groove barrels.

Stocks

The M1903A4 rifle was standardized with the Type C full pistol grip stock. As was the case with the telescopes, the Ordnance Department assumed responsibility for providing M1903A4 stocks to Remington. Initially, Type C stocks were procured from Springfield Armory and were modified at Remington by having the bolt notch cut into the side and inletted for the '03A3 barrel guard ring. These stocks can be identified by the "S" (Springfield) stamped in the cutoff recess. As production continued, both Type C and the semi-pistol grip scant stocks were procured from the Keystone Company. These were stamped with a "K" in the recess. While not discussed in available ordnance documents, it is likely that the unfinished stock blanks for the Keystone wart hog

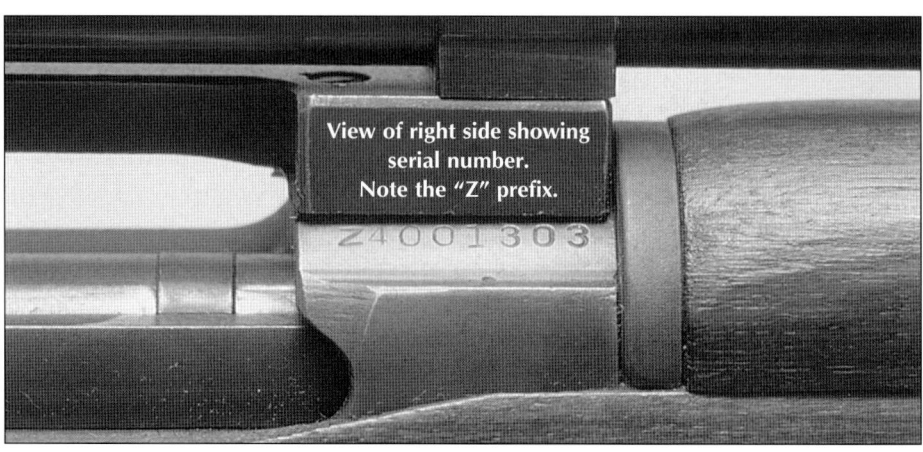

View of right side showing serial number. Note the "Z" prefix.

Swell! The Same Mount I Used Back Home!

SURE, the boys know they can put those shots right in there where they count! This Redfield Junior Mount is a familiar old friend to thousands of American sportsmen now in the armed forces—the same mount they used "back home" on favorite hunting and target rifles.

STANDARD
REDFIELD SIGHTS
ADOPTED BY ARMED FORCES
without change!

• Besides the Redfield Junior Scope Mount, adopted for snipers' rifles, the Ordnance Department chose two of Redfield's famous MICROMETER sights... picked them out from stock models... just as YOU would choose a REDFIELD sight from your dealer's shelf or from our catalogue.

Now, of course our entire output goes to the armed forces

REDFIELD
GUNSIGHT CORP.
3315 Gilpin St., Denver, Colorado.

Advertisement which appeared in the November 1943 issue of *American Rifleman* magazine.

stocks were furnished by Remington from the large quantity of blanks left over from the aborted British rifle contract. The WWII-production Type C stocks were noticeably different from the prewar variety in that they were fatter and not quite as well finished. The use of Type C and scant-grip stocks by Remington was apparently confined to the production of M1903A4 rifles, although a large number of both types of stocks saw extensive use in post-WWII overhauls on M1903 and M1903A3 rifles. The M1903A4 stocks had the same type of marking format as found on Remington M1903A3 rifles.

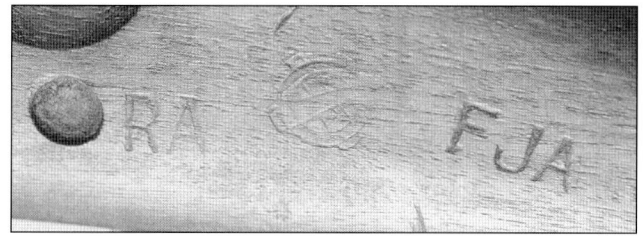

View of Remington M1903A4 stock markings. Note the "FJA" (Col. Frank J. Atwood), "RA" (Remington Arms) and Ordnance Department escutcheon. Most Remington M1903A3s had the same stock marking format.

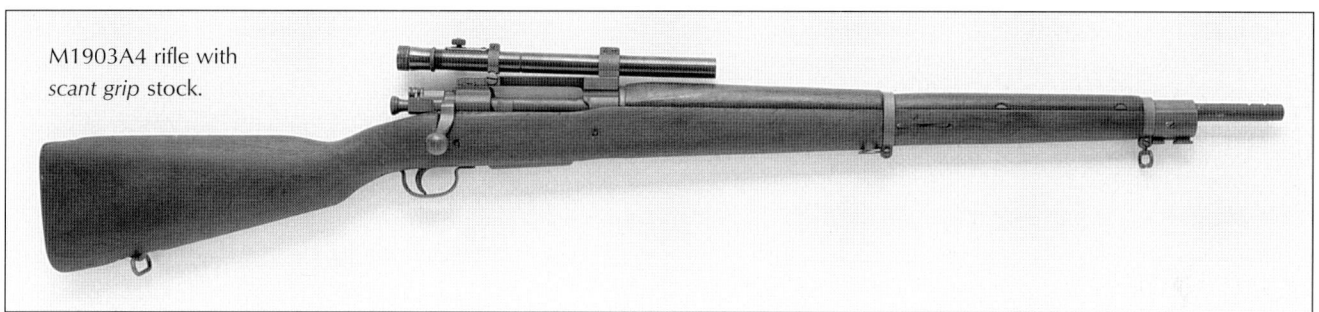

M1903A4 rifle with *scant grip* stock.

Barrel Guards
Same as used on M1903A3 rifles.

Rear Sights
The M1903A4 rifle was not fitted with a rear sight, and the rear section of the Redfield mount was configured to fit on the standard receiver dovetail.

Finish
Same as the M1903A3 rifle; green or greenish/gray parkerizing. The Redfield mounts were also parkerized.

Furniture
As was the case with the M1903A3 rifle, early and mid-production '03A4 rifles typically had blued furniture and bore the same "R" marking. As production continued, some parkerized furniture began to be used, most commonly the upper band. Even very late-production rifles, however, contained some blued furniture. Rifles with all parkerized furniture are almost certainly rebuilds or have had some of the furniture replaced.

The increasing demand for sniper rifles resulted in additional contracts being given to Remington for '03A4 production, and the company eventually delivered a total of 28,365 sniper rifles to the government. As soon as the weapons were shipped from the plant, many were delivered to overseas combat units and were soon in the thick of fighting in all theaters. Almost immediately, some deficiencies of the new sniping rifle became apparent. Most of the problems were attributable to the use of civilian components, primarily the Weaver telescope. The sight may have been satisfactory for a weekend deer hunt, but was unsuited for the hardships of combat. The Weaver just wasn't sturdy enough for such use, and many problems were encountered with the scope. The relatively low magnification was also cause for many complaints. There are numerous examples of M1903A4's widespread negative reputation. One of the more illustrative was related by Roy Dunlap in his classic book, *Ordnance Went Up Front*:

"I never considered the Remington-made 1903A4 sniper rifles very accurate, although I must confess I did not get a chance to shoot them with good ammunition. Most of these rifles were equipped with Weaver 330 scopes, in Redfield, Jr. mounts, a poor choice for the Pacific, as the Weaver just was not designed for that kind of a beating. When they came in to our instrument repair men, water could actually be poured out of many of them. They just were not weatherproof enough (please do not consider this a criticism of the Weaver as a telescopic sight, but only as a military accessory; I own three Weavers and am quite pleased with them). We never had any of these rifles equipped with Lyman Alaskan sights, although they are pictured in army manuals, using the same type of Redfield mount as the Weaver."

Similar feelings about the 'A4 were related more bluntly in Crossman's 1951 edition of *The Book of the Springfield*:

"The less said about the 1903 A4 'Sniper' rifle, the better. For a country which has developed the telescopic-sighted sporting rifle to highest accuracy and general effectiveness, we turned up the sorriest excuse for a combat man-killer in the war. So help me, the Japs had a better outfit!

"In the first place, the rifles weren't particularly good, not comparable with National Match Springfields, little or no attention was paid to bedding in the stock, and the scope selected — the Weaver 330 — was completely unsuited to its job. The scope is a nice little number for a .22 sporter, and a lot of them have been used on .30-06's, but it couldn't stand the rigors of war. I have myself personally poured at least a quart of water from these (collectively) in the Philippines, and never saw any which where in usable condition outside the supply tents.

"...as for the 1903 A4, the best report I have is from a rifleman who used one in Germany. He threw away the Weaver and had the Ordnance boys braze on a Russian sniper scope! After this, he got some fair results."

Despite the apparent problems with the rifle and its Weaver telescope, the 'A4 was the only U.S. Army sniper rifle to see issue and widespread use during World War II, other than a literal handful of M1C sniper rifles were used in the closing days of the war in the Pacific.

Use of the M1903A4 Rifle by the U.S.M.C.

There has been some confusion and erroneous statements regarding utilization of the M1903A4 sniper rifle by the U.S. Marine Corps during WWII. Some sources, including some supposedly knowledgeable "authorities," have flatly stated that the Marines never acquired any 'A4 rifles during the war. This assertion is incorrect according to official Marine Corps documents and photographic evidence. Official WWII-vintage Marine Corp photographs exist that clearly depict U.S. Marines armed with M1903A4 rifles in combat during several Pacific campaigns. U.S.M.C. use of the M1903A4 rifles is also confirmed in several official documents. One of the most pertinent is a memo dated February 10, 1944, from the Headquarters, U.S. Marine

U.S. Marine sighting a M1903A4 rifle. Although most '03A4s were issued to the Army, a number were apparently acquired by the Marine Corps to augment their other types of '03 sniper rifles. (*U.S.M.C.*)

American soldiers in France, August of 1944. The soldier in the center is holding a M1903A4 sniper rifle with the issue Weaver 330C/M73B1 scope. The GI behind him has an M1 Garand fitted with an M7 grenade launcher. *(U.S. Army)*

Corps in Washington, D.C., to Lt. Col. W.A. Kengla, Division of Plans and Policies which stated:

"...Unofficial information from Army Ordnance this date indicates approximately 2,000 M1903A4 rifles on hand, not obligated, and it is believed up to 1,000 of these could be obtained by the Marine Corps through proper channels."

This was followed by memo dated February 16, 1944, from the Commandant of the Marine Corps to the Quartermaster which stated:

"...upon exhaustion of depot stocks of Unertl telescopes, please take steps to substitute the rifle U.S. cal. .30, M1903A4 (Snipers) equipped with Sight, Telescope Assembly (Weaver 330C)."

Apparently, some M1903A4 rifles were obtained by the Marines prior to these early 1944 directives. The total number of '03A4s procured by the Marine Corps during WWII is not known, but some of the weapons definitely saw combat service in the hands of the Leathernecks.

At the end of WWII, the M1903A4 remained in service, although it was supplanted by the semi-automatic M1C and M1D rifles. As was the case with other U.S. weapons, large numbers of M1903A4s were overhauled after WWII. Many of these were fitted with replacement stocks, including a number of the scant grip *wart hog* variety. Rebuilt rifles can usually be identified by the initials of the rebuilding facility stamped on the left side of the stock and the fact that the rifles, including furniture, were generally reparkerized.

The 'A4 saw a fair amount of use during the Korean War. The Weaver was still the predominate telescope used with the rifle during this period, but some M81 and M82 scopes were utilized during the early 1950s as well. The Weaver and the M81/M82 scopes were eventually replaced by the M84 telescope on the M1903A4 rifles. It is doubtful if any of the M84 scopes were used during the Korean War. The M84 was utilized on M1C, M1D and M1903A4 sniper rifles from circa mid-1950s. M1903A4 rifles with M84 scopes remained in the military's inventory through the mid-1970s, and some of the weapons saw use in Vietnam. *A Technical Manual* for the M1903A4 rifle and M84 scope was printed at least as late as 1970.

After the '03A4 rifles were withdrawn from service, many were sold under the auspices of the Director of Civilian Marksmanship (DCM) and, later, the Civilian Marksmanship Program. Most, if not all, of these rifles were sold without telescopes, and the majority had been rebuilt at least once. M1903A4 rifles were not wildly popular with collectors until the past few years. Now, original examples are among the most popular U.S. martial arms on the market, with the expected rapid increase in price. The fact that virtually all of the M1903A4 rifles were sold without telescopes has resulted in many collectors seeking correct scopes for their rifles. Genuine WWII military issue Weaver 330C, M73B1 and 330-M8 scopes have always been rather scarce, and the current popularity of the 'A4 rifle has exacerbated the situation. This dearth of available examples and resultant high prices has resulted in some tenuous theories being crafted to justify the acquisition of scopes that were never used on the rifles by the military. For example, several types of commercial Weaver telescopes superficially resemble the desirable military examples and can be found much easier and much less expensively than the scopes actually issued with 'A4 rifles. This has resulted in a theory along the lines of "...the government bought any type of Weaver telescope and used them on '03A4 rifle; we were at war, so any type of telescope could have been used." This theory may sound fine, and may possess a modicum of logic, but is incorrect. The government specifications for telescopes authorized for use with the M1903A4 rifle were clear. The approved telescopes were specifically cited, and those were the only types authorized to be procured and issued with the sniper rifles. Any rationalization regarding the use of other types of scopes is a case of wishful thinking, and has crafted an erroneous or questionable theory to justify the presence of incorrect scopes on a rifle.

A collector owning a rebuilt 'A4 rifle will have an easier time finding the correct telescope as M84s are more common and usually less expensive than the elusive WWII Weavers. A M81 or M82 would also be correct for display with a M1903A4 rifle in post-WWII trim, but these scopes are about as scarce and expensive as the Second World War Weavers. The fact that the Lyman Alaskan was stan-

U.S. Army sniper sighting M1903A4 rifle from concealed position. *(U.S. Army)*

dardized for issue with the 'A4 rifle during WWII results in some people assuming that this scope would be correct for display with the rifle. This is good illustration of the fact that what may have been standardized for a particular weapon was not always actually used with that weapon. A few Alaskan scopes are known to have been teamed with M1C rifles in the Korean War, but there is little evidence to suggest this was also done with M1903A4 rifles. The same is true with the Weaver K-4 scopes of the late 1960s period. Some of these are known to have been issued with M1D rifles in special 1-inch mounts. Some collectors have theorized that since the K-4s were used with M1D rifles during this period, they must have also been used with 'A4s. Again, this may be possible, but there is no known evidence to even remotely hint that this occurred. In summary, the following telescopes are the only types confirmed to have been procured for, and issued with, the M1903A4 rifles in government service:

World War II — Weaver 330C, M73B1 and 330-M8
Post-WWII — The above Weaver scopes (until the early 1950s), then the M81, M82 and M84. The M84 was, by far, the most commonly used after the early 1950s.

Unlike virtually all other U.S. military sniper rifles, the M1903A4 is almost impossible to fake due to the unique placement of the markings on the receiver ring. Even though fake M1904A4 receivers are essentially out of the question, this does not mean that every rifle encountered is unquestionably original. While a receiver may be genuine, every feature must be examined to determine if the balance of the weapon is legitimate. Some examples may be commercially reparkerized, the barrel may have been replaced, the stock could be a replacement or has had fake markings applied, and the scope mount and/or scope could be incorrect. Also, the vintage of the telescope should match the vintage of the rifle in question. For example, a rifle that has been through a later post-WWII overhaul, as evidenced by the arsenal stamps on the stock, would probably not have a WWII-vintage Weaver scope mounted. On the other hand, a rifle remaining in its Second World War factory configuration probably would not have a M84 scope attached. Such combinations are certainly not impossible but would be rather unlikely.

The M1903A4 was made in larger numbers than all other previous U.S. military sniper rifles combined. While the 'A4 was clearly not an optimum sniping weapon, it provided yeoman-like service to the U.S. Army when no other telescopic-sighted rifles were available. Despite whatever shortcomings it may have possessed as a sniper rifle, the '03A4 remains one of the classic United States infantry weapons of the Second World War, and an original example is a worthy addition to any collection.

Pfc. Edward J. Foley of the 143rd Infantry, 36th Division, cleaning his M1903A4 sniper rifle before moving out to the front lines near Velletri, Italy, May 29, 1944. It is interesting to note that even at this late date in the war, most of the soldiers shown in this photo are armed with M1903 rifles. *(National Archives)*

U.S. Marine Corps Sniper Rifles

While the M1903A4 was the only sniper rifle to be fielded in any appreciable numbers by the U.S. Army in WWII, the picture was quite different in Marine Corps service. Unlike the Army, which discarded its First World War M1903/Warner & Swasey sniper rifles in the 1920s, the Marines held on to their M1903/Winchester A5 sniper rifles. The relatively few rifles of this type on hand after WWI were sufficient to meet the needs of the small U.S. Marine Corps throughout the 1920s and 1930s. On the eve of the Second World War, however, it was apparent that the Marines would need additional sniping weapons.

M1903 Rifles with Winchester A5 and Lyman 5A Telescopes

The Sniper and Rifle Team Rifles left over from the First World War were still in the Marine Corps' inventory and ready for immediate issue. Some of the earlier Winchester A5 telescopes were apparently replaced by the slightly improved Lyman 5A telescopes. The only substantive difference between the Winchester and Lyman scopes was the presence of a rib on the latter to better secure the tube in the mount. Otherwise, the two scopes were almost identical. A number of Marine Corps documents dating from the immediate pre-WWII period use the terms A5 and 5A almost interchangeably when referring to rifle telescopes, and it is often unclear exactly which scope is being referenced.

The Marine Corps apparently considered the issue of more modern telescopes to replace the Winchester/Lyman sights. These included the Lyman Alaskan, Noske and Weaver (330 and 440), as evidenced by their mention in a October 22, 1940, letter from the Marine Barracks, Quantico, Virginia, to the Commandant. This was followed up a few days later by a memo dated October 28, 1940, which related:

"There are 887 sights, telescopic, accessory, M-1903 rifle, now on hand at the Depot of Supplies, Philadelphia, Pennsylvania, these are Lyman, 5A type which were procured during the last war. They have never proved satisfactory, and it is considered that any of the sights mentioned (the Alaskan, Noske, and Weaver) in the basic letter are superior for use as a sniper's sight. It is believed that the various manufacturers would agree to furnish sample sights without cost to the Marine Corps for experimental purposes, in comparison with the Lyman, 5A sight if the need for such equipment is apparent."

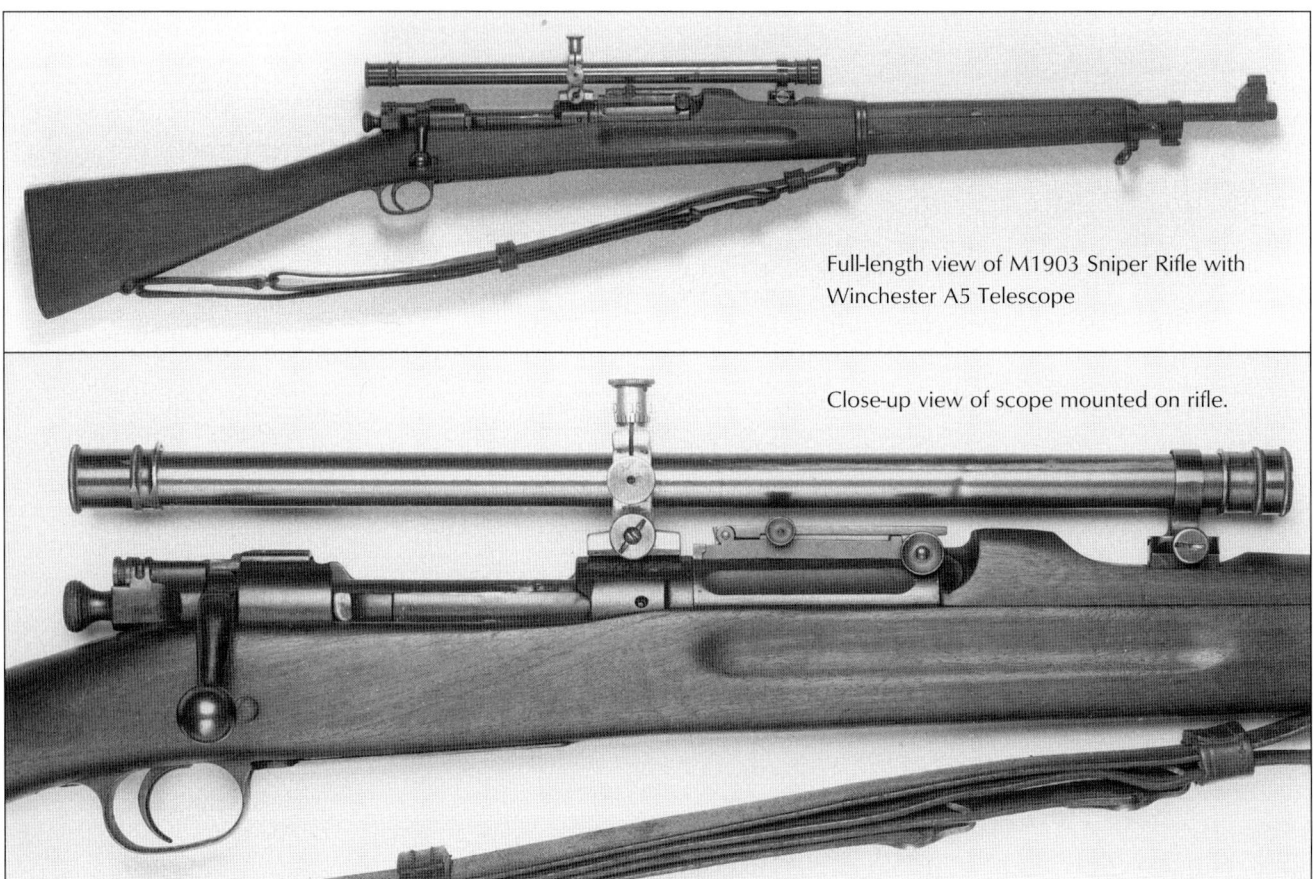

Full-length view of M1903 Sniper Rifle with Winchester A5 Telescope

Close-up view of scope mounted on rifle.

Marine Scout-Sniper with M1903/A5 sniper rifle training in WWI. *(U.S. Marine Corps, courtesy Alec Tulkoff)*

Since the memo stated that the telescopes "were procured during the last war," it must be assumed that they were, in reality, the earlier Winchester A5 scopes. This was followed by a letter dated November 13, 1940, from the Commandant to the Quartermaster with the Subject of "Test of Lyman 5A type telescopic sights. The letter stated:

"Reference (a) recommended that several types of telescopic sights now available commercially be purchased and tested for possible use by snipers.

"Reference (b) approves the recommendation contained in (a) and further approves having the Marine Corps Equipment Board make comparative tests of the several types now available commercially with the Lyman 5A type now on hand at the Depot of Supplies, Philadelphia, Pa.

"The Quartermaster is requested to make the necessary arrangements with the manufacturers to have one (1) each of the Lyman, Noske and Weaver sights recommended in reference (a) submitted to the Marine Corps Equipment Board for comparative test with the Lyman 5A type sight. The Quartermaster is further requested to make the necessary arrangements to have five (5) of the Lyman 5A type sights delivered to the Marine Corps Equipment Board.

"By copy of this letter the Marine Corps Equipment

Board is requested to make the necessary comparative test and advise this Headquarters of the results; make recommendations regarding the suitability of the types submitted; and if the Lyman 5A should be retained, modified, or discarded."

The results of the requested tests have not been discovered, but apparently none of the telescopes under consideration and tested against the 5A were recommended for adoption. The A5/5A remained the Marines' sole sniper telescope during this period and a March 27, 1941, memo stated, in part:

U.S. Marine Scout-Sniper undergoing training during WWII. *(U.S. Marine Corps)*

"With respect to the Lyman 5A (sometimes designated as the Winchester A5) telescopic sight, of which the Marine Corps has about one thousand units in stock, it is recommended that these sights be retained as an article of issue for elementary training of Sniper-Observer-Scouts."

While the search for a satisfactory sniper scope was being conducted, the Marines were faced with the immediate prospects of obtaining sufficient telescopic-sighted rifles for the training of new snipers. To this end, a Marine Corps memo dated April 8, 1941, to the Commandant stated:

"...the Equipment Board recommends the procurement of one thousand (1,000) sets of telescopic sight equipment for the use of snipers estimated at five hundred (500). The estimated cost of such a purchase would amount of approximately $220,000. Present table of organization do not provide for special personnel for such duty.

"It is believed, therefore, that sniper training should be conducted within combat units using such equipment as is available at least initially. It is proposed, therefore, to equip forty M-1903 rifles with the Lyman 5A sights in stock and send twenty to each Division for training purposes."

This was followed by a memo dated April 26, 1941, from the Quartermaster to the Depot Quartermaster, Marine Corps, Philadelphia, Pa., which ordered:

"...for your information and necessary action: 1. That forty M-1903 rifles be equipped for employment of Lyman 5A sights and that twenty rifles with serviceable telescopic sights be furnished each Marine Division for test and training."

The M1903 rifles fitted with A5 or 5A scopes were clearly considered unsatisfactory, and their utilization was a stop-gap measure borne of necessity. As an interim measure, the Marine Corps approved the procurement of thirty M2 .22 caliber rifles fitted with Winchester A5 telescopes for use in training sniper candidates until the issue of a standardized sniper rifle could be settled. The dissatisfaction with the Winchester and Lyman scopes by the Marines should not be construed to mean that the '03 rifles fitted with these telescopes did not see combat action in WWII.

U.S. Marine on Guadalcanal sighting his M1903 sniper rifle with Winchester/Lyman scope. This was the standard U.S.M.C. sniper rifle during the early Pacific campaigns. *(U.S. Marine Corps)*

To the contrary, they were utilized until very late in the war, and experimentation was ongoing in an attempt to improve the performance of the A5 telescope. As an example, a Report on Telescopic Sight, 1903 Rifle, A5, with Coated Lenses, Project #188 prepared by the Experimental Section of the Marine Corps Equipment Board dated May 21, 1944, detailed extensive testing done with M1903 rifles fitted with A5 telescopes. Some of the scopes had a special magnesium fluoride coating applied to the lens to determine if this would improve the utility of the sight. The conclusion of the report stated that, "Coating the lenses of the Telescopic Sight, 1903 Rifle, A5 does not improve its effectiveness."

The Marines engaged in a study to determine the best candidates for a new Marine Corps sniper rifle and telescope. Eventually, the Winchester Model 70 rifle was recommended as the best available rifle for the Marine Corps' needs. The Model 70 was among the most popular civilian bolt-action rifles of the day, and it enjoyed an enviable reputation as a quality firearm. Many types of civilian telescopes were considered for use with the Model 70, but a 8X power target-type scope made by the Unertl Company was selected as the best choice. This scope was referred to in numerous Marine Corps documents of the period as the Unertl "Sniper" Telescope. John Unertl gave a telescope of this type to the Marines for evaluation. It was recommended that the Marine Corps immediately purchase 20 of the scopes from Unertl, and that a quantity order for 1,000 be placed as soon as practicable. This request was turned down by the Commandant.

Consideration of Winchester Model 70 Rifle and Unertl Telescope

The Marine Corps eventually purchased 373 Model 70 rifles from Winchester, but only a handful were fitted with scopes for evaluation purposes. The disposition of the balance of the rifles is not known, but they were not fitted with scopes and issued as sniping weapons. The Model 70 rifle and Unertl scope found favor with most of the Marines who tested them, and the combination was recommended for adoption. Any hopes that the Model 70/Unertl sniping rig would be adopted by the Marine Corps were firmly dashed by a July 29, 1942, memo from the Depot Quartermaster which stated:

"...The subject rifles (Winchester Model 70) are not considered suitable for general service use for the following reasons:

(a) Not sufficiently sturdy
(b) Parts are not interchangeable with M1903 and M1 rifle parts.
(c) Replacement parts will be difficult to procure.
(d) Not fitted with sling swivels.

These rifles are not considered suitable for use as sniper rifles. The 1047 rifles, U.S. caliber .30, M1903, "Snipers Equipment" on hand at this Depot...are believed to be superior to the subject rifles both in accuracy and durability. The parts for these rifles are interchangeable with those of the standard M1903 rifle."

M1903A1 Rifle and Unertl Telescope (M1941 Sniper Rifle)

The disapproval of the Winchester Model 70 as the Marines' new sniping weapon was not really surprising for a number of reasons, not the least of which was the fact that there were many perfectly suitable and perfectly accurate Springfield rifles in the Marines' inventory. The accuracy of specially selected and prepared M1903 rifles was well known, and the Springfield was certainly more durable as a combat arm than the civilian Model 70. Spare parts and maintenance procedures for the '03 were well established, which would not have been the case if the Model 70 was adopted. The 1,047 M1903 rifles referred to in the above memo as Sniper Equipment were match and target rifles currently in the Marines' inventory. A July 4, 1942, memo from the U.S.M.C. Quartermaster Department, Philadelphia, Penn., contained the following information on the 1,047 rifles slated to be converted to sniper configuration:

"Subject: M1903 Rifles, national match and special target.

1. There are on hand at this depot the following rifles, U.S. cal. .30, M1903:
    104 Rifles, U.S. cal. .30, M1903 national match, held for U.S. Marine Corps Reserve Rifle Team.

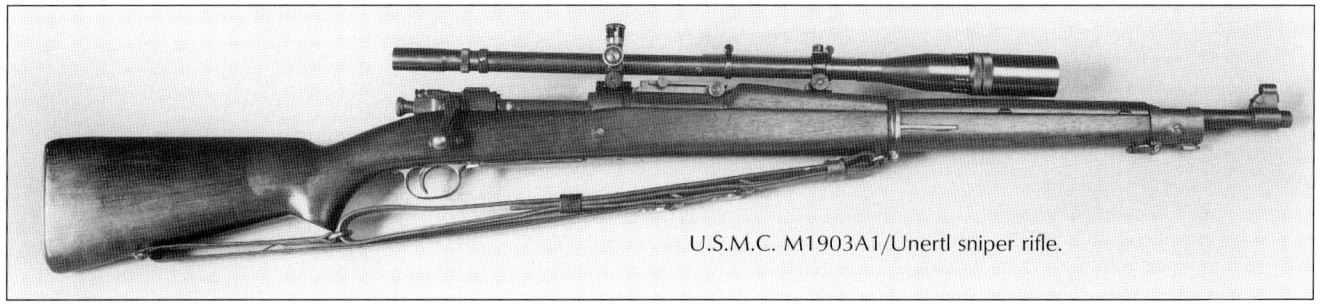

U.S.M.C. M1903A1/Unertl sniper rifle.

A Marine sniper firing his M1903A1/Unertl sniper rifle in WWII. The rifle has just been fired as the telescope is still in the forward position. The lack of a return spring necessitated that the scope be manually retracted into battery after each shot. *(Courtesy Peter Senich)*

U.S. Marine Scout-Sniper firing M1903A1/Unertl sniper rifles on Saipan. Note that the rifle at left has been fitted with a Style S stock with grasping grooves rather than the full-pistol grip Style C stock used on most of these weapons. *(USMC)*

U.S. Marine Scout Sniper student and instructor training with M1903A1/Unertl sniper rifle. *(U.S. Marine Corps)*

U.S. Marine sniper cleaning his M1903A1/Unertl sniper Rifle. *(U.S. Marine Corps)*

  369 Rifles, U.S. cal. .30, M1903, national match, held for U.S. Marine Corps Rifle Team.
<u>574</u> Rifles, U.S. cal. .30 M1903 special target rifles, held for Division, Marine Corps and Elliott Trophy Team matches.
1,047 Total

2. All the above rifles have bright bolts (polished and not parkerized). It is recommended that they be taken up as rifles, cal. 30, M1903 and issued as may be directed.
3. If and when national matches are again held, the U.S. Rifle, M1 undoubtedly will be the required rifle, except in the National Rifle Assn. matches the M1903 rifle will probably be permitted, in which case rifle could be selected from stock, re-barreled and otherwise fitted as special target rifles."

The term *special target rifle* denoted a service rifle that was specially *tweaked and tuned* for greater accuracy as a match rifle rather than being originally manufactured as such. Such rifles were capable of accuracy comparable to any National Match rifle and, functionally, there was no real difference between the two types. These rifles chosen for conversion to sniper configuration were also referenced in a 1942 report which stated:

> "There are available at the Quartermaster Depot at Philadelphia approximately 1,000 star-gauged rifles which are the property of the Marine Corps Rifle Team and which could be used for equipping snipers. Suitable telescopic sights would have to be provided for these rifles."

While the Model 70 was not chosen as the new sniper rifle, the Unertl telescope did find favor in the eyes of the Marines, and was the Corps' choice as a "...suitable telescopic sight." Marine Captain George Van Orden called the Unertl Snipers telescope "...the only completely satisfactory sighting telescope available in the United States." In January 6, 1943, the Commandant approved the purchase of 1,000 telescopes, mounts, blocks (front and rear) and carrying cases from Unertl for use with the 1,047 M1903 match rifles referenced above. The scopes were the 8X target-type previously tested with the Winchester Model 70 rifles and utilized $\frac{1}{4}$-minute external adjusting mounts. The carrying cases were made of micarta painted green, with cartridge belt hooks. The scopes were serially numbered and stamped "USMC-SNIPER" on top of the tube. Even though marked "8", the scopes were actually of 7.8X power.

Most, if not all, of the M1903 National Match and Special Target rifles were converted to sniper configuration at the U.S.M.C. Philadelphia depot. These rifles typically had the serial number hand-etched on top of the bolt body. One modification of these rifles that was adopted early in the conversion program was bluing of the bright bolts, presumably to aid in concealment purposes in combat. This is confirmed by a July 10, 1942, memo which stated:

> "Subject: Rifles, M1903, national match and special target. It is requested that the bolts of these rifles...be put through a blueing process and that rifles be taken up as rifles, caliber .30, "Snipers Equipment," and held in store pending instructions from this office."

By the virtue of being Rifle Team arms, these rifles were capable of sufficient accuracy for sniping purposes. Conversion to sniper configuration was a relatively easy procedure for the experienced Marine armorers. It must be noted that the armorers converted the match rifles to sniper rifles on, literally, a one-at-a-time basis, and some variances will be found from rifle to rifle. Normally, these variances are rather subtle in nature and reflect the individual preferences of the various armorers who performed the work. The major alterations were mounting of the front and rear bases and modification of the handguard to provide clearance for the front base. The handguard required a hole to be cut into the middle, and the swell on top had to be machined down. The quality of the workmanship found on the altered handguards ranged from professional to crude. Specifications also stated that "...Type 'C' stocks should be provided if available..." While the vast majority of the newly converted sniper rifles were, indeed, fitted with Type C stocks, a few retained the older Type S stocks, presumably on either the preference of the armorer or the unavailability of the Type C stocks. Initially, the Type C stocks were of prewar manufacture, but the supply was augmented by newly made Type C stocks acquired from Springfield Armory in the 1942–1943 period. The relatively few existing stocks that were retained for use can be identified by the presence of the pre-WWII markings (inspection cartouche and proof stamp). Most of the new replacement stocks were never stamped with inspection or proof markings. Some of the Type S stocks used with the new sniper rifles were also procured from Springfield Armory, which manufactured 4,000 of the stocks specifically for the Marine Corps in early 1941. These were not marked with inspector cartouches or proof marks. If the original stock was a Type C and was serviceable, it was retained. National Match stocks were typically stamped on the underside of the stock with the receiver serial number. Apparently, the stocks were sometimes swapped around because original rifles with non-matching stock numbers have been observed. It has been reported that some of the new replacement stocks were also marked with serial numbers. If so, relatively few were marked in this manner, as most replacement stocks used with the sniper rifles were unmarked. Some of the stocks were varnished to provide a measure of water-proofing.

Likewise, if the original barrel was found to be unserviceable, it was replaced by a new barrel, either selected from replacements on hand, or from a batch of new barrels acquired from Springfield Armory in 1940. The majority of rifles retained their original barrels since they were typically well maintained, given their former status as match rifles.

Although there are a few oblique citations in vintage documents to *Model 1941* or *Model 1942* sniper rifles, virtually all official documents refer to the rifles as *M1903A1 Rifle, Sniper, with Telescope, Sighting, Unertl 8X*. Therefore, it is doubtful if the Model 1941 (or Model 1942) designation was ever the weapon's official nomenclature, although this term is frequently tossed around today. These rifles will be referred to in this book as M1903A1/Unertl sniper rifles. While there will be some variances noted in original specimens, the following features are typically found on U.S.M.C. M1903A1/Unertl sniper rifles:

Serial Number Range

Authentic rifles have been observed from the 900,000 range to the low 1,500,000. Most were in the 1,200,000 to 1,500,000 ranges. All verified examples were of Springfield Armory manufacture. While possible, the use of receivers by any other manufacturer has not been confirmed and remains doubtful.

Barrels

All confirmed original rifles had Springfield Armory barrels, most with mid- to late-1930s dates. Although it cannot be categorically discounted, none of the WWII-vintage replacement Sedgley "USMC"-marked barrels are known to have been used on the sniper rifles. The majority of these rifles had star-gauged barrels with the familiar asterisk-like stamp on the muzzle crown. However, a number of original rifles did not have star-gauge marked barrels. Therefore, the absence or presence of this marking does not signify originality or lack thereof.

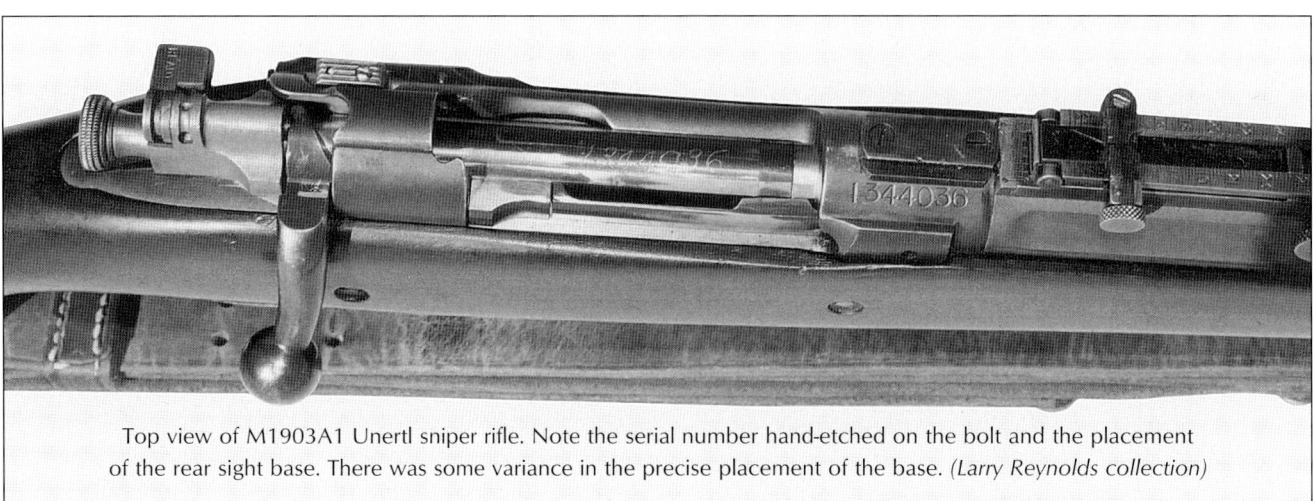
Top view of M1903A1 Unertl sniper rifle. Note the serial number hand-etched on the bolt and the placement of the rear sight base. There was some variance in the precise placement of the base. *(Larry Reynolds collection)*

Receivers

Some of the rifles had the top of the receiver ring slightly filed or milled down to make attachment of the rear base easier. Virtually all examples had the bolt guide rails polished, which was a common feature of National Match and other finely tuned target rifles. Pre-1936 receivers had the gas escape hole (the so-called Hatcher Hole) added to the left side.

Bolts

Bolts were originally polished and hand-etched with the receiver serial number. Specifications called for the bright bolts to be blued. The bluing was of a distinctive type that had a somewhat watery appearance. Bolts with a single gas hole often had the hole enlarged by Marine armorers. Later bolts had two gas escape holes and were not usually modified. While blued bolts were the norm, some of the rifles retained the bright finished bolts as evidenced by WWII-vintage photographs.

Scope Mount Blocks

Standard Unertl target-type blocks were procured for use with the U.S.M.C. sniper rifles. The rear block was marked "O", and the front block marked "E" for identification purposes. Original specimens will exhibit some variation in the placement of the rear base on the receiver ring. Most had the edge of the base flush against the rear sight base, while some had the block centered on the middle of the receiver. The use of some non-standard (non-Unertl) blocks has been reported but remains unconfirmed. Most original rifles will exhibit a small punch mark on the bottom of the barrel directly opposite the front block.

Stocks

As with some of the other components, there were some variances found regarding the types of stocks. The full pistol grip Type C stock was the preferred style. Original stocks that were retained for use with the sniper rifles had the pre-WWII markings (cartouche, proof mark, etc.) left intact. Newly acquired replacement stocks were typically unmarked. Some were varnished to provide waterproofing and some weren't. A few rifles utilized straight-grip Type S stocks but, by far, the most common style of stock used with these sniper rifles was the Type C.

Handguards

The handguards were modified by milling down a portion of the swell and cutting a hole in the top to provide clearance for the front scope block. Some collectors believe that a hallmark of original handguards is the workmanship involved in routing out the hole in the handguard, and that less-than-arsenal-quality work is a sign of fake handguards. This is untrue, because some crudely modified handguards have been observed on original rifles, and some fakes have professionally modified handguards. This feature is not a litmus test. Some original handguards were marked with chalk on the inside with the initials of the armorer who performed the conversion and, occasionally, the date of conversion. Of course, it may be impossible to ascertain the genuineness of any such markings encountered today.

Iron Sights

The type of sights used with the M1903A1/Unertl sniper rifles is also the subject of some confusion and disagreement. Examples with standard M1905 front and rear sights have been observed, as have some with the special No. 10 Marine Corps sights. Although the standard sights are more commonly encountered, either type could be considered as correct.

Unertl Telescopes

Original telescopes were marked "USMC-SNIPER" on top of the tube and serially numbered from 1000 to just

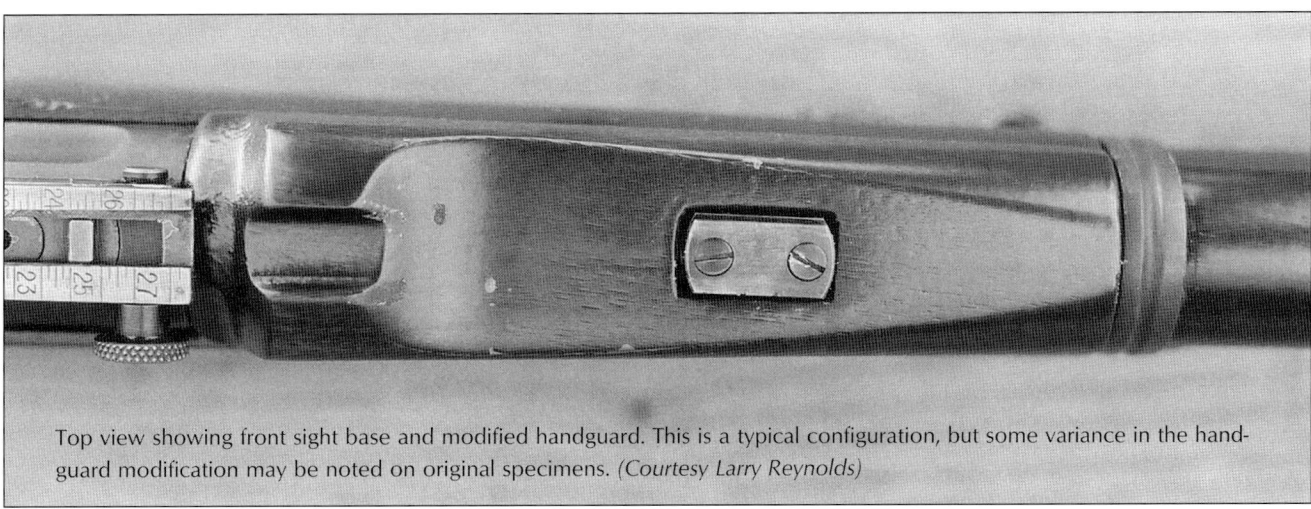

Top view showing front sight base and modified handguard. This is a typical configuration, but some variance in the handguard modification may be noted on original specimens. *(Courtesy Larry Reynolds)*

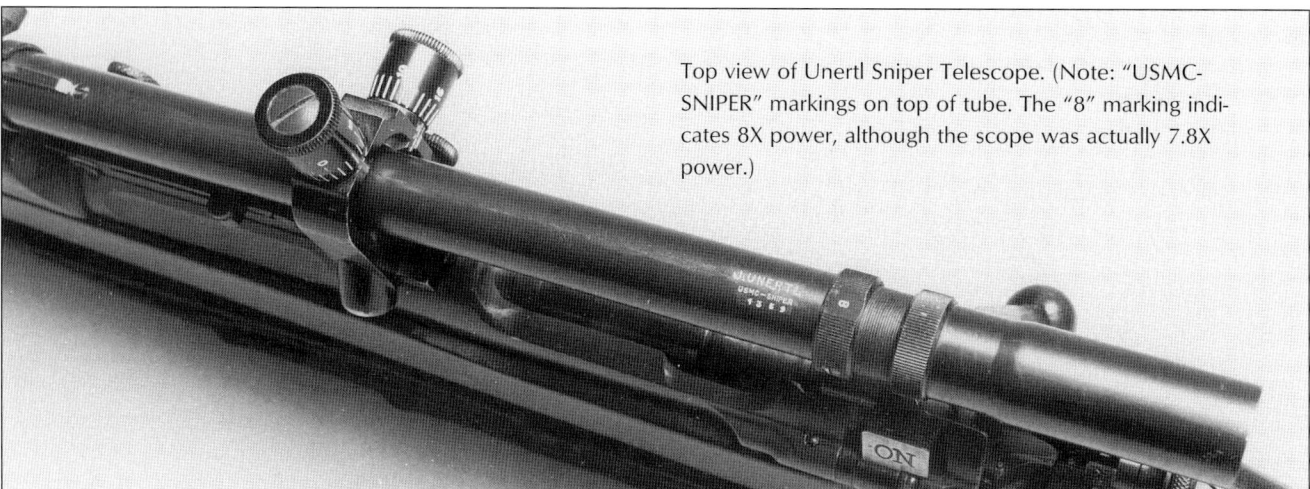

Top view of Unertl Sniper Telescope. (Note: "USMC-SNIPER" markings on top of tube. The "8" marking indicates 8X power, although the scope was actually 7.8X power.)

under 3000. The scopes were also marked "8" to denote the power, although they were actually 7.8X. It is believed that all of these telescopes were originally blued, although a few parkerized examples have been reported. It is presumed that these were refinished, either under U.S.M.C. auspices or by subsequent civilian owners.

The Unertl sniper telescopes did not have return springs, and the scopes had to be manually retracted after each shot. It has been theorized that the springs were eliminated in Marine Corps service to prevent sand and dirt from marring the tubes, but this remains a matter of conjecture. Another and probably more important reason for elimination of the spring was because the tube could easily hit the shooter in the eye when the rifle was fired and automatically brought back into battery by the spring. The return springs were more commonly used on civilian Unertl telescopes teamed with .22 caliber rifles for this reason. It has been reported that some enterprising Marine snipers fashioned makeshift return springs from slices of rubber inner tubes and these worked satisfactorily. Two different types of reticles have been observed on genuine U.S.M.C. Unertl sniper telescopes: medium cross hairs and cross hairs with a ¼-minute dot. Either type could be considered as correct. The scopes were issued with screw-on metal dust covers.

Carrying Can

The Unertl sniper telescopes were issued with cylindrical carrying cans constructed of green-painted micarta. The lid of the canister was retained by a canvas strap. The bottom of the container was spring-loaded to reduce rattle. The cans were fitted with wire cartridge belt hooks. A few carrying cans made of aluminum were fabricated but are rarely encountered. The micarta cans were seldom used in the field due to their bulk and the fact that the scopes were rarely removed from the rifles. The aluminum cans were also very noisy and would reportedly "ring like a bell" if struck by a tree branch or dropped on the ground. Original Unertl carrying cans are prized collectibles. A 1945 Marine Corps memo states that a total of 2,565 micarta carrying cans were procured.

Presenting the above information is very much a two-edge sword. It can be argued that giving this information makes it easier for a forger to create a more realistic fake sniper rifle. On the other hand, a potential buyer of such a rifle should have as much reliable information as possible before making a purchase decision. Regardless, many of the fakers already know much of this information.

As the M1903A1/Unertl sniper rifles began to be shipped from the Philadelphia Depot, they were immedi-

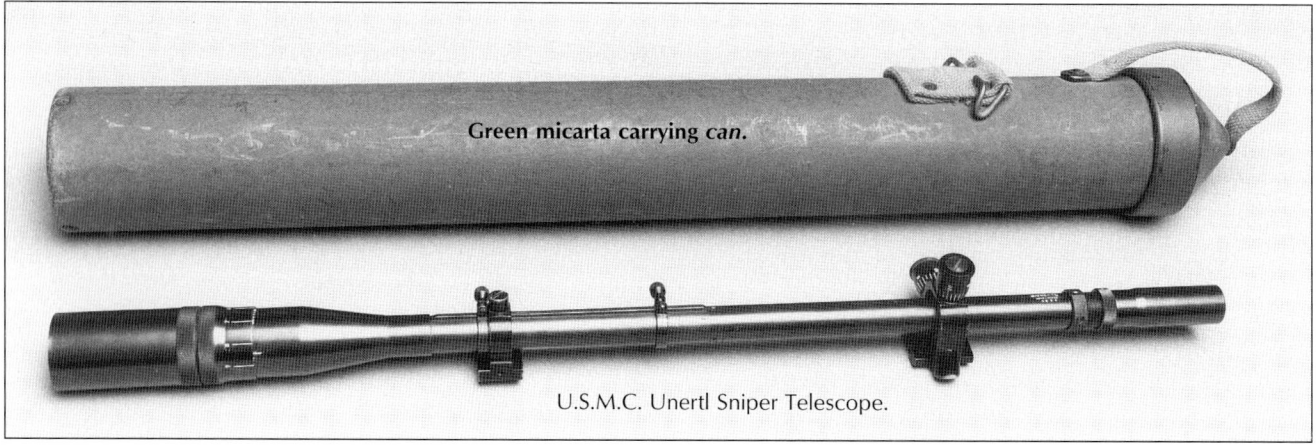

Green micarta carrying can.

U.S.M.C. Unertl Sniper Telescope.

ately issued to Marine Corps units. Marine Corps documents reflect that 250 of the sniper rifles with Unertl telescopes were shipped to the Headquarters First Marine Amphibious Corps beginning in February 1943. A Marine Corps memo dated September 23, 1943, contained the following proposed distribution of these sniper rifles to the Fourth Marine Division:

> "Each Inf. Bn. Hq. Co.   1
> Each Rifle Co.   2
> Each Sct. Plat., Sct. Co.   1
> Sct. Sniper Teams   67
> Total Snipers' Rifles   87"

Some students of the subject have suggested that the 250 rifles cited above represented the entire number of M1903A1/Unertl sniper rifles that were deployed to overseas combat zones. This is possible but unlikely. The total number of M1903A1 rifles converted to sniper configuration by the Marines is unconfirmed. The Unertl Company received an initial contract for 1,000 telescopes, and a second contract for 2,500 was granted. However, this second contract was cancelled before completion, and the number of telescopes actually delivered to the Marine Corps is unknown. An April 20, 1945, memorandum from the Marine Corps Quartermaster confirms that at least 1,750 Unertl scopes were obtained prior to cancellation of the order. Sniper historian Peter Senich reports a U.S.M.C.-Unertl telescope serially numbered 2774, the highest reported number. This would suggest that at least 1,774 telescopes were procured since serial numbers apparently started at 1,000. If true, this would mean that only some 774 scopes were delivered prior to cancellation of the second contract. There may well be higher serial numbers, but it is doubtful if more than 2,000 scopes were eventually delivered. It is known that 1,047 suitable match/target rifles were available for conversion to sniper configuration as evidenced by the July 4, 1942, memo. However, there were almost certainly some additional rifles converted to sniper configuration. An August 18, 1945, Marine Corps document stated:

> "There are...approximately 800 Rifles, U.S. Cal. .30, M1903A1 in depot stocks which either have mounting blocks assembled thereto or have been set aside for use as sniper rifles."

It is important to note that these rifles were in addition to the 1,047 National Match and Special Target rifles cited previously since they were specifically identified as M1903A1 rifles. The earlier rifles were specifically identified as National Match or Special Target rifles. It seems clear that some non-match M1903A1 rifles were fitted with Unertl telescopes and were then issued as sniper rifles. This is contrary to a number of published writings that maintain that ONLY national match and other special target rifles were converted to sniper rifles. This is refuted by primary U.S.M.C. documentation. How many of these later M1903A1 rifles were utilized during World War II is unknown, but it is likely that some saw use in Korea in the early 1950s.

The M1903A1/Unertl sniper rifles were shipped to Marine units overseas and soon employed in combat. Although the specially tuned '03 rifles and target-quality Unertl telescopes were capable of superb accuracy, reports of the effectiveness of the weapons in combat varied widely. The dense jungle terrain of the islands that composed much of the Pacific Theater often mitigated the use of telescopic-sighted rifles. However, the topography of some of the later Pacific island campaigns, such as Iwo Jima, Okinawa and Saipan, offered ample opportunities to employ telescopic-sighted sniper rifles. Even though it can be logically argued that the M1903A1/Unertl rig was the best American sniper rifle of WWII, there were mixed reports of the weapon's effectiveness in combat. Peter Senich related several positive comments regarding the M1903A1/Unertl sniper rifles in combat. Regarding the Unertl telescope, one observer stated:

> "It (the Unertl telescope) was, theoretically, too long, too fragile, too whatever. But infantrymen and Marines — and even Navy sharpshooters at times — went on aiming with it and squeezing them off, and enemy soldiers kept dropping. It's hard to argue with results like that."

Senich also related the comments of a veteran 2nd Division Marine Scout-Sniper who served on Tarawa, Saipan and Tinian who stated:

U.S.M.C. Bougainville Raiders. Most are armed with M1903 rifles. *(U.S.M.C.)*

"We found it quite adequate. We found no faults with the scope."

On the other hand, there are numerous examples of negative reports from units that fielded these sniper rifles, including some from members of the 2nd Marine Division on Tarawa. To be fair, much of the criticism was of telescopic-sighted rifles in general, and not of the M1903A1/Unertl rifle specifically. As an example, an after action report by a Marine Raider Battalion on New Georgia Island bluntly stated:

"U.S. Rifle, cal. .30, M1903 (snipers)
Should be substituted by the M1. The M1 is just as accurate, for any firing to be done in the jungle and has greater fire power."

The sniper rifles cited in this report were likely the M1903s fitted with Winchester A5 or Lyman 5A scopes rather than the M1903A1/Unertl rifles. However, the Unertl scope did come in for a fair amount of criticism in its own right. It is surprising that a number of U.S.M.C. documents that condemned the Unertl praised the Weaver 330C. Several of these documents requested that M1903A4 rifles with Weaver scopes be procured to replace the M1903A1/Unertl sniper rifles. A brief handwritten memo dated February 11, 1944, from the Headquarters, U.S. Marine Corps, Washington, D.C., to the M-4 Section stated:

"Recommend cancellation of unfilled portion of Unertl contract. Recommendations from 2nd Division condemn Unertl and commend Weaver. Don't believe there is any vital need for any scoped rifles but feel that Army standard (sniper rifle)...will provide what scoped rifles we need..."

A subsequent memo dated February 16, 1944, from the Commandant to the Quartermaster was even more to the point:

"The Unertle [sic], 8X, sniper telescope has not proved effective in combat. Accordingly you are requested to cancel existing contracts for this item. Upon exhaustion of depot stocks of Unertl telescopes, please take steps to substitute the rifle U.S. cal. .30, M1903A4 (Snipers) equipped with Sight, Telescopic Assembly (Weaver 330C)."

It seems surprising that the Marine Corps clearly wished to replace their M1903A1/Unertl sniper rifles with M1903A4 rifles, especially given the latter's less-than-stellar performance in the war. Nevertheless, the official position of the Marine Corps was clear preference for the '03A4 rifle and Weaver scope over the '03A1 and Unertl scope. Even though the Marines wanted to replace the M1903A1 rifles and Unertl scopes, these weapons remained in inventory and in use through the end of WWII and beyond. It was envisioned that the new M1C Garand sniper rifle would replace the '03 sniper in Marine Corps service. This was alluded to in an August 1944 U.S.M.C. memo:

"...authorized the issue of M1903A1 Rifles (Sniper) W/Telescope, Sighting, Unertl, 8X, on a basis of 108 per Marine Division and directed that the Commandant be notified when present stocks of this Sniper Rifle are depleted in order that another rifle could be authorized. It is expected that the M1C Rifle will be authorized."

As reflected in a number of WWII documents and memos, the official Marine Corps policy regarding the use of sniper rifles was confusingly ambivalent. On the one hand, an April 23, 1945, memo from the U.S.M.C. Division of Plans and Policies bluntly stated that, "...the sniper rifle is not considered to be a necessary weapon for any phase of Marine Corps training at present."

On the other hand, a memo from the General Supply Subsection, written only four days later, contained the following opinions and recommendation regarding sniper rifles and telescopes in Marine Corps service:

"Opinion:
 1. As so often happens, it appears that the experiences of one unit in one operation; i.e. Raider Battalion at New Georgia, have been sufficient to effectively damn a piece of equipment.
 2. The Unertl 8X scope was evidently procured early in the war because it appeared, at that time, to answer the requirements.
 3. Because the Unertl scope was not satisfactory does not mean that all scope-fitted rifles are useless for Marine Corps operations. The 1st Division at Cape Gloucester was unable to use effectively scope-fitted rifles because of climate and terrain. The 2nd Division at Saipan used scope-fitted rifles very effectively.
 4. Every military organization in this war maintains sniper units who have proved of considerable worth.

Recommendation:
 1. That the enclosed Mailgram be sent to FMF Pac to determine their opinion regarding the retention of a scope-fitted sniper's rifle. (The comparative value of the Rifle, U.S. Cal. .30, M1903A4, with Telescope, Weaver, 330C, and the Rifle, U.S., Cal. .30, M1C, with telescope, M81, is currently undergoing test by the Marine Corps Equipment Board."

Although it was clear from numerous late WWII official

documents that the Marine Corps wished to replace the M1903A1/Unertl sniper rifles with M1903A4 and M1C sniper rifles, this wasn't accomplished before the end of the war. An April 1945 memo stated that the U.S. Navy requested 400 scope-mounted sniper rifles from the Marines for use in mine-sweeping operations. Based on a handwritten notation on the memo, it appears that the Marines provided at least 100 M1903A1/Unertl sniper rifles pursuant to this request. It is likely that at least some of these rifles were converted from the 800 M1903A1 (non-match) rifles that were mentioned in the same memo.

The M1903A1/Unertl remained the standard Marine Corps sniper rifle at the end of the Second World War, even though limited numbers of M1903A4 rifles were utilized. The Marines eventually adopted the semi-automatic M1C sniper rifle, but tests on the weapon were still being conducted at the war's end. V-J Day found the M1903A1/Unertl sniping rifle still firmly entrenched in the Marine Corps' inventory in spite of the negative comments found in numerous documents and reports.

Post-WWII Use of the M1903A1/Unertl Sniper Rifle

The end of WWII resulted in little additional development or acquisition of sniper rifles by the Marine Corps beyond formal adoption of the M1C sniper rifle. The sudden outbreak of hostilities in Korea in 1950 found the '03A1/Unertl as the only sniper rifle available to the Marine Corps in any quantity, as few M1Cs were in inventory. Some of the M1903A1/Unertl sniper rifles were still left over from WWII, but the immediate requirements resulted in additional M1903A1 rifles being converted to sniper configuration for use in Korea. The number converted during this period is not known, but was certainly less than were converted in WWII. The remaining unused Unertl sniper scopes were taken out of storage and utilized. When the supply of Unertl scopes was depleted, a few Fecker and Lyman target scopes and bases that were in Marine inventory for use on target rifles were reportedly pressed into service. The M1903A1 rifles converted to sniper configuration during Korea were similar to those converted in WWII, although some minor differences, such as un-numbered parkerized bolts, may be noted. Some of these bolts may have had a notch milled on the bolt handle to provide clearance for the scope.

The open terrain common to much of the Korean peninsula was tailor-made for the use of scope-sighted sniper rifles, and the M1903A1/Unert rifles proved to be quite effective. Nevertheless, the Marine Corps was firmly committed to the M1C as the new standardized sniper rifle. As the Marines were able to acquire more of the semi-automatic sniper rifles, the M1C and M1903A1/Unertl weapons served side-by-side in Korea. Despite the M1903A1/Unertl sniper rifle's proven effectiveness in Korea, the weapon was declared Limited Standard and the Unertl scope declared Obsolete as related in as late 1951 memo:

"1. The U.S. Rifle, Caliber .30, M1903A1 now in use and in stock as snipers' rifles be declared limited standard.
2. The Unertl 8X Telescope be declared obsolete.
3. The U.S. Rifle, Caliber .30, M1C, with telescope, cheekpad and flash-hider, be standardized for the Marine Corps."

The end of the Korean War spelled the end of the M1903A1/Unertl sniper rifle in Marine Corps service.

U.S. Marine Snipers in Korea. M1903A1/Unertl and M1C sniper rifles were often employed side-by-side in Korea. The sniper at left is firing a M1903A1/Unertl rifle, and the snipers in the center and far right are firing M1C sniper rifles. *(National Archives)*

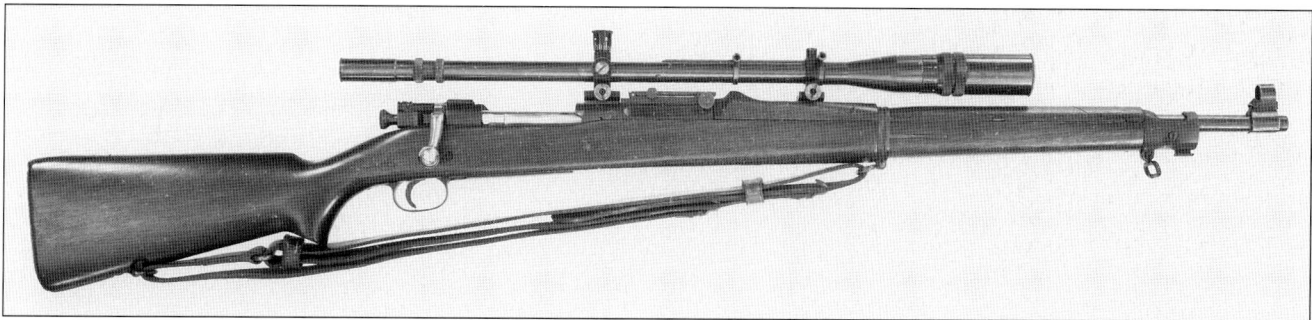

Another U.S.M.C. M1903A1/Unertl sniper rifle. Note the rather subtle variances between this rifle and the one depicted on page 153 including the slightly different configuration of the modified handguard and the polished bolt. *(Courtesy American Rifleman)*

ABOVE – Marine Sniper in Korea, early 1950s. The wide-open terrain common to much of the Korean Peninsula was tailor-made for the employment of telescopic-sighted sniper rifles. *(U.S. Marine Corps)*
ABOVE, LEFT – U.S. Marine Corps Scout-Sniper posing with his M1903A1/Unertl sniper rifle. *(U.S. Marine Corps)*
LEFT – U.S. Marine sniper firing his M1903A1/Unertl sniper rifle, Korea. *(National Archives)*
BELOW – Marine sniper in Korea with M1903A1 Unertl sniper rifle. This photo is unusual as the sniper has a M1905 bayonet attached to the rifle! *(National Archives)*

A few of the rifles were sold to individual Marines, normally sans scope, and most were undoubtedly destroyed or converted back to standard M1903A1 configuration and eventually discarded. A few original rifles with Marine Corps bills of sale are known, but these are very much the exception, and precious few can be documented as genuine. Peter Senich in his excellent book *U.S. Marine Corps Scout Sniper: World War II and Korea* aptly summed up the three types of M1903A1/Unertl rifles that may be encountered:

"From a collector's standpoint, there are, in effect, three categories of M1903A1 Marine Corps sniper rifles: those originating within the Marine Corps during World War II; those owing their origins to the Marine Corps following the war, particularly those intended for use in Korea; and finally, those surreptitiously 'put together' for sale on the collector's market. Unfortunately, in most cases, it is all but impossible to tell these weapons apart."

Regrettably, these comments are absolutely correct, and positive identification of a M1903A1/Unertl sniper rifle can be extremely difficult, if not impossible, for even experienced collectors. The fact that the rifles were converted by Marine armorers on an individual basis, and that even the originals varied somewhat from rifle to rifle, make it very difficult to properly ascertain the originality of a particular rifle of this type. Any competent gunsmith today can create a realistic-looking fake U.S.M.C. 1903A1/Unertl sniper rifle if they have the correct components and a bit of knowledge. Very few U.S.M.C. sniper rifles have accompanying documents, such as government bills of sale, so it is important to learn the features found on genuine examples. As with most U.S. military sniper rifles, any undocumented example is really worth no more than the value of the sum of the parts. Genuine Unertl U.S.M.C. sniper telescopes still surface from time to time and typically bring a large sum of money. Since there are few original rifles of this type around today that are missing their scopes, the obvious conclusion is that these scopes are being used to create more fake sniper rifles. It is unquestionably true that the vast majority of rifles of this type encountered today are fake, but proving it, one way or the other, can be a futile task. Nevertheless, a U.S.M.C. M1903A1/Unertl sniper rifle is a visually impressive weapon, and one of the most popular U.S. sniper rifles available to collectors.

It is puzzling that none of the several types of '03 sniper rifles proved to be very successful in United States military service given the weapon's well-deserved reputation as a superbly accurate and reliable rifle. It must be concluded that the '03 sniper rifle's relative lack of success was due more to the types of telescopes employed, rather than any inherent problem with the rifles.

Although a few M1903A4 sniper rifles lingered on in the military's inventory as late as 1970, the Korean War effectively marked the end of the M1903 rifle's utilization as a combat arm by American armed forces. Some of the venerable weapons remain in limited use today by military color guards and similar duties, but by the early 1950s, the glory days of the '03 as a combat weapon were clearly over.

Postwar Disposition of M1903 Rifles

Following the end of World War II, most of the '03 rifles in government inventory, except for the Army and Marine Corps sniper rifles, were deemed obsolete. After the war, large numbers of '03 rifles were overhauled by several ordnance facilities, including Springfield Armory and Rock Island, Ogden and Raritan Arsenals. (See **Table 14** on page 227). In addition to the overhaul work performed at the government installations, Remington Arms Company also received a contract near the end of WWII for rifle rebuilding. This contract was identified as "Remanufacture Rifles, U.S. Cal. .30, M1903A1, A3 & A4." Contract terms called for 43,000 of these rifles to be reconditioned, with delivery to be between April and October 1945. The work generally consisted of gauging all parts, replacing any unserviceable barrels, refinishing the stocks as necessary and proof firing. After proof firing, the stocks were stamped with a small circled "P" marking, which is normally the only way to identify one of the Remington-overhauled rifles.

Even though the '03s were no longer envisioned for use by U.S. military forces, the weapons required refurbishment to make them suitable for sale on the surplus market and for foreign military aid requirements. A large number of spare parts, such as barrels and bolts, were necessary for use in these extensive postwar overhaul programs. Remington Arms Company received a contract for 95,000 spare barrels, 1,859 bolts and other spare parts near the end of the company's production run. Remington, along with Smith-Corona, made spare M1903A3 rear sights and other parts. The commercial firm of Hadley Special Tool Co. also produced rear sight assemblies, sears, triggers, safeties and other replacement parts in the late-WWII or immediate postwar period. In addition, Springfield Armory manufactured a number of '03 and 'A3 replacement parts in the late-WWII period.

Several erstwhile allies were the recipients of M1903 rifles from the immediate post-WWII period into the early 1950s. Also beginning in the early 1950s, the Director of Civilian Marksmanship (DCM) began the sale of M1903, M1903A1 and M1903 Modified rifles to qualified members of the National Rifle Association. The rifles were graded either *Serviceable*, and listed for $30.00 plus shipping, or *Unserviceable* for $15.00 plus shipping. The Unserviceable designation did not mean that the rifles were necessarily unusable, only that they were not thoroughly inspected and were sold *as is*. Most were perfectly suitable for use.

Brand-new M1903A3 rifles were also sold during this period for $50.00 plus shipping. In 1957, used M1903A3 rifles began to be offered for the same price as the Serviceable and Unserviceable '03s. In early 1963, the rifles had been sold and the program was discontinued. Many of the former DCM rifles are still encountered. A number of these weapons, especially M1903A3s, were coated in cosmoline and packed for long-term storage after rebuild. It is not unusual today for someone to encounter one of these rifles and reach the logical but erroneous conclusion that they have acquired a rifle unused since it left the factory. These rebuilt rifles appear to be new because they were never used since their overhaul, which further reinforces the factory new myth. A few such rifles were, in fact, untouched since they left the factory, but new production rifles were not originally packed in cosmoline. Many of the DCM '03s were sporterized in the late 1940s into the 1960s. The weapons were not considered as collectible by many people at this time, and these DCM rifles were seen by most buyers as a source of low-cost hunting and target rifles. Such sporterized examples have no value as collectibles. It has been correctly said that the definition of sporterizing is taking a $500 rifle, spending $300 on it, and turning it into a $200 rifle!

In the spring of 2002, the Civilian Marksmanship Program (CMP), successor of the DCM, acquired a relatively large quantity (reportedly about 45,000) of M1903 and M1903A3 rifles and offered them for sale to qualified buyers. These weapons were previously in the hands of a foreign country to which they had been sent after WWII for military aid. When that nation had no further use for the rifles, they were returned to the United States government and subsequently transferred to the CMP. Although the original recipient nation was not revealed by the CMP, it is certain that the country was Greece, which had need for military weapons to battle Communist insurgents after WWII. Most of the rifles were refurbished by the Greeks, and many were refinished in a distinctive black-tinted phosphate that was not as durable as traditional parkerizing. The majority of these rifles will show hard use and signs of various modifications while in Greek service. The CMP prices ranged from $375 to $525 depending on maker, variant and type of stock. The variants offered were Springfield and Rock Island high and low numbers, Springfield Mark 1s, Remington M1903s and Remington and Smith-Corona M1903A3s. All types were available in Type S or Type C stock configuration with the latter bringing a higher price.

Accessories, Accouterments and Appendages

The many variants of the M1903 rifle make it a fertile field for collecting. It is sometimes forgotten that the large number of related items used with these rifles can be extremely interesting collectibles as well. Some of these accessories, accouterments and appendages are common and inexpensive, while others can rival many of the rifles in rarity and value. Whether they are worth a few dollars, or thousands of dollars, such items can add a lot of color and interest to the rifles in a collection.

Slings

The sling is often overlooked by some collectors but is an important part of the rifle as the weapon is, technically speaking, incomplete without the proper sling. As collector interest in the '03 continues to grow, original slings are often in short supply and prices are rapidly escalating.

M1887 Sling

The early prototype rifles were used with the leather M1887 sling as issued with all variants of the U.S. Krag service rifle. The M1887 sling was $68\frac{1}{2}$ inches inches in length and $1\frac{1}{4}$ inches wide. The sling utilized a brass frog for adjustment, and the lower end was secured by a single brass button. Some M1887 slings were constructed of two pieces of leather sewn together. When the M1903 rod bayonet rifle was adopted, the M1887 sling remained in use. However, the difference in spacing of the '03's sling swivels as opposed to the Krag resulted in some problems with the old sling. Some of the older M1887 slings were reportedly shortened to 51 inches for use with the new rifle.

M1903 Sling

A new pattern sling was adopted that was supposedly more suitable for use with the '03 rifle. This sling was 48 inches long and had the same type of brass adjustment frog and button as the M1887 sling. The M1903 slings were dated (1903 and 1904 dates have been observed), and all examples are believed to have been made by Rock Island Arsenal. While marginally adequate as a carrying sling, it was not long enough to be useful as a shooting aid and the M1903 sling was not very popular. While uncommon, as compared to the later M1907 leather slings, a seemingly disproportionate number of M1903 slings may be found in excellent condition, which suggests that many were never issued. Unlike the later slings, reproduction M1903 slings are not common today, but one should not be oblivious to that possibility.

M1907 Sling

The lack of the M1903 sling's utility as a shooting aid resulted in vociferous complaints from shooters who decried the new sling and lobbied for a better design, or even the reintroduction of the M1887 sling. The Chief of Ordnance responded by approving the adoption of a sling reportedly designed by a colonel in the Ohio National Guard in 1906. This new sling was designated as the *Model of 1907*. The M1907 sling was constructed of two sections of leather and had two brass adjustment frogs. The sling was easily adjusted for use as a carrying sling and as a shooting aid. Most, if not all, of the initial production

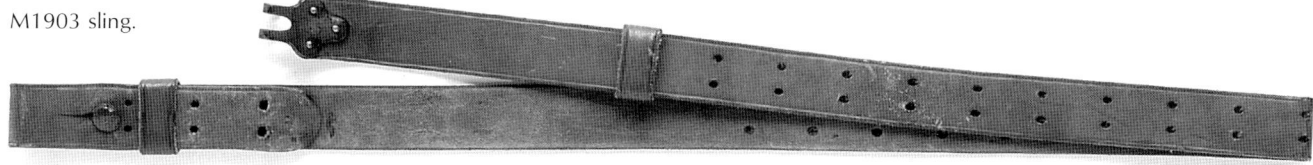

M1903 sling.

M1907 slings were fabricated by Rock Island Arsenal and marked with the identity of the maker, the initials of the inspector and the year of production. Original M1907 slings from this period are somewhat scarce and are sought after by today's collectors.

The demands of the First World War resulted in contracts being given to a number of firms for production of the M1907 sling. There were no distinctive variants of the pre-WWII slings. Many, but not all, were stamped with the identity of the maker, inspector initials, and the date of production. The most commonly encountered date is 1918. Any original M1907 sling in decent condition is a desirable collectible, but the dated slings will normally bring a premium over the unmarked variety.

The M1907 sling was standardized for use with the M1903 and M1917 rifles, as well as the 12-gauge *trench guns* adopted in WWI. On the eve of the Second World War, the M1907 remained the standard service rifle sling, and new contracts were given to a number of firms. The only substantive difference between the WWII contract slings and those made earlier was the use of parkerized steel frogs rather than the blackened brass frogs. Some very early WWII production slings still utilized brass hardware, but by late 1942, the steel variety was the norm. Many of the WWII-vintage slings were marked with the identity of the maker and the date of production.

Many collectors wish to have slings on their rifles that are dated to match the vintage of the rifle. There is nothing wrong with this approach but, in actual military service, the

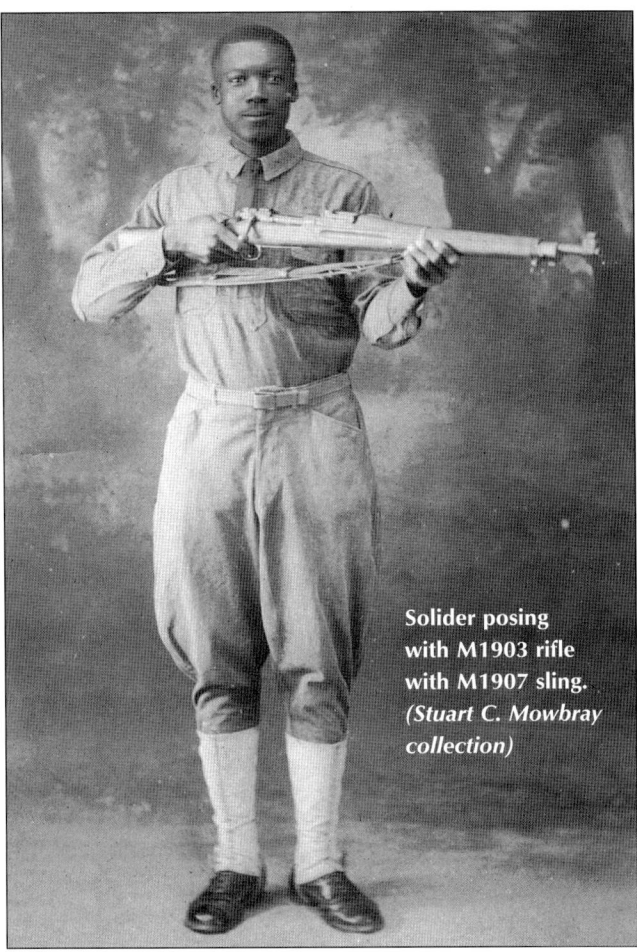

Solider posing with M1903 rifle with M1907 sling. (Stuart C. Mowbray collection)

Markings on M1903 sling.

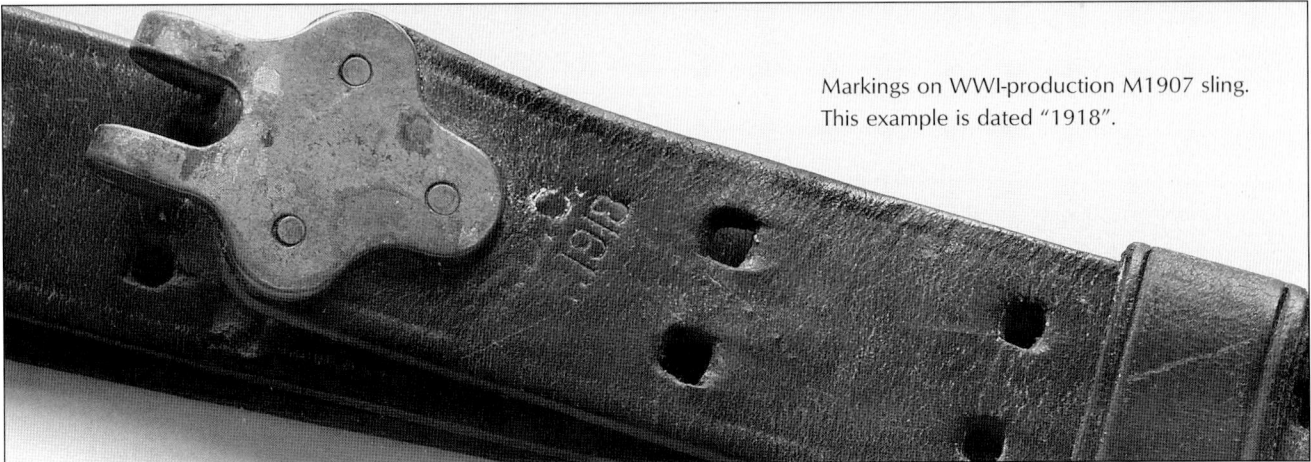

Markings on WWI-production M1907 sling. This example is dated "1918".

M1907 sling (pre-WWII with brass hardware).

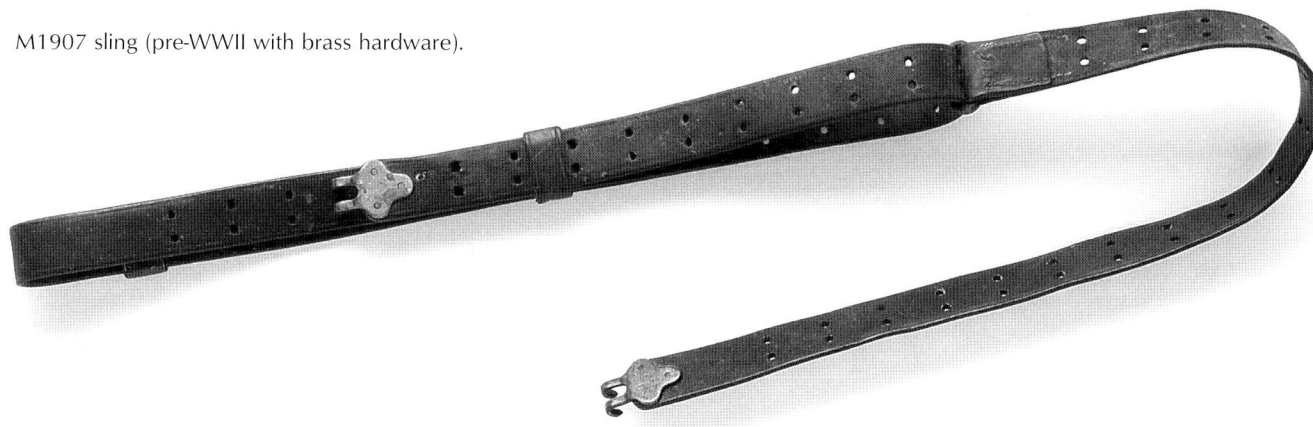

WWI U.S. Doughboys. Note M1903 rifle with
M1907 sling and fixed M1905 bayonet. *(National Archives)*

vintage of the sling and the vintage of the rifle were often years apart. Large numbers of WWI (and earlier) slings were used in WWII. Conversely, a later sling was often put with an earlier rifle to replace a missing or worn sling. Nevertheless, there is some appeal to many collectors to have, for example, a 1942-dated sling on their 1942-vintage Remington '03. On the other hand, a 1918 sling on the same rifle would be, historically speaking, just as accurate.

M1917 Kerr Sling

Although the M1907 was the predominate service rifle sling in WWI, another variety was adopted as a supplemental sling to meet the huge demand. This sling, developed by the Kerr Adjustable Strap Company, was standardized as the *Sling, Gun, M1917 (webbing)*. The sling was termed the "No-Buckl" by the company and was made of gray or greenish-gray canvas material and had stamped sheet metal snaps for adjustment. The sling was less expensive and a bit lighter than the leather M1907 sling.

The Kerr sling was standardized for use with the M1903, M1917 and Krag rifles in WWI. Some people have

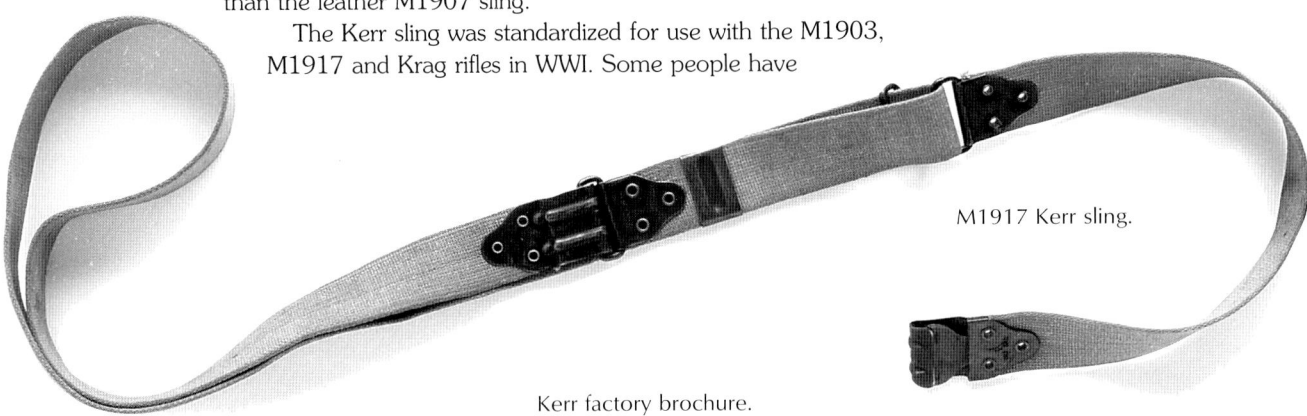

M1917 Kerr sling.

Kerr factory brochure.

Group of U.S. Marines from the WWI or immediate post-WWI era with Lewis machine gun. The Marines also have M1903 rifles slung over their backs. The rifles are fitted with M1917 Kerr slings. Note also the M1910 bayonet scabbards. *(U.S. Marine Corps)*

M1923 Sling

The M1923 sling was developed as an alternative for the relatively costly and heavy M1907 sling. It was adopted as the *Sling, Gun, M1923 (webbing)*. Although adopted prior to the Second World War, the sling was not put into quantity production until late 1941 or early 1942. The sling was intended to be issued with the modified .303 caliber Remington M1903 rifles that were to be made for the British. Upon cancellation of the British rifle contract, the M1923 slings were reportedly utilized on some of the M1917 rifles and Thompson submachine guns sent to Great Britain for Lend-Lease purposes. Some of the slings were also issued to American troops. In theory, the M1923 sling was judged better than either the M1907 sling or the M1917 Kerr slings. The web material was lighter and less prone to deterioration than the leather M1907 sling, and the M1923 sling was supposed to be easier and faster to adjust. In reality, any theoretical advantages were greatly offset by the fact that the sling was complicated to install and adjust. Even today, a number of collectors scratch their heads at the complexity of this supposedly superior sling. The sling was equally disliked by the troops during WWII for the same reasons.

assumed that the Kerr sling was intended for use with the M1917 rifle because of the sling's M1917 designation. This is not correct, as the M1917 designation referred to the year of adoption. A somewhat similar sling, designated as the M3, was adopted in WWII for use with the Thompson Submachine Gun. The *M3* sling was shorter than the M1917 sling, the web material was of a different color and the blued sheet metal snaps were unmarked. Few of the Kerr slings were utilized overseas during WWI.

Original M1917 Kerr slings were commonly found until just a few years ago. They are still far from rare, although nice examples are getting harder to find and prices are rising. A M1917 sling would be technically correct for a WWI or WWII-vintage '03 although, in reality, the sling saw much less use with the weapon as compared to the M1907 sling.

Despite the M1923's unpopularity with most of its users, it is nevertheless a very collectible item, and prime examples are getting to be harder to find. Early examples were made of a khaki-colored material, while later examples were olive green. Most were marked with the initials of the maker. The most common marking is "S.M. Co." which represents Schlegel Manufacturing, Rochester, New York. The slings were also stamped with the date of production (1942 to 1944 dates will be encountered). Some of these slings will be seen marked with dates as late as the 1950s, and stamped "M.R.T." These dates are not the dates of production but, rather, indicate that the slings received Mildew Resistant Treatment on the specified date. It is highly unlikely that any of these unsatisfactory M1923 slings were manufactured after WWII.

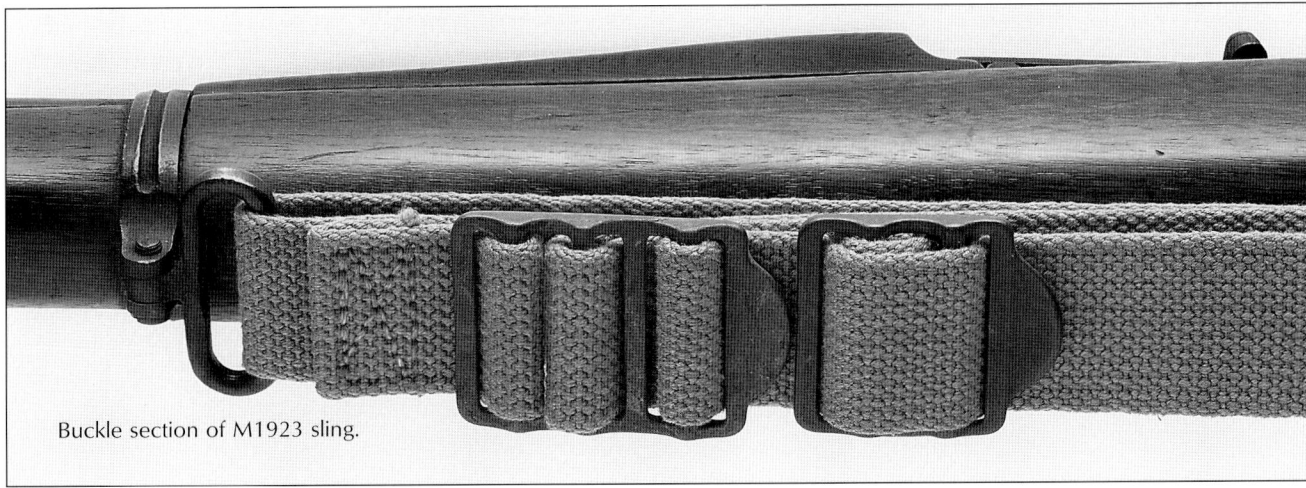

Buckle section of M1923 sling.

M1 Sling

By early 1942, the War Department requested a rifle sling that was less expensive, simpler and lighter than either the M1907 or M1923 slings. After evaluating several designs, the *Sling, Gun, M1 (webbing)* was adopted and put into production by several firms. The M1 sling was made of web material with a sheet-metal adjustment buckle. As with the M1917 sling, the M1 designation had nothing to do with the type of rifle(s) it was intended for but, rather, was simply the sling's model designation.

The M1 sling was capable of use with all varieties of U.S. service rifles and shotguns. The M1 sling was fine for carrying the rifle, but was not as well suited as the M1907 sling for marksmanship purposes. Earlier versions were constructed of khaki material, and later examples were olive green. Some were ink-stamped with the initials of the maker and the year of production.

The M1 sling began to be issued in 1943, but never replaced the M1907 sling in service during WWII. After the war, the M1 sling was retained as the standardized U.S. service rifle sling, and the basic design remains in use even today. Post-WWII slings can be identified as having been made from dark olive green web with a denser weave and had a different style adjustment buckle. WWII M1 slings, especially in excellent condition, are increasingly hard to find and prices are rising. Post-WWII M1 slings are still relatively common and inexpensive. An original WWII M1 sling would be correct for use on a M1903 rifle that remained in service after 1942 until the end of the war.

Original U.S. military rifle slings have become highly desired collectibles due to the dramatic increase in collector interest in U.S. martial arms. There are reproductions of all types of slings (with the possible exception of the M1923). A reproduction sling can be fine for shooting or hunting purposes, but has no place on a collectible rifle. Some of the reproductions are stamped with the name of a genuine government contractor and date of production (WWI and WWII dates may be noted). A reproduction sling of this type can usually be spotted without too much difficulty if someone knows what to look for. The configuration of the metal frogs and rivets is especially important. Original rivets were flush with the frog, while many of the reproductions have rivets with rounded heads that protrude above the frog. While a genuine sling in unused condition may be encountered, in most cases, a sling that appears too new for a 60+-year-old item should be viewed with the utmost suspicion. Original slings often change hands today for surprisingly high prices. If a collector wishes to pay a lot of money for a pristine original example that is his prerogative. However, a collector should not pay a premium price for a sling he believes is a genuine example when it is not. Regardless, an original sling of the correct type and vintage is a great addition to any collectible '03 rifle.

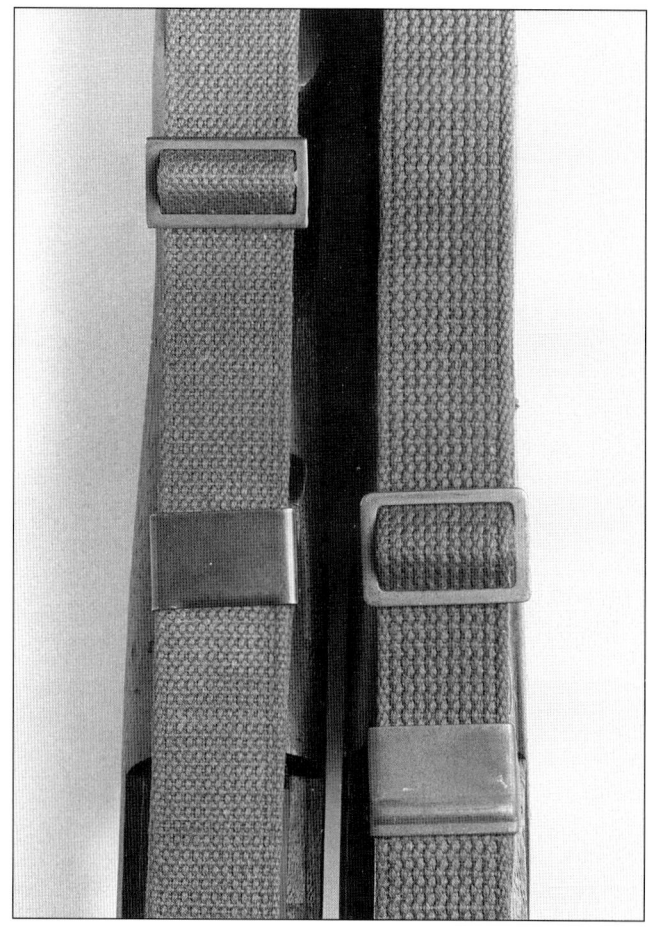

M1 Slings (left): WWII M1 Sling, (right) Post-WWII sling. Note the difference in the configuration of the metal buckle and loop between the WWII and post-WWII slings. The postwar sling also has a thicker weave to the web material.

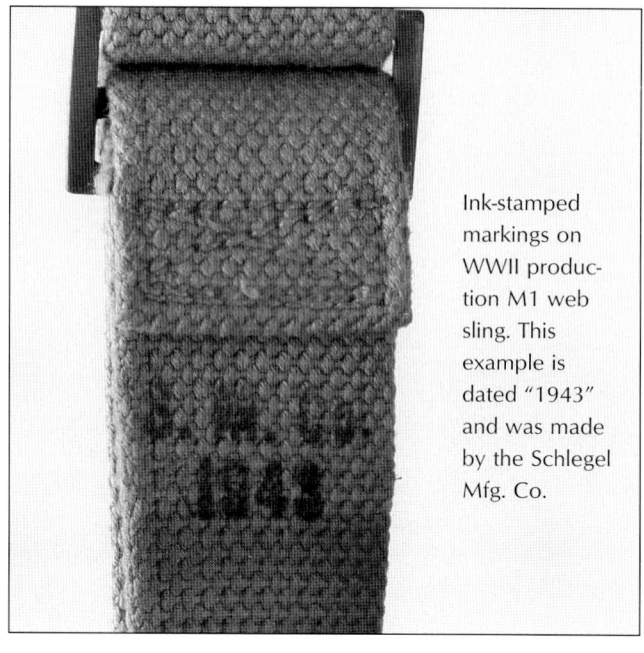

Ink-stamped markings on WWII production M1 web sling. This example is dated "1943" and was made by the Schlegel Mfg. Co.

Oiler and Thong Case

Except for extremely early rifles, a cylindrical nickel-plated brass case was issued to be carried in the butt trap recess. One end of the case contained a reservoir for oil, with a threaded cap containing a dropper for application of the oil. The other end, which also closed with a threaded cap, contained a compartment for a thong and bristle brush for cleaning the bore of the rifle. In 1908, the bristle brush was replaced by a bronze brush with threaded brass weight. The bronze brush was more effective in removing metal bore fouling than the earlier bristle brush. Versions of the oiler and thong case were used through the Second World War and beyond. A plastic oiler and thong case was adopted and issued during WWII. One of these would be proper for a M1903 rifle remaining in service from circa 1943 until the end of the war.

WWII production plastic oiler and thong case.

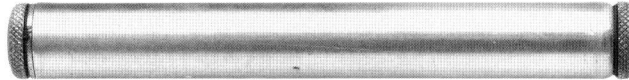

Pre-WWII metal oiler and thong case.

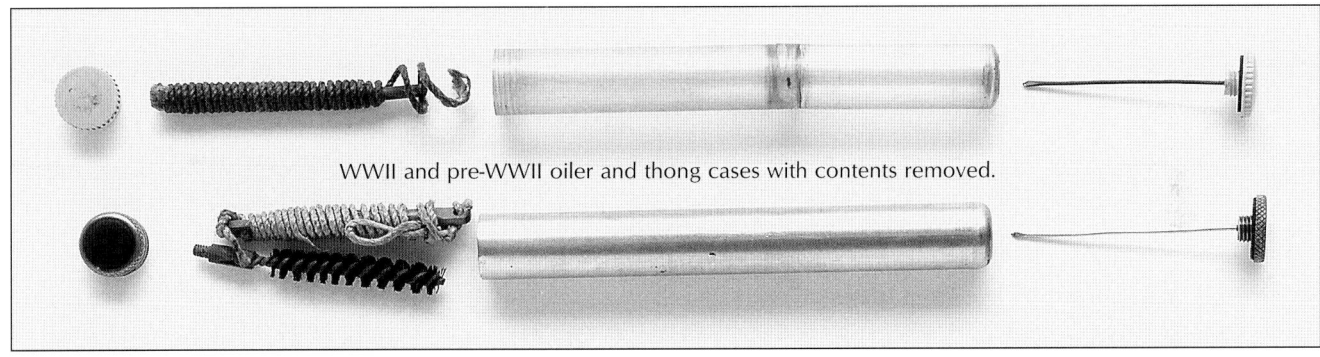

WWII and pre-WWII oiler and thong cases with contents removed.

Spare Parts Container

The Container, Spare Parts for the M1903 rifle was adopted in 1911. This item consisted of a wooden cylinder that was configured to hold a spare striker, firing pin assembly, and extractor for the rifle. The sear notch on the cocking piece required that a slot be machined into the bottom of the stock recess in order to provide clearance. Rifles manufactured from the time of the container's adoption in 1911 through 1917 were made with this slot in the recess. The vast majority of the spare parts containers were made of walnut, although the use of other types of wood was also approved.

The containers were to be carried in alternate rifles. It was eventually determined that it was more important to have cleaning materials readily available in the buttstock recess since breakage of the parts carried in the container was relatively uncommon. By 1918, the spare parts containers were withdrawn from use. Original surviving examples are uncommon, although some well-made reproductions were produced in the mid-1980s. These can usually be identified because of their brand-new condition as compared to the originals. Any example of an '03 spare parts container is a great find.

Wooden spare parts container.

Oiler and thong case.

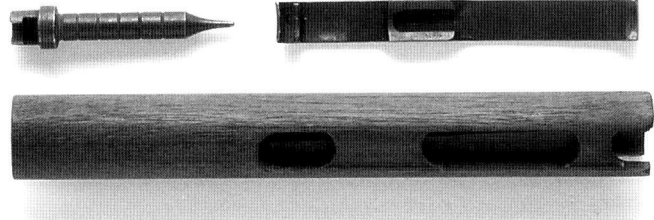

Spare parts container with spare parts removed.

Bayonets and Bayonet Scabbards

M1905 Bayonet and Scabbard – 1905 to 1910

When it was determined that the unsatisfactory rod bayonet had to be replaced, an Ordnance committee was appointed to evaluate various types of bayonets and to make recommendations regarding which pattern should be adopted. Several types of improved rod bayonets were tested along with a conventional knife bayonet. Multi-purpose bayonets, including a design intended for entrenching use, as well as a wide-blade bolo bayonet, were also evaluated. The committee eventually selected a conventional knife bayonet, similar to the Krag bayonet but with a 16-inch blade. It is interesting to note that all of the knife bayonets tested had 16-inch blades, rather than the shorter 10-inch blade used with the previous Krag bayonet, to compensate for the reduced reach of the shorter '03, as compared to the longer Krag rifle. The initial pattern bayonet considered for the new rifle had the same type of Mauser-influenced, side-mounted transverse locking plunger as the Krag bayonet. This was soon changed to a plunger, located underneath and behind the guard, which was less prone to accidental release. On April 3, 1905, the War Department officially approved the recommendations of the committee and adopted the *Bayonet, Model of 1905*.

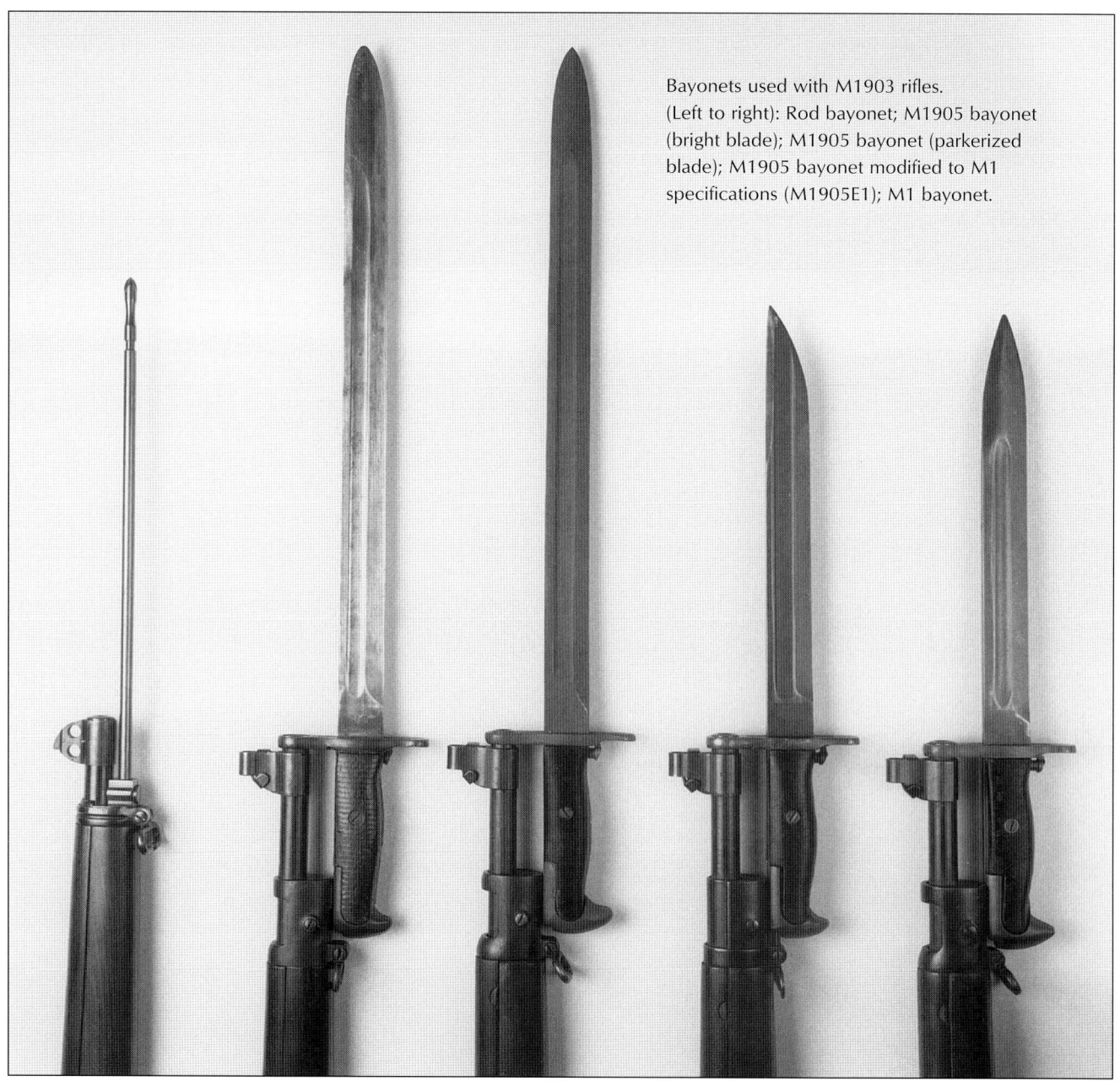

Bayonets used with M1903 rifles.
(Left to right): Rod bayonet; M1905 bayonet (bright blade); M1905 bayonet (parkerized blade); M1905 bayonet modified to M1 specifications (M1905E1); M1 bayonet.

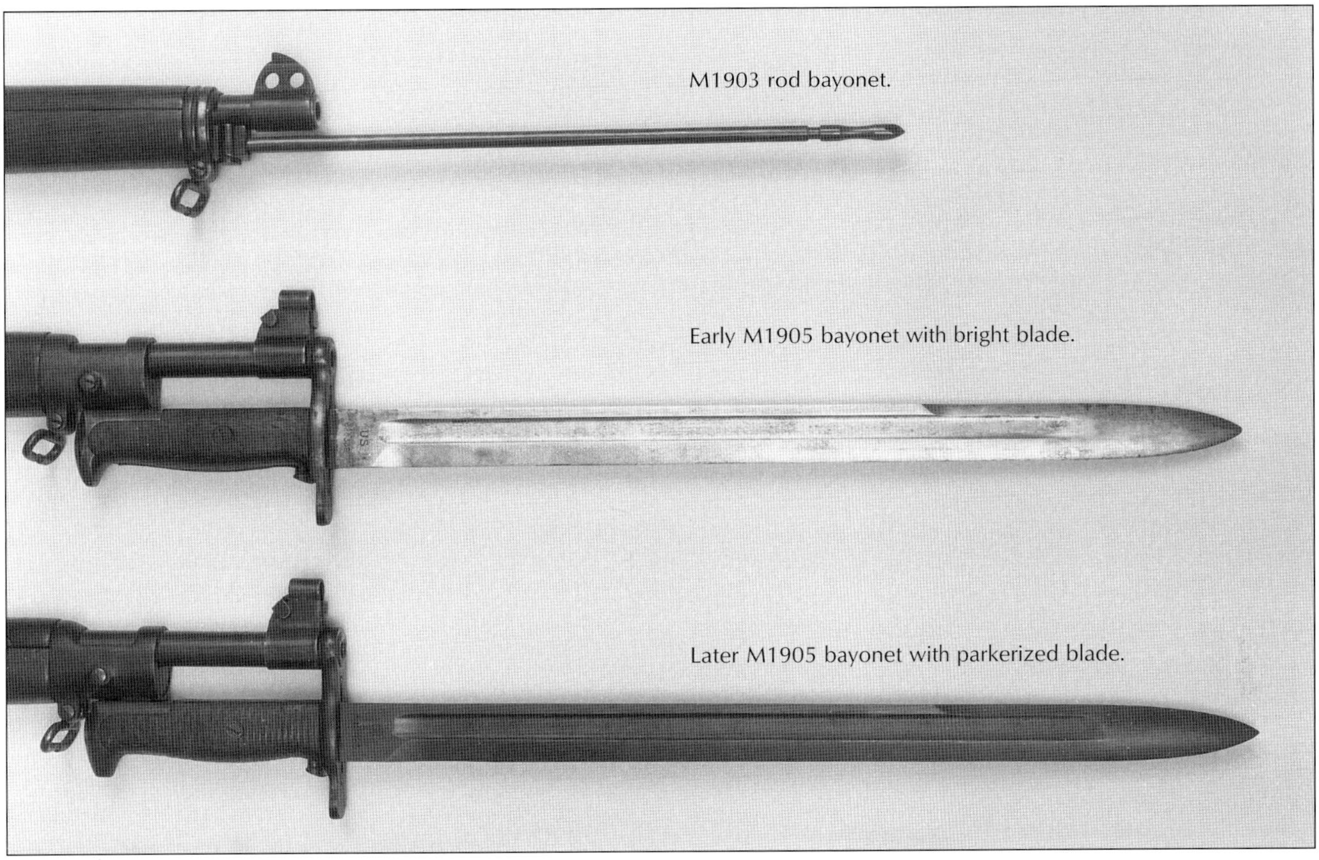

M1903 rod bayonet.

Early M1905 bayonet with bright blade.

Later M1905 bayonet with parkerized blade.

Early M1905 bayonet (bright blade) with unmodified M1905 scabbard. (front view)

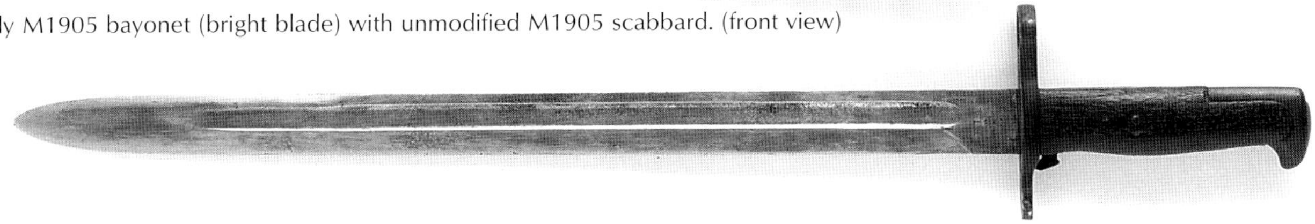

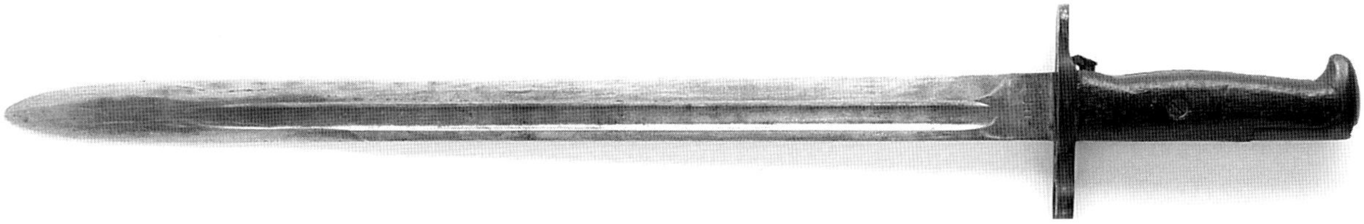

Same as above (back view).

M1903 rifles with M1905 bayonets firing from trench position in WWI. *(National Archives)*

Doughboy of the 33rd Division on guard duty in France during WWI. Note the M1903 Rifle and M1905 bayonet. *(U.S. Army)*

World War II U.S. soldier on sentry duty armed with a M1903 Springfield rifle and M1905 bayonet. *(U.S. Army)*

BELOW – American soldiers in WWI France with 1905 bayonets.

WWI soldier on guard duty with M1903 rifle and M1905 bayonet affixed. *(U.S. Army)*

Soon after its adoption, the Model of 1905 bayonet was put into production at Springfield Armory and Rock Island Arsenal. Early examples were not serially numbered, but after 1906, serial numbers were marked on the blade. It should be noted that it was never intended to issue rifles and bayonets with matching serial numbers. The reason for serially numbering the bayonets was because the bayonet was considered an important item of issue, and this allowed for better inventory control and accountability. The M1905 bayonet had walnut grips with shallow scalloping. The hilts were blued in order to retard corrosion under the grips. The blued area extended for about ¼ inch beyond the crossguard, but the balance of the blade was polished bright. The bayonets were marked with the year of production, the initials of the maker, "S.A." or "R.I.A.", and the Ordnance Department flaming bomb insignia. The M1905 bayonet was issued with a scabbard constructed of a wooden body under a leather covering. The scabbard was also standardized as the Model of 1905. Model of 1905 scabbards manufactured prior to 1910 had the same type of wire belt hanger as found on late-production Krag bayonet scabbards. In 1907, the bayonet catch was redesigned to eliminate the propensity of the older bayonet catch to inadvertently release when the rifle was fired. The modified bayonets typically had an "A" stamped near the bayonet lug slot. Concurrent with adoption of the M1905 bayonet, the

Markings on early production (1907) M1905 bayonet made by Springfield Armory.

Reverse side of very early RIA bayonet. Note the lack of a serial number.

WWI soldiers undergoing trench warfare training in gas masks. Note fixed M1905 bayonets. *(Frank Trzaska)*

Markings on M1905 scabbard. This example was made by Rock Island Arsenal in 1907. "F.P.B" is the arsenal inspector.

Markings on very early (1906) M1905 bayonet made by Rock Island Arsenal.

Reverse side of 1907-dated bayonet. Note "US" and serial #.

Blade markings on 1908 production Springfield M1905 bayonet.

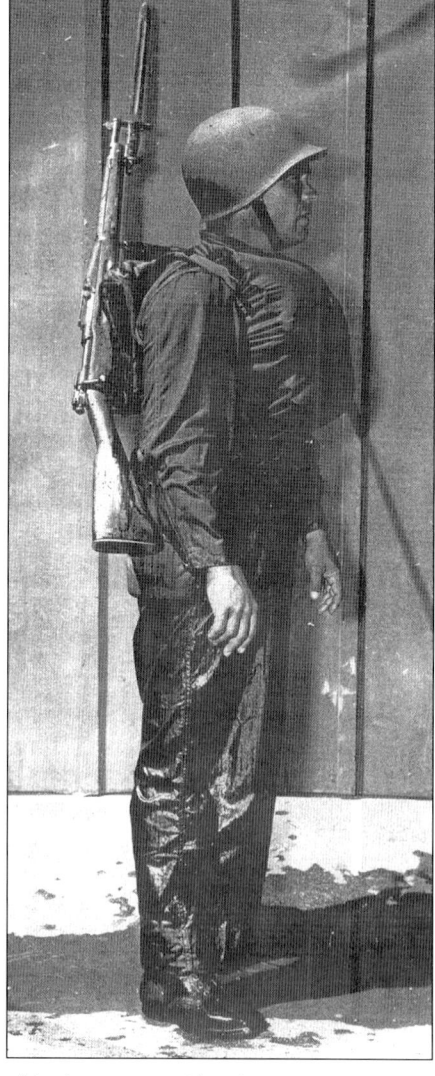

LEFT – Pre-WWI U.S. Army soldier with M1903 rifle. Note the M1905 bayonet in an unmodified M1905 scabbard. *(Frank Trzaska)* CENTER – Burl Kincaid of Colorado. Note the M1905 bayonet and the M1905 scabbard suspended from his belt. This photo was taken at the Post Studio, Fort Logan, Colorado. *(Courtesy Stuart C. Mowbray collection)* RIGHT – WWII U.S. Marine with experimental flotation bladder. Note the M1903 rifle with fixed M1905 bayonet. *(U.S.M.C. – Courtesy Alec Tulkoff)*

M1903 rifle was modified to incorporate the necessary hardware for attachment of the new bayonet and elimination of the rod bayonet and related mechanism. In 1910, a M1905 bayonet with a modified guard for use with limited-issue Maxim silencers was produced. Surviving examples of these modified bayonets are uncommon.

M1910 Bayonet Scabbard

In 1910, a new pattern bayonet scabbard was adopted for use with the M1905 bayonet. Unlike the earlier M1905 scabbard which had a leather cover, the M1910 scabbard had a canvas covering with a leather tip, either brown and black. The single metal belt hangar was replaced by the now-familiar cartridge belt hooks that saw use on all types of equipment (canteens, pistol holsters, first aid pouches, etc.) even as late as today. The M1910 scabbards were typically unmarked, although

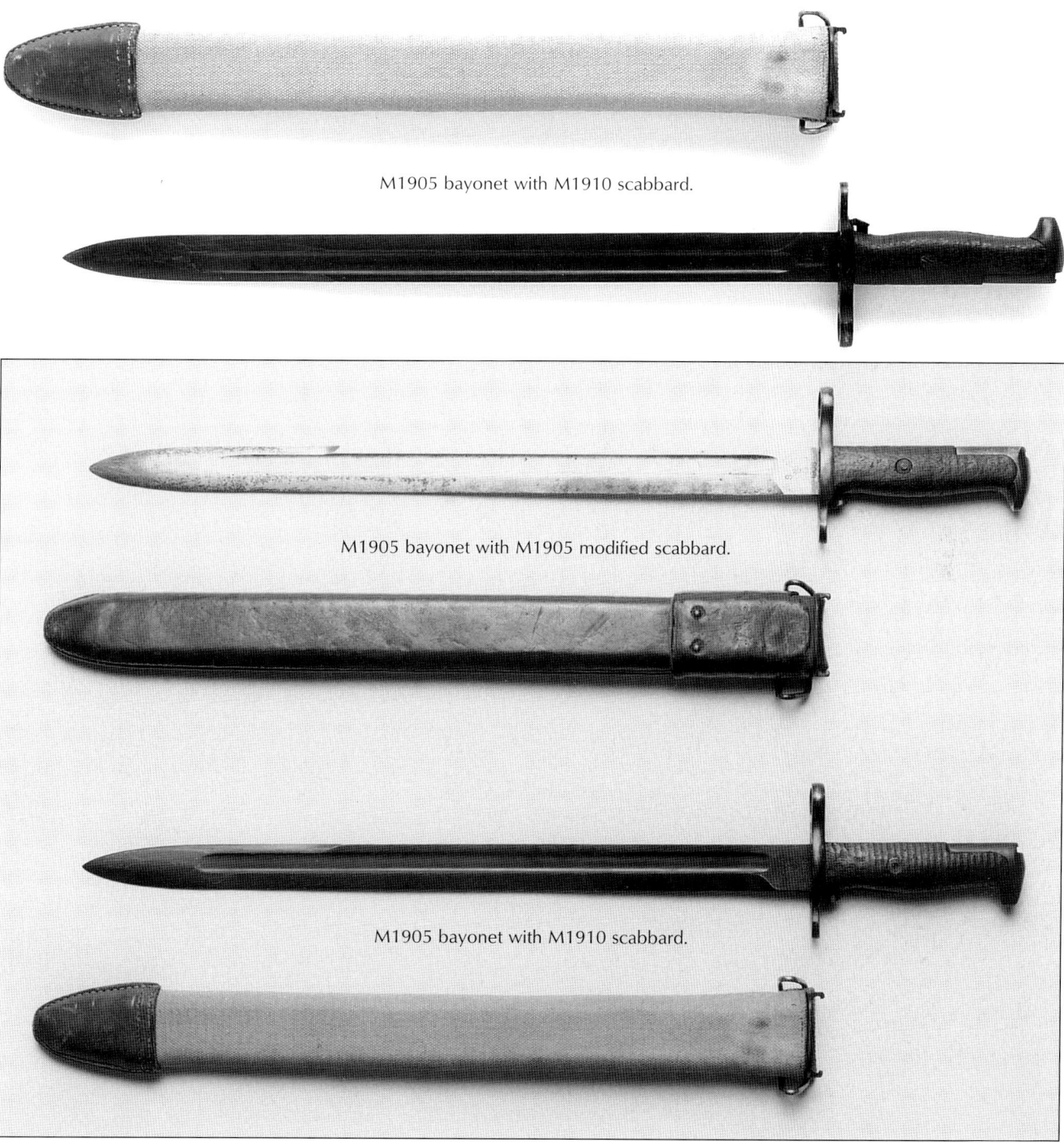

M1905 bayonet with M1910 scabbard.

M1905 bayonet with M1905 modified scabbard.

M1905 bayonet with M1910 scabbard.

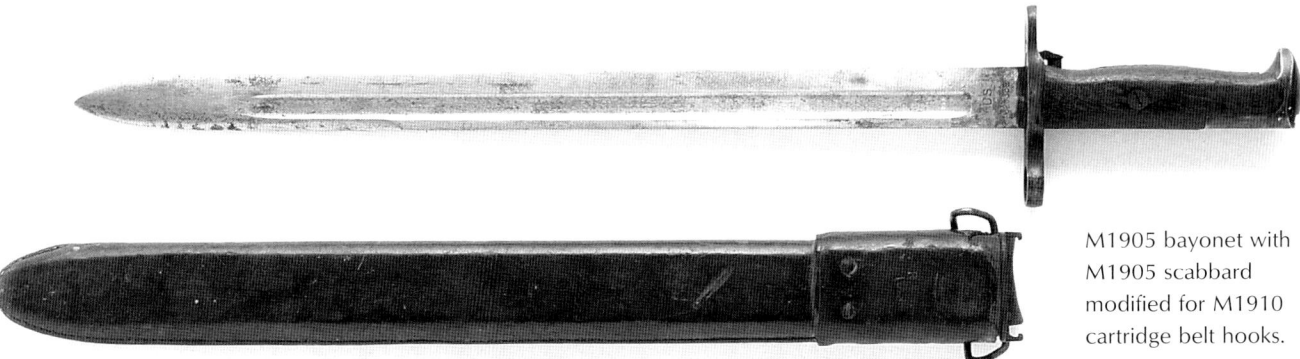

M1905 bayonet with M1905 scabbard modified for M1910 cartridge belt hooks.

some had unit designation stenciled or written on the canvas cover. Many of the earlier M1905 scabbards were modified to incorporate the M1910-pattern wire belt hooks.

Model of 1915 Bolo-Bayonet

While the M1905 was a serviceable bayonet, the Ordnance Department evaluated the concept of multipurpose implements that could serve as tools and bayonets. Such an item would theoretically allow a soldier to carry a single implement that could serve as a bayonet, entrenching tool and blade for brush cutting and similar duties. A bolo-bayonet had been fabricated in limited numbers and was issued with the Krag rifle just prior to the adoption of the M1903 rifle. Several types of experimental combination edged weapons of the type were fabricated and tested for use with the M1903 rifle including designs based on the standard M1909 and M1910 Bolos. The bolo was a knife with a wide and heavy blade that was used as an edged tool and, in extreme cases, as a combat weapon.

In 1915, a combination bolo-bayonet was adopted as the Model of 1915 and a production order for 6,002 was placed with Springfield Armory in May of 1915. A total of 3,200 were made in Fiscal Year 1916 and 2,802 in FY 1917. It is reported in Ordnance Department documents that the items were intended for issue to the Philippine Scouts. A total of 5,800 of the M1915 bolo-bayonets were shipped to the Philippines, and 202 were sent to Rock Island Arsenal.

WWI Doughboy in trench position with his M1903 rifle close by. Note the modified M1905 bayonet scabbard. *(National Archives)*

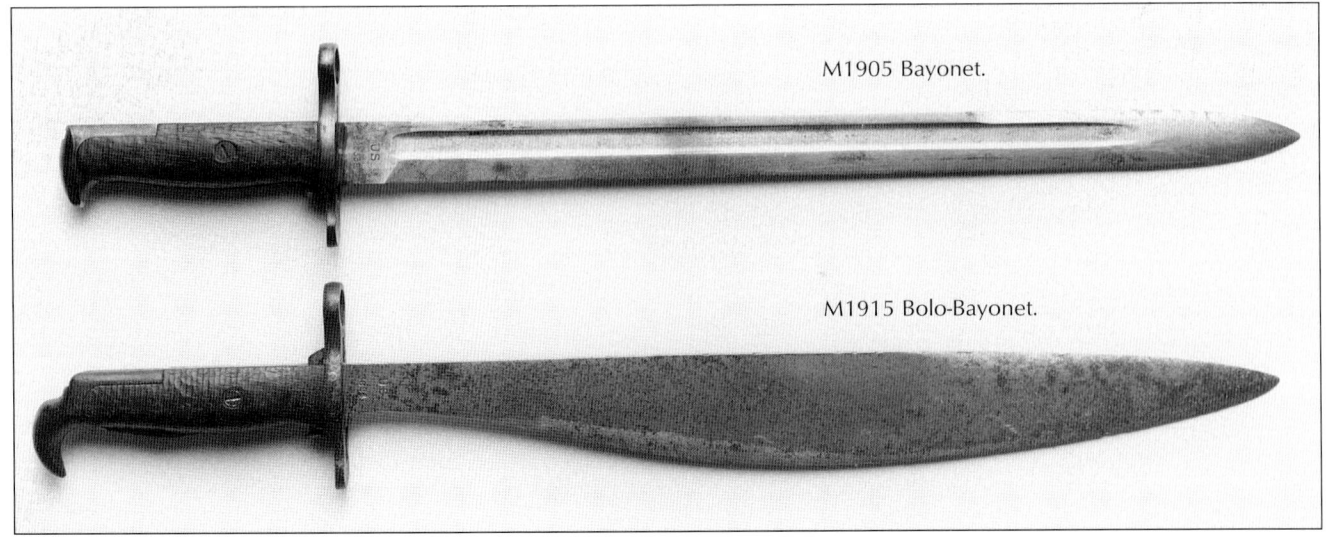

M1905 Bayonet.

M1915 Bolo-Bayonet.

The M1915 bolo-bayonet featured a 15 13/16-inch bright finished blade with walnut grips and a rather unusual hooked pommel. As was the case with the standard M1905 bayonet being manufactured during this same period, the hilt of the M1915 bolo-bayonet was blued under the grips to retard corrosion. The M1915 bolo-bayonet attached to the '03 rifle in the same manner as the M1905 bayonet. The reverse ricasso was marked "S.A." over a flaming bomb insignia and the year of production, "1916" on most examples. The obverse ricasso was stamped "U.S." over the serial number. The bolo-bayonet was issued with a wide leather-bound scabbard. By the time of the First World War, the M1915 bolo-bayonets began to be withdrawn from service, and all but handful destroyed. Surviving examples are quite rare and valuable.

M1905 Bayonet and M1910 Scabbard – WWI

The M1905 bayonet continued in production during the First World War at Springfield Armory and Rock Island Arsenal. Except for the dates, there were no real changes between the WWI-vintage and earlier bayonets other than the fact that the formerly bright-finished blades were blued

Pre-WWI photo of Philippine Scouts (Moros) armed with M1903 rifles with rare M1915 Bolo-Bayonets. *(Frank Trzaska)*

beginning in 1917. Many of the older bright blades were subsequently blued in France during the war by a method referred to in ordnance reports as an "...Italian process." In very late 1918, new-production M1905 bayonet blades began receiving a parkerized finish, similar to that applied to the M1903 rifles manufactured in the same period.

The M1910 bayonet scabbard remained the standard pattern, and large numbers were produced and issued during the war along with some of the earlier modified M1905 leather scabbards. The M1910 remained the standard U.S. bayonet scabbard well into WWII.

FAR LEFT – Blade markings on 1918 production Rock Island Arsenal M1905 bayonet. LEFT – Serial number on 1918 production RIA M1905 bayonet.
BELOW – WWI postcard depicting bayonet training at Camp Upton (NY). *(Frank Trzaska)*

WWI photo showing M1905 bayonets being sharpened on a grinding stone. *(U.S. Army Military History Institute)*

M1917 Bayonet Scabbard

It is interesting to note that the M1917 Bayonet Scabbard was also approved for use with the M1905 bayonet in the event of shortages of the standardized M1910 scabbard. This is confirmed in a 1925 memorandum from the Chief of Ordnance confirming that, "The bayonet scabbard, M1917, will be issued when the bayonet scabbard, M1910, is not available." Some WWI-era photographs also confirm that a number of M1917 scabbards were indeed utilized with M1905 bayonets during this period. Due to shortages during the early days of the Second World War, the M1917 scabbard remained in limited use as an alternate to the standardized M1910 scabbard.

While not widely known today, the M1917 scabbard was authorized for use with the M1905 bayonet in both World Wars I and II.

(Left) M1917 Bayonet; (Center) M1917 Scabbard; (Right) M1905 Bayonet.

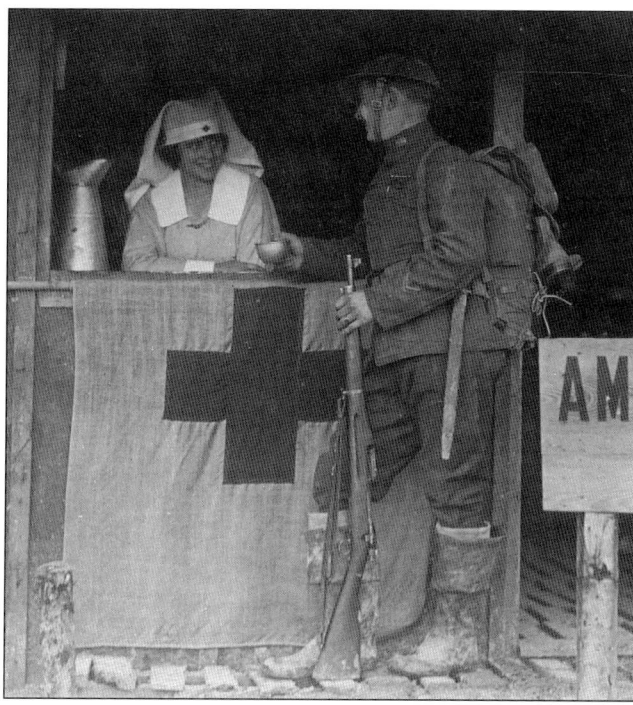

U.S. Army *Doughboy* chatting up a Red Cross volunteer. The soldier is armed with a M1903 Springfield rifle and has his M1905 bayonet in a M1917 scabbard. The M1917 was utilized as a substitute for the M1910 bayonet scabbard in WWI and WWII. *(National Archives)*

M1905 Bayonet – Post-WWI

Springfield Armory continued with production of the M1905 bayonet a few years after WWI, but only very limited numbers were made. Although examples dated as late as 1922 have been observed, bayonets manufactured later than 1918 are uncommon. The latest Rock Island M1905 bayonet observed is dated 1919 and it is doubtful if RIA produced any past this date. The vast majority of WWI and pre-WWI M1905 bayonets were overhauled during the 1920s and 1930s and this process included parkerizing the formerly bright blades.

M1905 Bayonet – World War II

The supply of M1905 bayonets and M1910 scabbards made during the First World War was sufficient to meet the demand until the eve of World War II. A number of these earlier bayonets had been refurbished during their tenure of service which typically resulted in parkerized blades and replaced grips.

Just prior to America's entrance into the Second World War, contracts were given to several firms for additional M1905 bayonets which were needed to equip the large number of new-production M1 rifles and Remington

e. In the summer of 1941
g six firms were granted
roduction as follows:

	Quantity
. . . .	440,336
. . . .	200,000
ompany	60,000
American Fork & Hoe	200,000
Pal Blade & Tool Company	200,000
Oneida, Ltd.	100,000

These new bayonets were of the same general configuration as the earlier Springfield Armory and Rock Island Arsenal M1905 bayonets, but were not as well crafted as the armory-made examples, and had grips made of plastic

WWII Marine in bootcamp, training with a M1905 bayonet.

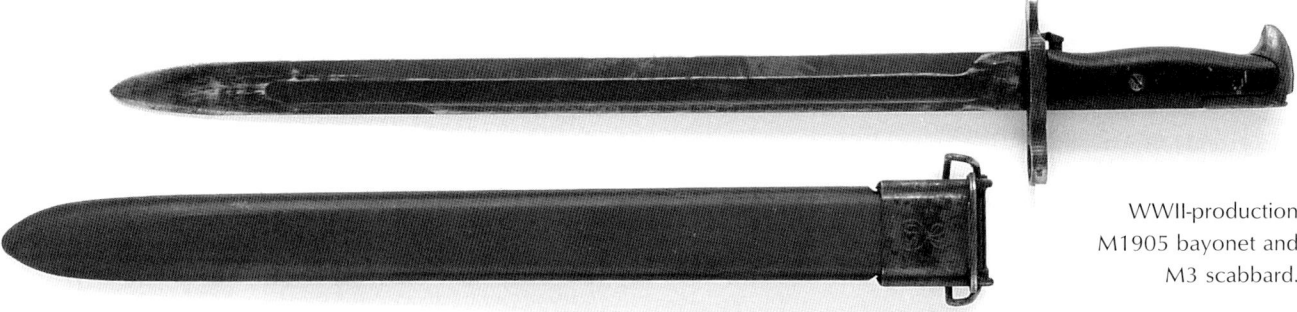

WWII-production M1905 bayonet and M3 scabbard.

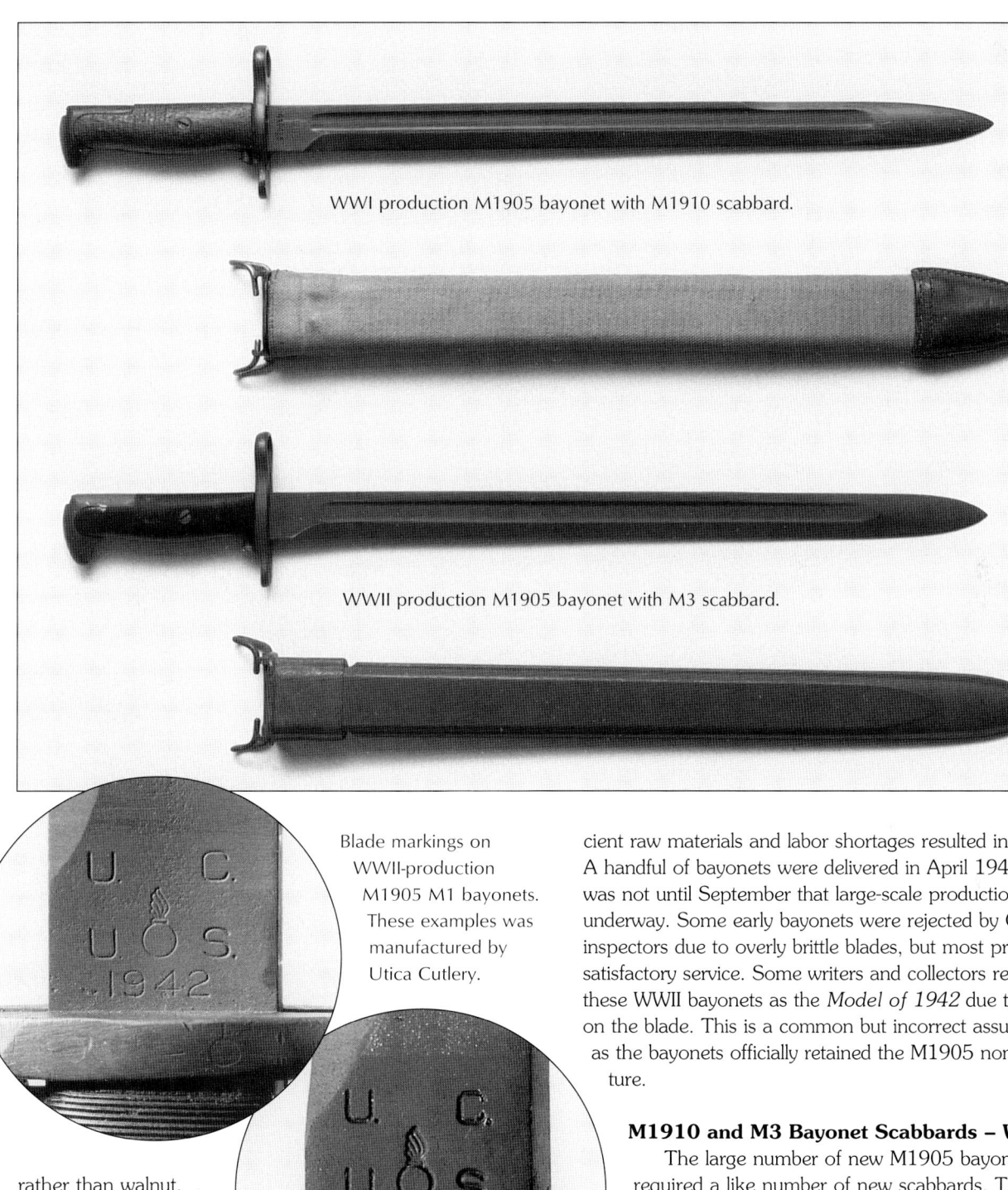

WWI production M1905 bayonet with M1910 scabbard.

WWII production M1905 bayonet with M3 scabbard.

Blade markings on WWII-production M1905 M1 bayonets. These examples was manufactured by Utica Cutlery.

rather than walnut. The bayonets were marked with the initials of the maker, a flaming bomb insignia, and the year of production (1942) on the reverse ricasso. The obverse was unmarked.

Although delivery of the new M1905 bayonets was slated to begin in January 1942, problems with obtaining sufficient raw materials and labor shortages resulted in delays. A handful of bayonets were delivered in April 1942, but it was not until September that large-scale production was underway. Some early bayonets were rejected by Ordnance inspectors due to overly brittle blades, but most provided satisfactory service. Some writers and collectors refer to these WWII bayonets as the *Model of 1942* due to the date on the blade. This is a common but incorrect assumption, as the bayonets officially retained the M1905 nomenclature.

M1910 and M3 Bayonet Scabbards – WWII

The large number of new M1905 bayonets required a like number of new scabbards. There were only some 6,000 M1910 scabbards in inventory, along with another approximately 48,000 modified M1905 scabbards. This number was totally inadequate given the large number of new bayonets that were in production. Use of the M1917 scabbard with the M1905 bayonet was also approved, but it was obvious that large numbers of new bayonet scabbards would be needed. The standard M1910 scabbard was put back into production during this period, but the item proved to be overly costly and was prone to damage and deterioration. The WWII

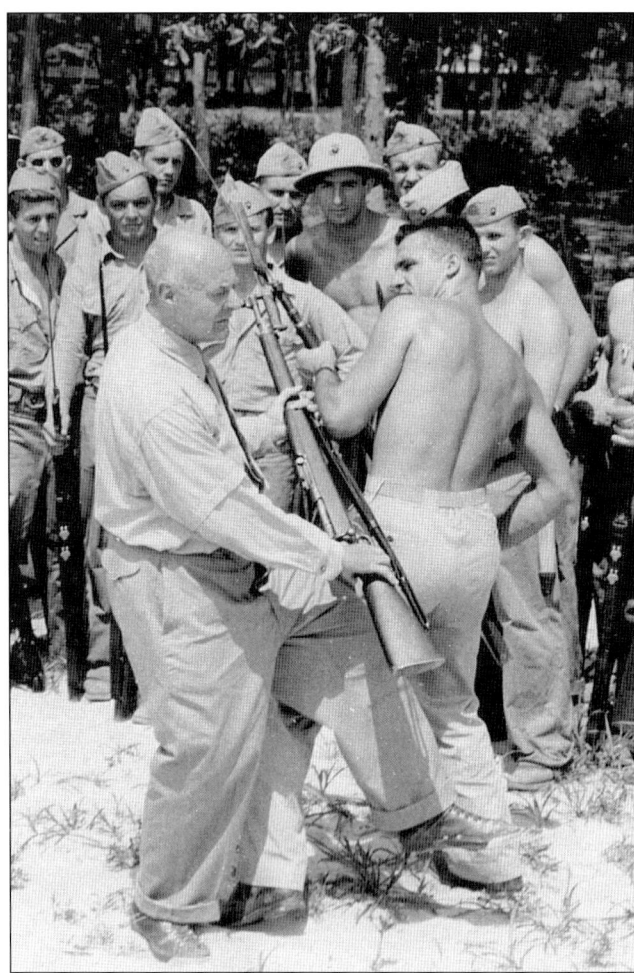

U.S.M.C. photo of recruits training in bayonet fighting at Parris Island by Col. Anthony Joseph Drexel Biddle. Col. Biddle was called back into duty at age 68 and served until the end of the war. Photo is dated August 1942. *(Frank Trzaska)*

Undated photo of U.S. Marines (3rd Regiment) during bayonet training in San Diego, California. Note the black leather tips on the M1910 bayonet scabbards. *(Frank Trzaska)*

U.S. Marine recruits training at Parris Island (South Carolina), June 14, 1942. Note the M1917 scabbard on the Marine (center, front). The M1917 scabbard was *Substitute Standard* for use with the M1905 bayonet during WWI and WWII. *(Frank Trzaska)*

U.S. Marine recruits training at Parris Island in June 1942. Note the parkerized M1905 bayonet at left and the bright-bladed M1905 bayonet at right. Also note use of the M1917 bayonet scabbard. *(U.S.M.C. photo courtesy of Frank Trzaska)*

Markings on throat of WWII-production M3 scabbard.

production M1910 bayonet scabbards can be differentiated from the WWI and earlier scabbards, by the tint and texture of the canvas covering and, in many examples, the configuration of the metal belt hooks. Most examples were unmarked.

Due to the cost of the M1910 scabbard and the problems encountered in service, the Beckwith Manufacturing Company developed a scabbard with a plastic body that could be made much faster and more at lower cost. Preliminary testing confirmed the superiority of the design, and the item was standardized as the *Scabbard, Bayonet, M3*. On November 17, 1941, contracts were granted to Beckwith and Detroit Gasket & Manufacturing Company for production of the newly adopted M3 bayonet scabbard. Upon adoption of the M3, the M1910 scabbard was redesignated as Substitute Standard, and the M1917 and modified M1905 scabbards were redesignated as Limited Standard. The M3 proved to be a durable and serviceable scabbard, and most of the newly made M1905 and many of these older arsenal-made bayonets were carried in these scabbards during WWII.

M1 Bayonet

Although the M1905 was an excellent bayonet, the relatively long 16-inch blade was the subject of some criticism as it proved to be cumbersome when troops were riding in trucks and on other vehicles. Another consideration was that the reduced emphasis on bayonet fighting largely mitigated the advantages of the longer blade. It was determined that a bayonet similar to the M1905 but with a 10-inch blade, would be equally serviceable as a weapon and would be less cumbersome in service. It was also realized that the shorter blade would save a large amount of critically needed steel.

To the end, a shortened version of the M1905 was designated as the *Bayonet, M1905E1*. The M1905E1 was made by simply shortening the blades of M1905 bayonets. The modified bayonet proved to be satisfactory, and the design was standardized on February 11, 1943, as the *Bayonet, M1*. In addition to being at least as effective when affixed to a rifle, the M1 bayonet was a better hand weapon and tool than the longer M1905 bayonet. Upon standardization of the M1 bayonet, contracts for manufacture of the M1905 were modified for production of the new bayonet. The various contractors were allowed 30 days for the changeover. Some of the firms also received contracts for modification of the M1905 bayonets to M1 configuration by shortening the blades. Two different types of blade modification were done. One resulted in a standard spear point, while the other had a distinctive clipped-point blade, sometime imaginatively referred to as a *Bowie point* by collectors. Both WWII and pre-WWII M1905 bay-

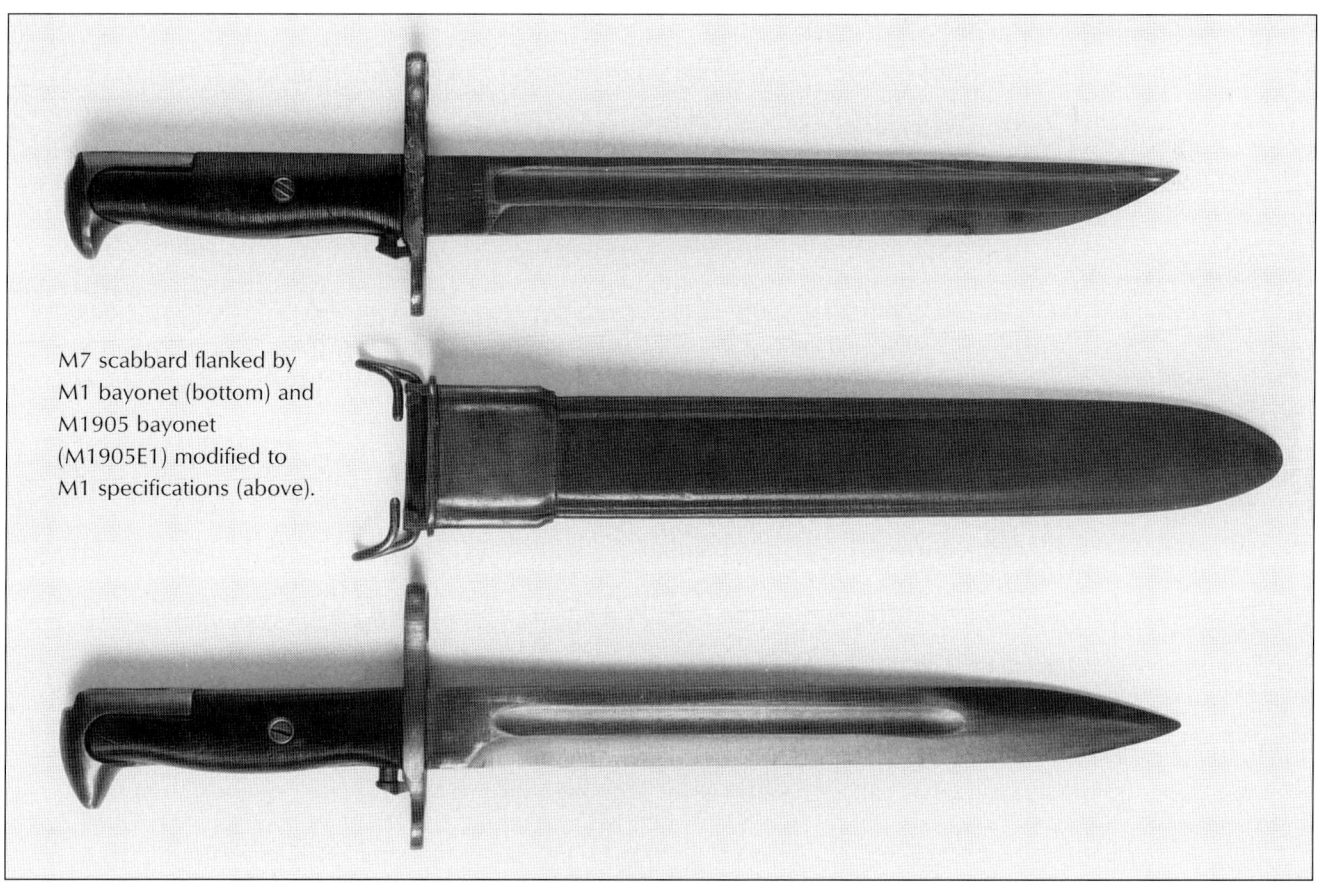

M7 scabbard flanked by M1 bayonet (bottom) and M1905 bayonet (M1905E1) modified to M1 specifications (above).

ABOVE, LEFT – Cpl. George W. Page thrusts a M1903 rifle with M1 bayonet at instructor Lt. Daniel B. Hopkins at Camp Patrick Henry Officer's School, WWII. ABOVE, RIGHT – Page and Hopkins training with M1 bayonet. This image depicts how the shorter M1 bayonet was better suited as a hand-held weapon than the longer M1905 bayonet. *(Frank Trzaska)*

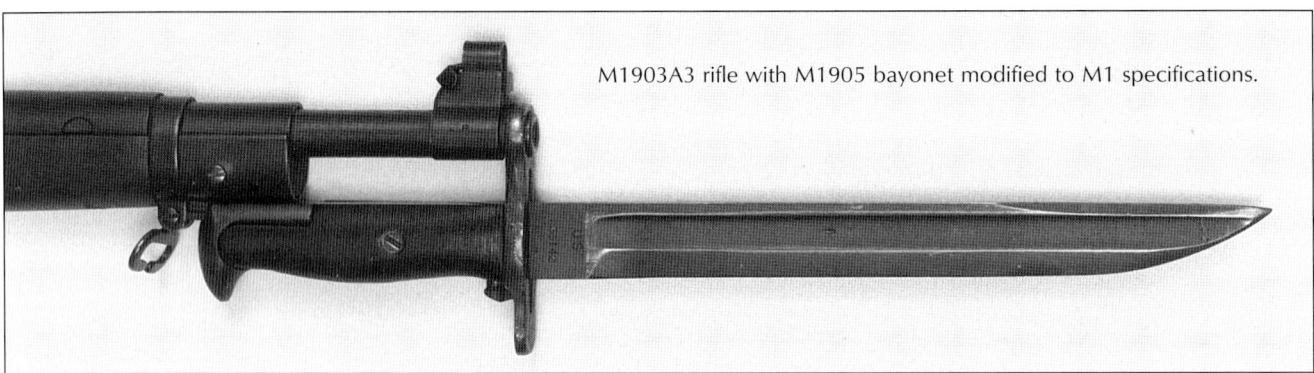

M1903A3 rifle with M1905 bayonet modified to M1 specifications.

onets were shortened to M1 configuration, and the initials of the firm that performed the modification were typically stamped on the back strap. In addition to the original markings on the blade, an M1 bayonet made from a shortened M1905 can be identified because the fuller runs the entire length of the blade. A total of 1,007,671 M1905 bayonets were shortened to M1 configuration, which partially accounts for the relative scarcity of unmodified examples. As the supply of available M1905 bayonets became depleted, contracts were given for production of new M1 bayonets beginning in April 1943. Except for Union Fork & Hoe and Wilde Drop Forge & Tool Company, the same firms that produced the M1905 bayonet during WWII also made new production M1 bayonets.

M7 Bayonet Scabbard

The standardization of the M1 bayonet resulted in a need for a scabbard similar to the M7 but appropriately shortened to accommodate reduced blade length. Such a scabbard was standardized on February 10, 1943, as the *M3A1*, but the designation was changed to *M7* on April 6, 1943. A number of M3 scabbards were shortened to the M7 length, but most were newly made. The M1 bayonet and M7 scabbard remained items of issue into the early 1960s.

The M1905 and M1 bayonets were designed for use with various M1903 rifle variants as well as the M1 Garand. A couple of the manufacturers are uncommon today, but most remain available to collectors at relatively reasonable prices.

Front Sight Covers

The rod bayonet rifles were issued with a detachable sheet metal combination muzzle cover and sight protector. This item was blued and was unmarked. When the M1905 pattern sight was adopted, a metal cover for protection of the front sight was adopted. The cover was intended to be removed prior to firing, but it was sometimes left in place, even though the top of the front sight blade could be partially obscured. Prior to WWII, the '03 front sight covers were made of blackened steel and were unmarked. There were two variants of pre-WWII front sight covers; one made from thick sheet metal and another made from noticeably thinner metal. There was also a front sight cover produced for the U.S.M.C. No. 10 sight. It was similar to the standard cover but had a higher profile to accommodate the taller front sight. These covers are not rare but can be hard to find today.

The '03 front sight cover was put back into production in the early days of WWII. Unlike the pre-WWII variety, there were several varieties of the WWII front sight covers. The most common was the type made by Remington. These are easily identified, as they are blued sheet metal and marked "R" on one side and stamped with "U.S." and a flaming bomb on the other. Several other contractors made front sight covers during WWII, and these were often stamped with a code marking to identify the manufacturer. Some were also stamped with the component's drawing number (C64157-4). With the exception of the rod bayonet and U.S.M.C. varieties, none of the '03 front sight covers can be considered uncommon.

Cavalry Saddle Scabbard

Since the M1903 rifle was standardized for cavalry use as well as infantry use, a saddle scabbard was necessary to carry the weapon on horseback. The *Model of 1904* scabbard was adopted and put into production at Rock Island Arsenal. The leather scabbard had two leather straps, with metal snaps, for attachment to the standard cavalry saddle. The lower strap had a metal retaining ring. The name of the maker, "RIA", and date of production were stamped on the scabbard. The earliest observed date is 1904. A similar scabbard was later adopted as the *Model of 1918* which differed from the M1904 scabbard primarily in that the lower portion was slightly narrower and the lower strap did not have the metal retaining ring. The Model 1918 examples were typically stamped with the initials of the maker and the year of production, with 1918 being the most common. Some of the M1918 scabbards were later modified for use with the M1 Garand. Unmodified examples are not rare, but are getting increasingly harder to find. Any decent specimen would make a fine addition to a collection. Judging from vintage photographs, a number of M1 Garand leather scabbards were also used to carry M1903 rifles on jeeps and motorcycles.

Front Sight Covers

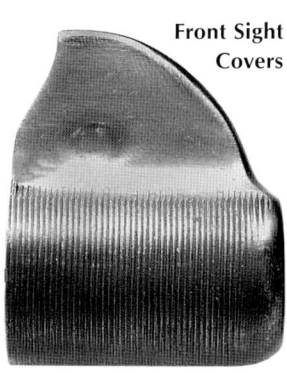

M1903 *rod bayonet.*

Pre-WWII.

WWII marked with drawing number.

WWII cover made by Remington Arms marked with "R" on one side and "U.S." with "flaming bomb" on the other.

ABOVE, LEFT – M1 leather scabbard attached to motorcycle and side car. (Stuart C. Mowbray collection) ABOVE, RIGHT – WWII photo of Col. William Darby (*Darby's Rangers*) on motorcycle. His M1903 rifle is in an M1 rifle leather scabbard.

An excellent view of the M1904 saddle scabbard. *(Stuart C. Mowbray collection)*

M1903 rifle above M1904 saddle scabbard.

Cartridge Belts • Pre-World War I

M1903 Cartridge Belt

The Krag rifle was issued with web belts having individual loops for the cartridges. Since the M1903 rifle was designed for use with 5-round chargers (stripper clips), it was necessary to adopt a cartridge belt having individual pockets to hold the clipped cartridges. The belt, adopted as the Model of 1903, was constructed of woven web canvas material and featured nine pockets that each held two five-round chargers. Both infantry versions and cavalry versions of the M1903 cartridge belt were manufactured, with the latter having a saber hanger attachment. Initially, all of the M1903 infantry and cavalry belts were manufactured by the Mills Woven Cartridge Belt Co. of Worcester, Massachusetts, but by 1907, the belts were also being manufactured by the Russell Manufacturing Company of Middleton, Connecticut.

M1903 woven cartridge belt. Note two *stripper clips* of .30-03 cartridges.

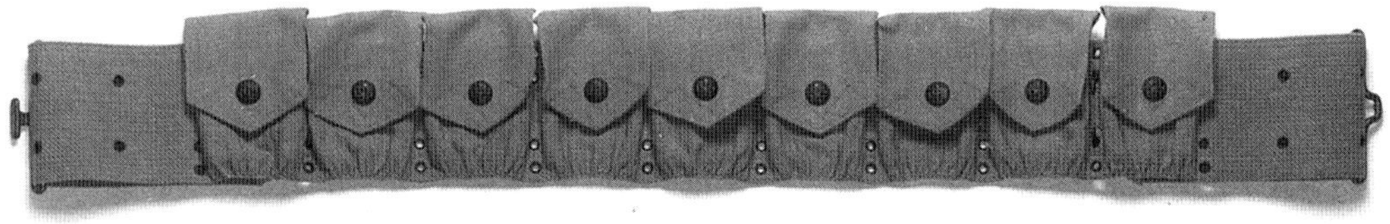

Early Mills belt.

WWI M1910 Mills belt.

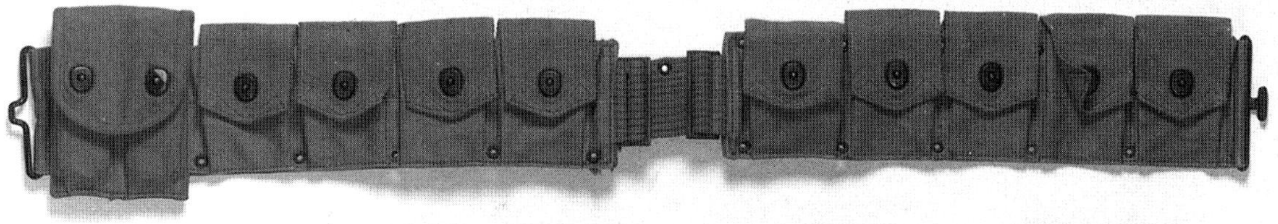

M1918 WWI Sewn construction belt (mounted).

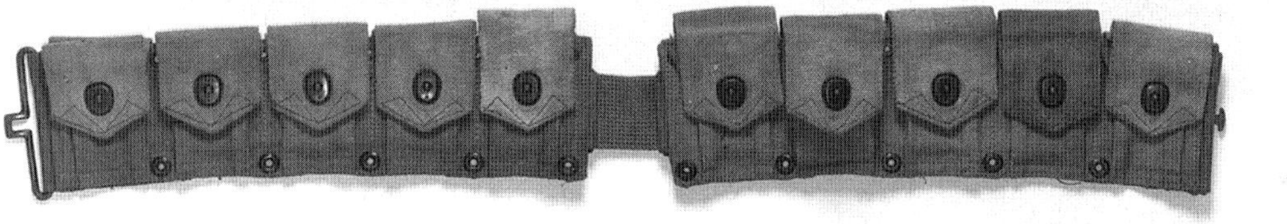

Early WWII M1923 belt.

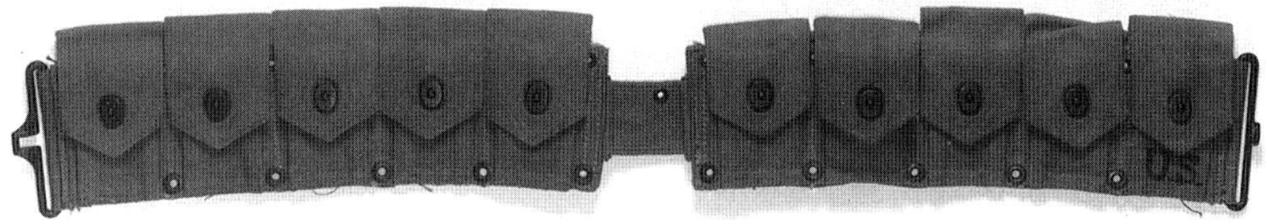

Later WWII M1923 belt.

U.S. Army soldiers with M1903 rifles and M1905 bayonets. Note the early M1903 cartridge belts. *(Stuart C. Mowbray collection)*

The early M1903 cartridge belts manufactured for the .30-03 cartridge can be identified from later variants by the configuration of the material at the bottom of each pocket. Later belts made for the sharp-pointed spitzer cartridge have puckered pockets for reinforcement, while the early .30-03 belts lacked this feature. All variants of the M1903 cartridge belt had metal snaps with eagle-head markings.

Pre-WWI *eagle-head* snap.

M1909 Cavalry Cartridge Belt

The adoption of the spitzer bullet of the M1906 cartridge caused some problems with damage to the bottom of the original pattern M1903 cartridge belt due to the tips of the sharp-pointed bullets. A cartridge belt with a puckered bottom on each pocket to reinforce the belt in that area was adopted as the *Model of 1909* Cavalry Cartridge Belt. The belt was manufactured by the Mills Woven Cartridge Belt Company. Other than the configuration of the bottom of the pocket, the M1909 belt was essentially identical to the earlier M1903 cavalry cartridge belt except for the addition of two pockets on the belt to hold revolver cartridges.

M1910 Cartridge Belt

While the M1903 and M1909 cartridge belts proved to be satisfactory in service, some fault was found in the design and placement of the clip pockets and the adjustment strap. The *Model of 1910* cartridge belt was adopted to correct these deficiencies. As was the case with the previous cartridge belts, the M1910 was made by the Mills Company in both mounted pattern for cavalry use and dismounted pattern for infantry. The M1910 cartridge belt had revised pocket arrangements for the rifle ammunition, ten pockets for the infantry and eight for the cavalry. The cavalry version also had four pockets for revolver ammunition.

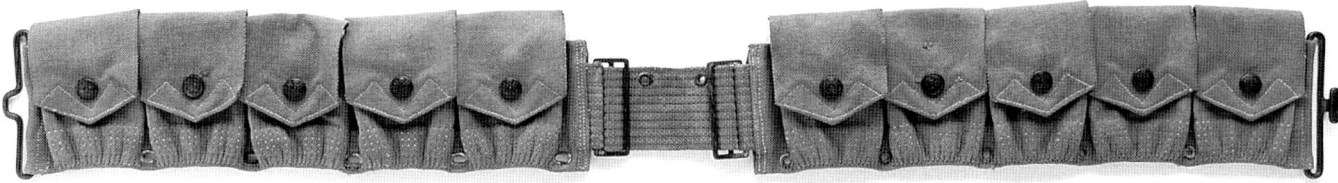

WWI-vintage M1910 woven cartridge belt.

M1912 Cavalry Equipment and M1912 Cartridge Belt

The M1912 cartridge belt was part of the *M1912 Cavalry Equipment* which consisted of the belt, a leather bucket which held the rifle's buttstock and a padded ring into which the upper portion of the rifle was inserted when on horseback. The M1912 belt contained a leather picket pin holder, the aforementioned padded ring for the rifle barrel and a leather strap which was snapped into the rifle's triggerguard to further secure

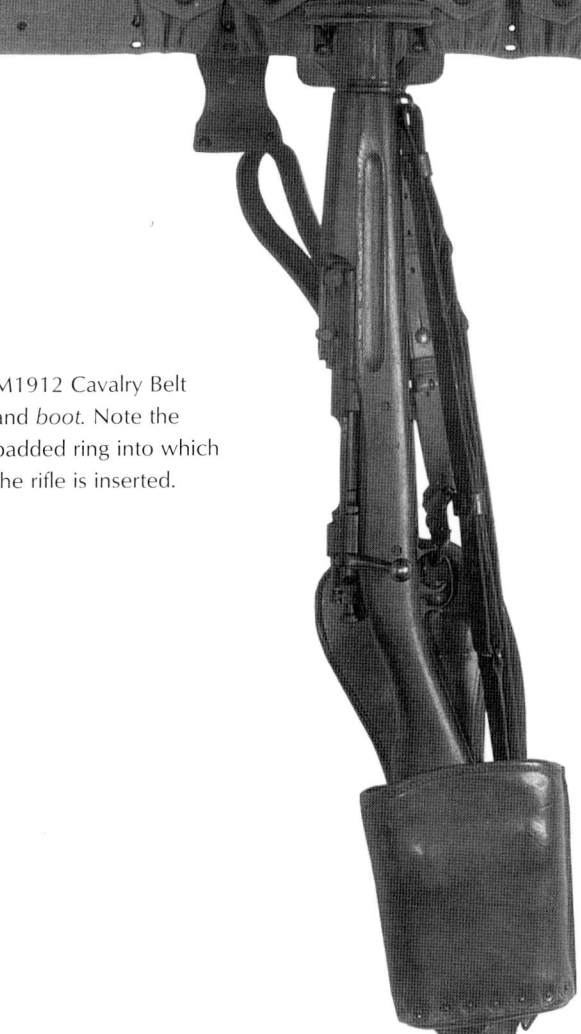

M1912 Cavalry Belt and *boot*. Note the padded ring into which the rifle is inserted.

the weapon while on horseback. The M1912 cartridge belt and related items were manufactured by Rock Island Arsenal. The M1912 Cavalry Equipment was something of a *Rube Goldberg* contraption that was not very popular with cavalrymen and saw little actual field use although versions were produced as late as 1918. The rig is an example of an idea that may have looked good on the drawing board but was a failure in the field.

M1912 Cavalry equipment.

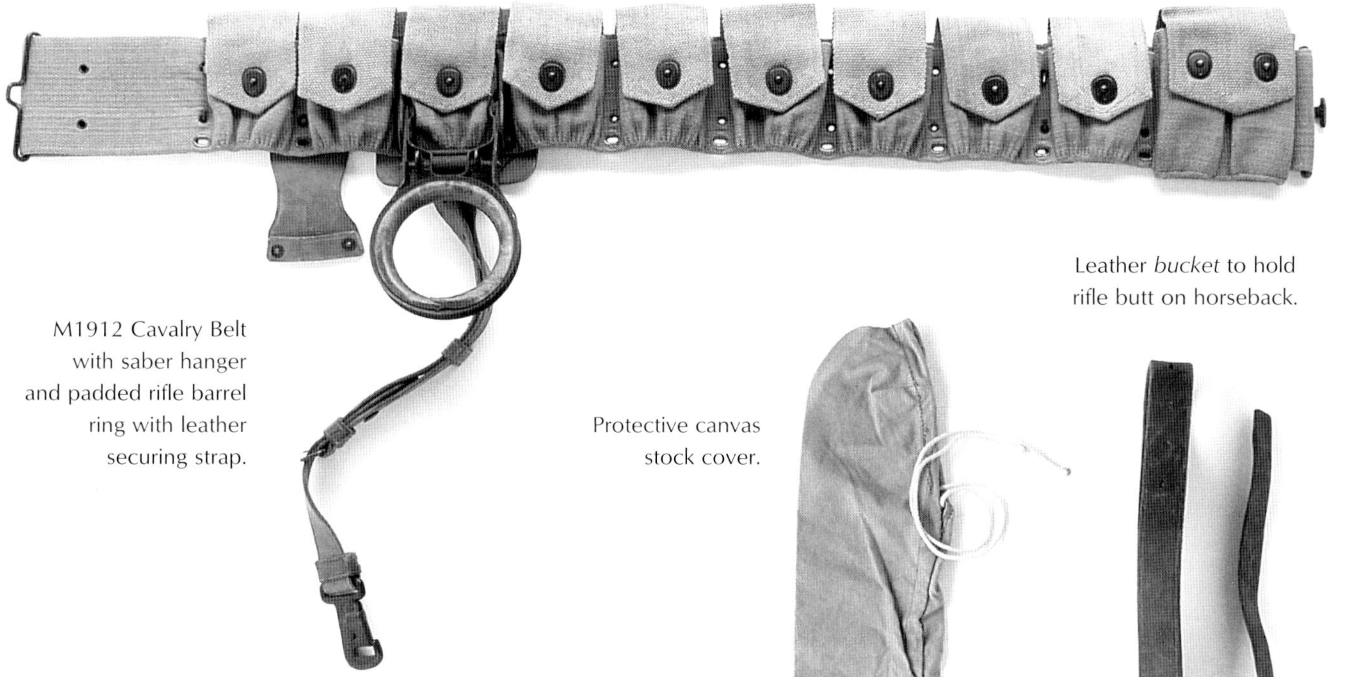

M1912 Cavalry Belt with saber hanger and padded rifle barrel ring with leather securing strap.

Protective canvas stock cover.

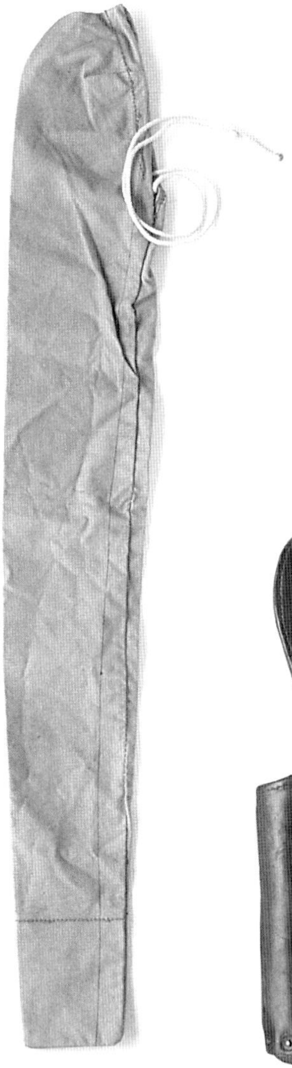

Leather *bucket* to hold rifle butt on horseback.

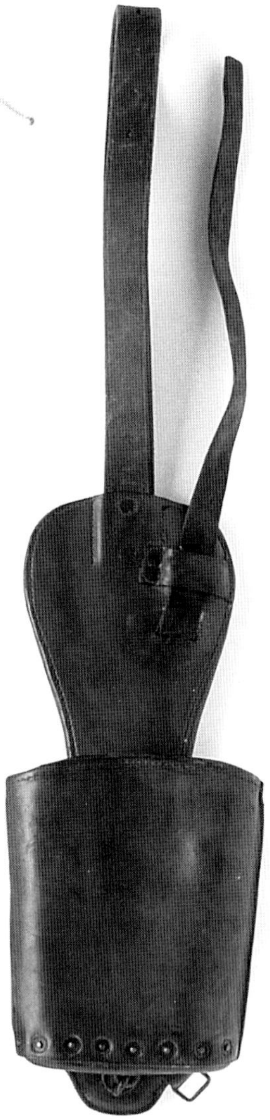

M1914 Mounted Cartridge Belt

The M1914 cartridge belt differed from the M1910 belt primarily in the addition of a provision for the attachment on the left side of the belt of a two-pocket pouch for the M1911 .45 pistol magazines. Some of the M1914 belts were subsequently modified by removing the pistol magazine pouch and sewing on an extra pocket for rifle cartridges. These were referred to as *M1914 Mounted Cartridge Belt - Modified*. While there was not a M1914 dismounted (infantry) belt standardized, it is likely that M1914-Modified belts were issued for infantry use.

World War I Cartridge Belts

The M1910 cartridge belts were items of standard issue at the beginning of the United States' entrance into the war. As the demand rapidly increased with the expansion of the U.S. armed forces, additional quantities of the woven cartridge belts were ordered, but the combined total of the Mills and Russell plants was inadequate to meet the demand.

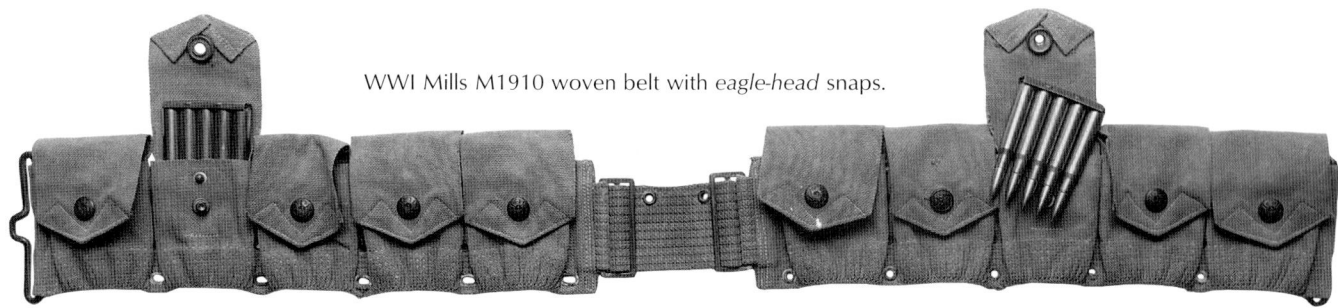

WWI Mills M1910 woven belt with *eagle-head* snaps.

M1917/M1918 Cartridge Belts

To increase production, the standard M1910 belt was redesigned to utilize sewn canvas material rather than the woven fabric originally used. This simplified production, decreased cost and broadened the manufacturing base of potential contractors. The resulting belt was standardized as the *Model of 1917 Dismounted Belt*. The belt had ten pockets each of which held two five-round stripper clips for either the M1903 or M1917 rifles. Like its predecessors, the M1917 belt had grommets on the lower edge for attachment of bayonet scabbards, canteens, first-aid pouches and other equipage.

In order to reduce production time and cost, the eagle-head snap fasteners on each pocket flap were replaced by the simpler and less-expensive *Lift-the-Dot* closures. The bottoms of the clip pockets were smooth but were reinforced by canvas in order to prevent damage from the sharp-pointed bullets. Large numbers of the M1917 belts were manufactured during WWI by Plant Brothers of Boston, Massachusetts, R.H. Long Co. of Framingham, Massachusetts, and L.C. Chase Co. of Watertown, Massachusetts.

There was a cavalry version of the belt adopted as the *Model 1918 Mounted cartridge belt* which differed from the M1917 infantry belt only in the deletion of one pocket which left space for the substitution of a M1911 .45 pistol pouch. After WWI, a number of the M1918 Mounted belts were modified by adding a pocket for the rifle clips in place of the M1911 .45 pistol magazine pouch. The modified belts can be identified by the fact that the added pockets were made from a different color material than the rest of the belt. A number of Model of 1912 pattern cavalry belts were also constructed of sewn canvas material during the WWI period. Most of these belts saw little or no use, and examples in near-new condition can still be found.

Original WWI-vintage M1917 and M1918 cartridge belts can still be found but, as with all U.S. martial items, prices are rising and decent examples are now harder to find. Some reproduction cartridge belts of this type may also be encountered, but can usually be identified by the markings and the general condition. Originals were usually stamped on the back of the belt with the identity of the maker and the date of production. An original M1917 cartridge belt in excellent condition will show some evidence of patina or other signs of being nearly ninety years old.

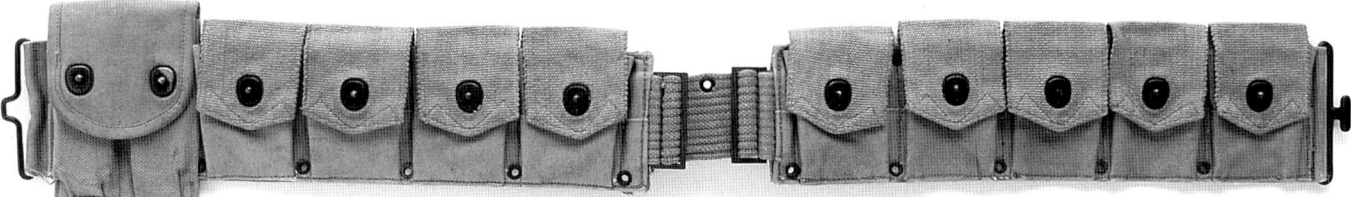

WWI-vintage M1917 *Mounted* belt. Note pocket for two M1911 .45 pistol magazines.

World War II and Postwar Cartridge Belts

M1923 Cartridge Belt

Despite large number of surplus M1917 and M1918 cartridge belts left over from First World War stocks, the U.S. Army adopted a new cartridge belt in 1923. This design, standardized as the *Model of 1923*, would remain the basic American military cartridge belt for the next 35 years. The M1923 cartridge belt differed from its predecessors primarily in the method of adjustment and details of construction. The M1923 cartridge belt used the same type of Lift the Dot snap fasteners as found on the M1917/M1918 belts. Initially, both Mounted and Dismounted M1923 cartridge belts were produced but decreased emphasis on cavalry and related equipage resulted in far larger numbers of M1923 infantry (Dismounted) belts being produced as compared to the M1923 cavalry (Mounted) belt. The Mounted belt had nine pockets and space for a pistol magazine pouch, while the Dismounted belt had ten pockets. Even though adopted in 1923, relatively few of these belts were manufactured prior to WWII because of

Early WWII khaki M1923 cartridge belt. Note "U.S." stamp on front.

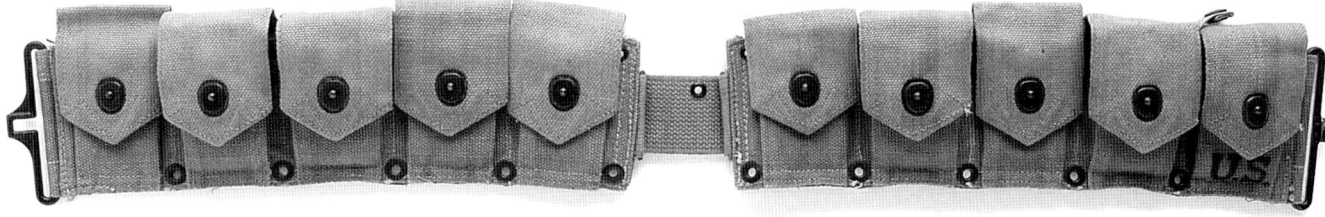

the low demand and because of the large number of WWI cartridge belts still on hand.

Large numbers of M1923 cartridge belts were ordered from several contractors during WWII. Although initially designed for use with the 5-round chargers for the M1903 rifle, the M1923 cartridge belt was also capable of carrying the 8-round M1 Garand clips. Until mid-WWII, the M1923 belts featured a clip-retaining strap in each pocket to separate the two five-round chargers. As the M1 rifle replaced the M1903 in widespread service, these straps were eliminated, except for U.S.M.C.-contract belts. M1923 belts had grommets on the bottom for attachment of bayonet scabbards, canteens, first-aid pouches and other equipage. The belts also had grommets on the top edge for attachment of loading-bearing suspenders.

Early production M1923 belts were made of khaki material, and later belts were darker olive drab. Some examples may be seen made with both khaki and olive drab material. Many M1923 belts were marked "U.S." on an outside pocket flap, and most were stenciled on the inside of the belt with the name of the maker and the year of production. Marine Corps belts were also usually stenciled "U.S.M.C." The M1923 belt remained in production after WWII, and examples dating into the 1950s will be encountered. These belts were very common until just a few years ago, but are beginning to be harder to find, especially in excellent or better condition. Reproductions are now on the market, so a collector should be wary of a belt that looks brand new, even though some M1923 belts can still be found in such condition. Some WWII-vintage M1923 belts, made of dark blue material and unmarked except for a "U.S." stenciled in black ink on a front pocket, were manufactured. These belts are uncommon, and it is assumed that they were made for the U.S. Navy.

The collecting of web gear has become quite popular recently, and prices for collectible examples are rapidly increasing. The days of inexpensive cartridge belts and other items found in neighborhood surplus stores are a thing of the past. Regardless, an original cartridge belt of the proper vintage and type is a great accompaniment to a M1903 rifle in a collection.

Rifle Grenade Launchers

V-B Grenade Launchers – WWI

Although grenades were used in warfare for several centuries, the First World War saw a renewed emphasis on such weapons. While the hand grenade was a useful weapon in the trench warfare environment, the weapon possessed a handicap in that its maximum range was no greater than the strength and skill of the thrower. The ability to project a grenade farther than possible by hand could obviously be a valuable weapon, and several types of grenades capable of being launched from rifles were developed and fielded.

Prior to WWI, the United States and other nations experimented with several types of rifle grenades having long metal stems that could be inserted into the bore of the rifle and launched by means of a special round similar to a blank cartridge. The Babbit rifle grenade was adopted by the United States Army in 1911 and fielded in limited numbers. The Babbit grenade, like all rifle rod grenades, had several disadvantages. These included:

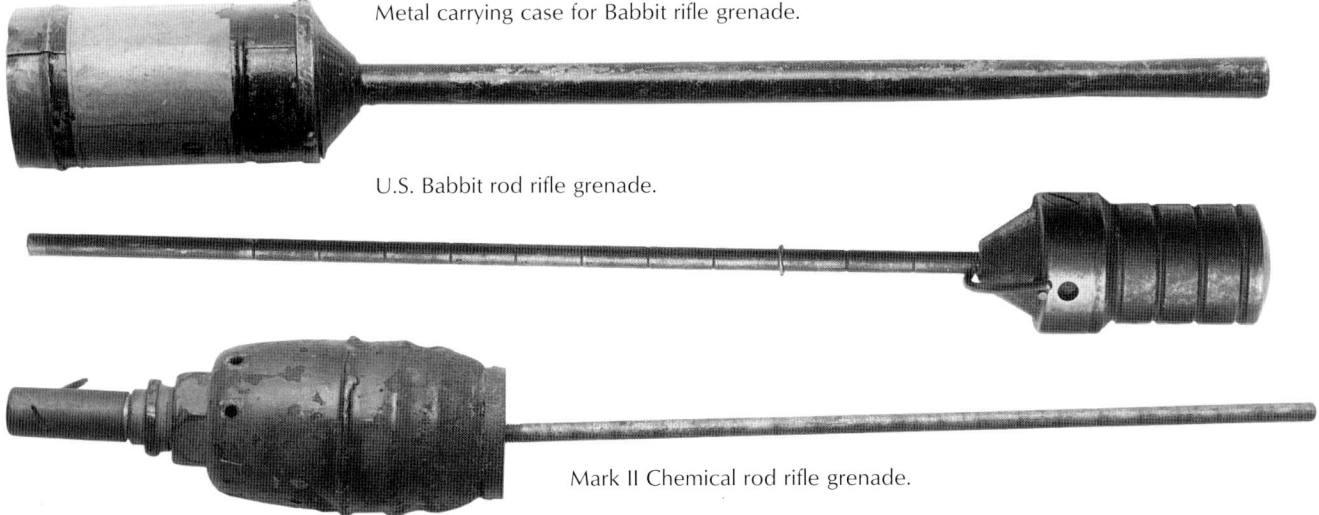

Metal carrying case for Babbit rifle grenade.

U.S. Babbit rod rifle grenade.

Mark II Chemical rod rifle grenade.

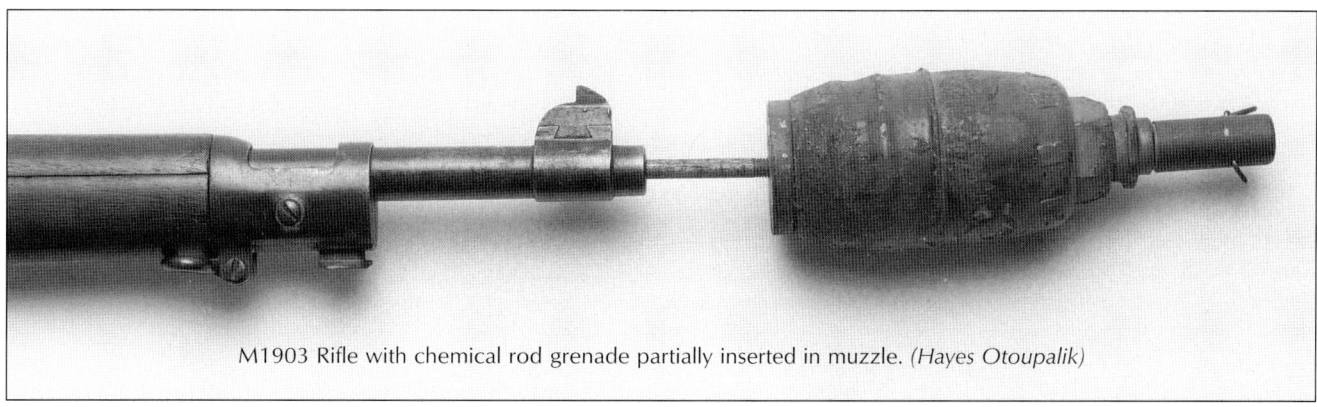
M1903 Rifle with chemical rod grenade partially inserted in muzzle. *(Hayes Otoupalik)*

WWI Mark III V-B grenade launcher on M1903 rifle.

(1) Damage to the rifle's barrel as the metal stem wobbled back and forth as it was being projected out of the rifle.
(2) The long stem resulted in a cumbersome item that was awkward to carry.
(3) The use of such rod grenades required a special cartridge which could cause logistical problems.

These problems resulted in the acquisition by the U.S. Army in WWI of a rifle grenade launcher that had been previously adopted and widely used by our French allies. This launcher was termed the *V-B* after the initials of its inventors, Jean Viven and Gustave Bessiere. The V-B launcher, called a tromblon, was a heavy metal cup that was placed onto the rifle's barrel. The V-B grenade had a hole in the middle which allowed the standard rifle bullet to pass through, and the cartridge gasses propelled the grenade up to a maximum range of about 200 yards. This eliminated the necessity of a separate grenade launching cartridge.

The V-B launcher was officially adopted by the U.S. Army on July 16, 1917. The first variant of the U.S. V-B launcher, the Mark I, was made in France under American contract. This was followed by the U.S.-made Mark III and Mark IV launchers, which were produced for both the M1903 and M1917 rifles. There was not a Mark II launcher manufactured. The Mark III had a straight slot that was placed over the barrel and held in place by a sheet metal shim, and the Mark IV had a spiral slot that allowed the launcher to be more securely attached to the rifle.

The Mark I, Mark III and Mark IV launchers for the M1903 and M1917 rifles were not interchangeable between the models of rifles, even though they were virtually identical in design. The launchers were marked on the outside of the body with the designation of the appropriate rifle, "M1903" or "M1917". The V-B launchers were carried on the cartridge belt in a leather carrying case having wire cartridge belt hooks. Soon after the end of WWI, the leather cases were replaced by canvas carrying cases, as the former wore out or deteriorated.

Despite some training accidents and other problems, the V-B launchers were used with good effectiveness by our Doughboys during the war. The weapon bridged the gap between the effective range of hand grenades and trench mortars. One negative aspect of the V-B launcher was the heavy recoil when a grenade was fired. This resulted in a number of broken rifle stocks which was reportedly the primary reason for the introduction of a second reinforcing stock screw for the '03 rifle.

Despite its effectiveness during WWI, the V-B grenade dropped out of widespread use by the U.S. Army a few years after the Armistice but some of the V-B launchers continued to see use, primarily for the launching of pyrotechnic devices. There is some evidence that a few V-B

Text continued on page 200.

Illustration from WWI U.S. Army manual depicting procured for firing rod rifle grenade from M1903 rifle. *(U.S. Army)*

① Open bolt

② Insert grenade and pull pin

③ Load

④ Fire

FIGURE 12.—Firing from the kneeling position

Members of Company A, 126th Infantry, 32nd Division, Alsace, France, June 14, 1918. The *Doughboy* at left is preparing to fire a V-B grenade from a M1903 rifle with attached V-B launcher. *(U.S. Army)*

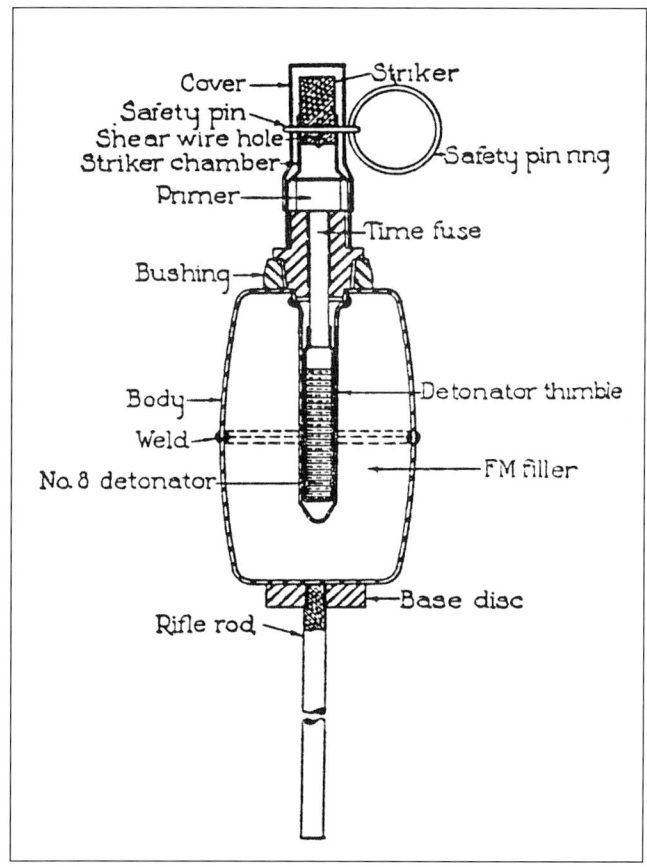

ABOVE – Illustration from WWI U.S. Army manual of *Mark I Smoke* rod rifle grenade. *(U.S. Army)*
BELOW – *Doughboy* from *Gas Headquarters Co.* 1st Corps, U.S. Army, preparing to launch white phosphorous (WP) chemical rod rifle grenade from '03 rifle. France, October 6, 1918. *(National Archives)*

ABOVE – French soldier with V-B grenade/launcher on Berthier rifle. The U.S. copied the V-B grenade and launcher from our French allies. *(National Archives)*
BELOW – Mark III V-B Grenade Launcher for M1903 rifle. This example was manufactured by the Westinghouse Company as evidenced by the circled "W" logo. *(Hayes Otoupalik)*

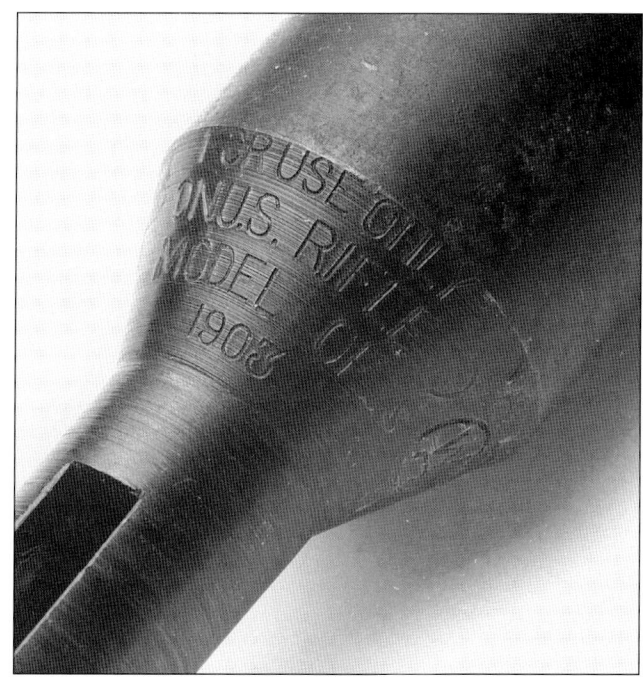

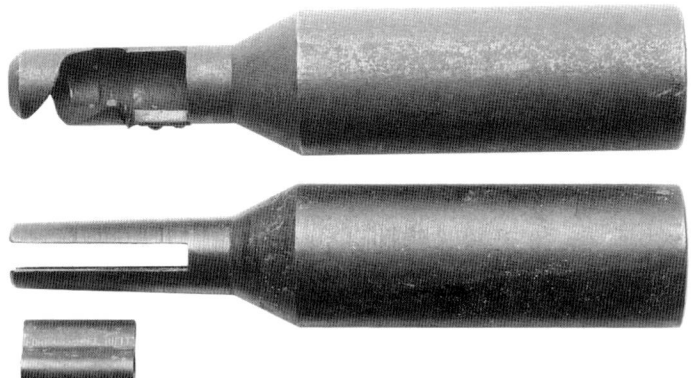

ABOVE – V-B Rifle Grenades (Left to Right): Sectionalized V-B grenade; V-B grenade with protective brass cover in place; Right-side view of V-B grenade showing fuse; Bottom view of V-B grenade showing hole through which the bullet passes.
LEFT – U.S. V-B Grenade Launchers: (Top) Mark IV for M1903 rifle. Note spiral slot; (Bottom) Mark III for M1903 rifle. Note sheet metal shim. *(Hayes Otoupalik)*
BELOW – U.S. soldiers training in WWI. The soldier at left is loading his M1903 rifle and preparing to launch a V-B rifle grenade. Note the fixed M1905 bayonet on the '03 rifle at right. *(National Archives)*

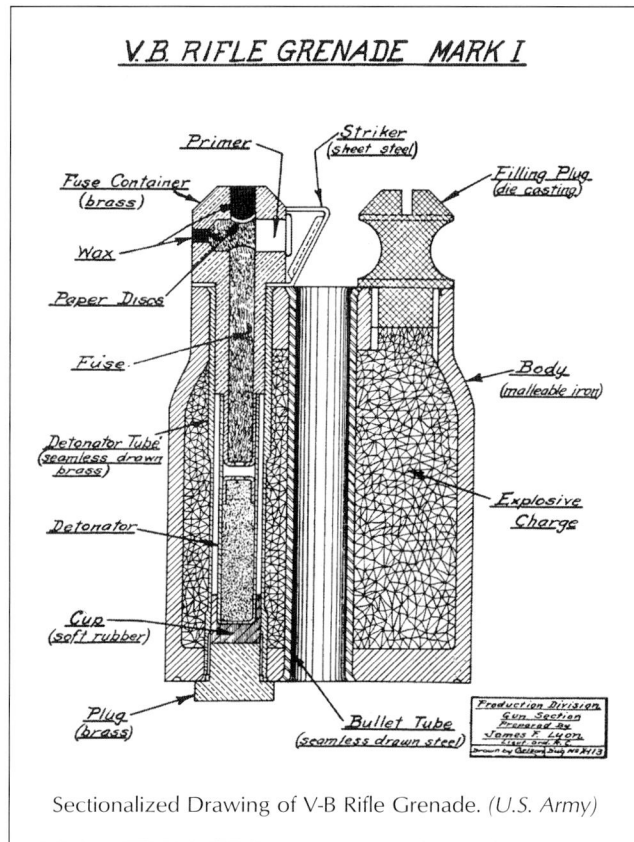

Sectionalized Drawing of V-B Rifle Grenade. *(U.S. Army)*

ABOVE – U.S. soldier preparing to launch V-B grenade from Mark IV launcher on M1903 rifle. Note the M1905 bayonet in M1910 scabbard on his pack and grenade bandoleer below the scabbard. This soldier is identified as Private John Dafnomiles, Company F, 2nd Battalion, 6th Regiment, 5th Infantry Division. Photo taken September 24, 1918, at Moselle, France. *(U.S. Army Military History Institute)*

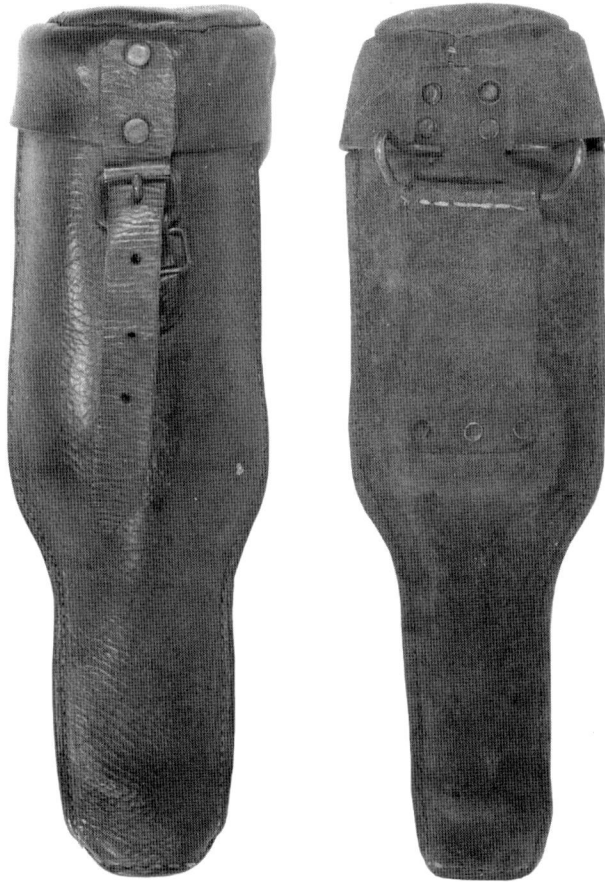

LEFT – Front and rear views of leather carrying case for V-B launcher. Note belt hooks. *(Hayes Otoupalik)*

RIGHT – Post-WWI canvas carrying case for V-B launcher. Rock Island Arsenal ("R.I.A.") marking and 1920 date.

Canvas 11-pocket bandoleer for V-B grenades.

Text continued from page 195.

launchers may have remained in U.S. Marine Corps service into the early Second World War. If so, U.S.M.C. use of the V-B launcher during WWII was very limited and, as was the case with the U.S. Army following the end of WWI, was restricted to launching flares and other signaling devices.

Surviving examples of V-B rifle grenade launchers are rare today, as most were disposed of as scrap metal after World War I. Inert V-B grenades can still be found from time to time but are far from common. The leather carrying cases are more rare than original launchers, although the later canvas carrying cases are common. Any original V-B launcher is a rare and desirable collectible.

M1 Launcher – WWII

The U.S. military did not have an issue rifle grenade launcher from the time of the abandonment of the V-B until the eve of the Second World War. When the M1 rifle was adopted, development of a suitable grenade launcher began, but the Garand's gas system proved to be a vexing problem for ordnance designers. While a suitable grenade launcher for the Garand rifle was under development, a launcher for the M1903 rifle was adopted.

The fact that the M1903 was a manually operated bolt-action rifle greatly simplified the efforts to develop a suitable grenade launcher. A prototype launcher, designated as the T3, was tested and found to be satisfactory. The Knapp-

Text continued on page 205.

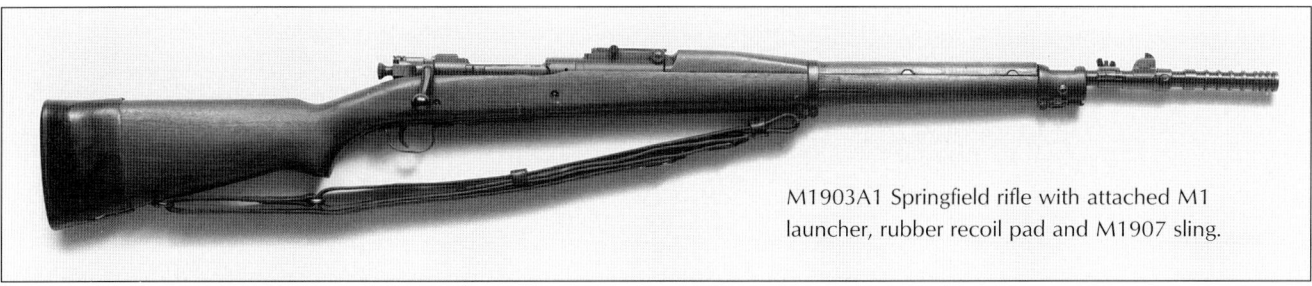

M1903A1 Springfield rifle with attached M1 launcher, rubber recoil pad and M1907 sling.

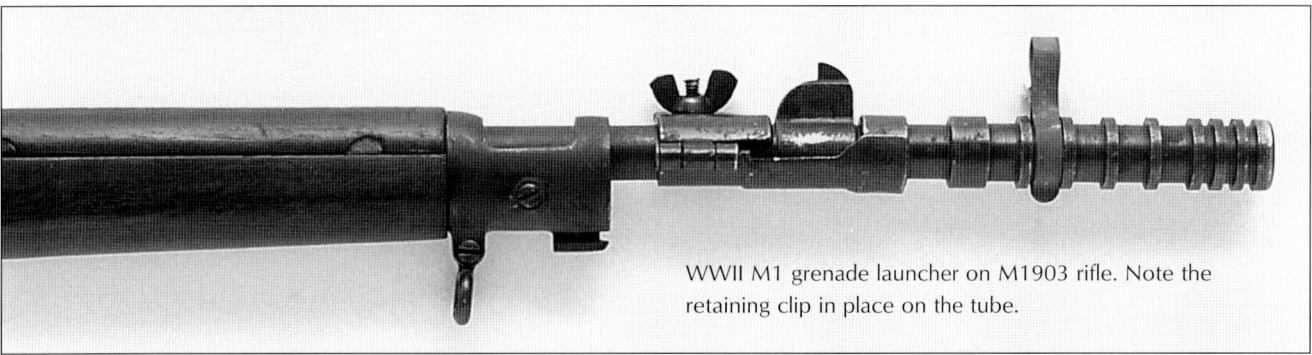

WWII M1 grenade launcher on M1903 rifle. Note the retaining clip in place on the tube.

BELOW – 1943 U.S. Army Ordnance photograph (taken in England) depicting a variety of signaling and anti-tank weapons. Note the two M1903 rifles with M1 launchers arrayed in the center. Two M9A1 anti-tank rifle grenades are in front of the launchers. *(U.S. Army)*

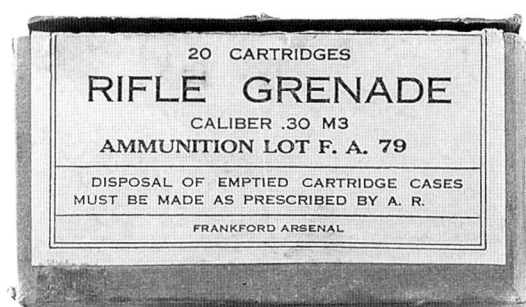  

Assortment of WWII-vintage rifle grenade launching ammunition.

Markings on M1 grenade launcher.

Note "M1903A1" rifle nomenclature and Knapp-Monarch name and logo.

RIGHT – Mark 11 Practice grenade (dated 7-42) used to simulate M9 Anti-tank rifle grenade in practice. *(Garand Stand collection)*

Unidentified WWII photo depicting a soldier carrying two M1903 rifles fitted with M1 launchers ashore. *(U.S. Army)*

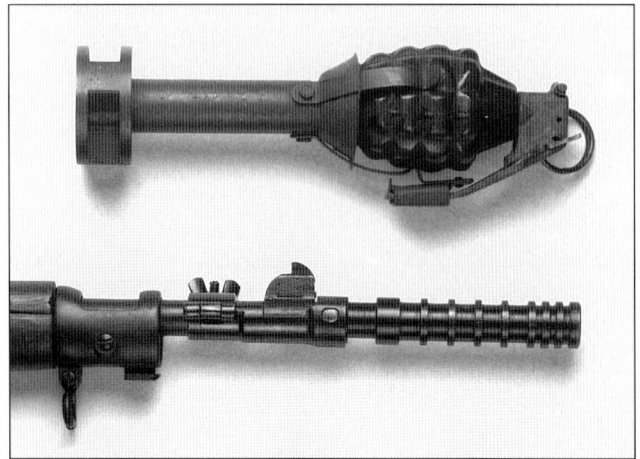

WWII M1 launcher on M1903 rifle. A Mark II fragmentation hand grenade with launching adapter is shown above.

Rubber recoil pad as issued with M1 grenade launchers.

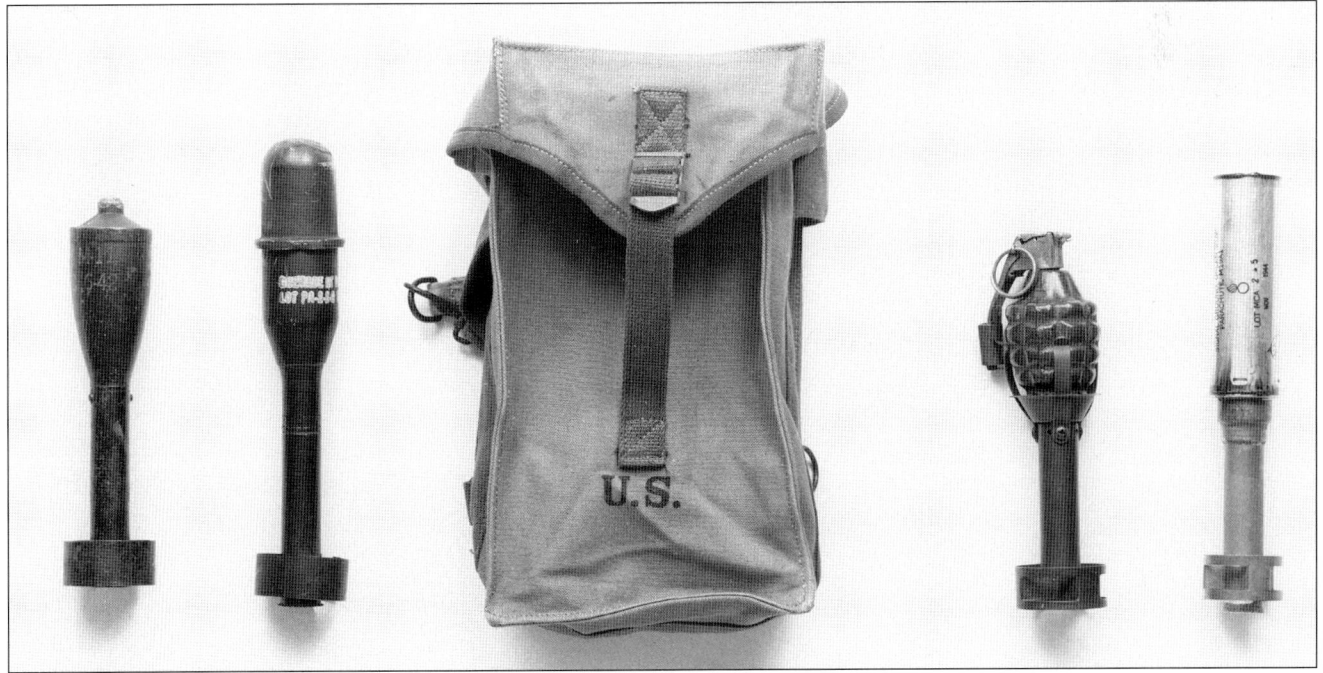

WWII Marine gunnery sergeant holding a M1903 rifle with M1 grenade launcher and Mark II fragmentation grenade with adapter. The rifle is fitted with an experimental grenade launching sight that is believed to be the predecessor to the M15 sight. *(U.S.M.C. - Courtesy Alec Tulkoff)*

WWII rifle grenades and carrying case (Left to right): MII Practice grenade; MIIA1 Practice grenade; Rifle grenade carrying case; Mark II fragmentation hand grenade on M1 adapter; Ground signal parachute flare.

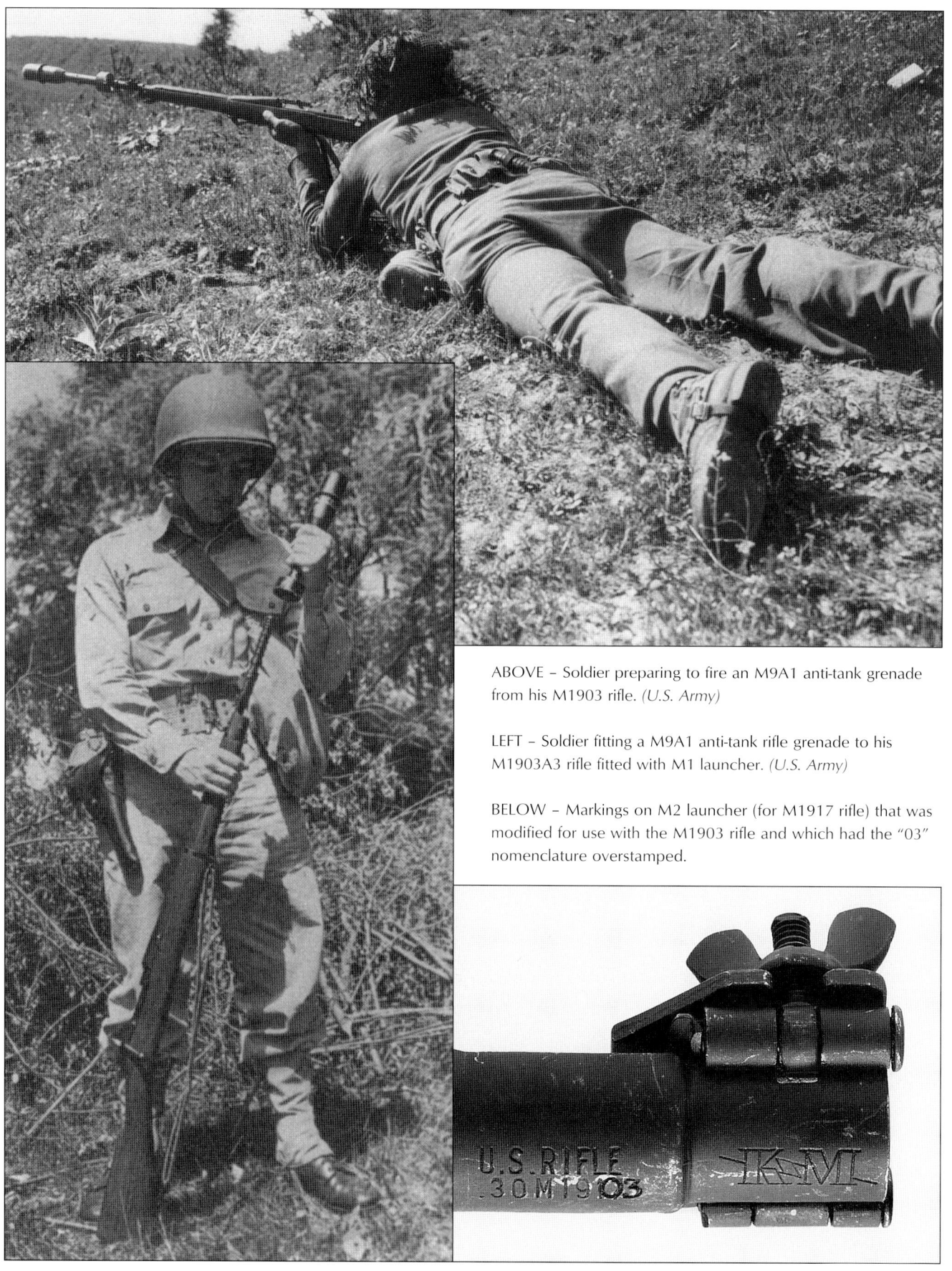

ABOVE – Soldier preparing to fire an M9A1 anti-tank grenade from his M1903 rifle. *(U.S. Army)*

LEFT – Soldier fitting a M9A1 anti-tank rifle grenade to his M1903A3 rifle fitted with M1 launcher. *(U.S. Army)*

BELOW – Markings on M2 launcher (for M1917 rifle) that was modified for use with the M1903 rifle and which had the "03" nomenclature overstamped.

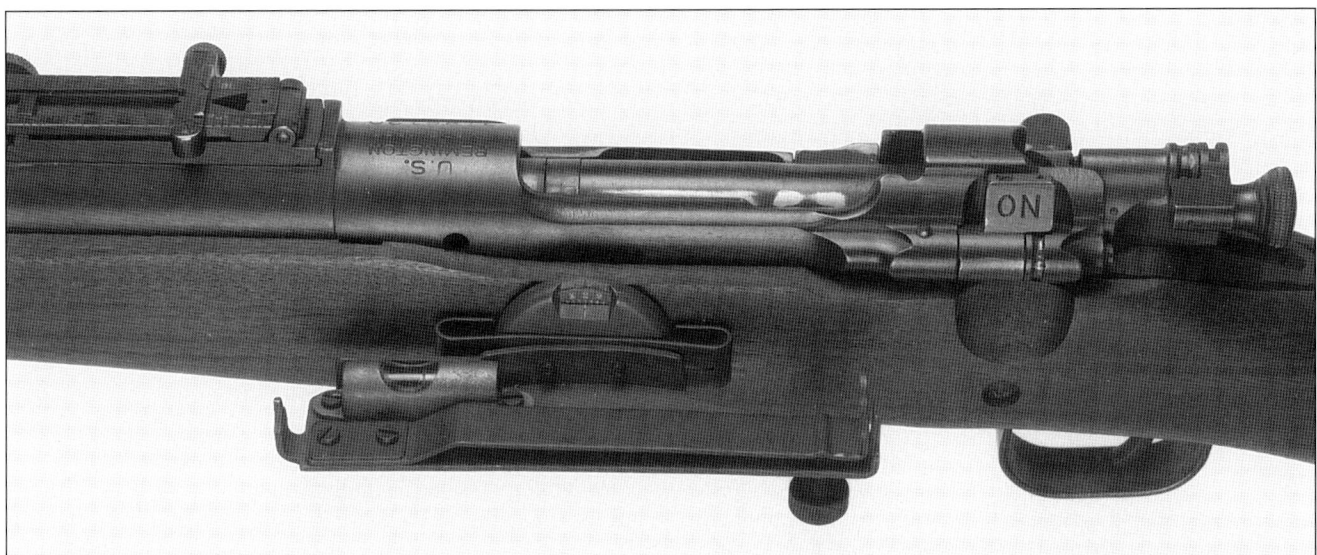

M15 grenade launching sight on M1903 rifle. This sight was also standardized for use with the M1917 rifle, M1 rifle and M1 carbine. Original examples are still very common.

Text continued from page 200.

Monarch Company of St. Louis, Missouri, was given a contract to manufacture 150,000 of the launchers. Before production could begin, the launcher was slightly redesigned and designated as the *T9*. On September 9, 1941, the T9 was officially standardized as the *Launcher, Rifle Grenade, M1*. A very similar design, the *M2*, was also adopted for use with the M1917 rifle. The M1 launcher was a simple design that consisted of a cylindrical body that slipped over the rifle muzzle and was held in place by a clamp which was fastened by a wing nut. The tube of the launcher had a number of rings which determined the range of the rifle grenade. The launcher was used with the M3 grenade launcher cartridge which can be identified by the crimped head. An auxiliary cartridge, the *M7*, was sometimes used to increase the range of the rifle grenade. The M7, dubbed the *vitamin pill*, was dropped into the tube of the launcher prior to attaching the grenade. Although it increased the range, it also increased the recoil when firing a rifle grenade.

Knapp-Monarch's contract was revised and called for the production of 100,000 M1 launchers, with half earmarked for foreign aid requirements (Lend-Lease, etc.) and half for delivery to the U.S. Army. The company began production of the M1 launchers in November 1941. The M1 launchers were blued and were marked with the Knapp-Monarch logo ("K-M" with a lighting bolt). Knapp-Monarch was given additional contracts for production of the M1 launcher, and a total of 322,892 launchers were manufactured by the time production stopped in May 1943.

The launchers were used with several different types of rifle grenades including anti-tank, fragmentation, and pyrotechnic/signaling devices. An adapter that permitted launching a standard hand grenade from a rifle was widely used during WWII. Retaining clips were provided that could be snapped onto the tube to hold the grenade at the proper position on the launcher for the desired range. Two types of grenade launching sights were developed for the M1903 rifle. The first consisted of front and rear apertures attached by a wire and fastened to the rifle by means of a spring clamp. These sights are very rare today and likely saw little use. The later variety consisted of an aperture and a spirit-bubble level that fastened to a metal mounting plate screwed to the left side of the stock. The sight, adopted as the M15, was carried in a canvas pouch along with range instructions. The M15 sight was standardized for use on the M1903, M1917 and M1 rifles and the M1 carbine. Large numbers were made, and examples can still be found today for just a few dollars. A black rubber pad was issued with the M1 launcher which was intended to reduce the recoil force when firing a rifle grenade. These pads had an Ordnance Department flaming bomb insignia and drawing number on the face.

Some Knapp-Monarch M2 launchers were converted to M1 specifications for use with M1903 rifles. These were usually parkerized and had the "17" in (M1917) overstamped to "03". Even though fairly large numbers were made, M1 launchers are surprisingly scarce today, and original examples are typically quite hard to find and usually rather expensive. Unlike some other U.S. military rifle grenade launchers, reproduction (fake) M1 launchers have not been reported, but one should not be oblivious to that possibility, especially given the price tag typically involved. An original M1 launcher is a great collectible and a fine addition to a WWII M1903 rifle.

25-Round Extension Magazine

An accessory for the '03 rifle intended to be utilized for trench warfare in the First World War was an extension magazine designed to increase the firepower of the weapon. The magazine replaced the standard '03 floorplate and allowed the rifle to hold a total of 25 rounds rather than 5 rounds. The magazine could be easily installed but was not a detachable box magazine as was used with the Browning Automatic Rifle (BAR) and other weapons. The magazine assembly was accompanied by a sheet metal cover and was issued in a brown cardboard box.

The 25-round extension magazine was utilized with the rare Air Service rifles and Cameron-Yaggi Trench Periscope rifles. Some people are of the opinion that the extension magazine was intended to be used only with these two prototype or limited-issue weapons. Analysis of the available information appears to refute this assumption, and it is likely that the magazines were also intended to be issued with standard '03 rifles for trench warfare purposes. This conclusion is based on several factors, including the illustration in a WWI Ordnance Department catalog of a standard '03 fitted with a 25-round extension magazine. The ordnance publication stated that, "...large numbers (of the magazine)...have been constructed for tests..." Also, General Julian S. Hatcher stated that the magazine was "...made up in fair number..." in response to requests from front-line infantrymen.

The exact number of extension magazines manufactured is not known, but an Ordnance Department memo dated March 17, 1920, stated that 2,723 of the items had been delivered to Springfield Armory in 1918, so it can be ascertained that at least that number of magazines had been manufactured. The fact that relatively large numbers of the magazines were manufactured strongly suggests that the intention was to issue the items for front line use. Since the Air Service and Cameron-Yaggi rifles were made in quite limited numbers, the large quantity of extension magazines manufactured would not have been needed if utilization was restricted solely to these two quasi-experimental weapons. In addition, a status report issued by Springfield Armory in early 1918 stated that the extension magazine "...would be adopted for aeroplane, Sitascope, and similar special uses, and possibly for general issue."

Some collectors today have theorized that the extension magazines were utilized with the M1903/Warner & Swasey sniper rifles, but there is absolutely no evidence to suggest that this was the case. The Germans fielded a similar exten-

Twenty-five-round extension magazine attached to M1903 rifle.

sion magazine for their Mauser rifles during WWI, and it is probable that the U.S. extension magazine was, at least in part, developed as a response. Apparently the war ended before any significant number of the extension magazines could be issued. In certain applications, such as repelling massed infantry assaults, the added firepower of the extension magazine could have proven to be of value. On the other hand, the protrusion of the magazine from the bottom of the rifle made it difficult to assume the proper prone position and would have made the rifle heavier and more cumbersome. Examples of the 25-round extension magazine are no longer commonly found but are still far from rare.

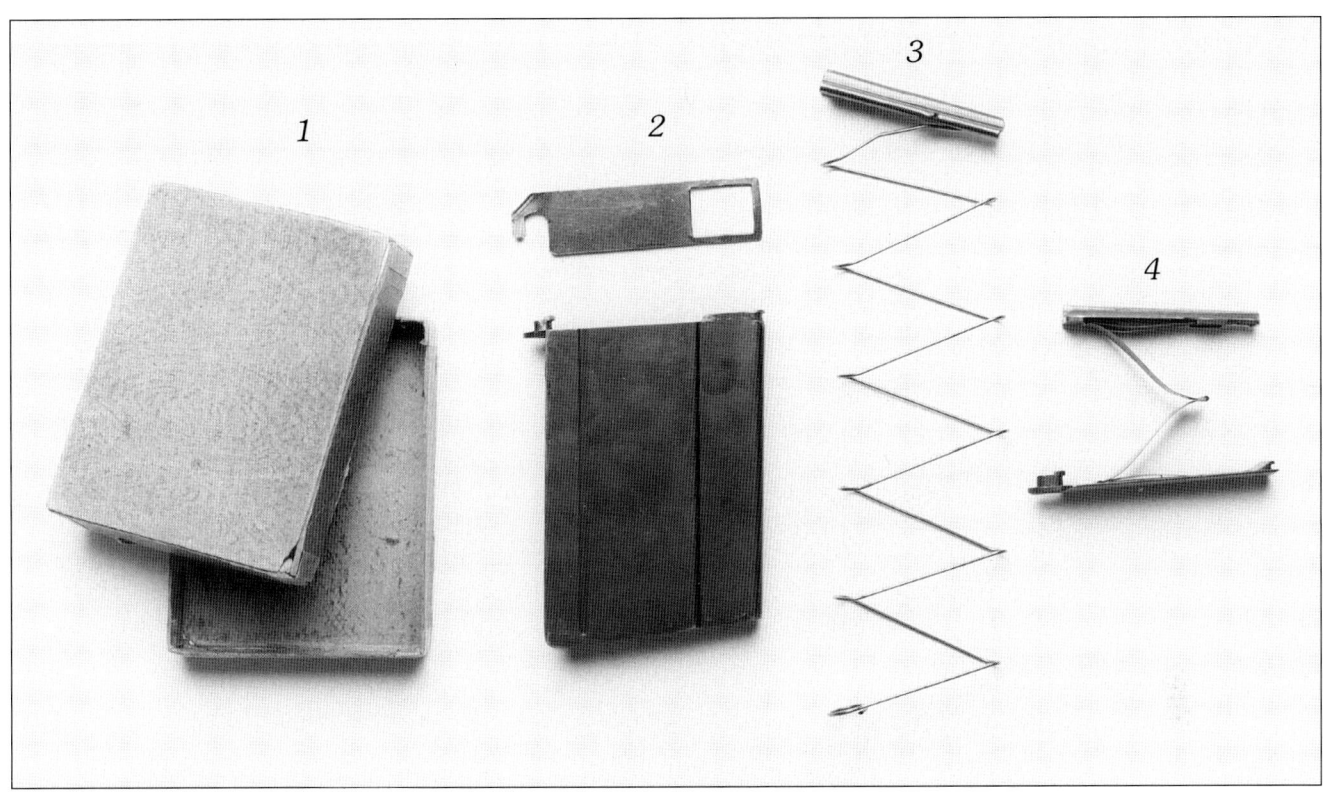

(Left to right) - (1) Cardboard box in which extension magazines were issued, (2) magazine with sheet metal cover (above), (3) extension magazine follower and spring, (4) standard M1903 rifle follower and spring. *Note the difference in length between the extension magazine follower spring and the standard rifle follower spring.*

Illustration from WWI Ordnance Catalog depicting a standard M1903 rifle fitted with a 25-round extension magazine. This is highly suggestive that the magazines were intended for general issue.

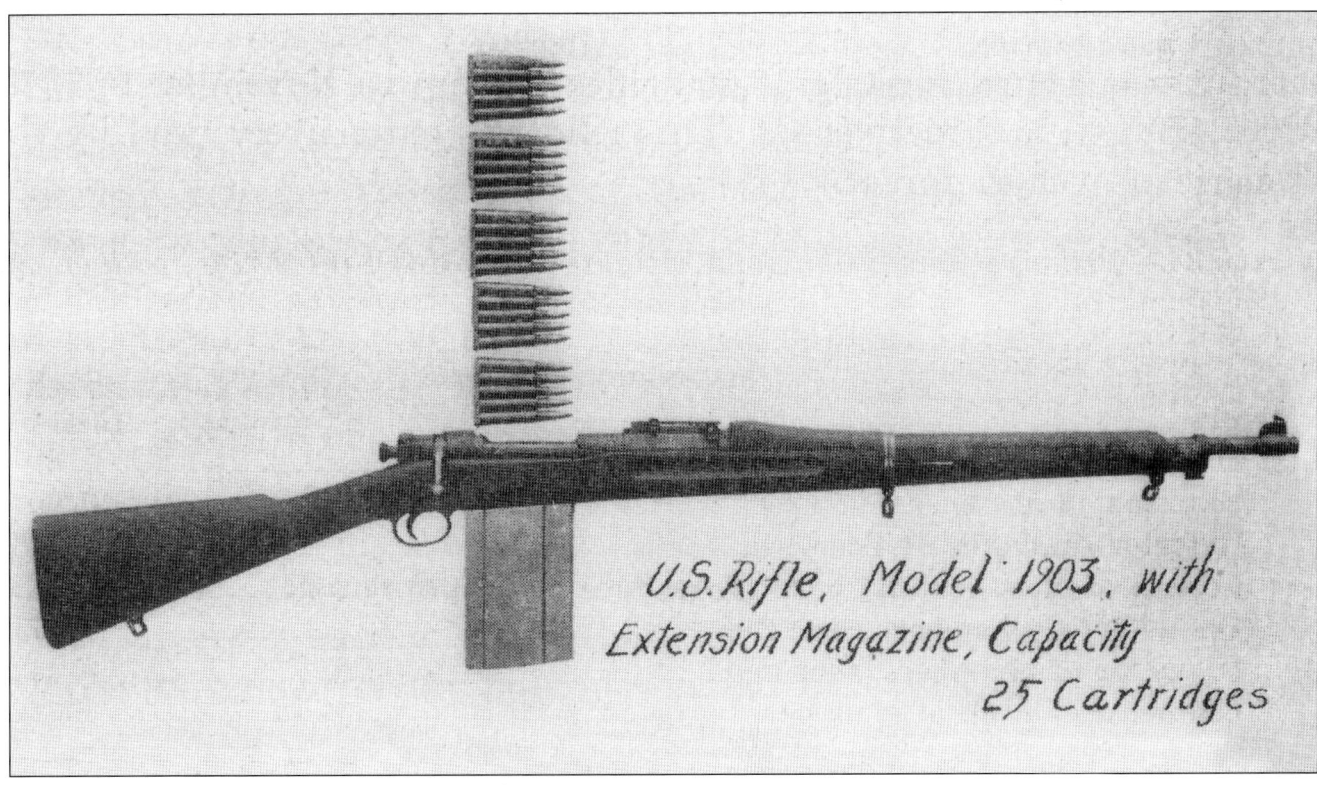

Manuals, Handbooks and Ammunition

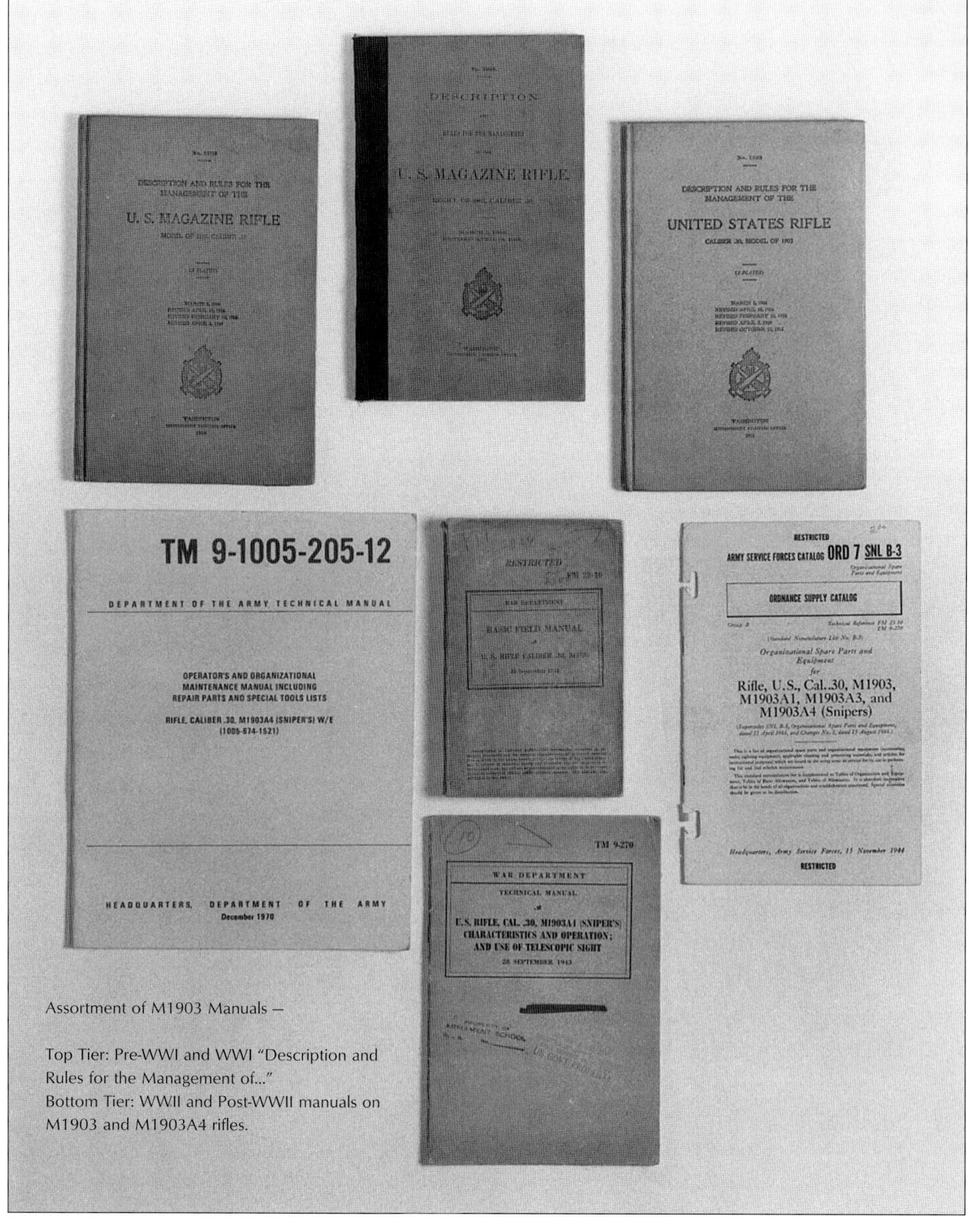

Assortment of M1903 Manuals —

Top Tier: Pre-WWI and WWI "Description and Rules for the Management of..."
Bottom Tier: WWII and Post-WWII manuals on M1903 and M1903A4 rifles.

A sometimes overlooked field for collectors are the various manuals and handbooks printed for the '03. The earliest examples are the "Description and Rules for the Management of..." manuals that were printed between 1904 and 1918. There were several editions of these manuals printed when noteworthy changes to the rifles were made. The manuals were made with hardcovers. Original editions are rather scarce, and examples in good condition are highly collectible. Many have been commercially reprinted in recent years with soft covers.

There was a "Soldier's Handbook" printed during WWI with blue-colored cloth binding. These are also rather scarce and are fine additions to a collection. Several types of scorebooks for recording firing range data were also printed during this period.

Several types of Field Manuals (FM) and Technical Manuals (TM) were printed during WWII for all variants of the '03, including the M1903A4 sniper rifle. Originals can still be found but are getting harder to find.

The last manual printed for the '03 was as 1970-dated *Technical Manual for the M1903A4 Sniper Rifle*. This edition depicted the weapon fitted with the M84 telescope. It is interesting to note that manuals for the '03 were still being printed some 67 years after adoption of the weapon!

Some of these manuals are more common than others but all are quite collectible. Reprints are also around, so a potential collector should be careful not to buy a reprint if he is seeking an original.

LEFT – "Description and Rules for the Management of..." dated 1917.

BELOW – 1909-dated Manual for M1903 Rifle.

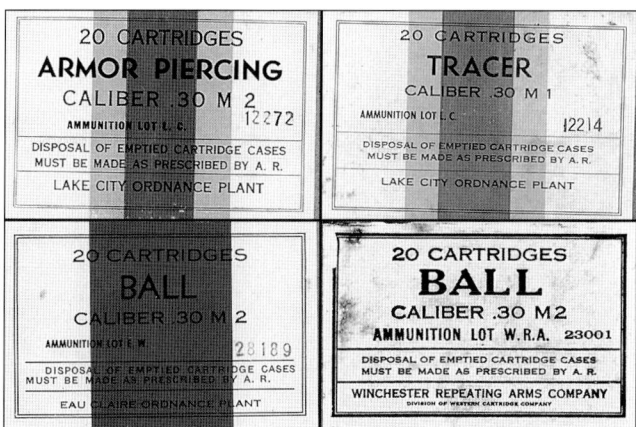

Assortment of WWII .30 caliber ammunition: (Clockwise from top, left) M2 armor-piercing; M1 tracer; M2 ball; WWII-vintage M2 ball manufactured by Winchester Repeating Arms Co.

The various Accessories, Accouterments and Appendages made for the M1903 rifle can be an interesting collecting genre in its own right. Some of the items are very common and inexpensive, and others are quite rare and valuable. All are interesting and add much color to a rifle collection.

The M1903's days as a military service rifle are long gone. Few weapons have served the United States military as long, or as well, as the venerable old *Oh Three*. The weapon's long association with our armed forces, including use during two World Wars, the myriad variants and accessories, and the undeniable mystique of the rifle, all combine to make the M1903 an ideal collecting theme. The '03's popularity with collectors is at an all-time high, and there is no sign that this popularity will be abating anytime soon. Hopefully, this book will be a useful tool for collectors, or potential collectors, to better enjoy this fascinating and rewarding hobby.

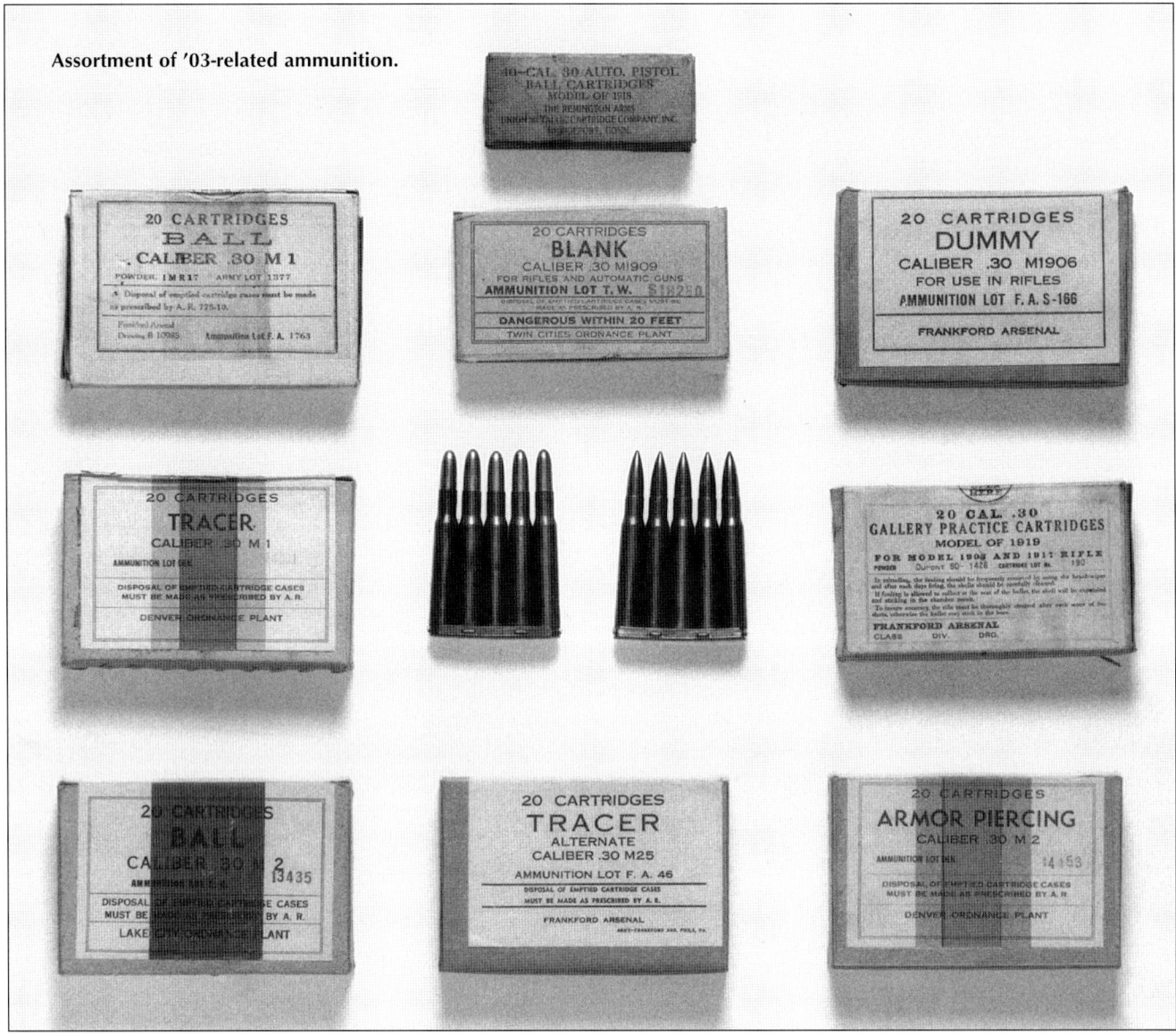

Left Tier (Top to Bottom): 1930s-vintage M1 Ball; WWII M1 Tracer; WWII M2 Ball.
Center Tier (Top to Bottom): 40-round box of .30 caliber M1918 Pedersen Device ammunition; Clip of .30-03 cartridges; Clip of .30-06 cartridges; WWII M25 Tracer.
Right Tier (Top to Bottom): M1906 Dummy cartridges; Gallery Practice cartridges; WWII M2 armor-piercing.

Table 1

Springfield M1903 Rifle Serial Numbers at Start of Calendar Years

Serial No.	Year	Serial No.	Year	Serial No.	Year
1	1903	570561	1914	1267101	1925
87000	1904	595601	1915	1270301	1926
125000	1905	620121	1916	1274765	1927
192000	1906	632826	1917	1285266	1928
269451	1907	761758	1918	1305901	1929
337862	1908	1055092	1919	1338406	1930
358085	1909	1162501	1920	1370000	1931
398276	1910	1211300	1921	1404000	1932
456376	1911	1239641	1922	1426000	1933
502046	1912	1252387	1923	1442000	1934
531521	1913	1261487	1924	1492000	1935

The above are estimated serial numbers for Springfield M1903 rifles. Serial numbers for 1903–1906 are estimates based on Springfield Armory payroll records for 1904–1906 and are courtesy of Springfield Research Service. Serial numbers for 1907–1930 are based on Crossman's Book of the Springfield. Serial numbers for 1931–1935 are courtesy of Springfield Research Service and are based on Hatcher's records for 1907–1935. (Used with permission)

Table 2

Rock Island Arsenal M1903 Rifle Serial Numbers at Start of Calendar Years

Serial No.	Year	Serial No.	Year
1	1904	187000	1911
700	1905	209000	1912
19000	1906	225000	1913
50000	1907	236000	1914
82000	1908	261000	1918
118000	1909	318000	1919
157000	1910	347000	1920

Note: These dates are for the vintage of the receiver. The date of receiver production and date of assembly could vary by several years, particularly for pre-1909 Rock Island Arsenal rifles. These estimated serial numbers are based on information extrapolated from Fiscal Year data reported in Rock Island Arsenal records. Courtesy of Springfield Research Service. (Used with permission)

Table 3

Memorandum of Changes made 1903–1914

(Courtesy Springfield Research Service)

Memorandum of Changes that have been made in the U.S. Rifle, Cal. .30, Model of 1903 (O.O. 37888/2916, S.A. 38-5)

1. The original rifle had a small oiler which was carried in the butt of the stock, together with the cleaning rod head, the latter screwing on the end of the rod bayonet. In the latter part of 1903, the combination oiler and thong case was adopted, replacing the previous oiler and the cleaning rod head.
2. The original sight of the 1903 rifle, known as the "Dickson" sight, was modified in 1904 by the adoption of a plate for a peep sight.

3. The rear face of the front sight stud was serrated in 1904, in order to prevent any reflection of light from this surface interfering with the aiming.
4. In 1904, the barrel bed of the stock and the handguard was relieved so as to reduce the charring effect of a heated barrel on these components.
5. The cartridge for this rifle was originally loaded with a 220-grain bullet giving a muzzle velocity of 2,300 f.s. It was found, however, that the erosion of the barrels was excessive, and extensive tests were made to see if this defect could be overcome; and it was found that a reduction of the muzzle velocity by 100 f.s., while not materially decreasing the remaining energy or increasing the ordinates of trajectories at ranges up to 1,000 yards would, however, double the number of rounds that could be fired before the barrel was sufficiently eroded to affect the accuracy of same for target practice and would still leave the arm more powerful than any other military musket known to the department. It was therefore decided in 1905 to adopt a muzzle velocity of 2,200 f.s. for this rifle until such extended experiments in service and improvements in powder and barrel steel would warrant a return to the higher velocity.
6. In order to fulfill the new conditions imposed by the revised infantry drill regulations, viz., that the piece be carried loaded and cocked, it was necessary in 1905 to redesign the safety lock and cocking piece so as to stand the wear of such repeated setting and unsetting.
7. In 1905, the rod bayonet was discarded and the knife bayonet adopted. This change in bayonet necessitated a new design of upper band and front sight stud.
8. In 1905, a new rear sight was adopted, being a modification of the Springfield sight, model 1888, and the 1901 Krag sight, the new sight being known as the model of 1905 sight.
9. In 1905, the front sight stud was made in two parts, the fixed stud and the movable stud, this being done to permit correction of alignment of front and rear sights.
10. In 1905, the handguard was altered at the rear end so as to afford protection for the rear sight.
11. In 1906, the rear sight was improved by the addition of an automatic compensating device on the windage knob to take up the wear.
12. In 1906, the lower band which had previously been made as a closed ring was cut so as to facilitate disassembling.
13. In 1906, the bolt was browned to prevent any reflection of light from its surface.
14. In 1907, the bayonet catch was redesigned, as it was found that the old model catch would release when the bayonet was fixed to the rifle during firing.
15. In 1907, drift slides with different size peep holes and peep notches were supplied in addition to the regular drift slides furnished with each 10 rifles. Two drift slides with peep hole .04 diameter and peep notches .035 diameter, and two with peep hole .06 diameter and peep notches .055 diameter being furnished, it having been found that the different sizes were necessary owing to the difference in vision of the soldier.
16. In 1907, the sharp pointed bullet weight 150 grains and having a velocity of 2,700 f.s. was adopted. Length of bullet was slightly reduced and neck of cartridge shortened later in the same year. The adoption of this bullet required the shortening of the barrel and the stock in order to take the new ammunition. The graduations of the leaf of the rear sight were also extended from 2,500 to 2,850 yards.
17. In 1907, the fixed base was changed by omitting the lightening cut underneath the band. This change was made as it was found that in assembling the fixed base to the barrel, it was possible to spring the base and thus throw the rear sight out of alignment.
18. In 1908, the stock was strength by a stock screw. The addition of this screw was found necessary in order to prevent the recoil of the rifle splitting the stock at the rear end of the receiver.
19. In 1908, two steel handguard clips were added to the handguard in order to prevent splitting of this component.
20. In 1909, a groove was cut in the top side at rear end of the handguard in order to enlarge the field of view when sighting the rifle at 100 yards.
21. In 1909, the barrel bearing at the front end of the stock and handguard was relieved in order to prevent distortion of the barrel by warping of either of these components.
22. In 1910, a spare part container was furnished with every alternate rifle in place of the combination oiler and thong case. The spare parts container holds three spare parts: a striker, an extractor, and a firing pin.
23. In 1910, the buttplate was checked for the purpose of insuring a firmer seat at the shoulder when firing.
24. In 1910, serrations were cut in the finger piece of trigger to prevent slipping of the finger.
25. In 1910, the stock around the receiver was changed in outline to do away with the sharp corners and to prevent splitting off of the thin portions of the stock.

Springfield Armory, Massachusetts, February 12, 1914.

Note: This Springfield Armory memorandum provides a handy, and authoritative, means to ascertain the various changes that took place in the components of the M1903 rifle from the time of its adoption until early 1914.

Table 4

Serial Numbers of M1903 Rifles with M1908 Warner & Swasey Musket Sights Cited in Government Documents and Records

(Courtesy of Springfield Research Service)

Rifle #	Sight Type and #	Date Cited	Unit/Usage
155268	M1908 sight, no # cited	7/15/09	Office Chief of Ordnance to SA***
207211	M1908 sight, #452	10/3/08	Scope test/Springfield Armory
207213	No type or # cited	2/20/23	Troop G, 5th Cavalry*
207622	No type or # cited	2/20/23	Troop G, 5th Cavalry*
207630	M1908 sight, no # cited	4/03/14	Scope test/SA
220597	No type or # cited	2/02/10	Maxim silencer – sent to SA***
259173	No type or # cited	10/10/09	RIA Silencer Test***
313536	M1908 sight, #199	10/6/09	Issued to 22nd Infantry
337862	M1908 sight, no # cited	5/09/08	Presented to Ambrose Swasey
352248	No type or # cited	2/13/23	Troop F, 1st Cavalry*
352271	M1908 sight, no # cited	6/07/09	Issued to 22nd Infantry
352340	M1908 sight, #248	6/10/09	Issued to 15th Infantry
352355	M1908 sight, no # cited	6/08/09	Troop F, 14th Cavalry, sight test
"	"	3/12/23	Post Ord. Office, Ft. Huachuca
352358	M1908 sight, #701	6/14/09	Co. F, 16th Infantry, sight test
352359	M1908 sight, no # cited	6/10/09	Co. M, 11th Infantry, sight test
352367	M1908 sight, no # cited	6/31/09	Co. F, 1st Infantry, sight test
352376	M1908 sight, #265	6/13/09	Troop C, 2nd Cavalry, sight test
352377	M1908 sight, no # cited	5/26/09	Co. I, 3rd Engineers, sight test
352378	M1908 sight, #961	6/13/09	Troop C, 2nd Cavalry, sight test
352380	M1908 sight, #912	10/03/10	Issued to 14th Infantry
352395	M1908 sight, #185	9/30/10	Issued to 14th Infantry
352401	M1908 sight, #876	10/03/10	Issued to 14th Infantry
352404	M1908 sight, #671	10/03/10	Issued to 14th Infantry
352416	No Type cited	1/22/23	Troop E, 2nd Sqdn., 12th Cavalry*
352418	M1908 sight, #389	8/05/09	Issued to 14th Infantry
352425	M1908 sight, #997	10/3/10	Issued to 14th Infantry
352446	M1908 sight, #166	6/12/09	Issued to Troop M, 2nd Cavalry
352447	M1908 sight, #947	10/03/10	Issued to 14th Infantry
352451	M1908 sight, no # cited	6/16/09	Co. E, 1st Infantry, sight test
352453	M1908 sight, no # cited	7/15/09	22nd Infantry, sight test
352455	M1908 sight, no # cited	7/21/11	Repaired at Rock Island Arsenal
352459	M1908 sight, no # cited	7/15/09	22nd Infantry, sight test
352462	M1908 sight, no # cited	6/08/09	Troop K, 14th Cavalry, sight test
352467	M1908 sight, no # cited	7/15/09	22nd Infantry, sight test
352469	M1908 sight, no # cited	7/29/09	Co. H, 1st Infantry, sight test
352473	M1908 sight, #694	9/30/10	Issued to 14th Infantry
352479	M1908 sight, #95	6/02/09	Issued to Co. E, 3rd Infantry
352480	No type or # cited	5/05/25	To Rock Island Arsenal*
352481	No type or # cited	2/07/16	Co. H, 24th Infantry*
352483	M1908 sight, #107	6/07/09	Issued to Troop A, 8th Cavalry
352486	M1908 sight, no # cited	7/31/11	Issued to Co. L, 8th Infantry
352495	M1908 sight, #418	12/19/10	Issued to Co. G, 24th Infantry
352500	M1908 sight, #256	7/27/09	Issued to Troop L, 4th Cavalry
352505	M1908 sight, no # cited	6/16/09	Co. L, 9th Infantry, sight test
352513	M1908 sight, #409	9/30/10	Issued to 14th Infantry
352514	M1908 sight, no # cited	12/20/09	Issued to Co. F, 25th Infantry
352516	M1908 sight, #756	10/03/10	Issued to 14th Infantry
352520	M1908 sight, #717	8/05/09	Issued to 14th Infantry
352533	M1908 sight, no # cited	12/20/09	Issued to Co. M, 25th Infantry
352534	M1908 sight, no # cited	11/27/09	Issued to 12th Infantry
352537	M1908 sight, #844	9/30/10	Issued to 14th Infantry

Rifle #	Sight Type and #	Date Cited	Unit/Usage
352540	M1908 sight, #902	0/03/10	Issued to 14th Infantry
352542	M1908 sight, #812	9/30/10	Issued to 14th Infantry
352545	M1908 sight, no # cited	8/25/09	Issued to 6th Cavalry
352554	M1908 sight, no # cited	6/07/09	Co. G, 16th Infantry, sight test
352555	M1908 sight, #931	8/05/09	Issued to 14th Infantry
352558	M1908 sight, no # cited	5/26/09	Co. I, 3rd Engineers, sight test
352572	M1908 sight, no # cited	5/13/09	Co. A, 9th Infantry, sight test
352574	M1908 sight, #829	9/30/10	Issued to 14th Infantry
352579	M1908 sight, no # cited	12/20/09	Issued to Co. F, 25th Infantry
352582	M1908 sight, no # cited	12/20/09	Issued to Co. F, 25th Infantry
352583	M1908 sight, no # cited	7/29/09	Co. H, 1st Infantry, sight test
352591	M1908 sight, #404	10/03/10	Issued to 14th Infantry
352596	M1908 sight, no # cited	12/20/09	Issued to Co. F, 25th Infantry
352601	No type or # cited	7/19/15	Co. D, 10th Infantry*
352608	M1908 sight, #894	7/14/09	Issued to Co. M, 3rd Infantry
"	"	3/14/23	Co. E, 25th Infantry
352609	M1908 sight, no # cited	6/22/09	Issued to Troop F. 12 Cavalry
352610	M1908 sight, #805	8/05/09	Issued to 14th Infantry
352617	M1908 sight, #648	9/30/10	Issued to 14th Infantry
352624	M1908 sight, no # cited	6/25/11	Issued to 16th Infantry
352627	M1908 sight, #944	10/03/10	Issued to 14th Infantry
352630	M1908 sight, #454	9/30/10	Issued to 14th Infantry
352632	M1908 sight, #957	10/03/10	Issued to 14th Infantry
352633	M1908 sight, #933	8/05/09	Issued to 14th Infantry
352637	M1908 sight, #908	8/05/09	Issued to 14th Infantry
352639	No type or # cited	5/05/25	To Rock Island Arsenal
352642	M1908 sight, #973	10/03/10	Issued to 14th Infantry
352645	M1908 sight, #461	----------	Reported
352650	M1908 sight, #768	8/05/09	Issued to 14th Infantry
352651	M1908 sight, #775	8/05/09	Issued to 14th Infantry
352677	M1908 sight, #897	10/03/10	Issued to 14th Infantry
352684	M1908 sight, no # cited	7/09/09	Issued to 12th Cavalry
352697	M1908 sight, #696	8/23/09	Issued to 4th Infantry
352700	No type or # cited	3/12/23	Post Ord. Office, Ft. Huachuca*
352704	M1908 sight, #804	9/30/10	Issued to 14th Infantry
352706	M1908 sight, no # cited	6/07/09	Co. G, 16th Infantry, sight test
352707	M1908 sight, #277	8/06/09	Issued to Co. G, 2nd Infantry
352710	M1908 sight, no # cited	6/06/09	Troop D, 8th Cavalry, sight test
352712	M1908 sight, no # cited	6/16/09	Co. H, 9th Infantry, sight test
352716	M1908 sight, no # cited	12/20/09	Issued to Co. F, 25th Infantry
352717	M1908 sight, no # cited	12/20/09	Issued to Co. H, 25th Infantry
352719	M1908 sight, #810	10/03/10	Issued to 14th Infantry
352720	M1908 sight, no # cited	7/28/09	Co. I, 1st Infantry, sight test
352725	M1908 sight, no # cited	3/12/12	At Benicia Arsenal
352734	M1908 sight, no # cited	6/06/09	Troop D, 8th Cavalry, sight test
352736	M1908 sight, #510	9/30/10	Issued to 14th Infantry
352740	M1908 sight, no # cited	12/20/09	Issued to Co. K, 25th Infantry
352742	M1908 sight, no # cited	12/20/09	Issued to Co. E, 25th Infantry
352743	M1908 sight, no # cited	8/29/09	Co. D, 25th Infantry, sight test
352751	M1908 sight, #744	10/03/10	Issued to 14th Infantry
352754	M1908 sight, #707	8/05/09	Issued to 14th Infantry
352757	M1908 sight, #731	10/03/10	Issued to 14th Infantry
352768	M1908 sight, #193	7/22/09	Issued to 22nd Infantry
352780	M1908 sight, no # cited	6/10/09	Co. B, 15th Infantry, sight test
352785	M1908 sight, #914	9/30/10	Issued to 14th Infantry
352788	M1908 sight, #442	9/30/10	Issued to 14th Infantry
352789	M1908 sight, no # cited	6/16/09	Co. H, 9th Infantry, sight test
352794	M1908 sight, #953	9/30/10	Issued to 14th Infantry
352795	No type or # cited	5/05/25	To Rock Island Arsenal
352802	M1908 sight, #980	8/05/09	Issued to 14th Infantry

Rifle #	Sight Type and #	Date Cited	Unit/Usage
352806	M1908 sight, #561	10/03/10	Issued to 14th Infantry
352807	M1908 sight, #473	8/05/09	Issued to 14th Infantry
352808	M1908 sight, #927	9/30/10	Issued to 14th Infantry
352812	M1908 sight, #964	9/30/10	Issued to 14th Infantry
352813	M1908 sight, #971	8/05/09	Issued to 14th Infantry
352815	M1908 sight, #990	10/03/10	Issued to 14th Infantry
352816	No type or # cited	12/23/23	Troop E, 2nd Sqdn.,12th Cavalry*
352819	M1908 sight, #951	10/03/10	Issued to 14th Infantry
352825	M1908 sight, #881	10/03/10	Issued to 14th Infantry
352827	M1908 sight, #519	10/03/10	Issued to 14th Infantry
352830	No type or # cited	2/13/23	Troop F, 1st Cavalry*
352839	M1908 sight, #33	----------	Reported
352845	M1908 sight, #168	8/05/09	Issued to 14th Infantry
352846	M1908 sight, no # cited	12/20/09	Issued to Co. L, 25th Infantry
352847	M1908 sight, no # cited	6/31/09	Co. F, 1st Infantry, sight test
352858	M1908 sight, #711	8/05/09	Issued to 14th Infantry
352861	No type or # cited	7/17/16	Issued to Troop L, 2nd Cavalry
352863	M1908 sight, #395	7/14/09	Issued to Co. B, 3rd Infantry
352873	M1908 sight, #190	6/10/09	Issued to Co. E, 15th Infantry
352877	M1908 sight, #970	9/30/10	Issued to 14th Infantry
352883	M1908 sight, no # cited	7/15/09	22nd Infantry, sight test
352885	M1908 sight, no # cited	12/20/09	Issued to Co. F, 25th Infantry
352886	M1908 sight, #478	12/20/09	Issued to Co. M, 25th Infantry
"	"	7/31/21	Camp S.D. Little
352887	M1908 sight, #484	9/30/10	Issued to 14th Infantry
352889	M1908 sight, #424	9/30/10	Issued to 14th Infantry
352890	No type or # cited	6/12/14	Issued to Co. M, 14th Infantry
352902	No type or # cited	6/12/14	Issued to Co. M, 14th Infantry
352907	M1908 sight, #507	10/03/10	Issued to 14th Infantry
352908	M1908 sight, #613	----------	Reported
352913	M1908 sight, #265	7/22/09	Issued to 22nd Infantry
352920	M1908 sight, #346	7/14/09	Issued to Co. I, 3rd Infantry
352922	M1908 sight, #758	9/30/10	Issued to 14th Infantry
352923	M1908 sight, no # cited	7/15/09	22nd Infantry, sight test
352931	M1908 sight, no # cited	6/16/09	Co. L, 9th Infantry, sight test
352932	M1908 sight, #677	7/14/09	Issued to Co. L, 3rd Infantry
352934	M1908 sight, #167	7/22/09	Issued to 22nd Infantry
352938	No type or # cited	9/ 8/19	Telescope purchased
352946	M1908 sight, #965	10/03/10	Issued to 14th Infantry
352947	M1908 sight, no # cited	6/14/09	Co. C, 16th Infantry, sight test
352948	M1908 sight, #807	9/30/10	Issued to 14th Infantry
352949	M1908 sight, no # cited	6/10/09	Co. B, 15th Infantry, sight test
352954	M1908 sight, #644	9/30/10	Issued to 14th Infantry
352960	M1908 sight, no # cited	6/14/09	Co. C, 16th Infantry, sight test
352971	M1908 sight, #601	7/22/09	Issued to 22nd Infantry
352976	M1908 sight, no # cited	6/10/09	Co. A, 15th Infantry, sight test
352977	M1908 sight, #821	10/03/10	Issued to 14th Infantry
352980	M1908 sight, #440	9/30/10	Issued to 14th Infantry
352985	M1908 sight, #741	8/05/09	Issued to 14th Infantry
352986	M1908 sight, no # cited	8/10/09	Issued to Troop F, 13th Cavalry
"		12/02/23	Troop E, 2nd Sqdn., 12th Cavalry
352987	M1908 sight, no # cited	6/14/09	Co. C, 16th Infantry, sight test
352988	M1908 sight, #428	10/--/10	Issued to 4th Infantry
352997	M1908 sight, #462	7/22/09	Issued to 22nd Infantry
353003	M1908 sight, #333	5/16/09	Issued to 3rd Cavalry ***
353004	M1908 sight, no # cited	12/20/09	Issued to Co. F, 25th Infantry
353009	M1908 sight, #296	----------	Reported
353011	No type or # cited	5/05/25	To Rock Island Arsenal*
353012	No type or # cited	7/19/15	Co. D., 10th Infantry*
353021	M1908 sight, #819	9/30/10	Issued to 14th Infantry

Rifle #	Sight Type and #	Date Cited	Unit/Usage
353022	M1908 sight, #652	9/30/09	Issued to 14th Infantry
353025	M1908 sight, #260	6/21/09	Issued to Co. M, 2nd Infantry
353028	M1908 sight, #921	10/03/10	Issued to 14th Infantry
353029	M1908 sight, no # cited	12/20/09	Issued to Co. L, 25th Infantry
"	"	3/13/23	Co. L. 25th Infantry* (still in use)
353032	M1908 sight, no # cited	12/20/09	Issued to Co. M, 25th Infantry
"	"	7/31/21	Camp S.D. Little
353033	M1908 sight, no # cited	12/20/09	Issued to Co. I, 25th Infantry
353034	M1908 sight, #816	10/03/10	Issued to 14th Infantry
353036	M1908 sight, #721	6/28/09	Issued to Co. L, 28th Infantry
353040	M1908 sight, #470	7/09/09	Issued to 12th Cavalry
353046	M1908 sight, #543	7/14/09	Issued to Co. A, 3rd Infantry
353050	M1908 sight, #401	9/30/10	Issued to 14th Infantry
353055	No type or # cited	2/13/23	Troop F, 1st Cavalry*
353058	M1908 sight, #449	12/19/10	Issued to Co. G, 24th Infantry
353060	M1908 sight, no # cited	12/20/09	Issued to Co. H, 25th Infantry
353075	No type or # cited	1/23/23	Troop F, 2nd Sqdn., 12th Cavalry*
353079	M1908 sight, no # cited	6/10/09	Co. A, 15th Infantry, sight test
353094	M1908 sight, #998	10/03/10	Issued to 14th Infantry
353098	M1908 sight, no # cited	6/10/09	Co. B, 15th Infantry, sight test
353102	M1908 sight, #900	9/30/10	Issued to 14th Infantry
353104	M1908 sight, no # cited	6/14/09	Co. C, 16th Infantry, sight test
353112	M1908 sight, #882	10/03/10	Issued to 14th Infantry
353114	M1908 sight, #435	10/--/10	Issued to 4th Infantry
353122	M1908 sight, #751	10/03/10	Issued to 14th Infantry
353123	M1908 sight, #554	9/30/10	Issued to 14th Infantry
353124	M1908 sight, #848	10/--/10	Issued to 4th Infantry
353126	M1908 sight, no # cited	7/15/09	22nd Infantry, sight test
353139	M1908 sight, no # cited	7/29/09	Issued to Troop K, 4th Cavalry
353152	M1908 sight, #948	10/03/10	Issued to 14th Infantry
353153	Type not cited	1/07/24	Presidio of Monterey
353155	M1908 sight, no # cited	7/21/11	Repaired at Rock Island Arsenal
"	"	5/05/25	To Rock Island Arsenal
353159	M1908 sight, #275	----------	Reported
353160	M1908 sight, #465	10/03/10	Issued to 14th Infantry
353173	M1908 sight, no # cited	12/20/09	Issued to Co. K, 25th Infantry
353179	M1908 sight, no # cited	5/13/09	Co. A, 9th Infantry, sight test
353187	M1908 sight, #916	9/30/10	Issued to 14th Infantry
353192	M1908 sight, #684	9/30/10	Issued to 14th Infantry
353196	M1908 sight, #504	10/03/10	Issued to 14th Infantry
353197	M1908 sight, #446	6/10/09	Issued to Co. E, 15th Infantry
353203	M1908 sight, #429	10/--/10	Issued to 4th Infantry
353205	M1908 sight, no # cited	6/16/09	Co. E, 1st Infantry, sight test
352212	M1908 sight, #364	10/03/10	Issued to 14th Infantry
353218	M1908 sight, no # cited	7/15/09	22nd Infantry, sight test
353225	M1908 sight, #939	8/05/09	Issued to 14th Infantry
353228	M1908 sight, no # cited	12/20/09	Issued to Co. H, 25th Infantry
353232	M1908 sight, #895	10/03/10	Issued to 14th Infantry
353236	No type or # cited	1/23/23	Troop F, 2nd Sqdn., 12th Cavalry*
353237	M1908 sight, #506	10/03/10	Issued to 14th Infantry
353240	M1908 sight, # 40	6/14/09	Issued to 16th Infantry
353247	M1908 sight, #524	10/03/10	Issued to 14th Infantry
353248	M1908 sight, #952	10/03/10	Issued to 14th Infantry
353254	M1908 sight, no # cited	12/20/09	Issued to Co. F, 25th Infantry
"	"	2/13/23	Troop G, 1st Cavalry
353261	M1908 sight, no # cited	5/16/09	Co. L. 17th Infantry, sight test
353262	M1908 sight, #798	----------	Reported
353264	M1908 sight, #556	10/03/10	Issued to 14th Infantry
353272	M1908 sight, no # cited	6/10/09	Co. A, 15th Infantry, sight test
353283	M1908 sight, no # cited	6/08/09	Troop K, 14th Cavalry, sight test

Rifle #	Sight Type and #	Date Cited	Unit/Usage
353285	M1908 sight, no # cited	6/25/11	Issued to 16th Infantry
353288	No type or # cited	2/07/16	Co. H, 24th Infantry*
353289	M1908 sight, no # cited	6/16/09	Co. L, 1st Infantry, sight test
353291	M1908 sight, no # cited	12/20/09	Issued to Co. F, 25th Infantry
353292	M1908 sight, no # cited	12/20/09	Issued to Co. F, 25th Infantry
353299	M1908 sight, no # cited	6/08/09	Troop F, 14th Cavalry, sight test
353301	M1908 sight, no # cited	12/20/09	Issued to Co. F, 25th Infantry
353310	M1908 sight, no # cited	7/25/09	Co. I, 16th Infantry, sight test
353315	No type or # cited	4/06/16	Manila Ord. Dept to SA*
353317	M1908 sight, #799	10/03/10	Issued to 14th Infantry
353326	M1908 sight, #729	8/05/09	Issued to 14th Infantry
"	"	4/06/16	Manila Ord. Depot to SA
353327	M1908 sight, #733	10/03/10	Issued to 14th Infantry
"	"	2/07/25	To Rock Island Arsenal
353330	M1908 sight, #361	10/06/09	Issued to Co. D, 25th Infantry
353442	M1908 sight, #793	----------	Reported
353448	M1908 sight, #928	10/03/10	Issued to 14th Infantry
353522	M1908 sight, #366	7/14/09	Issued to Co. K, 3rd Infantry
353594	M1908 sight, no # cited	7/28/09	Co. I, 1st Infantry, sight test
353915	No type or # cited	2/20/23	Troop G, 5th Cavalry*
363228	No type or # cited	7/31/21	Camp S.D. Little
409417	M1908 sight, no # cited	----------	---------------
409455	No type or # cited	2/13/23	Troop F, 1st Cavalry*
409457	M1908 sight, #1056	3/12/23	Post Ord. Office, Ft. Huachuca*
409460	No type or # cited	4/06/16	Manila Ord. Depot to SA*
409468	"	4/12/23	Troop F, 10th Cavalry*
409472	"	3/12/23	Troop E, 10th Cavalry*
409494	"	5/05/25	To Rock Island Arsenal*
409548	"	1/10/23	Ft. McIntosh Ord. Officer*
409563	"	1/05/10	26th Infantry (Hunting)*
409594	M1908 sight, #1063	3/12/23	Post Ord. Office, Ft. Huachuca*
409601	No type or # cited	1/10/23	Ft. McIntosh Ord. Officer*
409636	"	1/23/23	Troop F, 2nd Sqdn., 12th Cavalry*
409655	"	5/05/25	To Rock Island Arsenal*
409656	"	3/12/23	Post Ord. Office, Ft. Huachuca*
409685	"	1/10/23	Ft. McIntosh Ord. Officer*
409703	"	4/06/16	Manila Ord. Depot to SA*
409778	"	1/10/23	Ft. McIntosh Ord. Officer*
409782	"	3/12/23	Post Ord. Office, Ft. Huachuca*
409784	M1908 sight, #1179	----------	Reported
452539	No type or # cited	7/24/25	U.S. Army – China*
452696	"	7/24/25	U.S. Army – China*
453062	"	7/25/25	U.S. Army – China*
454477	"	12/22/10	Manufactured*** *
468504	"	1/10/23	Ft. McIntosh Ord. Officer*
483648	M1908 sight, #651	----------	Reported

* Specific type of telescope not cited in ordnance documents.
*** Fitted with Maxim Silencer.

Reported numbers are primarily from serial numbers stamped inside of extant M1908 W&S sights – Compiled by W.P. Eyberg, 1983.

Note that a few duplicate serial number citations are listed. This was typically a case of the sniper rifle in question being transferred from one unit to another in the course of its tenure of issue, or being sent to Rock Island Arsenal circa 1925 for destruction or conversion to service rifle configuration. There is also an instance of one sniper rifle, serial #353029, remaining in the same unit (Co. L, 25th Infantry) from December 20, 1909 to March 13, 1923, a span of over 13 years.

Table 5

M1903 Rifles with M1913 Warner & Swasey Musket Sights cited in government documents and reports

(Courtesy of Springfield Research Service)

Rifle Serial #	Date cited	Details	Sight #
577890	12/23/23	Troop E, 2nd Sqdn., 12th Cavalry	
577891	12/23/23	Troop F, 2nd Sqdn., 12th Cavalry	
577920	2/13/23	Troop E, 1st Cavalry	
577947	2/13/23	Troop B, 1st Cavalry	
586004	----------	Reported	2130
612940	12/01/25	To Rock Island Arsenal	
625375	Known AEF Rifle	Reported	2454
625424	----------	Reported	2308
625441	2/05/24	Co. I, 25th Infantry	
625442	7/31/21	Camp S.D. Little	
625447	3/13/23	Co. I, 25th Infantry	
625448	----------	Reported	2359
625450	7/31/21	Camp S.D. Little	
625462	3/13/23	Co. L, 25th Infantry	
625463	3/13/23	Co. K, 25th Infantry	
625464	7/31/21	Camp S.D. Little	
625469	3/08/23	Co. C, 25th Infantry	
625539	----------	Reported	2451
625608	----------	Reported	2490
625560	----------	Reported	2492
632065	----------	Reported	2579
632084	2/13/23	Troop E, 1st Cavalry	
632089	2/13/23	Hq. Troop, 1st Cavalry	
632163	----------	Reported	2642
632175	----------	Reported	2761
632205	10/21/18	Camp Gordon, GA	
632206	10/21/18	Camp Gordon, GA	
632207	10/21/18	Camp Gordon, GA	
632208	10/21/18	Camp Gordon, GA	
677762	5/05/25	To Rock Island Arsenal	
677820	5/05/25	To Rock Island Arsenal	
677889	----------	Reported	3261
677900	----------	Reported	3463
677959	5/05/25	To Rock Island Arsenal	
678268	5/05/25	To Rock Island Arsenal	
689442	N/A	Used by U.S. Sniper in Argonne Campaign, WWI*	
697844	3/10/26	At Ft. Riley, KS	
699832	----------	Reported	3194
709619	----------	Reported	3102
712992	5/05/25	To Rock Island Arsenal	
714815	----------	Reported	2918
716339	5/05/25	To Rock Island Arsenal	
779046	12/01/25	To Rock Island Arsenal	
779312	12/01/25	To Rock Island Arsenal	
780154	12/01/25	To Rock Island Arsenal	
783913	12/01/25	To Rock Island Arsenal	
785153	12/01/25	To Rock Island Arsenal	
785823	12/01/25	To Rock Island Arsenal	
786031	12/01/25	To Rock Island Arsenal	

Rifle Serial #	Date cited	Details	Sight #
786291	12/01/25	To Rock Island Arsenal	
786537	12/01/25	To Rock Island Arsenal	
927664	2/13/23	Troop B, 1st Cavalry	
"	3/10/23	Ord. Warehouse, Camp Harry J. Jones	
928836	12/01/25	To Rock Island Arsenal	
929184	12/01/25	To Rock Island Arsenal	
931856	2/13/23	Troop C, 1st Cavalry	
934465	5/05/25	To Rock Island Arsenal	
934897	5/05/25	To Rock Island Arsenal	
934825	2/13/23	Troop C, 1st Cavalry	
935384	3/10/23	Post Ord. Office, Camp H.J. Jones	
935386	5/05/25	To Rock Island Arsenal	
935403	2/13/23	Troop B, 1st Cavalry	
935450	2/13/23	Troop C, 1st Cavalry	
935557	5/05/25	To Rock Island Arsenal	
935703	2/13/23	Troop B, 1st Cavalry	
936382	3/10/23	Post Ord. Office, Camp H.J. Jones	
936416	3/10/23	Ord. Warehouse, Camp Harry J. Jones	
936429	2/13/23	Troop F, 1st Cavalry	
936527	2/13/23	Troop C, 1st Cavalry	
936618	----------	Reported	7239
937139	----------	Reported	7813

*Rifle currently in Springfield Armory Museum collection. Receiver still has traces of camouflage paint.

Reported numbers privately compiled and primarily taken from serial numbers stamped inside of extant M1913 W&S sights, believed to be original.

Table 6

M1903 Rifles Fitted with Winchester A5 Telescopes Cited in Government Documents and Records

(Courtesy of Springfield Research Service)

Rifle Serial #	Date cited	Details
468493	2/28/14	Fitted with A/5 scope by WRA Co.
470498	2/28/14	Fitted with A/5 scope by WRA Co.
470555	2/28/14	Fitted with A/5 scope by WRA Co.*
470836	2/28/14	Fitted with A/5 scope by WRA Co.
471503	2/28/14	Fitted with A/5 scope by WRA Co.
472373	2/28/14	Fitted with A/5 scope by WRA Co.
473105	2/28/14	Fitted with A/5 scope by WRA Co.
473298	2/28/14	Fitted with A/5 scope by WRA Co.
473398	2/28/14	Fitted with A/5 scope by WRA Co.
473553	2/28/14	Fitted with A/5 scope by WRA Co.
473633	2/28/14	Fitted with A/5 scope by WRA Co.
474180	2/28/14	Fitted with A/5 scope by WRA Co.*

*Currently in Springfield Armory Museum collection

Note: There is no indication in the government records cited regarding the purpose of these 12 '03 rifles fitted with A5 scopes by Winchester Repeating Arms Company or whether the scopes were fitted under the auspices of a military contract.

Rifle Serial #	Date cited	Details
611365	7/15/30	U.S.M.C. – Nicaragua
620267	7/15/30	U.S.M.C. – Nicaragua
646068	7/15/30	U.S.M.C. – Nicaragua
646136	7/15/30	U.S.M.C. – Nicaragua
646237	3/10/26	U.S.M.C. – Philadelphia Depot
646241	7/15/30	U.S.M.C. – Nicaragua
646475	3/10/26	U.S.M.C. – Philadelphia Depot
671408	7/15/30	U.S.M.C. – Nicaragua
673163	7/15/30	U.S.M.C. – Nicaragua

Note: These seven U.S.M.C. '03 rifles with scopes cited in government records as being in Nicaragua are intermixed with a much larger number of standard '03s in close serial number proximity. This strongly suggests that these were standard '03 service rifles converted for sniper use in Nicaragua in the late 1920s. The rifles cited at the U.S.M.C. Philadelphia Depot were, likewise, in close serial number proximity of standard M1903 U.S.M.C. rifles at the same location during the same period.

Rifle Serial #	Date cited	Details
785409	2/16/23	Troop E, 5th Cavalry
785424	2/16/23	Troop E, 5th Cavalry

According to Ordnance Department records, Troop G of the 5th Cavalry was also equipped with other types of telescopic-sighted rifles. Although the type of scope mounted was not recorded, they were presumably M1908 and M1913 Warner & Swasey sights based on the serial numbers. Only the two above rifles were specifically cited as having Winchester A5 scopes.

Table 7

Mark I Pedersen Devices Cited in Government Documents and Records

(Courtesy of Springfield Research Service)

Device Serial #	Date of Citation	Details
4829	3/09/28	To SA from Fort Thomas
6704	3/09/28	To SA from Fort Benjamin Harrison
9404	3/09/28	To SA from Fort Benjamin Harrison
16313	3/09/28	To SA from Fort Benjamin Harrison
16744	3/09/28	To SA from Fort Thomas
18748	3/09/28	To SA from Fort Benjamin Harrison
20882	3/09/28	To SA from Fort Benjamin Harrison
22660	3/09/28	To SA from Fort Benjamin Harrison
28753	3/09/28	To SA from Fort Benjamin Harrison
29691	3/09/28	To SA from Fort Thomas
30454	3/09/28	To SA from Fort Benjamin Harrison
31547	3/09/28	To SA from Fort Thomas
32648	3/09/28	To SA from Fort Thomas
32930	3/09/28	To SA from Fort Benjamin Harrison
35643	3/09/28	To SA from Fort Benjamin Harrison
36050	3/09/28	To SA from Fort Thomas
38470	3/09/28	To SA from Fort Benjamin Harrison
38533	3/09/28	To SA from Fort Thomas
40782	3/09/28	To SA from Fort Benjamin Harrison
40852	3/09/28	To SA from Fort Thomas
40969	3/09/28	To SA from Fort Thomas
41427	3/09/28	To SA from Fort Thomas
41908	3/09/28	To SA from Fort Thomas
42665	3/09/28	To SA from Fort Thomas
42956	3/09/28	To SA from Fort Benjamin Harrison
43472	3/09/28	To SA from Fort Thomas
44287	3/09/28	To SA from Fort Benjamin Harrison
44971	3/09/28	To SA from Fort Thomas
45521	3/09/28	To SA from Fort Thomas
45797	3/09/28	To SA from Fort Thomas
46351	3/09/28	To SA from Fort Thomas
46848	3/09/28	To SA from Fort Thomas
47665	3/09/28	To SA from Fort Thomas
48682	3/09/28	To SA from Fort Benjamin Harrison
52736	3/09/28	To SA from Fort Benjamin Harrison
57545	3/09/28	To SA from Fort Benjamin Harrison

Note: These Pedersen Devices were among those tested at several U.S. Army bases. After the testing, the devices were sent to Springfield Armory and Rock Island Arsenal for storage and subsequent destruction. The 37 devices cited here were among those tested at Fort Benjamin Harrison and Fort Thomas that were returned in early 1928 to Springfield Armory for storage prior to their destruction three years later (1931).

Table 8

Serial Numbers of M1903 Cameron-Yaggi Trench Periscope Rifles Cited in Government Documents and Records

(Courtesy of Springfield Research Service)

Serial #	Date of Citation	Details
247954	12/01/25	To Rock Island Arsenal
258196	12/01/25	To Rock Island Arsenal
259142	12/01/25	To Rock Island Arsenal
259623	12/01/25	To Rock Island Arsenal
259914	12/01/25	To Rock Island Arsenal
260972	12/01/25	To Rock Island Arsenal
263167	12/01/25	To Rock Island Arsenal
266635	12/01/25	To Rock Island Arsenal

Note: These eight M1903 Cameron-Yaggi Trench Periscope rifles were cited as being in inventory and directed to be shipped to Rock Island Arsenal. The rifles were either destroyed or the trench periscope apparatus removed and scrapped, and the rifles converted to standard service rifle configuration.

Table 9

Percentage of components found to be unserviceable in lot of 10,000 rifles sent to Springfield Armory for overhaul in the 1920s

Source: Army Ordnance article, July–August 1928, by Lt. J.E. McInerney, Ord. Dept., U.S.A.

Principal Component	% Found Unserviceable	Principal Component	% Found Unserviceable
Barrel assemblies	91%	Firing pin assemblies	5%
Receivers	85%	Stacking swivels	5%
Handguards	53%	Buttplates	4%
Windage screw assemblies	34%	Lower band swivels	4%
Magazine springs	23%	Upper bands	3%
Bolt assemblies	22%	Extractors	3%
Stocks	19%	Main springs	3%
Sears	19%	Guards	2%
Slide & cap assemblies	12%	Sleeves	2%
Cut-offs	8%	Floor plates	2%
Ejectors	6%	Rear sight leaves	2%
Strikers	6%	Movable base	1%

Table 10

Remington M1903 and M1903A3 Production and Serial Numbers

(Compiled by William Hansen. Used with Permission)

Calendar Month	Monthly Production '03	Monthly Production '03A3	Calculated Serial Number Month-End	Calendar Month	Monthly Production '03	Monthly Production '03A3	Calculated Serial Number Month-End
1941				**1943**			
Oct.	10	0	3000009	Jan.	10,934	33,484	3384420
Nov.	1,273	0	3001282	Feb.	283	51,603	3458758
Dec.	4,681	0	3005963	Mar.	105	58,960	3520614
				Apr.	0	50,287	3573277
1942				May	0	35,980	3710958
Jan.	11,372	0	3017335	June	0	66,640	3780746
Feb.	11,981	0	3029316	July	0	42,094	3824829
Mar.	21,889	0	3051205	Aug.	0	60,565	3888272
Apr.	25,982	0	3077187	Sept.	0	64,080	3995409
May	28,691	0	3105878	Oct.	0	65,253	4023778
June	32,941	0	3138819	Nov.	0	62,141	4088927
July	31,137	0	3169956	Dec.	0	56,251	4147887
Aug.	28,981	0	3198937				
Sept.	25,072	0	3224009	**1944**			
Oct.	34,284	0	3258293	Jan.	0	37,822	4187457
Nov.	37,178	0	3295471	Feb.	0	20,560	4209000
Dec.	41,291	1,909	3338671				
				Totals	**348,085**	**707,629**	

Table 11

M1903A4 Sniper Rifle Production Data and Serial Numbers

(Compiled by William Hansen. Used with Permission)

Calendar Month	Actual Rifle[1] Production	Principal Barrel[2] Date Range	Calculated Month-End Serial Number[3]
1943			
February	102	1, 2–43	3407193
March	1,403	1 to 3–43	3408656
April	409	2, 3–43	3409166
May	119	2 to 4–43	3409290
June	2,342	2 to 6–43	3411732
July	2,654	2 to 9–43	3414499
August	3,276	7 to 9–43	3417914
September	2,839	7 to 9–43	3420874
October	1,563	8 to 10–43	3422503
November	1,405	8 to 10–43	3423968
December	852	8 to 10–43	3424856

Table 11 Continued on next page

1944

Month	Production		Date Range	Serial Number
January	3,179	(2,140)	8 to 11–43	3427087
		(1,039)[4]	9–43	Z4001083
February	3,496	(1,820)[4]	9 to 12–43	Z4002980
		(1,676)[5]	12–43 to 1–44	4993747
March	2,933		12–43 to 1–44	4996805
April	1,619		12–43 to 1–44	4998493
May	62		12–43 to 1–44	4998558
June	31		12–43 to 1–44	499859X[7]
Total	**28,365**[6]			

Notes and Assumptions

Serial Number Assignments:
1st Block: 20,000 numbers assigned January 18, 1943, from SN 3407088 to 3427087.
2nd Block: 15,000 numbers assigned June 20, 1943, from SN 4000001 to 4015000 from which a second authorization totaling 8,365 rifles was to come. It was initiated on September 11, 1943, upon the Lyman Corporation's scheduled entry into scope production for the Snipers program expansion as previously announced on August 2, 1943. However, this Second Block was suspended after about 2,980 numbers were used due to an overrun of the '03A3 production into the 2nd block in mid-October. These Snipers rifles were then ordered "Z prefixed" per an August 11, 1943, Ordnance directive changing the methodology for avoiding serial number duplicates.
3rd Block: Upon discovery of the 2nd Block snafu, Remington was authorized to begin use of a new Block of numbers on October 19, 1943, beginning with SN 4992001 for the much expanded M1903A3 and A4 program that never materialized. As it turns out, therefore, only the Snipers program was to use any of the SN block.

1. Actual production each month does not reflect the number of complete rifles in the month shown, but the number of complete rifles certifiably accepted after final inspection approval, including spare parts and accessories. The base data was provided by Clark Campbell (See U.S. Martial Arms Collector #90).
2. Since rifle production did not follow serial number order or date sequence, the actual range of barrel dates noted on production rifles may extend both before and after the dates or periods shown. Also, the First In-Last Out phenomena was much more aggravated than normal in the Snipers program due to frequent interruptions in rifle assembly (i.e. erratic production cycles) caused primarily by scope supply delays. As a result, there was a greater mix of older serially stamped receivers emerging later on in the assembly process mated to newer barrels, as well as older dated barrel stragglers mated to newer serially stamped receivers. This was especially prevalent in the July and August 1943 production.
3. The end-month serial numbers are calculated and, therefore, represent a hypothetical estimate of what possibly could have been, but never was. Since rifle production never occurred in serial number order, no such records were ever required, let alone maintained by Ordnance or the manufacturer.
4. It is observed that the total actual Snipers rifles assembled, those with the "Z" prefix were not certified for acceptance until the months of January and February 1944, even though their receivers had been serially numbered sometime between September 11 and October 19, 1943. This unusually long delay typified the lag time in the Snipers program. Finished rifles from this Block certified for acceptance approval were still delayed to February 1944 due primarily to the scope supply problems.
5. Receivers stamped with the Third Block of SNs beginning with SN 4992001 began sometime after assigned on October 19, 1943. However, due to suspension of the expanded M1903A4 program for lack of scopes, rifle assembly and approval momentum was severely interrupted once again. And even though well back on track by December pursuant to winding down the Snipers program, finished rifles from this Block certified for acceptance approval were still delayed to February 1944 due primarily to the scope supply problem.
6. Even though there were actually 26,365 rifles certified for acceptance under the Snipers contract, it is unknown how many serially stamped overrun receivers made their way into production as unauthorized M1903A4 rifles as opposed to reverting to M1903A3s.
7. This is an approximated end-number only based on current extant evidence and bears no resemblance to any last known Snipers serial number in existence.

Table 12

L.C. Smith and Corona Typewriters, Inc - M1903A3 Rifle Production Date/Serial Number Table

(Compiled by William Hansen. Used with permission)

Calendar Year and Month	Actual Rifle Production[1]		Calculated End-Month Serial Number[2]
1942			
December	5,540 [3]		3613711
1943			
January	9,560		3623568
February	10,030		3633908
March	13,560		3647887
April	17,366		3665790
May	18,100		3684449
June	16,880		3701851
July	20,420	(5,964)	3707999 (End of 1st Block)
		(3,880)[4]	C3711999 [4]
		(10,576)[5]	4718902 [5]
August	22,762		4742368
September	22,780		4765852
October	22,500		4789047
November	20,250		4809923
December	15,750		4826160
1944			
January	13,500		4480077
February	5,582 [6]		4845831 [7]
Total	234,580 [8]		

Notes and Assumptions
Contract Rifle Authorization and Serial Number Assignments

Authorized Rifles	Description
100,000	Initial letter Purchase Order (P.O.) issued 25 February, 1942, became Contract No. W-740-ORD-2259 awarded 12 March 1942. First Block serial numbers assigned to S-C were from SN **3608000 to 3707999**.
280,000	Second Letter Purchase Order (P.O.) issued 10 July, 1942 under rifle Contract No. W-740-ORD-2412. A total of 284,000 serial numbers were assigned from SN **4708000 to 4992000.**
600	Supplement No. 1 issued 25 October, 1942, among other approval actions, increased rifle authorization.
824	Supplement No. 2 issued 8 January, 1943, among other approval actions, further increased rifle authorization.
381,424	**Total M1903A3 rifles authorized under the S-C contract.**

1. Actual production each month reflects the number of complete rifles certifiably accepted by the Ordnance Department after final inspection and approval for payment. The data came from an official "Production-World War II" report dated 10 March, 1944, prepared by the Rochester Ordnance District (ROD), Small Arms Branch – Industrial Service.
2. The end-month serial numbers are calculated and therefore represent a hypothetical estimate of what possibly could have been, but never was. Since rifle production never occurred in serial number order, no such records were ever required or maintained by either Ordnance or the manufacturer.

Table 12 continued on next page

3. While Remington, along with S-C, actually assembled M1903A3 rifles beginning October 1942, all approvals were rescinded, resulting in suspension of S-C "fully assembled" rifles pending major redesign of the rear peep sight by Remington. Reportedly, S-C had 864 such rifles initially approved by the end of October 1942. Resumption of completed rifle assembly, inspections and approvals were not reinstated containing the new rear sight until December. Therefore, this production total reflects the earlier accumulation beginning with SN 3608000 and September 1942 dated barrels.
4. S-C inadvertently overran its initial (1st) serial number block into the 2nd M1903A3 Remington block beginning with SN 3708000. Based on extant evidence of such S-C overruns as high as SN 3711893, it is estimated that approximately 4,000 such S-C serial numbers were stamped, then ordered prefixed by Ordnance with a hand-stamped "C" in order to avoid duplicate serial numbers.
5. The 2nd Block of S-C assigned serial numbers beginning with 4708000 was inaugurated after resolution of the "overrun snafu."
6. While the actual approved production of February 1944 was 5,000 rifles, a postcontract audit of S-C production provided for "reinstatement" of 582 rifles on 4 May, 1944. This addition is attributed to the last month of production since all normal contract production terminated on 19 February, 1944.
7. SN 4845831 is a known quantity appearing on the last S-C contract production rifle.
8. While 234,580 rifles were approved and accepted by Ordnance under the formal S-C contract, it is estimated that about 28,000 additional receivers (approximated) were allowed to be serially stamped and retained in Ordnance stores. SN 4873338 is an example of a known "high number" sighting, with numbers as high as 4882XXX also reported. Such receivers were likely used in postwar rifle assembly for defense aid to foreign government purposes and are not considered S-C contract production rifles.

Table 13

Comparison of Remington and Smith-Corona M1903A3 Rifles

	Remington	Smith-Corona
Receiver Markings:	"Remington"	"Smith-Corona"
Barrel Markings:	"RA"	"SC"
Rifling:	Four- or two-groove	Six-, four-, or two-groove
Serial # Ranges:		
Stock Markings:	"FJA/Flaming Bomb/ RA" (sometimes)	Same but no "RA" stamp
	7/16" circled "P" proof stamp	1/2" circled "P" proof stamp
	Four to twelve geometric sub-inspection stamps in front of floorplate	Typically four such stamps
Band spring recess:	Square	Rounded
Bolt:	Marked "R" at root	Marked "X" on top of handle or unmarked
Buttplate checkering:	16 squares per inch	10 or 11 squares per inch

Table 14

WWII and Post-WWII Ordnance Rebuild Facilities

Large numbers of U.S. military weapons, including many M1903 rifles (and variants) were overhauled (rebuilt) at several U.S. Ordnance facilities. Regulations mandated that the initials of the facility be stamped on the stock. There were instances where rifles were only inspected and cleaned at the facility, so a rebuild stamp does not always indicate a complete tear-down and overhaul. This is particularly common with rifles bearing "OG" and "RA-P" stamps. The following is a list of the most often encountered WWII and post-WWII rebuild/inspection markings.

Marking   **Facility**

"SA"   Springfield Armory (Massachusetts)
This marking was often enclosed in a box and sometimes followed by a one- or two-letter suffix that is assumed to be the identify of the supervising inspector.

"RA" or "RA-P"   Raritan Arsenal (New Jersey)
Recent documentation has verified that the "RA-P" stamp indicates "Raritan Arsenal-Peterson." Harry Peterson was Chief Inspector at Raritan. The less commonly encountered "RA" rebuild stamp should not be confused with the Remington Arms factory marking on M1903, M1903 and M1903A4 rifles.

"RIA"   Rock Island Arsenal (Illinois)
This marking is usually followed by "FK" (Frank Krack) or "EB" (Elmer Bjerke). Krack was the foreman of small arms inspection from 1941 to 1946, and Bjerke held the position from 1947 to 1958. This makes it possible to determine the general time-frame in which a rifle was rebuilt.

"OG"   Ogden Arsenal (Utah)
There were three basic types of Ogden rebuild/inspection stamps. The "OG" stamp typically found on the left/middle of the buttstock is a post-WWII stamp and is often found on M190A3 rifles (especially Smith-Corona) that appear to remain in their factory-new configuration. This would indicate that such rifles were only inspected and packed for storage at Ogden. However, some rifles with "OG" stamps were subjected to a complete overhaul.

"O.G.E.K." and "OGEK"
These other two Ogden stamps are of late-WWII or early post-WWII origin. The last two letters represent the supervising inspectors. The "O.G.E.K." stamp (typically enclosed in a box) represents Elmer Keith who gained fame as a gun writer in the 1940s and 1950s. The "O.G.E.K." stamp (not enclosed in a box) represents inspector Ed Klouser.

"MR"   Mount Rainer Ordnance Depot (Washington)
MR stamps were typically applied to the right side of the stock.

"SAA"   San Antonio Arsenal (Texas)
This marking was often had a letter prefix. The marking may be found on the left or right side of the stock.

"HOD"   Hawaii Ordnance Depot
This is a relatively uncommon marking.

"RRA"   Red River Arsenal (Texas)
"RRAD"   Red River Army Depot
This facility changed names circa the 1960s.

"AN"   Anniston Arsenal (Alabama)
This marking was often followed by a letter suffix.

"AA"   Augusta Arsenal (Georgia)
Typically followed by a letter suffix.

"BA"   Benicia Arsenal (California)
Usually consisted of "BA" over a two- or three-letter suffix.

A casual barrack room scene showing '03 Springfields in a rack and against the brick wall. Note the very civilian clock, the barred door and the litter and sloppy beds to the right. This photo is an experimental double exposure. If you look carefully to the right of the rifle rack, you can see the transparent "ghost" image of a soldier. *(Stuart C. Mowbray collection)*

Bibliography

Books

Berry, Henry. *Make the Kaiser Dance: Living Memories of a Forgotten War*, Doubleday & Co., Garden City, N.Y., 1978

Brophy, Lt. Col. William S. *The Springfield 1903 Rifles*, Stackpole Books, Harrisburg, Penn., 1985.

Brophy, Lt. Col. William S. *Arsenal of Freedom – The Springfield Armory, 1890–1948*, Andrew Mowbray, Inc., Lincoln, RI, 1991.

Campbell, Clark S. *The '03 Springfield Rifle's Era*, Campbell Books, Richmond, Virginia, 2003.

Canfield, Bruce N. *A Collector's Guide to the '03 Springfield*, Andrew Mowbray Publishing, Inc., Lincoln, R.I., 1989.

Canfield, Bruce N. *U.S. Infantry Weapons of World War II*, Andrew Mowbray Publishing, Inc., Lincoln, R.I., 1994.

Canfield, Bruce N. *U.S. Infantry Weapons of the First World War*, Andrew Mowbray Publishing, Inc., Lincoln, R.I., 2000.

Colvin, Fred H. and Ethan Viall, *Manufacture of the Model 1903 Springfield Service Rifle*, (Reprint) Wolf Publishing Co., Inc, Prescott, Arizona, 1984.

Crossman, Edward C. *The Book of the Springfield*, Small Arms Technical Publishing Co., Georgetown, S.C., 1951.

Crowell, Benedict, Asst. Secretary of War, *America's Munitions: 1917–1918*, Washington Printing Office, Washington, D.C., 1919.

Dorsey, R. Stephen, *U.S. Martial Web Belts and Bandoliers: 1903–1981*, Collector's Library, Eugene, Oregon, 1993.

Dunlap, Roy F. *Ordnance Went Up Front*, R&R Books, Livonia, N.Y., 1948.

Ferris, C.S. *The Rock Island '03*, C.S. Ferris, Arvada, Colorado, 1992.

Ferris, C.S. and John Beard, *Springfield Model 1903 Service Rifle – Production and Alteration – 1905–1910*, C.S. Ferris, Arvada, Colorado, 1995.

George, Lt. Col. John. *Shots Fired in Anger*, National Rifle Association, Washington, D.C., 1981.

Harllee, John. *Marine from Manatee: A Tradition of Rifle Marksmanship*, National Rifle Association, Washington, D.C., 1984.

Hatcher, Julian S. *Hatcher's Notebook*, The Military Service Publishing Co., Washington, D.C., 1947.

Hicks, Major James E. *U.S. Military Firearms*, Borden Publishing Co., Alhambra, California, 1962.

Johnson, George B. and Hans Bert Lockhoven, *International Armament – Vol. 1*, International Small Arms Publishers, Cologne, Germany, 1965.

Mallory, Frank. *Serial Numbers of U.S. Martial Arms, 1st Edition*, Springfield Research Service, Silver Spring, Maryland, 1983.

Mallory, Frank. *Serial Numbers of U.S. Martial Arms, Volume 2*, Springfield Research Service, Silver Spring, Maryland, 1986.

Mallory, Frank. *Serial Numbers of U.S. Martial Arms, Volume 3*, Springfield Research Service, Silver Spring, Maryland, 1990.

Mallory, Frank. *Serial Numbers of U.S. Martial Arms, Volume 4*, Springfield Research Service, Silver Spring, Maryland, 1995.

McBride, H.W., *A Rifleman Went to War*, Small Arms Technical Publishing Co., Plantersville, S.C., 1935.

Senich, Peter R. *The Complete Book of U.S. Sniping*, Paladin Press, Boulder, Colorado, 1988.

Senich, Peter R. *U.S. Marine Corps Scout-Sniper*, Paladin Press, Boulder, Colorado, 1993.

Articles

Campbell, Clark S. "No. 10 Sights and Unertl-Scope '03s", *U.S. Martial Arms Collector and Springfield Research Newsletter*, Number 97, October 2002.

Campbell, Clark S. with Larry Reynolds, "USMC Unertl-Scoped Rifles Revisited," *U.S. Martial Arms*

Collector and Springfield Research Newsletter, Number 96, 2002.

Canfield, Bruce N. "The Warner & Swasey Musket Sights," *The Gun Report*, May 1984.

Canfield, Bruce N. "The M1903 Sniper Rifles of the Second World War," *The Gun Report*, January 1985.

Canfield, Bruce N. "The Springfield Snipers," *Man at Arms*, Nov./Dec. 1989.

Canfield, Bruce N. "An Olympic '03," *The Gun Report*, September 1991.

Canfield, Bruce N. "The 'Rod Bayonet' M1903 Springfield," *The Gun Report*, December 1991.

Canfield, Bruce N. "Identified – Rock Island's 'CN'," *The Gun Report*, September 1992.

Canfield, Bruce N. "The Cameron-Yaggi Trench Periscope Rifle," *Man at Arms*, Sept./Oct. 1993.

Canfield, Bruce N. "The Pedersen Device," *Man at Arms*, May/June 1994.

Canfield, Bruce N. "Rock Island – The Other '03," *Man at Arms*, February 1996.

Canfield, Bruce N. "Doughboy Sniper Rifles," *American Rifleman*, September 2000.

Canfield, Bruce N. "The First '03s," *American Rifleman*, November 2001.

Canfield, Bruce N. "The V-B Grenade Launcher," *The Gun Report*, December 2001.

Canfield, Bruce N. "Making the Most of GI Marksmanship – the M1903A4," *American Rifleman*, January 2002.

Canfield, Bruce N. "The Remington '03s," *American Rifleman*, November 2002.

Canfield, Bruce N. "Built for the Trenches," *American Rifleman*, January 2003.

Canfield, Bruce N. "100 Years of the '03 Springfield," *American Rifleman*, March 2003.

Canfield, Bruce N. "Never in Anger: The Pedersen Device," *American Rifleman*, June 2003.

Ewalt, Frederick M., LCDR USN (Retired), "The M1903 Air Service Rifle," *U.S. Martial Arms Collector and Springfield Research Newsletter*, Number 98, August 2003.

Gagner, Wayne P. "The M1903 Cavalry Carbine Manufactured for the Cavalry Board," *U.S Martial Arms Collector and Springfield Research Newsletter*, Number 64, October 1993.

Gagner, Wayne P. "The Elusive Bushmaster Carbine," *U.S. Martial Arms Collector and Springfield Research Newsletter*, Number 91, January 2000.

Hansen, William R. "The World War II Model 1903 Rifle; From Myth to 'Modified,'" *U.S. Martial Arms Collector and Springfield Research Newsletter*, Number 96, April/June 2001.

Hansen, William R. "Snarls, Snafus and 'Snipers' – Stories Behind the M1903A4 Story," Unpublished draft, 2003.

Hansen, William R. "The Remington M1903...No Trivial Pursuit," Unpublished draft, 2003.

Marvin, Stephen D. "Typology for the Remington '03 Rifles," *U.S. Martial Arms Collector and Springfield Research Newsletter*, Number 74, October 1995.

McInerney, Lt. J.E., Ord. Dept. U.S.A. "Overhauling the Service Rifle," *Army Ordnance*, July/August 1928.

Reynolds, Larry. "Two Marine M1903 Springfields," *U.S. Martial Arms Collector and Springfield Research Newsletter*, Number 97, October 2002.

Reynolds, Larry. "Collector Notes: U.S.M.C. M1903A1/Unertl Sniper Rifle," *U.S. Martial Arms Collector and Springfield Research Newsletter*, Number 94, October 2000.

Rutherford, H.K. "Telescopic Musket Sights," *Army Ordnance*, January/February 1924.

Government Reports, Memos and Documents

"History of Small Arms Procurement, 1939–1945." Written and compiled by S.H. Beach,1st. Lt., Ord. Dept. and Reviewed by H.A. Van Daalen, Capt., Ord. Dept., Declassified 8/29/91.

U.S. Marine Corps memoranda, reports and letters and dating from July 7, 1941 to April 27, 1945, pertaining to the acquisition, performance and disposition of sniper rifles and telescopes.

Numerous U.S. Ordnance Department, U.S. Army, U.S. Navy and U.S. Marine Corps memoranda, reports and related documentation from circa 1900 to 1951.

Military Manuals, Handbooks and Supply Catalogs

Handbook of Ordnance Data, Government Printing Office, Washington, D.C., 1919.

Description and Rules for the Management of the United States Rifle, Caliber .30, Model of 1903, Government Printing Office, Washington, D.C., March 3, 1904, April 15, 1906, February 14, 1908, April 2, 1909, October 17, 1911, March 22, 1914 and January 22, 1917.

Soldier's Handbook of the Rifle and Score Book for Special Course C, Arranged for the United States Rifle, Model of 1903, Government Printing Office, Washington, D.C., 1917.

TM 9-270, War Department Technical Manual, U.S. Rifle, Cal. .30, Model 1903A4 (Sniper's), Characteristics and Operation and Use of Telescopic Sight, 28 September, 1943.

ORD 7, SNL B-3, Ordnance Supply Catalog, Rifle, U.S., Cal. .30, M1903, M1903A1, M1903A4 and M1903A4 (Snipers), Headquarters Army Service Force, 15 November, 1944.

FM 23-10, War Department, Basic Field Manual, U.S. Rifle, Caliber .30, M1903, January 2, 1940 and

September 30, 1943.

Small Arms Firing Regulations, U.S. Navy, Government Printing Office, Washington, D.C., 1916.

TM 9-1005-205-12, Department of the Army Technical Manual, "Operator's and Organizational Maintenance Manual including Repair Parts and Special Tools Lists, Rifle, Caliber .30, M1903A4 (Snipers), W/E (1005-674-152). Headquarters, Department of the Army, December, 1970.

Remington Model 03-A3 Service Manual, Remington Arms Company, Ilion, N.Y.

Newsletters

Springfield Research Service Newsletters: Issue No. 7, November 16, 1978; Issue No. 8, February 15, 1979; Issue No. 19, Oct.-Dec., 1981; Issue No. 25, Apr.-June, 1983; Issue No. 30, Jul.-Sept., 1984; Issue No. 31, Sept.-Dec., 1984; Issue No. 32, Jan.-Mar., 1985; Issue No. 34, July-Sept., 1985; Issue No. 35, Oct.-Dec., 1985; Issue No. 36, Jan.-Mar., 1986; Issue No. 37, Apr.-June, 1986; Issue No. 47, Oct.-Dec., 1988; Issue No. 48, Jan.-March, 1989; Issue No. 54, July-Sept., 1990; Issue No. 55, Oct.-Dec., 1990; Issue No. 66, October, 1993; Issue No. 67, January, 1994.

Catalogs

Major Firearms Auction – April 28th and 29th, 2002 – Session I – The Jonathan Peck Collection, Little John's Auction Service, Inc.

The Fort Niagara, New York, shooting range during WWI. The photo above shows how it looked in front of the targets. Below is a rare view of what was behind the targets. *(Stuart C. Mowbray collection)*

Index

A

Aberdeen Proving Ground, 126
Adams, J. Sumnar, 32
Alien Property Custody Act, 26
Aircraft Armament Service Headquarters, 92
Air Service Rifle, 89–94, 206
Alaska, 22, 23
Alsace, France, 196
Alaskan Telescope, Lyman – See Telescopes
American Expeditionary Force (AEF), 55, 74, 91, 94
American Fork & Hoe Co., 182
American Rifleman, 88, 142, 144
Ames, T.L., Col., 103
Ammunition, 210
    .32 Colt ACP, 80
    .45-70, 13
    .30-40 Krag, 13,
    8mm Mauser, 13, 58
    1900/1901/1902, 13, 14
    .303 British, 45, 112, 113, 169
    .30-03 (M1903), 19, 25–27, 29, 30, 189, 190, 209, 210
    .30-06 (M1906), 26, 29, 30, 55, 76, 79, 210
        Pedersen Device, 76, 78–81, 209, 210
        Grenade Launching, 194, 202, 205
Anti-tank guns, 133
Appomattox, 61
Argonne, 68
Armistice, WWI, 55, 81, 99, 109, 200
Arms and the Man, 44, 87–89
Armstrong, Otto H., 56
Army Ordnance, 75, 100–102
Arnold, H.H., Col./Gen., 91
Artillery Board, 82
Artillery pieces, 133
Asia, 112
ATF – See Bureau of Alcohol, Tobacco & Firearms
Atwood, Frank J., Col., 118, 129, 145
Avis Rifle Barrel Co., 99

B

Babbit Rifle Grenade – See Grenades, Rifle
Balloons, observation, 90, 91
Bands, barrel, 14, 22, 30, 38, 91, 114, 120, 126, 127, 131, 145
Barnes, Lt., 50
Barrels, 14, 18, 19, 21, 27, 29, 30, 32, 37, 99–101, 103, 104, 113, 118, 125, 126, 129, 134, 140, 144, 156, 163
Barrel guard, 123, 126, 144, 145
Base, telescope mounting, 156, 157
Bausch & Lomb Company, 141
Bayonets:
    Krag, 14, 16, 27, 172
    Rod bayonet, 16–19, 22, 26, 27, 172, 173
    M1905, 26, 27, 50, 57, 94, 96, 98, 162, 167, 172–176, 178, 179, 181, 185, 186, 190, 198, 199
    M1905 modified for Maxim Silencer, 43
    Bolo, M1915, 178, 179
    M1905 Modified (M1905E1), 172, 185, 186
    M1905 WWII production, 181–183
    M1, 172, 185, 186
    M1917, 181
    M1942 – See M1905 WWII production
Bayonet scabbards – See Scabbards, Bayonet
Bazooka – See Rocket Launcher
Beatty, J.C., Capt., 80
Beckwith Manufacturing Co., 185
Belts, Cartridge
    M1903, 189, 190
    M1909, 189, 190
    M1910, 189, 190
    M1912, 40, 191, 192
    M1914, 192
    M1917/1918, 79, 189, 193
    M1923, 189, 193, 194
    U.S. Navy (WWII), 194
Berthier rifle, 81, 197

Bessiere, Gustave, 194, 195
Biddle, Anthony Joseph Drexel, Col., 184
Biloxi, Mississippi, 182
Blocks, telescope mounting, 157
Bluing, 21, 22, 31, 56, 120, 126, 131, 134, 145, 155, 157, 179, 180, 186
Blunt, S.E., Col., 34
Book of the Springfield, 66, 74, 145
Bolos
    M1909, 178
    M1910, 178
Bolo bayonet – See M1915 Bolo Bayonet
Bolts, 22, 58, 60, 84–87, 100, 101, 104, 105, 108, 116, 130, 131, 139, 140, 155, 157, 161
Bonney Forge Co., 130
Bonus Marchers, 109
Boston, Massachusetts, 193
Bougainville, 159
Bowie point bayonet – See Bayonet, M1905E1
Bowlin, Roy L., Col., 114, 118
British/Great Britain, 54, 83, 94, 112–115, 117, 169
British .303 Cartridge, 54, 55, 112, 113
Brown Precision Co., 131
Browning Automatic Rifle (BAR), 111, 132, 206
Buffalo, New York, 142
Buffington Rear Sight, 27
Bureau of Alcohol, Tobacco & Firearms, 44
Bureau of Indian Affairs, 107
Burma, 133
Buttplates, 22, 24, 30, 35, 40, 56, 106, 114, 131, 134, 135
Bushmaster Carbine, 137, 138
Butler, Smedley, 44

C

C-prefix serial numbers, 129, 226
Cameron-Yaggi Rifle, 82–90, 94, 206, 222
Cameron, James L., 83, 84, 88
Camp Perry, 66
Camp Upton, New York, 180
Camouflage, 68, 97, 115
Camp Patrick Henry, 186
Canada/Canadians, 68
Cape Gloucester, 160
Carbine, M1, See M1 Carbine
Carbine, Experimental M1903, 16, 103
Carding, 21
Caribbean, 109
Caribbean Defense Command, 137
Cartouches – See Inspection Stamps
Casehardening, 22, 31, 60
Cataract Tool & Optical Co., 61
Cavalry School, 81

Central Powers, 46
Chase, L.C. Co., 193
Chauchat Light Machine Gun, 53
China-Burma-India Theater (CBI), 133
Chicago, Illinois, 109, 110
China, 22, 109, 134
Chronograph, 18
Class A Steel, 104
Civil War – See War Between the States
Civilian Marksmanship Program (CMP), 42, 108, 148, 164
Cleveland, Ohio, 62, 83
Clip loading, 13, 14, 16, 18
Commandant, USMC, 147, 150–152, 160
Commercial Controls Co., 130
Commonwealth Forces, 114, 117
Congress Heights Rifle Range, 75
Control Board, Signal Corps, 91
Corps of Cadets – See West Point
Cosmoline, 103, 17, 132, 164
Crossman, E.C., 58, 66, 74, 104, 107, 145
Crozier, William, Gen., 26, 43, 75
Cuba, 12
Cutoff, magazine, 14, 22, 76, 81

D

D-Day, 117
Dafnomiles, John, Pvt., 199
Darby, William, Col., 187
Director of Civilian Marksmanship (DCM), 42, 44, 132, 148, 163, 164
Department of Justice, 107
Depot of Supplies, USMC, 150
Depression, The, 112
Destructive Devices, 44
Detroit Gasket & Manufacturing Co., 185
Diamond D Co., 67
Dickson Sight, 20, 211
Dirigibles, 94
Double heat treating, 58, 60, 103
Duetsch Waffen-und-Munitionsfabriken, 26
Dunkirk, 112
Dunlap, Roy, 18, 45, 145

E

Eagle-head snaps, 190
Eddystone Rifle Plant, 55
Eider, E.H., Maj., 88–90
Equipment Board, USMC, 151–153
Europe, 46, 56, 83, 108, 112
European Theater (ETO), 133
Experimental Rifles

    1900, 14–16, 19
    1901, 16–19
    1902, 16, 18, 19
Experimental Department, Springfield Armory, 103
Extension Magazine, 25-round, 61, 84, 90–92, 206–209

F

Federal Prison System, 107
Finger Grooves (stock) – See Grasping Grooves
First World War – See World War I
Floorplate, 115, 120, 126, 129, 131
Foley, Edward J., Pfc., 149
Forging problems, 31, 58
Fort Benjamin Harrison, 81
Fort Logan, Colorado, 176
Fort Riley, Kansas, 103, 108
Fort Thomas, 81
France/French, 45, 49, 53, 54, 56, 58, 67, 68, 73, 80–83, 91, 92, 95, 113, 147, 174, 179,180, 195–197
Framingham, Massachusetts, 193
Frankford Arsenal, 126, 142
Front Sight Covers – See Sight, Covers

G

Gas escape hole – See also Hatcher Hole, 38, 113, 118, 119, 157
George, John, Col., 135
Germans/Germany, 13, 26, 29, 59, 94, 146, 209
Gibbs, Stanley P., 107
Glendale, California, 136
Gorham Company, 81
Grand Offensive, WWI, 80
Grasping grooves, 102, 105, 108, 114, 117, 126
Great Britain – See British
Greece, 164
Grenade, Bandoleer, 200
Grenade Launchers
    V-B, 56, 194–200
    T3, 200
    T9, 205
    M1, 137, 200–205
    M2, 204, 205
Grenade Launching Adapter, 202
Grenades, Rifle
    Babbit, 194, 195
    Chemical, 194, 195, 197
    Ground Signal Flare, 203
    M7 (M1 rifle), 147
    M9 Anti-tank, 202
    M9A1 Anti-tank, 201, 204
    Mark II Fragmentation, 202, 203
    Mark II Practice, 202, 203
    Mark IIA1 Practice, 203
    V-B, 194–200
Grenade, Rifle, Ammunition
    M3, 202
    M7 Vitamin Pill, 202
Grenade Launcher carrying cases, 195, 199, 200
Grenade Launching Sights
    M15, 203, 205
    WWII Experimental, 203
Grenade Launching Recoil Pad, 201, 202, 205
Grenade Launcher retaining clips, 201, 205
Groton, Connecticut, 131
Guadalcanal, 135, 152
Guilderson rifle, 88

H

Hadley Special Tool Co., 163
Handguards, 19, 20, 27, 28, 31, 33, 38, 40, 58, 73, 90, 100–103, 106, 114, 119, 123, 126, 157, 161
Hansen, William, 139, 223, 225
Hanssen, William H., 56
Haiti, 109
Hatcher, Julian C., Gen., 58, 108, 206
Hatcher Hole, 108, 113, 118, 134, 135, 157
Hatcher's Notebook, 58
High Numbered rifles, 58
Hawaii, 46
High Standard Manufacturing Co., 128, 129
Hilbert, William H., 56
Hird, Fred S. (Capt.), 34, 42
Hoboken, New Jersey, 81
Hopkins, Daniel B., Lt., 186
Hoboken, New Jersey, 81
Hubbell, Lindley D., Lt. Col., 67

I

Infantry Board, 141
Infantry School, 81
Issur-Tille, France, 92
Inspection Stamps, 20, 29–33, 35, 36, 38, 56, 99, 105, 107, 108, 114, 118, 126, 129, 149, 156, 157
Italy, 149
Iwo Jima, 159

J

Japanese, 115, 133

K

Keesler Field, Mississippi, 182

Kengla, W.A., Lt. Col., 147
Kerr Adjustable Strap Co., 168
Keystone Co., 144
Kincaid, Burt, 176
Knapp-Monarch Co., 200, 202, 205
Korean War, 147, 148, 161–163
Krag/Krag Jorgensen, 12–14, 17–20, 22, 27, 35, 36, 42, 61, 165, 168, 178
    M1892 Rifle, 12, 13,
    M1896 Rifle, 13,
    M1896 Carbine, 13,
    M1898 Rifle, 13, 14, 17–20, 61
    M1898 Carbine, 13, 17,
    M1899 Carbine, 13

L

Leary, Daniel A., 107
Lee-Enfield rifle (British), 94, 112
Lend-Lease, 117, 169, 205
Lewis machine gun, 45, 88, 109, 169
Lift the Dot closures, 193
Lindsay, Ora E., 56
Long, R.H. Co., 193
Low Numbered rifles, 31, 58, 60, 61
Lyman Gun Sight Corp., 141, 143, 145
Lyman #48 sight, 103
Lyon & Coulson Co., 142

M

Madden Brothers, 136
Mail Guard, Marines, 109, 110
Malony, H.J., Lt. Col., 92
Manila, Philippines, 12
Mann-Niedner mounts, 72–74
Marines – See U.S. Marine Corps and Mail Guard Marines
Marine from Manatee, 94
Manuals, 147, 208, 209
Mauser rifle, 13, 14, 26, 54, 94, 172, 208
Maxim Co., 44
Maxim silencers, 43–45, 66, 67
Mediterranean Theater, 133
Mildew Resistant Treatment (MRT), 169
Military Police (MP), 133
M1 Carbine, 117, 123, 137, 205
M1 (Garand) Rifle, 75, 107, 112, 117, 123, 132, 134, 135, 137, 139, 153,155, 160, 186, 187, 194, 200, 205
M1C Sniper Rifle, 146, 148, 160, 161
M1D Sniper Rifle, 147, 148
M2 rifle (.22 cal.), 152
Model 10 shotgun, Remington, 75, 110
Model 51 pistol, Remington, 75
Model 70 Rifle, Winchester, 153, 155
Model 720 rifle, Remington, 139
M1895 machine gun, Colt, 45
M1903 Rifle Variants
M1903 Rod bayonet rifle, 17–31, 35
M1903 with M1905 modifications (.30-03), 27–31
M1903 Mark I, 58, 75–77, 80–82
M1903A1, 107, 108, 112, 128, 133, 134, 163, 201
M1903A2, 133
M1903 Remington, 114–117, 182
M1903 Remington Modified, 113, 117–121, 125, 127, 134, 163
M1903A3, 120, 123–133, 139, 140, 145, 164, 186, 204
M1903A4 – See Sniper Rifles
Model 1909 Benét-Mercie Machine Rifle, 64, 45
Model 1911 .45 pistol, Colt, 46, 53, 81, 109, 192, 193
M1917 (US Enfield) Rifle, 54, 55, 82, 94, 99, 106, 112, 134, 204, 205
Model 1917 Revolvers, 109
McBride, H.W., 68
Medal of Honor, 44
Mediterranean Theater, 133
Meek, Samuel W., Lt., 94
Metallurgical issues – See Single Heat Treatment, Low Numbered receivers, High Numbered receivers
Mexico, 44
Mexican Punitive Expedition, 45, 67
Micarta carrying can – See Telescope carrying cases
Middleton, Connecticut, 189
Mills Woven Cartridge Belt Co., 40, 189, 190, 192
Montana, USS, 45
Moselle, France, 199
Moros, 179
Mosin-Nagant Rifle, 81
Mounts, scope, 143, 145, 148
Mt. Vernon Silversmiths, 81
Musket Sights – See Telescopes, M1908 and M1913 Warner & Swasey

N

National Blank Book Co., 91
National Board for the Promotion of Rifle Practice, 42
National Firearms Act of 1934, 44
National Guard, 44, 74
National Match Rifles, 106–109, 146, 155–157, 159
National Park Service, 107
National Rifle Association (NRA), 42, 43, 99, 155, 163
NRA-markings, 42, 43
Nelson, Conrad, 32, 38,
New Georgia Island, 160
New Haven, Connecticut, 128
New Zealand, 116, 117

Nicaragua, 109, 111
Nickel steel, 58, 60, 103–105
No-Buckl Sling – See Slings, M1917 Kerr

O

Ogden (Utah) Arsenal, 132, 163
Ohio National Guard, 165
Oiler & Thong Case, 22, 35, 40, 122, 171
Olympics, 34, 42
Omaha Beach, 117
Oneida, Ltd., 182
Okinawa, 159
Ordnance Department, U.S. Army, 13, 14, 16–22, 25, 26, 27, 37, 40, 42, 46, 61, 62, 74, 75, 80–82, 84, 88, 90–92, 99, 101, 108, 112–114, 123, 126, 128, 129, 134, 139, 142, 143, 175, 178, 201, 205–207
Ordnance, Chief of, 16, 61, 72, 75, 80, 91, 165, 181
Ordnance Engineering Division, 81, 88
Ordnance Went Up Front, 145
Oval Office, 26
Overhaul, 100–102, 227

P

Page, George W., Cpl., 186
Pal Blade & Tool Co., 182
Panama, 82, 137
Panama Canal Zone, 81, 137
Parris Island, South Carolina, 60, 103, 105, 184
Patent Infringement Claims, 26
Pattern 1914 Rifle, British, 54, 55
Parker Rust Proofing Co., 56, 102
Parkerizing, 56, 58, 81, 99, 100, 102, 103, 107, 114, 117, 119, 120, 126, 127, 130,131, 134, 145, 147, 164, 166, 173, 179, 181, 184
Parkhurst Attachment, 13, 14
Pattern Painting, 68, 97
Pearl Harbor, 112, 114, 115, 134
Pedersen Device, Mark I, 58, 75–82, 90, 94, 221
  Mark II, 82
Pedersen, John D., 75, 76, 81
Penny, Major, 58
Periscopes, 82
Periscope sight – See Sitascope
Pershing, John, Gen., 80, 91
Philadelphia, Philadelphia, 152, 153, 155, 158
Philippine Islands, 22, 36, 44, 45, 146, 178
Philippine Scouts, 178, 179
Pine Camp, New York, 111
Pistol, Automatic, Model of 1918 – See Pedersen Device
Plant Brothers Co., 193
Plattsburg Barracks, 57, 82
Proof stamps, 21, 33, 38, 105, 113, 114, 126, 130, 157

Prototype Rifles – See Experimental Rifles
Pyrotechnic devices, 200

Q

Quantico, Virginia, 150
Quartermaster, USMC, 147, 151–153, 155, 160

R

Racks, Arms/Rifle, 46, 93,
Raiders, USMC, 135, 159, 160
Raritan Arsenal, New Jersey, 92, 132, 134, 138, 163
Rebuild – See Overhaul
Receivers, 31, 34, 37, 58, 60, 61, 70, 77, 81, 103, 108, 113, 114, 118, 121, 125, 127, 128, 134, 139, 140, 144, 148, 157
Red Cross, 181
Redfield Junior Mount, 140, 143–145
Remington M1903 Rifles – See M1903 Rifle Variants
Remington Arms Co., 55, 75, 81, 110–129, 132, 139, 141, 143–145, 163, 187
Rifle Teams, USMC, 72–74, 110, 153, 155
(A) Rifleman Went to War, 68
Rochester, New York, 169
Rochester Ordnance District, 114
Rock Island Arsenal, 19, 22–24, 27–29, 31, 32, 34–38, 40, 42, 43, 46–48, 56, 58, 60, 64, 67, 72, 81, 99, 101–105, 112–114, 117, 123, 127, 163–166, 175, 179, 182, 187, 191, 199, 211, 217–219, 222, 227
Rock Island Arsenal Museum, 47, 48
Rocket Launcher (Bazooka), 132, 201
Rod Bayonet rifle – See M1903 Rod Bayonet Rifle
Roosevelt, Theodore, 26, 27
Ross Rifle, Canada, 68
R.O.T.C., 57
Russell Manufacturing Co., 189, 192
Russia, 81
Russian sniper scope, 146
Russo-Japanese War, 27
Rust Blue – See Bluing

S

Safety, 20, 163
Saipan, 154, 159
San Diego, California, 184
Sandy Hook Proving Ground, New Jersey, 18
Saddle Scabbard, Cavalry
  M1904, 187, 188
  M1918, 187
Savage Arms Co., 112, 129
Scabbards, Bayonet
  M1905, 183, 173, 175, 176, 178

M1905 Modified, 177, 178, 180, 183, 185
M1910, 40, 57, 169, 177, 179-181, 183, 185, 199
M1915 Bolo Bayonet, 179
M1917, 181, 183-185
M3, 182-184, 186
M3A1, 186
M7, 185, 186
Schlegel Manufacturing Co., 169
Scope mounting blocks, Unertl -
Scout-Snipers, USMC, 151, 152, 154, 155, 159, 161, 162
Second World War – See World War II
Sectionalized rifles:
    Springfield Armory, 41, 42
    Remington, 42, 121-123
Secretary of War, 27, 29, 42, 81
Sedgley Co., 134, 135, 156
Senich, Peter, 159, 163
Serial Numbers, 17-19, 31, 32, 37, 58, 62, 65, 67, 70, 74, 88, 92, 101-104, 107, 108, 113, 118, 125, 128, 129, 138-141, 144, 156, 175, 176
Serial Number/Production Tables, 211, 213-226
Shelton, Mike, Cpl., 94
Shims, scope mount, 143
Shotguns, 109, 166, 170
Shots Fired in Anger, 135
Sitascope, 84, 85, 88, 206
Sights:
    Rear, 14, 20-22, 26, 27-30, 34, 40, 91, 100, 106, 115, 117, 118, 120, 123, 126, 130, 134, 145, 156, 157, 163
    Front, 20, 21, 100, 123, 134, 139, 157
    USMC #10, 106, 134, 157, 186
Sight Covers, Front, 21, 32, 35, 115, 127, 186, 187
Signal Corps, U.S. Army, 43, 91
Silencer, Model 15, 44
Single heat treating, 58
Slings:
    M1887, 165
    M1903, 20, 27, 165, 166
    M1907, 28, 29, 96, 98, 114, 124, 139, 165-168, 201
    M1917 Kerr, 168, 169, 170
    M1923, 119, 169, 170
    M1, 170
    M3, 169
SMLE rifle, 112
Small Arms Firing Regulations, 1904 and 1906, 61, 62
Small Arms Firing School, 74
Smith-Corona Typewriter Co., 126, 128-132, 163, 226
Spain/Spanish, 12, 13
Spanish-American War, 12-14
Spangler, Samuel, 56
Spare Parts Container, 35, 40, 171

Special Target Rifles, 109, 159, 155
Snipers, U.S. Army, WWI, 97
Snipers, USMC – See Scout, Snipers
Sniper & Rifle Team Rifles, USMC, 73
Sniper Rifles, 42, 45, 61-74, 120
    Krag Prototype, 61
    M1903/M1908 Warner & Swasey, 42, 62-66, 72
    M1903/M1913 Warner & Swasey, 42, 65-72
    M1903/Winchester A5/Lyman 5-A, 72-74, 150-153
    M1903A1/Unertl USMC, 106, 153-163
    M1903A4, 120, 128, 133, 139-149, 160, 163, 209, 223, 224
Spitzer Bullet, 26, 29
Sporterizing, 164
Springfield Armory, 13, 14, 16-19, 21, 22, 27-29, 31, 32, 34-38, 40, 42, 43, 46, 56, 58, 63, 64, 67, 68, 81, 82, 88, 91, 92, 99-109, 114, 123, 127, 134, 144, 156, 163, 164, 175, 176, 178, 179, 181, 182, 206, 211-213, 221, 222, 227
Springfield Armory Museum, 16, 19, 68, 88
St. Louis, Missouri, 205
Star-gauging, 63, 156
Stocks, 14, 19, 22, 27-33, 35, 38, 39, 56, 64, 70, 77, 100-102, 105, 107, 112, 118, 126, 129, 156, 163, 171
    Type S, 35, 107, 108, 112-114, 117, 118, 120, 126, 154, 156, 157
    Mark I, 77, 81
    Air Service rifle, 91, 92, 103
    Type C, 107, 108, 112-114, 120, 126, 134, 144, 145, 156, 157
    M1903A3, 124, 126, 129, 130
    M1903A4, 144, 145
    Scant grip, 120, 126, 145, 147
Stock screws, 28, 32, 33, 36, 38, 39, 56, 101, 102, 105, 113, 118, 124, 126, 129, 195
Stock pins, 124, 126, 129
Subcaliber device, 133
Swasey, Ambrose, 62
Swivel, sling, 91, 103, 120
Swivel, stacking, 22, 24, 127
Syracuse, New York, 128

T

Tarawa, 159, 160
Telescopes
    Alaskan, 141-143, 145, 148, 150
    Cataract Tool, 61
    Fecker, 161
    Lyman 5-A, 74, 150-152, 160
    Lyman commercial, 161
    M73, 141

M81, 147, 148, 160
M82, 147, 148
M84, 147, 149, 209
Noske, 150, 151
Frankford Arsenal M73B1, 142
Warner & Swasey M1908, 41, 42, 45, 62–67, 72, 139, 150, 213–217
Warner & Swasey M1913, 42, 45, 65–72, 74, 139, 150, 218, 219
Winchester A5, 72–74, 150–153, 160, 220
Winchester WWI, 92
Unertl USMC, 153–163
Weaver 330, 141, 145, 146, 150
Weaver 440, 150
Weaver 330C, 141, 146–148, 160
Weaver 330-M8, 140, 142, 148
Weaver M73B1, 141–143, 145, 148
Weaver K-4, 148
Telescope Covers, 142, 143, 158
Telescope Carrying cases
    Warner & Swasey, 64, 65
    Winchester A5, 73, 74
    Unertl micarta can, 155, 158
Texaco Co., 44
Texas, USS, 104
Thompson Submachine Gun, 111, 132, 169
Tinian, 159
Trapdoor Springfield, 12, 13, 16, 22
Trench guns – See Shotguns
Triggers, 22, 35, 40, 56, 80, 81, 85, 106, 163
Triggerguard, 38, 105, 115, 117, 120, 126, 131, 191
Trench Periscope Rifle – See Cameron-Yaggi Rifle
Tromblon, 194 – See also Grenade Launcher, Rifle, VB

U

U-Boats, 117
Unertl, John, 153
Unertl Co., 153
Union Fork & Hoe Co., 182, 186
Utica Cutlery Co., 183
U.S. Army, 13, 45, 49, 72, 74, 81, 94, 107, 108, 123, 132, 137, 139, 150, 194, 196, 200, 202, 205
U.S. Army Ordnance Department – See Ordnance Department
U.S. Coast Guard, 107
U.S. Marine Corps, 44, 60, 66, 67, 72–74, 99, 100, 101, 103, 106–111, 123, 134, 135–137, 146, 147, 150–163, 169, 176, 184, 194, 200, 202, 203,
U.S. Navy, 44, 45, 107, 123, 137, 139, 161, 161, 194
USS *Montana*, 45
USS *Texas*, 104

V

V-B Grenade – See Grenades, Rifle
V-J Day, 161
Vanier, Edgar L., 56
Villa, Francisco (Pancho), 45,
Van Orden, George, Capt., 155
Viven, Jean, 195
Vera Cruz, Mexico, 44, 45
Velletri, Italy, 149
Vietnam War, 147

W

Waffenfabrik Mauser, 26
War Between the States, 61
War Department, 14, 22, 27, 55, 62, 80, 81, 112, 138, 139, 172
Wart Hog stock – See Stock, scant grip
Washington, D.C., 75, 80, 91, 109, 147, 160
Warner & Swasey Co., 62 – See also Telescopes
Watertown, Massachusetts, 193
Weaver, W.R. Co., 141–144 – See also Telescopes
Westinghouse Co., 197
West Haven, Connecticut, 99
West Point, New York, 22, 25
Wilde Drop Forge & Tool Co., 182, 186
Winthrop, Maryland, 88
Winchester Repeating Arms Co., 55, 58, 73, 112
Winder, C.B., Col., 88
Worchester, Massachusetts, 189
World War I, 46–61, 67, 68, 70, 73, 74, 82, 89, 94, 97–99, 102, 106, 107, 114, 166, 167–169, 174, 178–181, 185, 192, 194–196, 200, 206–209,
World War II, 58, 61, 108, 109, 112, 113, 116, 117, 127, 132–134, 137, 139, 148, 149, 152, 154, 157, 161, 164, 166, 169, 170, 174, 181–184, 187, 193, 200, 209
Wrenches, adjustment
    Warner & Swasey scopes, 64, 65, 67
    Pedersen Device, 78

Y

Yaggi, Lawrence E., 83, 84, 88

Z

Z-prefix serial numbers, 125, 144